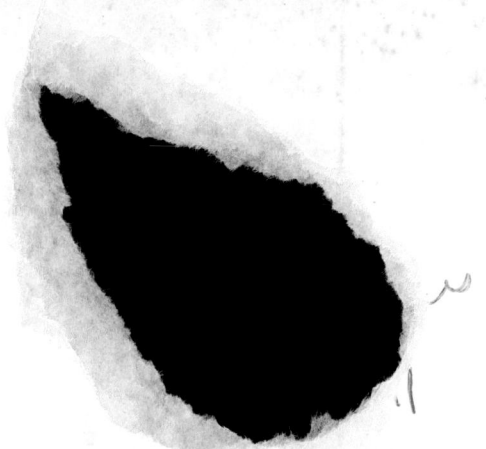

IS THE WORLD RUNNING DOWN?

Other books by Gary North

Marx's Religion of Revolution, 1968
An Introduction to Christian Economics, 1973
Unconditional Surrender, 1981
Successful Investing in an Age of Envy, 1981
The Dominion Covenant: Genesis, 1982
Government By Emergency, 1983
The Last Train Out, 1983
Backward, Christian Soldiers?, 1984
75 Bible Questions Your Instructors Pray You Won't Ask, 1984
Coined Freedom: Gold in the Age of the Bureaucrats, 1984
Moses and Pharaoh: Dominion Religion Versus Power Religion, 1985
Negatrends, 1985
Conspiracy: A Biblical View, 1986
Unholy Spirits: Occultism and New Age Humanism, 1986
Honest Money, 1986
Fighting Chance, 1986 [with Arthur Robinson]
Dominion and Common Grace, 1987
Inherit the Earth, 1987
The Pirate Economy, 1987
Liberating Planet Earth, 1987
Healer of the Nations, 1987
The Scourge: AIDS and the Coming Bankruptcy, 1988
Tools of Dominion, 1988

Books edited by Gary North

Foundations of Christian Scholarship, 1976
Tactics of Christian Resistance, 1983
The Theology of Christian Resistance, 1983
Editor, *Journal of Christian Reconstruction* (1974-1981)

IS THE WORLD RUNNING DOWN?

Crisis in the Christian Worldview

Gary North

Institute for Christian Economics
Tyler, Texas

Copyright © 1988
by Gary North

All rights reserved. Written permission must be secured from the publisher to use or reproduce any part of this book, except for brief quotations in critical reviews or articles.

Published in Tyler, Texas
by Institute for Christian Economics

Distributed by Dominion Press
7112 Burns Street, Fort Worth, Texas 76118

Typesetting by Thoburn Press, Tyler, Texas

Printed in the United States of America

ISBN 0-930464-13-3

This book is dedicated to
Arthur Robinson
who pushed me into an intellectual corner,
thereby decreasing my intellectual entropy.

TABLE OF CONTENTS

Preface ix
Introduction 1
  1. The Unnaturalness of Scientific Natural Law 13
  2. The Pessimism of the Scientists 40
  3. Entropy and Social Theory 67
  4. The Entropy Debate within Humanistic Science 91
  5. Christianity vs. Social Entropy 104
  6. The Question of Ethics 117
  7. Mysticism vs. Christianity 131
  8. Dominion and Sanctification 145
  9. Resurrection and Reconstruction 163
Conclusion 175
APPENDIX A — The Disastrous Quest for
  Scientific Common Ground 187
APPENDIX B — The End of Illusions:
  "Creationism" in the Public Schools 206
APPENDIX C — Comprehensive Redemption:
  A Theology for Social Action 219
APPENDIX D — Are Postmillennialists
  Accomplices of the New Age Movement? 257
APPENDIX E — The Division within Dispensationalism 281
APPENDIX F — Time for a Change:
  Rifkin's "New, Improved" Worldview 305
SCRIPTURE INDEX 325
GENERAL INDEX 329

PREFACE

But if there be no resurrection of the dead, then is Christ not risen: and if Christ be not risen, then is our preaching vain, and your faith is also vain. Yea, and we are found false witnesses of God; because we have testified of God that he raised up Christ: whom he raised not up, if so be that the dead rise not. For if the dead rise not, then is not Christ raised: and if Christ be not raised, your faith is vain; ye are yet in your sins (I Cor. 15:13-17).

This book asks and then attempts to answer one question: Which is more important, Adam's Fall or the bodily resurrection of Jesus Christ? It seems like such a simple question for a Christian to answer. The answer seems so easy. Obviously, the resurrection is more important, now and in eternity. If there had been no resurrection of Christ, our faith would be vain. But this answer immediately raises a second question: Which is more important, the *effects* of Christ's resurrection in history or the *effects* of Adam's Fall (God's curse of the ground) in history? My answer to this corollary question is going to make a lot of very dedicated Christians unhappy. I answer that the effects of Christ's resurrection are more important, as time goes by, than the effects of Adam's Fall. The implications of this statement, if believed and put into daily practice, would revolutionize the Christian world. In fact, they would revolutionize the entire fallen world. I will go farther: the implications *will* revolutionize the fallen world. Yet this is what most Christians categorically deny today. They deny it because they have been taught, implicitly and explicitly, that the effects of Adam's Fall are overwhelmingly, inevitably more powerful in history than Christ's resurrection. This book is my answer to this denial.

Scientific Methodology and Eschatology

I wish this book were not necessary. It will alienate some very dedicated Christians who have devoted their careers to refuting the fundamental world-and-life view of our age: Darwinian evolution.

What I present in this book is a Bible-based case against the prevailing apologetic[1] approach of most scientifically trained six-day creationists. Their arguments have yet to convince more than a few sporadic evolutionists, and not one of the prominent ones; but more important, this methodology has simultaneously weakened the case for biblical Christianity, for they have relied on a weak reed: an appeal to the second law of thermodynamics, sometimes referred to in textbooks as the law of entropy.

This is a book on theology, meaning *applied* theology, or *practical* theology. Before we begin, we must ask ourselves: What are the fundamental doctrines of Christianity? They are these: God the Trinity; God's creation of the universe out of nothing by the power of His spoken word in six consecutive and contiguous 24-hour days; God's creation of man as His image; God's covenant with man to exercise dominion over the earth as His lawful covenantal representative; the temptation of Adam by Satan; the ethical Fall of Adam; God's subsequent cursing of both man and the earth; God's judgment of the earth by a universal Flood; the preservation of mankind and land animals by means of an ark; God's scattering of rebellious mankind at the Tower of Babel through the confusion of language; God's covenantal adoption of Israel as a nation in history; God's giving to Israel His law for the establishment of a covenant law-order; the incarnation of Jesus Christ, born of a virgin; the death, bodily resurrection, and bodily ascension of Christ; the establishment of Christ's kingdom in heaven (definitively) and on earth (progressively); Christ's issuing of the "great commission" of world discipleship; the sending of the Holy Spirit at Pentecost; the second coming of Christ; the resurrection of all people at the final judgment; God's casting of Satan and his followers, including resurrected human covenant-breakers, into the eternal lake of fire; and the entrance of resurrected covenant-keepers into the sin-free, eternal new heavens and new earth. Remove any one of these doctrines, and you emasculate Christianity. Christians have long debated about the chronological order of the events after Pentecost, but to deny any of these doctrines is to abandon God's Bible-revealed plan for the ages.

Scientific Creationism[2] has openly emphasized four of these doc-

---

1. By "apologetics," I do not mean "saying we're sorry." I mean apologetic in the sense of the academic discipline of defending the Christian faith philosophically.

2. I use capital letters when referring to "scientific creationism" because it is a specific movement with an identifiable set of presuppositions and methodologies. There could be other six-day creationists who are scientific who do not share some of these presuppositions.

trines: the six-day creation out of nothing, God's curse of the ground, the universal Noachic Flood, and Christ's second coming. It has not dealt systematically with Christ's bodily resurrection. This neglect of the doctrine of Christ's resurrection has seriously crippled the Scientific Creation movement.

Without Christ's bodily resurrection, no event that followed the crucifixion would make sense, at least until the final judgment. Without His resurrection, there would be no need for God to postpone the final judgment, except to increase the number of people to be condemned to eternal torment. Without Christ's resurrection, Paul says, Christians' faith is vain (I Cor. 15:14-17). Yet it is this doctrine, the touchstone of Christianity and the primary offense to the fallen world, that Scientific Creationism relegates to secondary (or less) importance, preferring instead to emphasize the scientific importance of God's curse of the ground after Adam's rebellion, which they equate with the second law of thermodynamics. Until Scientific Creationists self-consciously begin to re-examine their worldview in terms of the doctrine of Christ's resurrection, its members will be hampered in their efforts to persuade Christians and non-Christians concerning the importance of the doctrine of the six-day creation. *A doctrine of creation without a doctrine of the resurrection is as erroneous as a doctrine of the resurrection without a doctrine of creation.* The first position —the six-day creation without Christ's resurrection—leads to Pharisaism, and the second position—Christ's resurrection without the six-day creation—leads step by step to neo-evangelicalism, Barthianism, and neo-orthodoxy.

Ignoring the Church's Foundation of Victory

There is no doubt in my mind that the Scientific Creation movement has been vital in challenging the major religion of the modern age: Darwinism. Scientific Creationists have been correct in pointing to the Bible's account of the Noachic Flood as the key event in the geological historical record of the earth. They have given Bible-believing Christians much-needed confidence in challenging the number-one secular humanist myth of our day. Certainly my own thought has been shaped by Scientific Creationism's conclusions regarding the inapplicability of Darwin's hypothesis to the earth's geological record. I read and generally accepted *The Genesis Flood* in 1963. I even used the libraries of Christian Heritage College and the Creation Research Society to gather information that I used in writing this book. But I have abandoned the most shaky pillar of their defense: their misuse of the entropy doctrine. That pillar has always rested on a foundation of humanist sand.

Strengthening the Case

What I want to do in this book is strengthen the case for six-day creationism. I have become convinced that the Scientific Creationists have been much too soft and academically gracious in their dealings with God-hating Darwinian scientists. These defenders of the faith have not "gone for the jugular" of their opponents, for they have accepted too many of their opponents' illegitimate ground rules in the debate.[3] Scientific Creationists have offered their intellectual opponents far too much ammunition. Scientific Creationists have allowed the Darwinists to establish the methodological starting point in the debate over the origins of the universe and man: *the autonomous mind of man*. The problem with this strategy is that if you acknowledge the legitimacy of your opponents' presupposition about man's autonomy, the best you can hope to achieve is to convince him that his starting point does not lead to the conclusions he has proclaimed. But you cannot rationally go from his erroneous presupposition to a correct conclusion; a person's starting point determines his conclusions. You cannot show him what is correct; you can only show him that what he has concluded cannot be true. You can at best demonstrate to him (or the audience) that he doesn't have a leg to stand on; but our goal should be to provide him with a pair of working legs, not simply to expose his artificial legs in public debate.

This insight regarding the proper starting point in all debate has been argued forcefully by Cornelius Van Til, and the unwillingness of the Creation Science movement to understand his point and adopt his apologetic method has crippled their efforts as surely as their debate points have crippled their Darwinist opponents. The problem is, the Darwinists are perfectly willing to continue to hobble along on their artificial legs, pretending that they are Olympic sprinters, rather than to go to the Bible for their source of scientific knowledge. Once you accept the premise of the autonomy of man's mind to sit in judgment on the truths God has revealed, you are forever condemned to hobble on artificial legs — legs that are themselves the gift of God in His common grace.[4] As a result, Scientific Creationists are

---

3. See Appendix A: "The Disastrous Quest for Scientific Common Ground."
4. Gary North, *Dominion and Common Grace: The Biblical Basis of Progress* (Tyler, Texas: Institute for Christian Economics, 1987).

limiting themselves to hobbling when they could sprint; they use only humanism's artificial legs, "for the sake of argument." Van Til writes:

> A deductive argument as such leads only from one spot in the universe to another spot in the universe. So also an inductive argument as such can never lead beyond the universe. In either case there is no more than an infinite regression. In both cases it is possible for the smart little girl to ask, "If God made the universe, who made God?" and no answer is forthcoming. This answer is, for instance, a favorite reply of the atheist debater, Clarence Darrow. But if it be said to such opponents of Christianity that, unless there were an absolute God their own questions and doubts would have no meaning at all, there is no argument in return. There lies the issue. It is the firm conviction of every epistemologically self-conscious Christian that no human being can utter a single syllable, whether in negation or in affirmation, unless it were for God's existence.[5]

Half a dozen of the most forensically skilled of the Scientific Creationists have been tactically successful in many brief public debates with Darwinists, but only because of the weak scientific case for Darwinism and the weak debaters who have foolishly agreed to show up. They have been public amputation sessions, not conversion sessions. These one-night successes have strengthened the self-confidence of Bible-believing Christians, and they have recruited a few science students and even fewer faculty members; nevertheless, Scientific Creationists and their associates have not yet begun to offer a systematic, comprehensive alternative worldview to the dominant Darwinian paradigm. They have failed to recognize clearly that the heart of Darwinism's hold on the thinking of the modern world is not the evolutionists' scientific case, which has been remarkably weak from the beginning, but rather the very worldview of Darwinism, for it conforms to the primary long-term goal of autonomous man: *to escape from God's judgments, historical and final.*

By narrowing the focus of their chosen intellectual battleground, Scientific Creationists have not yet successfully attacked the soft underbelly of Darwinism: *historical despair.* Scientific Creationists, by proclaiming the sovereignty of the entropy process, have also immersed their own worldview in historical despair. They can offer Darwinists and their followers only an escape from history: Jesus'

---

5. Cornelius Van Til, *A Survey of Christian Epistemology*, Vol. 2 of *In Defense of Biblical Christianity* (Phillipsburg, New Jersey: Presbyterian and Reformed Pub. Co., [1932] 1969), p. 11.

second coming. Historical escape is exactly what New Age mystics offer them, but without asking them to give up the fundamental principle of their Darwinian religion: an escape from God's judgments. Which, if either, of these escapist religious appeals should we expect to win the hearts of Darwinian humanists, New Age mysticism or Scientific Creationism? The answer is obvious. The New Age mystics allow secular humanists to retain the heart of their Darwinian religion: human autonomy.

An Alternative to Historical Despair

Christians need a better alternative than historical despair, both for themselves and for their presentation of Christ's gospel of redemption. We are at war with post-Darwinian evolutionism, and this war encompasses every area of life. Very few Christians recognize the comprehensive, literally life-and-death nature of this war, including members of the Scientific Creation movement. Marx understood it, Lenin understood it, but Christians don't. Occasional tactical victories during well-organized evening debates are motivationally encouraging to those Christians who happen to attend or listen to the tapes, but these tactical victories are not decisive to the outcome of the war. The Darwinists are still winning the visible war. Not a single liberal arts college or university has been captured for six-day creationism. (Christian Heritage College began with six-day creationism; it was not captured for it.) There has not even been a "close call." Not a single Christian denomination or association has adopted the doctrine of the six-day creation as a screening doctrine for the ordination of its pastors and deacons, let alone the faculty members at their underfunded, struggling colleges.

This indicates that the vast majority of Christians still do not believe that the doctrine of the six-day creation is relevant for Christian spiritual life. There is a reason for this: Scientific Creationists have written virtually nothing on how and why the doctrine of the six-day creation must reshape all of modern Christian theology and the entire Christian way of life. Christians have not been shown clearly and decisively that Darwinism is a total worldview, and that by accepting any aspect of this worldview, Christians compromise and weaken the presentation of the Christian worldview, as well as risk disobeying God. They have not been shown how evolutionism spreads like cancer from the geology or biology textbook to every area of personal ethics and public policy. Worse, they have not been shown why and how six-day creationism leads to a fundamentally unique worldview that encompasses things other than academic topics like historical geology and biology.[6] To win the battle with Darwinism, which is above all a *comprehensive worldview* justifying *comprehensive power*, six-day creationists must believe that the stakes are far larger than mere laboratory experiments or one-evening debates. Creation scientists must demonstrate to Christians that six-day creationism really makes a difference in every area of life.

Only a handful of Christians are ever willing to sacrifice their reputations and present associations for the sake of some rarified theological doctrine. The Scientific Creation movement has not yet persuaded Christians that its doctrinal position is anything more than a rarified theological opinion developed by ivory tower specialists in the natural sciences. The only people who seem to understand how much of a threat the six-day creation doctrine is to all of modern secular humanism are the best-informed secular humanists on one side and the Christian Reconstructionists on the other. The secular humanists reject the conclusions of the Scientific Creationists, and argue that the creationists' official methodology (the appeal to scientific neutrality) is a charade, while the Christian Reconstructionists accept the creationists' conclusions but reject their methodology as self-deception rather than a charade.

Saul's Armor

The Scientific Creationists' case against Darwinism has been narrowly focused and highly technical rather than a no-holds-barred attack: theology, philosophy, ethics, psychology, economics, law, and history. There is no single volume that has come out of Scientific Creationism that summarizes the nature of the war between creationism and evolutionism in the main areas of modern thought. There is not even a path-breaking scholarly monograph in any one of these outside fields. This is not because there are not intellectually competent people within the Creation Science movement. It is because of the self-imposed methodological armor that Scientific

---

[6]. If six-day creationism could be used to locate oil and mineral deposits less expensively than the methodology of evolutionism does, we would begin to see the abandonment of evolutionism, and also see last ditch efforts of university evolutionists to explain the creationists' success in terms of some other evolutionist theory. What we need is for evolutionism to start drilling more dry holes than we do. If nothing else, we could at least afford to fund a lot more creationist research projects.

Creationists have donned. They have worn Saul's armor into battle against Goliath, and it does not fit. It hampers an effective attack on the weak points in the enemy's defenses.

I think there are two glaring weaknesses in Creation Science: 1) reliance on the traditional apologetic method of empiricism rather than on Cornelius Van Til's biblical presuppositionalism; 2) an excessive reliance on the Fall of Adam and the resultant curses of God rather than on the resurrection of Christ and the resultant blessings of God. This second error is reflected in Creation Science's heavy reliance on the second law of thermodynamics as the basis of its case for creationism.

What I argue in this book is that any appeal to the second law of thermodynamics must remain *at best* essentially a negative critique of one technical aspect of Darwinian evolution. It involves taking a principle of humanistic physics—nineteenth-century physics at that—and arguing that evolutionists have disregarded the importance of this principle. Christians have told the evolutionists that humanistic science has been inconsistent in not acknowledging the overwhelming importance of the second law. Darwinian scientists have universally dismissed this challenge as ill-conceived, erroneous, naive, and inconsistent with "what science *really* teaches." (See Appendix A.) Because Darwinian evolutionists control virtually all the classrooms of the world, and not just the natural science classrooms, they have taken the position that they can safely ignore technical criticisms of their position, since the average student or voter will not grasp the importance of technical criticisms. They correctly understand that whether some technical accusation is accurate or not is politically irrelevant. The heart and soul of modern Darwinism is not scientific; it is political. Humanism's religion is above all a political religion, for they believe in social salvation by legislation.[7]

In any case, this tactic of appealing to the second law of thermodynamics is at best negative: showing an inconsistency in the other man's position. It has also created a kind of blindness on the part of the Creation Science movement. Creation Science has been needlessly yet so visibly dependent on this appeal to the second law that its leaders have neglected to discuss what should be an obvious point: the resurrection of Christ has in principle altered redeemed

---

7. R. J. Rushdoony, *Politics of Guilt and Pity* (Fairfax, Virginia: Thoburn Press, [1970] 1978).

man's relationship with God and nature, and it has therefore altered God's relationship with man and nature, for man is God's covenantal representative over the earth (Gen. 1:26-28).

Science and Motivation

You need to keep this question in mind as you read this book:

If the world is inevitably running down, what hope can Christians legitimately place in their earthy efforts, scientific and otherwise, to improve life on earth?

If Christians have no legitimate biblical or cosmic hope in achieving the gospel's goal of making God-honoring, worldwide improvements in the external condition of this world in history (Deut. 28:1-14) *before* Christ returns physically in judgment, then why should they sacrifice everything they possess to launch a doomed frontal assault against Darwinism? There is only one reason: because they believe that God has told them to do so. But the problem with this fall-back motivation is that the vast majority of those who deny that the church can be victorious in history *also* believe that God's law is no longer binding in New Testament times. Thus, the ethical motivation of obedience is undercut, for Christians do not know specifically what God requires them to do. Thus, they throw away their God-given tool of dominion, His law.[8] They have lost the motivation of victory (optimism) *and* the method of victory (God's law). They have therefore lost most of their cultural battles, and they have been involved in only a few since 1925 (the year of the Scopes "monkey trial").

Darwinists obviously control the major institutions of this world, including most of the churches. The readers of this book know this. So do the readers of Scientific Creationism's books. If the world cannot be comprehensively improved prior to Christ's second coming, then why should Christians risk everything they presently possess in trying to convert, dislodge, and replace the Darwinian princes of this world? Why not just stand on street corners and pass out gospel tracts and wait for the inevitable end?

This mental outlook of assured historical defeat creates a major problem for Scientific Creationism. There is nothing to be gained

---

8. Gary North, *Tools of Dominion: The Case Laws of Exodus* (Tyler, Texas: Institute for Christian Reconstruction, 1988).

culturally from tearing down Darwinism, since everything is under the "curse of entropy" anyway. The battle against evolutionism therefore appears to be an intellectual exercise indulged in by a tiny handful of obscure fundamentalist scientists. If Christians in general are unwilling to risk everything they possess in a broad-based challenge to Darwinian humanism in every area of life, how will Scientific Creationists ever prove their case to the Darwinists — not prove it technically in some narrow academic field, which has *never* been the main issue, but prove it ideologically and psychologically?

We are dealing with covenant-breakers who worship at the shrine of pragmatic politics. If we tell them that our worldview offers them no hope for the earthly future, how shall we lead them to Christ? Only by asking them to surrender in history for the sake of a promised victory outside of history. We are asking them to join the losing side in history. A few low-level humanist leaders may switch, by the grace of God, but most of them will not. Probably none of the top leaders will. Why should they? They believe in history but not in God. Scientific Creationists are asking them to believe in God but not in history. This has been Rushdoony's assertion for thirty years:

The humanists believe in history, but not in God. The fundamentalists believe in God, but not in history.

Furthermore, if Christian leaders, scholars, and writers become persuaded that the second law of thermodynamics has doomed this world to historical decline, why will they want to take the lead in proclaiming this inevitable defeat of the church to their present followers? Do Creation Scientists believe that politicians win votes by announcing in advance to their followers that a political victory will change nothing significant? That defeat is inevitable, no matter what the outcome of the election? If Creation Scientists believe that defeat is inevitable — and I believe that most of them do — they will be unsuccessful leaders in any movement for comprehensive social reform along biblical lines.

If a Christian believes that in the long run his earthly efforts are doomed, and if he also believes that the Darwinists will control the seats of power until Jesus comes again, then the smart tactic is to lie low, keep his mouth shut, and do the best he can to preserve the status quo until Jesus comes again and visibly smashes His enemies. Why would Christians risk sacrificing their life's work in order to launch an attack that calls public attention to their own weakness in the face of triumphant Darwinism in their respective fields? And even if they were willing to do so, where will they look to discover specifically what God requires of them in their areas of personal responsibility? Not in the Old Testament, surely; they have been told throughout their lives, "you're under grace, not law." So, they find themselves under humanist civilization, not Christian civilization.

Consider the Christian scholar. Careful scholarship takes a lot of work, a lot of money, and a lot of time. Rethinking any area of life in terms of Christian principles is a life-long task. If Christians are told from the beginning that no matter what they discover in their studies, the world is still going to run down, then very few of them will make the effort. (If they think that Jesus is coming again in the next few years, almost no one will make the effort. Who needs footnotes concerning the world on this side of the Rapture in a future Jesus-run international bureaucracy?) It is not random that there has yet to be written a single book by any Scientific Creationist in the social sciences or humanities that comprehensively exposes the Darwinian principles that govern his field, and which then offers a comprehensive, specific, detailed, Bible-based alternative to Darwinism. Yet the Scientific Creation movement is over a quarter century old.

Darwin published *The Origin of Species* in 1859. A quarter century later, the whole academic world had been reshaped in terms of his worldview. Darwinism dominated discussions in every academic discipline by 1885, all over the world. Scientific Creationism has yet to produce its first scholarly book in any field outside of natural science. This should warn us that there is a fundamental problem with Scientific Creationism. It is the problem of the resurrection. Scientific Creationists ignore it.

A Paradigm Shift is in Progress

I do not expect to persuade the founders of the Scientific Creation movement with the arguments in this book. Very few established scholars ever participate in a paradigm shift.[9] I *do* expect to persuade the best and the brightest of the younger members of the movement. Like the Darwinists, Scientific Creationists do not hold their position because of scientific arguments alone, or even primarily. They hold them because of the overall worldview they have

---

9. Thomas Kuhn, *The Structure of Scientific Revolutions* (2nd ed.; University of Chicago Press, 1970).

already adopted personally. They came to six-day creationism after their conversions to Christ; they did not begin with six-day creationism and then become Christians. (On this point, the Darwinists are correct: Scientific Creationism exists only to bolster the Christian religion. What they refuse to admit is that Darwinism exists only to bolster the anti-Christian humanist religion.) In short, a scientist's worldview generally determines the kind of science he does, not the other way around.

The prevailing Christian worldview is now changing. An *eschatological shift* is in progress in American fundamentalism: from premillennialism to postmillennialism.[10] The fundamentalists are beginning to recognize this.[11] The humanists are also beginning to recognize this.[12] An *ethical shift* is in progress: from antinomianism to theonomy (God's law).[13] An *apologetic shift* is also taking place: from natural law evidentialism to biblical presuppositionalism.[14] These parallel shifts involve a total restructuring of the prevailing fundamentalist outlook regarding time, ethics, and the impact of Christ's resurrection in history. As more and more Christians adopt one or more of these recently acknowledged (yet original New Testament) viewpoints, this will eventually produce a restructuring of the Scientific Creation movement. This restructuring will begin with a rethinking of the doctrine of Christ's resurrection.

Christ's Resurrection

Jesus Christ's resurrection in principle restored redeemed man's ethical relationship to God, thereby overcoming the break in mankind's personal relationship to God that took place when Adam rebelled. Creation Scientists understand that Christ's resurrection restored individual men to God, but they have not pursued another crucial implication of this altered ethical relationship: that *nature's*

---

10. David Chilton, *Paradise Restored: A Biblical Theology of Dominion* (Ft. Worth, Texas: Dominion Press, 1985).

11. Dave Hunt, *Beyond Seduction: A Return to Biblical Christianity* (Eugene, Oregon: Harvest House, 1987).

12. Frederick Edwords and Stephen McCabe, "Getting Out God's Vote: Pat Robertson and the Evangelicals," *The Humanist* (May/June 1987).

13. R. J. Rushdoony, *Institutes of Biblical Law* (Nutley, New Jersey: Craig Press, 1973); Greg L. Bahnsen, *Theonomy in Christian Ethics* (2nd ed.; Phillipsburg, New Jersey: Presbyterian & Reformed, 1984).

14. Cornelius Van Til, *Christian-Theistic Evidences*, Vol. 6 of *In Defense of Biblical Christianity* (Phillipsburg, New Jersey: Presbyterian and Reformed Pub. Co., [1961] 1978).

relationship to man and God has also been altered in principle by the resurrection, just as this relationship was altered by the curse which God placed on the cosmos when Adam rebelled. *Creation Scientists never discuss Christ's resurrection as the foundation of progressive cosmic restoration.*

The earth was brought under a curse by God in Genesis 3:17-19. This is the key biblical passage in the Creation Scientists' argument based on the second law of thermodynamics. But what about the resurrection? The resurrection was the great healing event in history. It *definitively* restored redeemed mankind as the legitimate heir of God.[15] This new ethical and legal relationship is to be worked out *progressively* in history. Therefore, these questions must be raised: What effects on the cosmos did Christ's resurrection produce? None? If not, then why not? If God's visible curses were placed on the cosmos because of Adam's covenantal rebellion, then why were there no blessings placed on the cosmos as a result of the death and resurrection of His Son, Jesus Christ? Was Adam's rebellion of greater consequence historically and cosmically than the resurrection of Jesus Christ, the Son of God? Why did the covenantal restoration of the resurrection produce no healing cosmic effects? Why is the curse of God in Genesis 3 still in full force in history?

The answer is: *it isn't*. There has been a progressive healing of the earth since Calvary. This has come sporadically in response to the sporadic covenantal faithfulness of God's people. There have been major scientific advances, remarkable medical progress, and economic growth, especially since the Protestant Reformation. Western civilization has brought these wonders to the common man[16] — the first civilization to do so — and Christianity was originally the foundation of the West. Redeemed men have been the primary agents of this healing. It is their responsibility self-consciously to carry out the dominion assignment of Genesis 1:26-28, which is why Christ delivered the Great Commission to the church (Matt. 28:18-20). The effects of death and decay are progressively rolled back when God's people faithfully transform their lives, institutions, and physical environments to conform to God's revealed laws.[17]

Christians need to start arguing that the *burdens* imposed by the

---

15. Gary North, *Inherit the Earth* (Ft. Worth, Texas: Dominion Press, 1987), ch. 5.
16. Fernand Braudel, *Civilization and Capitalism, 15th-18th Century*, 3 vols. (New York: Harper & Row, [1979] 1981-82).
17. Gary North, *Dominion and Common Grace*.

second law of thermodynamics could be progressively removed as a curse on man and the creation if mankind would repent before God. Even better, they should become prophetic: the second law of thermodynamics *will* be progressively removed *as a curse* on man and the creation *when* mankind repents before God. We never hear Creation Scientists arguing this way. It would destroy their original argument. They assume that the second law is a constant — a *uniformitarian* constant — in the external world (except when God performs a miracle). This constant never changes (except when God performs a miracle). Indeed, this explicit uniformitarianism is the heart and soul of the Scientific Creationists' technical criticism of evolutionism: the evolutionists supposedly do not adhere to the second law as a constant, they argue. Creation Scientists almost always argue as though the imposition of the second law of thermodynamics were God's *irrevocable* curse on Adam; they never argue that we can legitimately expect a reduction in these curses as a result of Christ's resurrection — the most astounding miracle in the history of man. They find themselves in the unenviable position of implicitly (and sometimes explicitly) arguing that the cursed effects of Adam's sin will remain cosmically dominant in history — except possibly during a millennium when Christ and His death-free resurrected saints will rule the earth — despite Christ's bodily resurrection.

We must abandon this presupposition. We must begin to work out the implications of Christ's resurrection for every area of life. Jesus offers us redemption — *comprehensive* redemption.[18] No area of life is exempt from the judgment of God, so no area of life is outside the redemptive work of Christ.

Am I arguing that the second law of thermodynamics will be progressively repealed in history as a result of the preaching of the gospel? No. It need not be "repealed" in history because *it was not imposed in history as God's curse*. The second law of thermodynamics was operating in the sin-free garden, and it will be operating in eternity, too. It is an aspect of the original creation, not a product of the curse. This may sound like a radical idea to Creation Scientists, but as I show at the end of Chapter Six (p. 127), Henry Morris himself has obliquely referred to this possibility. What we must say is that God has brought curses on us — death, decay, etc. — that did not exist in the

---

18. Gary North, "Comprehensive Redemption: A Theology for Social Action," *Journal of Christian Reconstruction* (Summer 1981). Reprinted in this book as Appendix C.

garden. God cursed Adam and the earth by altering the *effects* that the second law of thermodynamics has on man and the cosmos. As with everything else in life, there are now covenantal curses attached to man's environment. God used the second law of thermodynamics as a means of cursing us, just as He used the ground and our own bodies to curse us. The question is: Can these curses be reduced as a result of our obedience to God? The biblical answer categorically is *yes*. Read Deuteronomy 28:1-14 for proof.

God's covenantal judgment is a two-fold process: blessings and cursings.[19] The resurrection of Jesus Christ points to the cosmic reality of the potential blessings. *Christ's bodily resurrection implies that the cursed aspects of the second law of thermodynamics can be progressively removed in history in response to societies' increased covenantal faithfulness.* Until Christians begin to take seriously the promise of blessings that the resurrection has validated in history, they will not be able to offer a believable worldview as an alternative to humanism's various visions of long-term despair.

What Christians offer today is little more than an "*other*-worldview": a call to people to forsake the affairs of this life and to retreat into the supposedly safe womb of the local church, since nothing can be done to heal this world by means of the gospel and through the empowering of Christ's people by the Holy Spirit. The end result of such a retreat can be seen today in the Soviet Union: when the society outside the walls of the church falls to the satanic enemy, there are no more safety zones for Christians to flee to. Faithful members of God's church are sent to concentration camps. The "safe womb" of the institutional church can be smashed. Greek Christians have known this ever since Constantinople fell to the Turks in 1453.

Intellectual retreat is the second step toward surrender. The first step is theological: a denial of the comprehensive transforming power of the gospel. The Creation Scientists' misuse of the second law of thermodynamics is one aspect of this intellectual retreat from the battlefield of cultural ideas.

Who Is My Target?

I want to emphasize from the beginning that my primary target in this book is not the Creation Science movement. My primary tar-

---

19. Ray R. Sutton, *That You May Prosper: Dominion By Covenant* (Tyler, Texas: Institute for Christian Economics, 1987), ch. 4.

get is Jeremy Rifkin. To strengthen the case against Rifkin, I call into question some misguided and simplistic conclusions that many popularizers of modern humanistic science have proclaimed in the name of science — conclusions that Rifkin has adopted in order to attack Christian orthodoxy and Western civilization. In attacking the fundamental idea in Rifkin's thesis — that the second law of thermodynamics threatens to engulf and overcome Western civilization — I necessarily must challenge certain aspects of the apologetic methodology of the Creation Science movement. This methodology rests on an overemphasis on the second law of thermodynamics.

To repeat: because the Scientific Creationists have adopted the second law of thermodynamics as their biggest gun in the war against evolutionists, they have fallen into a trap: using the Fall of man and God's subsequent curses as the ordering principle of their scientific theory, rather than using the resurrection of Christ and God's subsequent blessings. This strategy has now backfired outside the realm of physical science, as we shall see. (I believe that a case can also be made that it has backfired within the realm of physical science, and I present suggestions along these lines in Appendix A. The key problem is the proper Christian use of humanistic science's hypothetically uniformitarian standards.) This strategy has created a Christian mind-set that plays into the hands of Rifkin, who also proclaims that he, too, has adopted the second law of thermodynamics as the ordering principle of his radical social theory. It should also be noted that this strategy has gained very few converts within the ranks of the physical science profession.

What I argue throughout this book is that Rifkin's growing popularity among otherwise conservative evangelicals has been aided by the reliance that conservative Christians have placed on "entropy" as the number-one intellectual weapon in their war against the evolutionists. Entropy, modern science informs us, is a measure of disorder, a disorder that does not decrease for the universe as a whole (maybe). When entropy is not actually increasing, the total disorder of the universe remains constant, "in equilibrium" (maybe). The concept of entropy has an almost hypnotic effect on many Christians who possess only a smattering of scientific knowledge.

Rifkin is an accomplished intellectual hypnotist. He has placed "entropy" at the end of a 12-inch chain, and he swings it back and forth in front of his Christian audience. His words are soothing: "You are growing sleepy. You are winding down. Your mind is wearing out. You are steadily losing IQ points. Everything is becoming confused. Now listen carefully as I tell you the scientific secret of the ages. Repeat after me: 'Entropy, entropy, entropy.'" He uses the word as a kind of talisman, a magical device to manipulate his chosen victims.

There is an old line: "You can't beat something with nothing." The concept of entropy has been misused to create *a philosophy of long-run nothingness*. Until Christians stop talking about the world's future in terms of "sovereign entropy," they will not be able to develop a believable and consistent positive alternative to modern humanism, meaning a positive program which will give people hope for solving *this* world's problems. As I argue in this book, to appeal to an *exclusively* other-worldly hope is to abandon hope for this world. It leads to social pessimism.

Apostle of a New Age

I am attempting to refute a new heresy, which is in fact a very ancient heresy: the New Age movement.[20] The New Age movement has made important inroads into Christian circles since 1979, and also inroads into the thinking of Christian leaders. One man, more than any other, is responsible for this successful infiltration: Jeremy Rifkin. What I argue in this book is that some of the key presuppositions of the Scientific Creation movement serve as the foundations for Rifkin's cosmological, economic, and social analyses. More than this: their *shared presuppositions* have made it very difficult for six-day creationists and other evangelicals to respond to Rifkin.

Yet Christians *must* respond to Rifkin. First, his general presuppositions are wrong. They are closer to Eastern mysticism than to Western rationalism. Second, his anti-rational arguments are initially disguised, for he appeals to what he (and the Scientific Creationists) say is the key fact of Western scientific rationalism, *the entropy law*,[21] in order to make his case against Western rationalism. Third, he has distorted the history of the West. Fourth, he has

---

20. Gary North, *Unholy Spirits: Occultism and New Age Humanism* (Ft. Worth, Texas: Dominion Press, 1986).

21. *The Entropy Law* was actually the proposed title of the book by Rifkin which was eventually published under the title, *Entropy*. Sometime in late 1979 or early 1980, the Peoples Business Commission, Rifkin's organization, sent out a brochure describing this forthcoming book, which also listed Noreen Banks as co-author, along with Ted Howard.

denied that economic growth is morally valid or even sustainable, long-term. Fifth, he has called Christians to adopt Eastern mysticism in the name of a new Christianity. Sixth, his recommended economic system would lead to the creation of a huge bureaucratic tyranny, yet he argues as if he were calling for a decentralized, minimal-State[22] form of government.

In short, Jeremy Rifkin is a specialist in deception. He is very clever and therefore a very dangerous man. He has self-consciously selected his target: Christians, especially the charismatics and the neo-evangelicals. He writes that "we are in the morning hours of a *second* Protestant Reformation. . . . [I]t is the evangelical community, with its resurgent spiritual vitality, that has the momentum, drive and energy that is required to achieve this radical theological transformation in American society."[23] He is determined to take advantage of this second Reformation, to redirect it along very different paths from those outlined in the Bible.

Overturning Capitalism

What kind of transformation is he talking about? Radical! At the very least, it will require a sharp reduction of America's economic wealth. "As long as we continue to devour the lion's share of the world's resources, squandering the great bulk of them on trivialities while the rest of the world struggles to find its next meal, we have no right to lecture other peoples on how to conduct their economic development."[24] You know the argument: 1) we eat; 2) they are hungry; 3) therefore. . . .

Then, just to make every successful person feel doubly guilty, "Today, the top one-fifth of the American population consumes over 40 percent of the nation's income."[25] Do you know why one-fifth of the population consumes over 40 percent of the nation's income? Because one-fifth *produces* over 40 percent of the nation's income. That fact, I assure you, Jeremy Rifkin and the professional guilt-manipulators never, ever tell you. I believe that people should not be made to feel

---

22. I capitalize State when I refer to civil government in general. I do not capitalize it when I refer to the administrative unit in the United States known as the state.

23. Jeremy Rifkin (with Ted Howard), *The Emerging Order: God in the Age of Scarcity* (New York: Ballantine, [1979] 1983), pp. x, xii.

24. Jeremy Rifkin (with Ted Howard), *Entropy: A New World View* (New York: Bantam New Age Books, [1980] 1981), p. 190.

25. *Ibid.*, p. 194.

guilty just because they are productive.[26] But it is Jeremy Rifkin's self-appointed task to make us feel guilty. Guilt-ridden people are more easily manipulated.[27]

"What do we need?" asks Rifkin. "What tremendous new economic breakthrough is called for?" Why, that same old utopian dream, that same old poverty-producing scheme: *economic planning.*[28] The question is: Who will be in charge of this planning? If the free market has not promoted such a plan, then we must need . . . well, he never really says. But bear in mind that if people refuse to do things voluntarily, then someone has to make them do it if they are going to get it done. "Regardless of which course we follow, the coming transition is sure to be accompanied by suffering and sacrifice. [This means *America's* suffering and sacrifice! — G.N.] But there is really no other choice. [We can't fight the inevitable! — G.N.] The fact is [and we can't argue with facts! — G.N.], the suffering will be minimized if the transition from the existing energy base to the new one is made now in a thoughtful, orderly manner, rather than later, out of sheer panic and desperation. We are rapidly approaching the absolute limits of the fossil fuel energy requirement. If we wait until we run smack up against the wall of this existing energy base, we will find that we have no energy cushion left to ease the transition process."[29]

Ah, yes, the old "existing energy base" argument. The old "we're running low on oil" argument. It all sounded so believable . . . in 1980. In the first three months of 1986, the cash price of oil fell from $29 a barrel to under $10. Let's see if I understand this. "Oil prices have dropped rapidly because we are running out of oil." Back to the drawing board!

Oil prices can go up, obviously. Oil is now again in the $20 per barrel range, as a result of Saudi Arabia's decision to stop selling all the oil it can produce. Terrorist attacks on the Mideast pipelines, or the expansion of the Iraq-Iran war into the Straits of Hormuz, or a Soviet invasion of the Middle East, could push prices even higher. The point is, contrary to Rifkin, there is no evidence that we are

---

26. David Chilton, *Productive Christians in an Age of Guilt-Manipulators: A Biblical Response to Ronald J. Sider* (4th ed.; Tyler, Texas: Institute for Christian Economics, 1986).
27. Rushdoony, *Politics of Guilt and Pity*, Section I.
28. Don Lavoie, *National Economic Planning: What Is Left?* (Cambridge, Massachusetts: Ballinger, 1985).
29. Rifkin, *Entropy*, p. 203.

running out of energy. *We are simply the victims of a government-created oil cartel.* Like all cartels, it has shown sporadic signs of falling apart, as members cheat on the previously agreed-to production limits. Hopefully, this will continue. In any case, we should have learned by now that capitalism tends to *lower* the price of raw materials if the free market is left alone. This is the testimony of two centuries of industrial production. The evidence is overwhelming.[30]

If we ever do run out of commercially available energy, it will be because we first ran out of freedom.

New Age Politics

What Rifkin wants is a "New Age politics."[31] What he wants is regional organic farms.[32] Who will run these small, regional enterprises? Why, our old favorites, The Workers: ". . . firms should be democratically organized as worker-managed companies."[33]

Does this begin to sound familiar? Haven't we seen all this before? Isn't this just warmed-over rhetoric from the 1968 counterculture? Isn't this language left over from some yellowing mimeographed platform statement of some faction of Students for a Democratic Society (SDS), the radical organization that, figuratively speaking, blew itself apart in 1969?

There will be no jet planes in the coming utopia. "A Boeing 747, for instance, simply cannot be manufactured by a small company employing several hundred individuals. Thus, a new ethic will have to be adopted. . . ."[34] No more jet bombers, either. No more missiles, I would imagine. Not in "Christian" America.

The trouble is, what if the Soviet Union doesn't go along with Rifkin's New Age politics, but the United States does? What then?

Now all this should begin to sound familiar.

Will life be prosperous in the New Age, the way it is today for most middle-class Americans? I fear not. "The entropy economy is one of necessities, not luxuries."[35] Don't expect much, but expect to be happy. Everyone who lives in a utopia is happy. That is the mark

---

30. Herman Kahn and Julian L. Simon (eds.), *The Resourceful Earth* (New York: Oxford University Press, 1984).
31. Rifkin, *Entropy*, p. 211.
32. *Ibid.*, p. 214.
33. *Ibid.*, p. 216.
34. *Idem.*
35. *Ibid.*, p. 245.

of utopias. You are required by law to be happy. That also is the mark of utopias. (*Utopia*: from the Greek words *ou* = "no" and *topos* = "place.") It is also the mark of Communist tyrannies.

There will be fewer people around to be happy, however. "Finally, the low-entropy age we are moving into will require a great reduction in world population."[36] But who will decide who lives, who doesn't, and who gets born? He refuses to say exactly—no use upsetting the potential victims in advance—but he mentions one possibility: having the government license parenthood.[37]

All this is offered in the name of a new, improved Christianity by a man who was once the head of something called the Peoples Bicentennial Commission.

Who Is Jeremy Rifkin?

Jeremy Rifkin is a best-selling co-author. He wrote *The Emerging Order* (with Ted Howard), published in 1979, *Entropy* (with Ted Howard), published in 1980, and *Who Shall Play God?* (with Ted Howard), a book critical of genetic engineering, published in 1977, which sold over 250,000 copies. He also wrote *The North Shall Rise Again* (with Randy Barber). Then came *Algeny* (with Nicanor Perlas). Who knows, someday he may write a best-selling book all by himself.

Before he became a best-selling co-author, he was the project director of the Peoples Bicentennial Commission, which employed both Mr. Howard and Mr. Barber. In his biographical summary that he included in his original proposal for the Commission, he listed a B.S. in economics from the Wharton School of Finance & Commerce (1967) and an M.A. in international affairs from the Fletcher School of Law and Diplomacy (1968). He also served as a VISTA volunteer in East Harlem.[38]

With this as his academic background, he now comes before us as the prophet of a new worldview, one that supposedly is based entirely on rigorous physical science. It is a lot easier to make a case for Rifkin as an academically qualified expert in social revolution than as an expert in thermodynamics.

---

36. *Ibid.*, p. 217.
37. *Ibid.*, p. 218.
38. *The Attempt to Steal the Bicentennial, The Peoples Bicentennial Commission*, Hearings Before the Subcommittee to Investigate the Administration of the Internal Security Act and Other Internal Security Laws of the Committee on the Judiciary, United States Senate, 94th Congress, Second Session (March 17 and 18, 1976), p. 110.

Rifkin's Strategy of Subversion

From the beginning of his public career, Rifkin has worked with a specific strategy of subversion. This strategy involves *the presentation of revolutionary goals to conservative Americans by wrapping them in the American flag*. In late 1971, Rifkin wrote concerning the need for a Peoples Bicentennial Commission: "At this critical stage in American history, it makes no sense for the New Left to allow the defenders of the system the advantage of presenting themselves as the true heirs and defenders of the American revolutionary tradition. Instead, the revolutionary heritage must be used as a tactical weapon to isolate the existing institutions and those in power by constantly focusing public attention on their inability to translate our revolutionary dreams into reality." He was quite explicit concerning the revolutionary tradition he had in mind: *communism*.

A genuine understanding of revolutionary ideals is what links Thomas Paine, Sam Adams, and Benjamin Rush, and the American people, with Lenin, Mao, Che, and the struggles of all oppressed people in the world. Not until the masses of Americans begin to re-identify with these principles and develop their own revolutionary struggle will they be able to form a real bond of fraternalism and solidarity with the struggles of all oppressed people.

He wrote this for the bimonthly newspaper of the New American Movement (Nov./Dec. 1971).[39] But in his introduction to *America's Birthday*, published by Simon & Schuster in 1974, he judiciously dropped the earlier references to Lenin, Mao, and Che Guevara.

A genuine understanding of American democratic ideals is what links the American people with the struggles of all oppressed people in the world. Indeed, the American Revolution has stood as an example for the revolutions of the Third World. Not until the majority of Americans begin to re-identify with our democratic principles and develop our own revolutionary struggle will we be able to form a real bond of fraternalism and solidarity with the struggles of all oppressed people.[40]

Jeremy Rifkin knew exactly what he was doing. He and John Rossen edited a book, *How to Commit Revolution American Style* in 1973, published by Lyle Stuart. Mr. Rossen wrote on page 149: "In the

---

39. *Ibid.*, p. 75; Appendix A.
40. *Ibid.*, p. 118.

Caribbean islands, new Black liberation movements are popping up all over. In Canada, the Quebecois Liberation Front has brought the fires of revolutionary nationalism right up to the U.S. frontier. On the European continent, similar fires are scorching the hides of imperialists. . . . In Asia the entire continent seethes with the movement. The victory of the first stage of the Chinese Revolution can be said to have struck the sparks that set off the whole world-wide phenomenon of revolutionary nationalism."[41]

What about the United States? On page 157, Rossen informs us that "the American version of the concept of revolutionary nationalism will be anti-capitalist and socialist in content, and national in form and rhetoric."[42]

Mr. Rifkin's partner specified in the March/April 1971 issue of *The New Patriot* (his own publication) what his understanding of Marx was:

> Marx laid the sturdy foundations for the scientific revolutionary-socialist methodology, and for any modern revolutionary to ignore those foundations would be as stupid as for a physicist to ignore the findings of Isaac Newton. But neither can a modern revolutionary limit himself to the findings of Marx. That is why I use the expression "scientific revolutionary methodology" rather than the expression "Marxism." The problem with most of those who call themselves Marxists today is that they accept Marxism as a dogma and not as a scientific tool, a revolutionary methodology which is constantly being refined, added to, improved on the basis of the revolutionary experience of the last century and a quarter.[43]

Co-authors Ted Howard, Randy Barber, and Rifkin were all associated with the Peoples Bicentennial Commission, which was later renamed the Peoples Business Commission. As he said to a *Washington Star* reporter in 1979, "Our job is to develop a politics for the '80s and '90s."[44]

A New Targeted Audience: Evangelicals

This was the original goal of the Peoples Bicentennial Commission: political change. Rifkin began to target evangelical Christians in the late 1970's with his book, *The Emerging Order*. This was simply a

---

41. *Ibid.*, p. 12.
42. *Ibid.*, p. 13.
43. *Ibid.*, p. 91
44. *Washington Star* (Jan. 24, 1979).

continuation of the strategy outlined by William Peltz, the Midwest regional coordinator of the Peoples Bicentennial Commission. At a meeting in Ann Arbor, Peltz argued that conservative Christians can be turned into promoters of revolutionary politics if you can show them that the Bible teaches revolution.

Interestingly, he cited Leviticus 25, the chapter that contains the Jubilee land laws, which required that the ownership of the land of Israel be returned to the original families every 50 years.[45] This has subsequently become a popular theme of numerous radical Christians, including Ron Sider and *Sojourners* magazine. It has also become a theme in certain fundamentalist groups. They have not understood that the Jubilee was an aspect of military conquest, an economic incentive to fight that was given to each Hebrew family before Israel invaded Canaan.[46] They also have not recognized that the Jubilee was fulfilled in principle by Jesus (Luke 4) and abolished historically when Israel as a nation ceased to exist.[47] But most of all, they have not bothered to tell their followers that if Leviticus 25 is still morally and legally binding, then lifetime slavery is still morally and legally valid, for it is only in Leviticus 25 that the Hebrews were told that they could buy and enslave foreigners for life, and then enslave their heirs forever (Lev. 25:44-46). It is time to abandon Leviticus 25 as the basis of social reform.

The Myth of Neutrality

This book deals in great detail with the writings of Jeremy Rifkin that are aimed specifically at a Christian audience. But it is not simply to refute Rifkin that I write this book. It is to refute the earthly pessimism that Rifkin's thesis promotes. Unfortunately, Bible-believing Christians have adopted a very similar view of the supposed "natural" decline of this "natural" world, and this has led to a similar debilitating outlook—a self-conscious effort on the part of Christians to remove "the supernatural" from scientific discussion, at least in the "preliminary" stages of discussion.[48]

---

45. *The Attempt to Steal the Bicentennial*, p. 36.
46. Gary North, "The Fulfilment of the Jubilee Year," *Biblical Economics Today*, VI (March/April 1983).
47. *Ibid.*
48. A good example of such an approach is John N. Moore's book, *How to Teach ORIGINS (Without ACLU Interference)* (Milford, Michigan: Mott Media, 1983). This presumes that Christians are being employed by officially neutral but in fact God-hating, humanist-operated schools. This perpetually ineffective strategy of subversion has yet to work, the latest defeat being the U.S. Supreme Court's decision in *Edwards v. Aguillard* (June 19, 1987). See Appendix B in this book.

This approach is based on the disastrous lure of the myth of neutrality. Van Til's warning is ignored: "If the theistic position be defensible *it is an impossibility for any human being to be neutral*. This is quite readily admitted when a centrally religious question is discussed. We need only recall the words of Jesus, 'He that is not against me is for me,' to remind ourselves of this fact. When two nations are at war no citizens of either of these two nations can be neutral."[49] This neutrality-based apologetic method assumes, erroneously, that the natural man can be led logically from his initial, agreed-upon belief that it is possible to discuss this world without any reference to God, to a conclusion that the God of the Bible exists and controls everything in the creation — a world in which God must be assumed in the first place in order to make sense of our environment. Such a line of argument assumes initially that the doctrine of creation is intellectually irrelevant to the argument, and then the force of logic supposedly will lead to the conclusion that the doctrine of creation is what the Bible says it is: the starting point of all knowledge. "In the beginning God created the heaven and the earth" (Gen. 1:1).

This apologetic approach is based on the assumption that rational men can discuss the first principles of science (or any other "secular" subject) on the basis of common-ground presuppositions about the true nature of the universe. This, of course, is precisely what covenant-breaking men have always wanted to assume: that they could reach "workable truths" without any appeal to, or judgment by, the God of the Bible. This is a false assumption. Christians should not make it when presenting their case for Christianity. If we allow the non-Christian to claim rightfully *any* theory-interpreted fact in the universe apart from God's sovereign control and interpretation of this fact, then we have thereby granted him the autonomy he demands, and that God denies to any aspect of the creation. Van Til's warning is crucial: "If the Christian position should prove to be right *in the end*, then the anti-Christian position was wrong, not only at the end, but already *at the beginning*."[50] In short, "Any method, as we pointed out above, that does not maintain that not a single fact can be known unless it be that God gives that fact meaning, is an anti-Christian method."[51]

---

49. Van Til, *A Survey of Christian Epistemology*, p. 19.
50. *Ibid.*, p. 8.
51. *Ibid.*, p. 10.

Christians have mistakenly argued against Darwinian evolution by appealing to the supposedly common-ground phenomenon of entropy. Rifkin's book dovetails too well with this entropy-based approach to refuting Darwinism. He, too, says that he is against Darwinism. He, too, bases his system on entropy. By accepting his starting point, Scientific Creationists are left at his mercy. This is a dangerous place to be.

Conclusion

Rifkin's thesis, if believed by Christians, can lead to emotional paralysis. He talks about mobilizing Christians, but anyone who takes his books seriously will be difficult to mobilize, because Rifkin's outlook, *if we believe what he says about entropy and the universe*, leads to pessimism and retreat, not revolution. Defeat has not been the expressed intention of the six-day creation movement, although eschatological pessimism has been common in Scientific Creationist circles. Pessimism regarding positive social change is where the entropy defense of the creation can lead, and usually does.

If God in His grace sends us a serious evangelical awakening, transforming the hearts and minds of literally billions of people, we will see a rebuilding of society, a healing of this cursed world on a scale that will dwarf the progress of the last two thousand years. For those who believe in such a coming revival, this is a time for optimism rather than retreat, a time for economic freedom rather than socialism's bureaucracy, a time for expansion and economic progress rather than a zero-growth economy. If we really believe in a coming worldwide revival, then ours is a time to start believing in a positive earthly future.

It is therefore time to abandon Jeremy Rifkin's worldview.

The purpose of Biblical history is to trace the victory of Jesus Christ. *That victory is not merely spiritual; it is also historical.* Creation, man, and man's body, all move in terms of a glorious destiny for which the whole creation groans and travails as it awaits the fulness of that glorious liberty of the sons of God (Rom. 8:18-23). The victory is historical and eschatological, and it is not the rejection of creation but its fulfilment.

This victory was set forth in the resurrection of Jesus Christ, Who destroyed the power of sin and death and emerged victorious from the grave. As St. Paul emphasized in I Corinthians 15, this victory is the victory of all believers. Christ is the firstfruit, the beginning, the alpha and omega of the life of the saints. Had Christ merely arisen as a spirit from the grave, it would have signified His lordship over the world of spirit but His surrender of matter and history. But by His physical resurrection, by His rising again in the same body with which He was crucified, He set forth His lordship over creation and over history. The world of history will see Christ's triumph and the triumph of His saints, His church, and His kingdom. History will not end in tribulation and disaster: it will see the triumph of the people of God and the manifestation of Christian order from pole to pole before Christ comes again. The doctrine of resurrection is thus a cornerstone of the Biblical dimension of victory.

The doctrine of the resurrection, however, does not last long in any church or philosophy which surrenders or compromises the doctrine of creation. Creationism asserts that the world is the creative act of the triune God, Who made it wholly good. Sin is a perversion of man and a deformity of creation. The goal of the Messianic purpose of history is the "restoration of all things" (Acts 3:21), their fulfilment in Jesus Christ, first in time and then in eternity.

R. J. Rushdoony[*]

---

[*]Rushdoony, *The Biblical Philosophy of History* (Phillipsburg, New Jersey: Presbyterian & Reformed, [1969] 1979), pp. 25-26.

INTRODUCTION

Thy raiment waxed not old upon thee, neither did thy foot swell, these forty years (Deut. 8:4).

And ye shall serve the LORD *your God, and he shall bless thy bread, and thy water; and I will take sickness away from the midst of thee. There shall nothing cast their young, nor be barren, in thy land: the number of thy days I will fulfil (Ex. 23:25-26).*

The first law of thermodynamics states that the total of "matter-energy" in the universe is constant throughout eternity, or at least after the "Big Bang" (the evolutionists' version of creation). The second law of thermodynamics states that *useful* energy is either constant (equilibrium conditions)[1] or decreasing (kinetic energy) in the universe as a whole. Useful energy *for the universe as a whole* therefore can never increase. (The underlying assumption of the second law is that the universe itself is a closed system, something like a giant container. Without this crucial assumption, the second law of thermodynamics loses its status as a universal law.)

We read: "Thy raiment waxed not old upon thee, neither did thy foot swell, these forty years" (Deut. 8:4). Thus, any consistent *scientific* application of the second law of thermodynamics to this verse would have to assert that God must have drawn energy from some external source in order to produce this *local* overcoming of entropy's effects. Perhaps God in some way rechanneled energy from the sun that otherwise would have been dissipated into space, or into the

---

1. A system is in equilibrium when its components are not moving in any particular direction. When a gas is in equilibrium in a container, its molecules are bouncing *randomly* against the walls of the container. In theory, no heat from outside the container passes through to the gas inside, and no heat from the gas inside passes through the container's walls to the outside. The random bouncing of the molecules of the gas does not produce measurable changes — heat, pressure — in the gas, *taken as a unit.*

ground, or wherever it was headed. But He had to get this energy from outside the "local system," namely, from outside the local environment of the clothing and the bodies of the Israelites. Problem: the Bible says nothing like this, and the kinds of miracles that take place throughout the Bible cannot be accounted for by any such rechanneling of physical energy. Thus, the second law of thermodynamics does not allow for events such as the miracles described in these Bible passages. In short, *if the second law of thermodynamics is universally true, then the Bible is wrong.*

This is why Christians must state categorically that the rule of the second "law" of thermodynamics is not universal. Above all, we must defend the resurrection of Christ against the humanists who do not want to believe it, and even if they feel compelled to acknowledge its historicity, refuse to accept the Bible's interpretation of its meaning.[2] For example, did Jesus' resurrection take place because God rechanneled some of the sun's energy into the tomb and then into Christ's dead body? How much energy (measured in "ergs") did it take to raise Jesus from the dead? If we could just figure out how to tap into this same energy source, would we also be able to raise people from the dead? We can see where this sort of reasoning leads to: *the deification of scientific man.*

Thus, the Bible testifies to the non-universal nature of the second law of thermodynamics. It is a *common feature* of man's environment, but *it is not universal.* Overcoming entropy from time to time is one way that God points to His own sovereign control over history. The second law is at most a common aspect of God's providential ordering of the cosmos. It is a secondary source of physical continuity. Continuity and discontinuity are always interpreted in reference to each other, and *the incarnation and bodily resurrection of Jesus Christ are the greatest discontinuities in mankind's history.* In short, the historic reality of God's miracles is a refutation of the asserted universality of the second law of thermodynamics.

It's a Miracle!

"It's a miracle!" People say this when they really mean, "It's terrific, but completely unexpected." But there really are miracles in

---

2. In the fall of 1964, I heard UCLA's Prof. Lynn White, Jr., say in the classroom regarding the resurrection: "Maybe it did happen. We live in a world in which anything can happen." By explaining the resurrection in terms of randomness rather than in terms of the decree of God, the humanist has denied the resurrection, even if he accepts the historical reality of the event. The "fact" of the resurrection of Christ's body from the grave proves little if anything. All facts are *interpreted* facts.

life, and they usually are unexpected. Not always, however. God promised Israel the miracle of genetic near-perfection: no miscarriages of man or beast in Israel, just so long as the people were covenantally faithful to God (Ex. 23:25-26). They knew in advance what was possible, but they did not obey, and they did not receive the blessing. Neither did their animals.

This book deals with miracles. It also deals with run-of-the-mill activities that involve the inevitable wear and tear of life. In the Book of Exodus, we find a notable verse that supports the thesis of this book, Exodus 3:2: "And the angel of the LORD appeared unto him [Moses] in a flame of fire out of the midst of a bush: and he looked, and, behold, the bush burned with fire, and the bush was not consumed." Why wasn't it consumed? Because God sustained it. But it was the oddness of a burning bush that was *not* being consumed that caught Moses' attention in the first place (Ex. 3:3). So the overcoming of entropy had its part to play in God's plan for the ages.

A similar comment applies to: 1) the manna of the wilderness which fed the Israelites for almost four decades; 2) the daily refilling of the oil pot of the widow of Zarephath, who fed Elijah for over three years; 3) the widow who poured oil out of a single small pot that filled a roomful of large containers; 4) Jesus' turning of water into wine; and 5) His feeding of thousands with a few fish and loaves of bread. Most notably, it applies to every account of resurrection from the dead, especially the resurrection of Jesus Christ.

If I were to come to you and insist that as a Christian, you have an intellectual responsibility to seek to identify the constant, universal, uniformitarian "natural law" that made any or all of these miracles possible, you would regard me as a fool. These were miracles; therefore, the normal cause-and-effect relationships of conventional physical science did not govern them.[3] This biblically reasonable response is precisely what has long angered humanistic scientists. They deny biblical miracles.

The idea that these miracles ever took place was rejected by all nineteenth-century Darwinian scientists. Very few scientists have ever affirmed faith in God's miracles, and never in their scientific papers does the subject of miracles come up. Miracles were under-

---

3. Sometimes I wonder if we make too much of a fuss trying to find the "mechanisms" of the Genesis Flood, or how Noah could have fed the animals, or how he squeezed them into the ark.

stood as irrelevant to science, and probably a denial of science. The reason for this rejection is clear enough: miracles could not be explained in terms of the categories of nineteenth-century science. The universe was explained as a sort of giant machine that is governed exclusively by mathematical laws. Miraculous biblical "discontinuities," if true, deny the universality of these hypothetical, unbreakable, mathematical, natural laws. Hence, in order to maintain their faith in the world of natural science, nineteenth-century scientists (and most of their successors) rejected the idea of biblical miracles. Typical of this outlook was a statement in 1910 by the American social scientist and progressive educator, G. Stanley Hall:

> We have largely evicted superstition from the physical universe, which used to be the dumping ground of the miraculous. . . . But we have great ground to rejoice that science is now advancing into this domain more rapidly than ever before, and that the last few years have seen more progress than the century that preceded. The mysteries of our psychic being are bound ere long to be cleared up. Every one of these ghostly phenomena will be brought under the domain of law. The present recrudescence here of ancient faiths in the supernatural is very interesting as a psychic atavism, as the last flashing up of old psychoses soon to become extinct.[4]

A tiny number of modern humanist scientists might be willing to accept the historical validity of some biblical miracles, but they would reject the biblical explanation, namely, a sovereign God who brought them to pass for His own purposes. These scientists are believers in the essential randomness of nature. "Anything is possible," they say.[5] Anything except the sovereign God of the Bible who controls all things in terms of His plan for the ages. *That* isn't possible.

We therefore discover a clash: the overwhelming majority of that minority of scientists who actually discuss epistemology ("what we can know and how we can know it") and cosmology ("origins and fate of the universe") vs. miracle-believing Christians who also discuss

---

4. G. Stanley Hall, "Introduction," Amy Tanner, *Studies in Spiritism* (New York: Appleton, 1910), p. xxxii.

5. Lyall Watson writes: "Science no longer holds any absolute truths. Even the discipline of physics, whose laws once went unchallenged, has had to submit to the indignity of an Uncertainty Principle. In this climate of disbelief, we have begun to doubt even fundamental propositions, and the old distinction between natural and supernatural has become meaningless. I find this tremendously exciting." Lyall Watson, *Supernature: A Natural History of the Supernatural* (Garden City, New York: Anchor Press/Doubleday, 1973), p. ix.

these topics. This is the century-old clash between some variant of Darwinism and creationism. *There is no biblically acceptable way to soften this confrontation.* There can be no "smoothing over of differences." The two systems are incompatible. This is not a case of semantic confusion; this is a case of all-out intellectual war. It is at root a war between rival religious worldviews, rival religious presuppositions concerning God, man, law, and time. We must heed Van Til's warning:

> In the first place, Christian theism must be defended against non-theistic philosophy. We have sought to do this in the course in apologetics. In the second place, Christian theism must be defended against non-theistic science. . . . Christianity is an historical religion. It is based upon such facts as the death and resurrection of Christ. The question of miracle is at the heart of it. Kill miracle and you kill Christianity. But one cannot even define miracle except in relation to natural law. Thus, we face the question of God's providence. And providence, in turn, presupposes creation. We may say, then, that we seek to defend the fact of miracle, the fact of providence, the fact of creation, and therefore, the fact of God, in relation to modern non-Christian science.[6]

The Intolerance of the Darwinists

The Darwinists have been much more consistent about the "no exceptions" nature of their position than the Christians have been. Those scientists who go into print in order to set the terms of acceptable scientific discourse on this crucial question of origins have defined creationism out of the debate. The comment by Harvard University's Stephen Jay Gould is typical: "As in 1909, no scientist or thinking person doubts the basic fact that life evolves. Intense debates about *how* evolution occurs display science at its most exciting, but provide no solace (only phony ammunition by willful distortion) to strict fundamentalists."[7] In addition to teaching paleontology, Gould also writes a monthly column in *Scientific American*. He is representative of mainstream public science.

Even less temperate are the remarks of Canadian Michael Ruse:

> . . . I believe Creationism is wrong: totally, utterly, and absolutely wrong. I would go further. There are degrees of being wrong. The Creationists are

---

6. Cornelius Van Til, *Christian-Theistic Evidences* (Phillipsburg, New Jersey: Presbyterian and Reformed Pub. Co., [1961] 1978), p. vii. I am quoting from the original edition, because a line has been dropped from the 1978 edition.

7. Stephen Jay Gould, *Hen's Teeth and Horse's Toes: Further Reflections in Natural History* (New York: Norton, 1983), p. 14.

at the bottom of the scale. They pull every trick in the book to justify their position. Indeed, at times, they verge right over into the downright dishonest. Scientific Creationism is not just wrong: it is ludicrously implausible. It is a grotesque parody of human thought, and a downright misuse of human intelligence. In short, to the Believer, it is an insult to God.[8]

Under no circumstances would I let Creationist ideas into [tax-financed school] biology classes, or anywhere else where they might be taken by students as possible frameworks of belief. I would not give Creationism equal time. I would not give it any time.[9]

It [Scientific Creationism] is intellectual Ludditism of the most pernicious kind. It is a betrayal of ourselves as human beings. And, it is therefore for this reason, above all others, that I argue that it should not be part of the material taught in schools.[10]

All must agree that there has to come a time when we have to cry "finis" to the teaching of certain ideas. After a while they become no longer tenable, and trying to make them so is positively harmful. It is an act of bad faith even to present such ideas as a possible basis of belief. . . . Scientific Creationism is fallacious by every canon of good argumentation. Thus, I say "Keep it out of the schools!"[11]

Such vitriolic language is almost never used in North American academic circles. When any group becomes the target of such verbal abuse, this indicates that the author is absolutely confident either that all his academic colleagues agree with his assessment or else that they will not dare to criticize it publicly. It is also indicative that the targets are not even remotely inside the academic guild, and therefore they are entitled to none of the guild's protection.

The most prolific American author of this century is Isaac Asimov, who had written over 350 books by 1986, up from "only" 200 in 1979. He has a book in each of the ten main divisions of the Dewey decimal system,[12] although he is most famous for his science fiction books and stories. He received a Ph.D. in chemistry in the 1940's, and he taught for a few years at the Boston University medical school, but as he freely admitted once, "I realized that I would never

---

8. Michael Ruse, *Darwinism Defended: A Guide to the Evolution Controversies* (Reading, Massachusetts: Addison-Wesley, 1982), p. 303.
9. *Ibid.*, p. 321.
10. *Ibid.*, p. 327.
11. *Ibid.*, p. 329.
12. Thomas Lask, "Book Ends," *New York Times Book Review* (Jan. 28, 1979).

be a first-rate scientist. But I could be a first-rate writer. The choice was an easy one: I just decided to do what I did best."[13] He gave up the classroom for the typewriter. But he is well respected by other popularizers of science. Astronomer-author (and television show personality of *Cosmos* in 1980) Carl Sagan describes him as "the great explainer of the age."[14] He is representative of conventional Darwinian science. Listen to the otherwise jovial Asimov in his dust jacket promotion of Willard Young's popularly written book, *Fallacies of Creationism*:

> In *Fallacies of Creationism*, Willard Young has assembled the clearest, fairest and most complete analysis of the nonsense offered up by those who wish to persuade others of their invented Creationist superstitions. Young quotes extensively from the writings of the Creationists to expose the manner in which they distort facts and misstate science in order to support the childish myths they are determined to believe. Young strikes out vigorously against these pernicious Creationist follies that no rational person can accept and that can only be designed to fasten medieval shackles on the human mind.[15]

His total confidence in the evolutionist's worldview is displayed in his religious affirmation concerning what every fact of every science teaches every time: "In fact, the strongest of all indications as to the fact of evolution and the truth of the theory of natural selection is that all the independent findings of scientists in every branch of science, when they have anything to do with biological evolution at all, *always* strengthen the case and *never* weaken it."[16] (Emphasis in the original.) Whenever we see the words "always" and "never" relating to what science teaches, or what scientists discover, we know that we are no longer dealing with science, but with *religious affirmation*. This is what this battle is all about: a battle over religion.

In 1986, 72 Nobel Prize-winning scientists signed a joint statement that affirmed that Scientific Creationism should not be allowed in the curricula of the public schools. This was the largest group of Nobel Prize-winning natural scientists to sign any document in the history of the Nobel Prize. These hostile statements by Darwinists

---

13. *Time* (Feb. 26, 1979), p. 80.
14. *Idem.*
15. Back cover of the dust jacket, Willard Young, *Fallacies of Creationism* (Calgary, Alberta: Detselig Enterprises, 1985).
16. "The Genesis War," *Science Digest* (Oct. 1981), p. 87.

concerning the biblical creation question are representative of the opinions of the scientific community as a whole. If such statements are not actually representative, they have nevertheless become representative by default. Those classroom and laboratory scientists who disagree, yet who remain silent, are inevitably tainted by this silence. In a war, guilt by association must be the Christian's operating hypothesis.

An intellectual war is going on. The Darwinian humanists have made it clear that they do not intend to take any academic prisoners. Neither should the creationists. Scientific neutrality is a myth. I cited Van Til's warning in the Preface, and I cite it again: "If the theistic position be defensible *it is an impossibility for any human being to be neutral*. This is quite readily admitted when a centrally religious question is discussed. We need only recall the words of Jesus, 'He that is not against me is for me'[17] to remind ourselves of this fact. When two nations are at war no citizens of either of these two nations can be neutral."[18]

The Curse

There is a traditional saying in America, "Nothing is sure except death and taxes." We see death as the ultimate and inescapable fact of life. But is death "normal"? The remarkable book by Arthur Custance, *The Seed of the Woman*, makes a strong case for all deaths as the result of either a disease that kills or an accident that kills. The living creature eventually loses its ability to fend off disease. Aging is, in this view, an interference with a normal process, life.[19]

The biblical accounts of resurrections from the dead indicate that the process of death can be overcome. So does Isaiah 65:20, which prophesies an extended life expectancy for sinners and righteous people before the day of judgment: "There shall be no more thence an infant of days, nor an old man that hath not filled his days: for the child shall die an hundred years old; but the sinner being an hundred years old shall be accursed." Yet we know that individual death is universal among higher animals.[20] We know that resurrections are

---

17. Mark 9:40.

18. Cornelius Van Til, *A Survey of Christian Epistemology*, Vol. 2 of *In Defense of Biblical Christianity* (Phillipsburg, New Jersey: Presbyterian and Reformed Pub. Co., [1962] 1969), p. 19.

19. Arthur C. Custance, *The Seed of the Woman* (Grand Rapids, Michigan: Zondervan, 1980). Custance is a theologian and a medical physiologist.

20. One-celled animals do not die; instead, they divide. The living material that they are made of continues on. Custance, *ibid.*

Introduction

a special miracle of God. Are we then prisoners in a world burdened by a constant curse? Is this curse a uniformitarian phenomenon, meaning the same during all periods of history and under all known circumstances? Can it accelerate or be retarded as a result of scientific activity or ethical activity?

When we bring up the question of uniformitarian rates of change, we thereby raise the issue of natural law. To what extent is a process of nature a "law"? To what extent is it a reliable regularity of nature? This is a fundamental question regarding the nature of reality.

Death, aging, and the decay of nature are regularities that we observe and use to formulate our plans and institutions. But are they uniformitarian processes? Are they inescapable? Are they constants? To what extent are they tied to God's curse of man and nature? If the curse should be steadily (or even sporadically) lifted, will these "constants" also change? Of course they will change: *this is how we will know that the curse has been lifted*. Then how can we legitimately describe them as uniformitarian processes? For that matter, is any process ultimately uniformitarian—the same, yesterday, today, and tomorrow? The Bible says no. The scientists say . . . ?

Entropy

Some Christians have argued that the curse of aging is an aspect of the phenomenon that scientists call entropy. Or better put, they argue that death, aging, and entropy are all the result of God's curse on man and nature. The physical degeneration and death of men certainly are part of the curse. But what about entropy, the supposedly universal "wearing out" of the universe? Is the curse of Genesis 3 the origin of entropy? For that matter, what exactly is the phenomenon of entropy?

Henry Morris, one of the founders of the post-1960 revival of creationism, or the Scientific Creation movement, places heavy reliance on the concept of entropy, which he equates with the second law of thermodynamics. He writes that

> there are three basic vehicles of physical reality associated with the entropy concept. In the structure of all systems, entropy is a measure of *disorder*. In the maintenance of all processes, entropy is a measure of *wasted energy*. In the transmission of all information, entropy is a measure of *useless noise*. Each of these concepts is basically equivalent to the other two, even though it expresses a distinct concept.

Always, furthermore, entropy tends to increase. Everywhere in the physical universe there is an inexorable downhill trend toward ultimate complete randomness, utter meaninglessness, and absolute stillness.[21]

This account of the second law of thermodynamics is not fundamentally different from what appears in many popular books written by humanistic scientists. Certainly, Jeremy Rifkin's interpretation of the second law conforms to this interpretation. But the Scientific Creationist always has an exception to the second law ready and waiting: "except when God miraculously intervenes to overcome the effects of entropy." This exception is rejected by modern science.

We usually think of a miracle as a one-time intervention by God in history. But what if the miracle of Christ's resurrection offers to God's people a way of steadily overcoming the *cursed effects* of the second law of thermodynamics? What if Christians' progressive (though incomplete) conformity to God's law through the empowering of the Holy Spirit were to result in a partial overcoming of the historic curse which God imposed on Adam and the earth? In short, why must occasional and unpredictable miracles by God be the only way to offset the world-deteriorating effects of entropy? Why can't entropy's unwanted effects—death at an early age, for example—be partially overcome through covenantal faithfulness (Ex. 20:12)? Isn't this possibility the primary potential social legacy of Christ's resurrection?

What if the greatest miracle of all—Jesus Christ's bodily resurrection from the dead—was only the first step in a new world order, meaning a *God-transformed, Bible-based, gospel-inaugurated new world order*, in contrast to the humanists' version of a central planning elite-transformed, legislation-based, politics-inaugurated new world order? If it was, then Christians have been given a momentous responsibility: to preach Christ's gospel of comprehensive redemption. (See Appendix C.) Because millions of Christians suffer from an inferiority complex in the face of temporarily triumphant humanism, they resist the idea that they have been given such comprehensive responsibility. They therefore resist the idea that God intends that His people work to establish His kingdom on earth in history. They prefer historical pessimism to historical optimism, for there is vastly more personal and institutional responsibility for Christians in a

---

21. Henry Morris, *The Troubled Waters of Evolution* (San Diego, California: C.L.P. Publishers, [1974] 1980), p. 121.

world of historical optimism. They also tend to prefer cosmic pessimism to cosmic optimism, for cosmic pessimism fits so much better into a worldview based on historical pessimism.

Negative Feedback

Scientists also speak of the process of negative feedback. "What goes up must come down," we are told from youth. Nothing multiplies forever. Things grow for a while, and then they stop growing. There are *limits to growth* in a finite world.

Christians acknowledge that negative feedback is a limiting factor in a cursed world. The animals are not allowed to multiply and overcome the land (Ex. 23:29). They are restrained by man or by "the forces of nature," meaning the environment's built-in limitations on the compound growth process. A multiplying species runs out of food or living space; some other rival species competes for the limited number of resources; still another species begins to prey on the expanding one, either externally ("beasts of prey") or internally (parasites). Similar restraints limit the development of human institutions in ethically rebellious civilizations.[22] Fallen man is never wholly free from sin. His institutions and his environment will never be wholly devoid of the process of negative feedback, in time and on earth.[23]

But is this system of cosmic negative feedback inescapable? Are there no exceptions? *What about the miracles in the Bible?* Aren't these classic examples of the non-universal nature of the entropy process (assuming what needs first to be proven, namely, that entropy is the physical basis of negative feedback)? This question should remain in the back of the reader's mind throughout this book. The question of how miracles fit into a world supposedly governed by unbreakable natural law should be the central question in all modern science. If natural law *is* breakable, then we must ask: How? Under what circumstances? Why? More to the point, what is the nature of "natural law"? Is it an autonomous, impersonal force that operates whether or not God intends otherwise?

---

22. Garrett Hardin, "The Cybernetics of Competition: A Biologist's View of Society," in Helmut Schoeck and James W. Wiggins (eds.), *Central Planning and Neomercantilism* (Princeton, New Jersey: Van Nostrand, 1964). Hardin, a dedicated evolutionist, does not discuss the possibility of the process of negative feedback being limited by the ethical character of a culture.

23. Garrett Hardin, *Nature and Man's Fate* (New York: Rinehart & Co., 1959), pp. 48-55.

Conclusion

Ultimately, this book asks three fundamental questions: 1) What is really fixed throughout world history: natural law, ethical law, or both? 2) How are these two forms of God-given law related? 3) Is there a discoverable relationship between how *mankind acts* and how the *world works*? In other words, does it make any difference to the operations of the external natural world whether people are generally covenant-keepers or covenant-breakers? Because Christians are divided over the answers to these three questions, we face a crisis in the Christian worldview.

1

THE UNNATURALNESS OF SCIENTIFIC NATURAL LAW

If the prospect of a dying universe causes us anguish, it does so only because we can forecast it, and we have as yet not the slightest idea why such forecasts are possible for us. A few figures scrawled on a piece of paper can describe the rate the universe expands, reveal what goes on inside a star, or predict where the planet Neptune will be on New Year's Day in the year A.D. 25,000. Why? Why should nature, whether hostile or benign, be in any way intelligible to us? All the mysteries of science are but palace guards to that mystery.

Timothy Ferris[1]

To a thoughtful humanist, this question boggles his mind: How can the mind of man grasp the nature of Nature? The Nobel Prize-winning physicist Eugene Wigner once wrote a scholarly paper for a professional mathematics journal: "The Unreasonable Effectiveness of Mathematics in the Natural Sciences."[2] Why is it, he asked, that mathematics, the product of man's mental artistry, is so useful in predicting the events of nature's independent environment? He had no answer.[3]

There *is* an answer. It is not one which is acceptable to humanists. It is this: *man is made in God's image*. God created the world, and then He created man to exercise dominion over it (Gen. 1:26-28).

---

1. Timothy Ferris, *The Red Limit: The Search for the Edge of the Universe* (New York: William Morrow, 1977), pp. 217-18.

2. Wigner, "The Unreasonable Effectiveness of Mathematics in the Natural Sciences," *Communications on Pure and Applied Mathematics*, Vol. 13 (1960), pp. 1-14.

3. He did not ask an even more important question: What produces the symmetry and coherence of mathematics in the mind of autonomous man? There is no humanism-based answer for that question, either. See Vern Poythress, "A Biblical View of Mathematics," in Gary North (ed.), *Foundations of Christian Scholarship: Essays in the Van Til Perspective* (Vallecito, California: Ross House Books, 1976), ch. 9.

Man's mind comprehends his environment—not perfectly, but adequately for a creature responsible before God to exercise dominion in God's name. It is only because mankind has this interpretive ability that science can exist. Even more crucial, *it is only because God created and actively, providentially sustains this universe that science can exist.*

Few Christians have been told that without three key doctrines that stem directly from Christian theology, modern science could not have been developed: first, the creation of the universe by a totally transcendent God out of nothing; second, the sustaining providence of God; third, linear (straight line) history. The pagan world, including Greece and Rome, did not believe these doctrines, and it did not develop theoretical science. Similarly, both Chinese and Islamic science failed to carry through on their hopeful beginnings in science because they rejected a Christian worldview. Because the West believed in these three doctrines, modern science became possible.

Because modern man has abandoned all three of these doctrines, modern science has become increasingly irrational, despite its tremendous advancement. As the experiments become more precise, physicists have lost faith in the coherence of the universe. The twentieth century has abandoned the stable, rational worldview of late-nineteenth-century physical science.

The roots of modern science began in the Middle Ages, an explicitly Christian era, and not in the supposedly atheistic, humanistic Renaissance.[4] (One reason for this is that the animist Renaissance was not atheistic; it was pantheistic and magical.)[5] Stanley Jaki—theologian, scientist, and historian—has written several books that demonstrate the truth that modern science was the product of a Christian worldview, but two of them are monumental: *Science and Creation* (1974) and *The Road of Science and the Ways to God* (1978). He is a member of the prestigious Institute for the Advancement of Science at Princeton, New Jersey. Albert Einstein was its most famous member.[6] What Jaki's books show is that modern physical science has become irrational to the degree that it has abandoned the

---

4. Pierre Duhem's pre-World War I studies in the history of Western science made it clear that science began in the Middle Ages. For this, his works were suppressed by hostile humanists in France for over four decades. Stanley L. Jaki, "Censorship and Science," *The Intercollegiate Review*, XXI (Winter 1985-86).

5. Frances Yates, *Giordano Bruno and the Hermetic Tradition* (New York: Vintage, [1964] 1969).

6. In 1987, Jaki won the Templeton Prize, which includes a check for $330,000. It is given to one person each year who offers mankind insights regarding the love of God.

doctrine of a Creator God. They chronicle science's abandonment of the idea of natural law and the independent nature that natural law was once believed to govern. Yet Christians continue to appeal to a long-dead version of Newtonian natural law, as if the physicists of the Copenhagen school sixty years ago had not blown away modern science's faith in a universe totally governed by such law. That such arguments impress untrained Christian laymen who maintain their faith in both God and popularized versions of Newton's worldview is not surprising. That such apologetic arguments defending creationism have not led modern scientists to embrace creationism or the Christian faith is even less surprising.

Natural Law: A Dead Humanist Faith

When Christians today speak of "natural law," they have in mind a universe that can be observed by man, and that conforms to rigorous mathematical laws, from the far reaches of the galaxy to the boiling water in the teakettle on the stove. Now, Christians do not really believe in a universe totally governed by such laws. They believe in miracles. These miracles are seen as miracles to the extent that they violate natural law. They also believe in human "free will" that is outside the mechanical cause-and-effect, clock-like predictability of Newtonian natural law. Nevertheless, except where man is concerned, Christians believe that the universe is coherent, and that God's creation reflects His own orderly nature.

Because most people have been influenced by this originally biblical worldview, they also believe in a world that is coherent, yet which also allows freedom and responsibility for human beings. The high school science textbooks of the public schools have not presented the case for twentieth-century quantum mechanics. The average person cannot grasp quantum mechanics. To this extent, the average person has been gracefully spared a personal confrontation with the impersonal and irrational world of modern physical science. Textbooks, in order to find a market, present a Newtonian worldview which physical scientists abandoned sometime between 1905 and 1925.[7] Here is how Paul Johnson begins his history of the twentieth century, probably the finest one-volume history of our century written so far:

---

7. Nick Herbert, *Quantum Reality: Beyond the New Physics* (Garden City, New York: Anchor Press/Doubleday, 1985), ch. 2.

The modern world began on 29 May 1919 when photographs of a solar eclipse, taken on the island of Principe off West Africa and at Sobral in Brazil, confirmed the truth of a new theory of the universe. It had been apparent for half a century that the Newtonian cosmology, based upon the straight lines of Euclidian geometry and Galileo's notion of absolute time, was in need of serious modification. It had stood for more than two hundred years. It was the framework within which the European Enlightenment, the Industrial Revolution, and the vast expansion of human knowledge, freedom and prosperity which characterized the nineteenth century, had taken place. But increasingly powerful telescopes were revealing anomalies. In particular, the motions of the planet Mercury deviated by forty-three seconds of an arc a century from its predictable behavior under Newtonian laws of physics. Why?

In 1905, a twenty-six-year-old German Jew, Albert Einstein, then working in the Swiss patent office in Berne, had published a paper, "On the electrodynamics of moving bodies," which became known as the Special Theory of Relativity. Einstein's observations on the way in which, in certain circumstances, lengths appeared to contract and clocks to slow down, are analogous to the effects of perspective in painting. In fact the discovery that space and time are relative rather than absolute terms of measurement is comparable, in its effects on our perception of the world, to the first use of perspective in art, which occurred in Greece in the two decades *c.* 500-480 B.C.[8]

This astronomical experiment confirmed in the minds of contemporary scientists Einstein's theory of special relativity. Johnson argues that this confirmation led to a fundamental restructuring of modern man's view of the universe. What he does not mention is the staggering fact that in that same year, 1905, Einstein published two other papers that had equally disrupting effects on modern science. The first, on the photoelectric effect, won him the Nobel Prize in physics in 1921; the second dealt with what scientists call Brownian motion: the peculiar wiggling of extremely tiny particles of matter when suspended in liquids. The first paper confirmed the reality of quantum mechanics, and this has led most theoretical physicists to deny the reality of a subatomic universe. The second paper showed how the reality of atoms could be decided experimentally. The experiments by Jean Perrin that were based on Einstein's suggestion later confirmed the existence of atoms.[9] Einstein's three papers

---

8. Paul Johnson, *Modern Times: The World from the Twenties to the Eighties* (New York: Harper & Row, 1983), p. 1.
9. Herbert, *Quantum Reality*, pp. 35-36.

almost singlehandedly shattered the worldview of Newtonian science — shattered it so completely that even Einstein, who later tried to pick up the pieces, could not put them together again.[10]

Newton's view of the universe was the product of Christian presuppositions. As those presuppositions have been borrowed and then abandoned by modern, officially atheistic or religiously skeptical scientists, this view of natural law has become increasingly unacceptable to scientists, as I hope to indicate in this chapter. Thus, any appeal to scientific natural laws as a defense of the Christian faith will prove increasingly useless, and has proved nearly useless for three decades. Modern scientists have steadily abandoned any reliance upon the traditional concept of natural law—itself an unstable mixture of Greek philosophical speculation and Christianity[11] — precisely because they have self-consciously abandoned Christianity.

This is why any attempt to refute evolutionists by an appeal to the second law of thermodynamics will inevitably backfire. The popularity in Christian circles of the writings of Jeremy Rifkin indicates that this appeal has already backfired. In short, it is a waste of effort to attempt a scientifically acceptable refutation of twentieth-century physical science by means of an argument based on nineteenth-century concepts of physical cause and effect.

I realize that at this point, most of my readers will not fully understand what I am saying. I have therefore decided to prove my case in Chapter One. Unfortunately, much of the material I use to prove my case is somewhat technical. So to help everyone get through it, I recommend that each reader put these words in the back of his mind: "These scientists must be crazy." You do not need to remember every argument. All you need to do is remember my

---

10. Though I am not sufficiently competent academically to judge the accuracy of the following book, let me at least suggest that Christian physicists would find intriguing the little-known published critiques of Einstein by Herbert Eugene Ives (1882-1953), collected and published in one volume, *The EINSTEIN Myth and the Ives Papers: A Counter-Revolution in Physics*, edited by Richard Hazlitt and Dean Turner (Old Greenwich, Connecticut: Devin-Adair, 1979). This could be a dead end, but at least it is a place to begin rethinking the shattered universe that Einstein bequeathed to mankind.

11. Archie P. Jones, "Natural Law and Christian Resistance to Tyranny," *Christianity and Civilization*, 3 (1983); Jones, "Apologists of Classical Tyranny: An Introductory Critique of Straussianism," *Journal of Christian Reconstruction*, V (Summer 1978); Rex Downie, "Natural Law and God's Law: An Antithesis," *Journal of Christian Reconstruction*, ibid.

conclusion: *modern science has lost its mind*. Science has lost its collective mind because scientists have abandoned faith in the God of the Bible.

But this raises a key question: Should Christians appeal to modern science, let alone nineteenth-century science, in order to defend their position? Should they build their case for creationism in terms of scientific concepts that have been abandoned by modern science, and which also lead them into the clutches of anti-Christian social theorists?

Before I answer these questions, I need to introduce you to a world of arrogant intellectuals who are in the process of going crazy.

An Autonomous (Self-law) Universe?

Do the laws of nature exist independently of man, man's observations, man's tools of observation, man's mathematics, and man's mind? The Bible says yes. The animals reproduced according to their kind before man arrived on the scene (Gen. 1:24-25). These laws do not exist independent of a Person, meaning God Himself, but they exist independent of man. Today, however, the idea of a law-governed universe independent from man has begun to bother many scientists. As they have become more self-consistent concerning epistemology — "What can man know, and how can he know it?" — they have placed all of nature's orderliness in the mind of man.

This sounds crazy to most people. Obviously, everyone agrees that the universe existed before man came on the scene. Nature must have operated in terms of fixed laws. Man only discovers these laws; he does not create them. But this common sense view has come under increasing attack ever since Immanuel Kant wrote his *Critique of Pure Reason* in 1787. Kant wrote: "Thus the order and regularity in the appearances, which we entitle *nature*, we ourselves introduce. We could never find them in appearances, had not we ourselves, or the nature of our mind, originally set them there."[12] We can know nothing of the universe as such, or as he called it, the thing-in-itself. We cannot say that nature is *autonomously* an orderly system. Only through the ordering processes inherent in the rational human mind can any orderliness of nature be described, Kant maintained. Modern science has become more and more consistent with Kant in

---

12. Immanuel Kant, *The Critique of Pure Reason* (1787), translated by Norman Kemp Smith (New York: St. Martin's, [1929] 1965), Sect. A 125, p. 147.

the twentieth century. He is *the* philosopher of the modern world.

Does this mean that modern humanist thought teaches that it is actually man who creates the orderliness of nature? Increasingly, this is exactly what is being said. Ferris writes of Sir Arthur Eddington, the brilliant British astronomer of the early twentieth century: "Eddington believed the laws of nature reside within our minds, are created not by the cosmos but by our perceptions of it, so that a visitor from another planet could deduce all our science simply by analyzing how our brains are wired. In Eddington's view, we know physical laws *a priori*, as Kant maintained, although where Kant conceived part of our *a priori* knowledge as inborn, Eddington felt it was derived from experience in observation and reasoning."[13] This is radical subjectivism, an obvious development of consistent humanism.

Prominent modern scientists have resisted the idea that the universe is not law-governed apart from man. Albert Einstein was one of those who resisted it.[14] Physicist Nick Herbert uses biblical imagery to describe Einstein's resistance: "Einstein, despite his numerous contributions to its success, never accepted quantum theory into his heart and stubbornly held to the old-fashioned belief that a realistic vision of the world was compatible with the quantum facts."[15] As Einstein wrote, "Belief in an external world independent of the perceiving subject is the basis of all natural science."[16] That he felt it necessary in the 1930's to make such an intuitively obvious statement indicates the extent of the epistemological crisis that had already begun to engulf modern physical science. Step by step, scientists have adopted subjective epistemologies that do not allow them to support such a faith in an independently lawful universe.[17]

---

13. Ferris, *Red Limit*, p. 116.

14. Stanley Jaki, "The Absolute Beneath the Relative: Reflections on Einstein's Theories," *The Intercollegiate Review*, XX (Spring/Summer 1985).

15. Herbert, *Quantum Reality*, p. 23.

16. Albert Einstein, *The World As I See It* (New York: Covici-Friede, 1934), p. 60.

17. Stanley Jaki, *The Road of Science and the Ways to God* (University of Chicago Press, 1978), ch. 13. Jaki stresses the attempt of physical scientists to retain their faith in an objective external world. As a Benedictine priest and a superb historian of science, Father Jaki is a believer in Roman Catholic philosophical realism — the reality of the laws governing the external world. His problem is that modern physics increasingly has abandoned philosophical realism in principle, despite the personal commitment of major scientists, including Einstein, to an unexplained and self-contradictory faith in the reality of the laws of the external world.

Twentieth-Century Quantum Mechanics

You are about to enter the realm of verbal, intellectual chaos—a chaos that modern physical scientists claim is so perfect that every experiment ever conducted in terms of it has confirmed it. To make our way through this chaos, we laymen must rely on popular works that explain the universe—perhaps only a mental universe—studied by modern physicists. A good place to begin is with Chapter Two of Nick Herbert's book, *Quantum Reality*. That chapter is titled, "Physicists Losing Their Grip."

Multiple Theories

Herbert begins his chapter with a quotation from Bryce DeWitt and Neill Graham: "No development of modern science has had a more profound impact on human thinking than the advent of quantum theory. Wrenched out of centuries-old thought patterns, physicists of a generation ago found themselves compelled to embrace a new metaphysics. The distress which this reorientation produced continues to the present day. Basically physicists have suffered a severe loss: their hold on reality."[18]

Herbert summarizes eight theories of how the world of subatomic particles (or waves, or nothing in particular) functions. Laymen should not expect many of these explanations to make sense. In fact, Herbert warns us: "Physicists' reality crisis is twofold: 1. There are too many of these quantum realities; 2. All of them are preposterous."[19] These theories, all of which supposedly produce reliable predictions of *observed, representative* behavior, are as follows:

1. There is no deep (underlying) reality.
2. Reality is created by observation.
3. Reality is an undivided wholeness.
4. There are many parallel universes.
5. The world obeys a non-human reasoning.
6. The world is made of ordinary objects.
7. Consciousness creates reality.
8. The world is twofold: potentials and actualities.

---

18. Herbert, *Quantum Reality*, p. 15.
19. *Ibid.*, p. 28.

Each of these theories is defended by brilliant scientists. My favorite, because of its sheer arrogance, is number 4, plural worlds. This can be regarded as the ultimate in magical reasoning, a scientific legacy of the Renaissance's theory of multiple worlds, or the "principle of plenitude," as Arthur Lovejoy called it.[20] Herbert summarizes: "Of all claims of the New Physics none is more outrageous than the contention that myriads of universes are created upon the occasion of each measurement act. For any situation in which several different outcomes are possible (flipping a coin, for instance), some physicists believe that *all outcomes actually occur*. In order to accommodate different outcomes without contradiction, entire new universes spring into being, identical in every detail except for the single outcome that gave them birth. In the case of a flipped coin, one universe contains a coin that came up heads, a coin showing tails."[21]

Our apologetic approach must recognize the reality of what has happened since 1905: "Just as Newton shattered the medieval crystal spheres, modern quantum theory has irreparably smashed Newton's clockwork. We are now certain that the world *is not* a deterministic mechanism. But what the world *is* we cannot say."[22]

Will Heathkit Eventually Offer One of These?

On the Science page of the *New York Times* (April 14, 1987) are two stories. These two stories summarize the Darwinian revolution better than anything I have ever seen or expect to see. The first discusses "the black skull." With its discovery in 1986, "the small contentious fraternity of paleoanthropology was stunned into a rare state of unanimity. Everyone agreed that the skull was the most significant early humanlike fossil to be found in more than a decade. Everyone agreed it would necessitate a major rethinking of the human family tree." Today, however, everyone is arguing again about how to fit the 2.5 million-year-old skull into the human family tree. Anyone who wants to learn more about this latest piece of Darwinian mythology is welcome to pursue it. The skull points once again to "man, the product of cosmic purposelessness." Man has only "recently" come out of a tree. Poor man, the grandson of apes.

---

20. See Arthur O. Lovejoy, *The Great Chain of Being: A Study of the History of an Idea* (New York: Harper Torchbook, [1933] 1960), chaps. 4, 5.
21. Herbert, *Quantum Reality*, p. 19.
22. *Ibid.*, p. xii.

But this myth of man's animal origins has always been only half of the Darwinian theology. It is always accompanied by the second part, "Man, the new sovereign of the universe."[23] On the same page of the *Times*, we are told of a new theory of physics. The title of the article tells all: "Physicist Aims to Create a Universe, Literally." Prof. Alan Guth of the Massachusetts Institute of Technology and several collaborators argue that it is theoretically possible for mankind to create a whole universe. He does not mean intellectually; he means really and truly, cross your heart and hope to live eternally.

If you have a sense of the ironic, you will appreciate his introductory essay on the subject, published in *Physics Letters*: "An Obstacle to Creating a Universe in the Laboratory." For all I know, there may be several such obstacles, half a dozen, perhaps, beginning with this one: man is not God. Here is what Dr. Guth expects the *Times* reader to believe: "The odd thing is that you might even be able to start a new universe using energy equivalent to just a few pounds of matter. Provided you could find some way to compress it to a density of about 10 to the 75th power grams per cubic centimeter, and provided you could trigger the thing, inflation would do the rest." I think he means inflation as in "Big Bang," not inflation as in "Federal Reserve System."

Where will this new universe fit in the scheme of things? I have a mental picture of a gunslinger coming up to the sheriff with the words, "This galaxy ain't big enough for both of us; one of us will have to leave." I hope Prof. Guth clears this experiment with the Environmental Protection Agency, or at the very least, with his local zoning board.

The reporter comments: "Does this mean that our universe could have been created as the conscious act of human beings in some other universe with which we no longer have any contact?" Prof. Guth's answer is straightforward: "Well, that is the possibility we're exploring. Nothing in our calculations so far has ruled out such a possibility." Man, the descendent of apes and amoebas, has suddenly become man, the creation of other men, who could be the creation of previous men, etc., etc., ad infinitum.

Personally, I think it is a lot cheaper to create quantum universes by flipping a coin.

---

23. Gary North, *The Dominion Covenant: Genesis* (2nd ed.; Tyler, Texas: Institute for Christian Economics, 1987), Appendix A: "From Cosmic Purposelessness to Humanistic Sovereignty."

"I Observe; Therefore You Are"

The most widely shared of the eight views is the second: reality is created by observation. Herbert says that this is the second aspect of the vision offered by the Copenhagen physicists, led by Niels Bohr and Werner Heisenberg. "Although the numerous physicists of the Copenhagen school do not believe in deep reality, they do assert the existence of *phenomenal reality*. What we see is undoubtedly real, they say, but these phenomena are not really there in the absence of an observation. The Copenhagen interpretation properly consists of two distinct parts: 1. There is no reality in the absence of observation; 2. Observation creates reality. 'You create your own reality,' is the theme of Fred Wolfe's *Taking the Quantum Leap*."[24] Herbert goes on to explain what all this means. (Note that he uses "she" as the personal pronoun when he refers to physicists—a sign of the cultural times, since not a single female physicist is referred to in his book.)

What's at stake in the quantum reality question is not the actual existence of electrons but *the manner in which electrons possess their major attributes*. Classical physicists imagined that every particle possessed at each moment a definite position and momentum; each field likewise possessed a particular field strength at every location. If we agree to call any entity—particle, field, apple, or galaxy—which possesses its attributes innately an "ordinary object" then the fundamental message of classical physics was this: the entire physical world consists of nothing but ordinary objects.

Quantum theory suggests, on the other hand, that the world is *not* made of ordinary objects. An electron, and every other quantum entity, does not possess all its attributes innately. An electron does possess certain innate attributes—mass, change, and spin, for instance—which serve to distinguish it from other kinds of quantum entities. The value of these attributes is the same for every electron under all measurement conditions. With respect to these particular attributes, even the electron behaves like an ordinary object.

However, all other attributes, most notably position and momentum, which, it was thought, classical particles possessed innately, can no longer be attached to the electron without qualification. These attributes—called "dynamic" to distinguish from the "static" attributes mass, change, and spin—do not belong to the electron itself, but seem to be created in part by the electron's measurement context. The fact of the matter is that nobody really knows these days how an electron, or any other quantum entity, actually possesses its dynamic attributes.

---

24. Herbert, *Quantum Reality*, p. 17.

According to the Copenhagen interpretation, the electron's dynamic attributes are *contextual:* what attributes it seems to have depends on how you measure it. An electron's so-called attributes belong jointly to the electron and the measuring device. When a Copenhagenist says, "There is no deep reality," she means that there is no hidden value of position that the electron "really has" when it is not being measured. Since position is an attribute that belongs jointly to the electron and its measuring device, when you take away the measuring device you take away the electron's position too.[25]

He concludes with these opaque words: "When you take away the measuring device the electron undoubtedly still exists, but it possesses no dynamic attributes at all; in particular it has no definite place or motion. We cannot picture such a state of being, but nature seems to have no trouble producing such entities. Indeed, such entities are all this world is made of."[26] You are reading this correctly. But to make sure we understand, he says it again: "Electrons cannot really be said to have dynamic attributes of their own. What attributes they seem to have depends upon how we choose to analyze them. A clock comes apart in only one way: it's made of definite parts. A wave, on the other hand, doesn't have parts; you can divide it up any way you please. However, none of these divisions is there to begin with; the kinds of parts a wave seems to have depends on how *we* cut it up. The world's wave nature makes us in a certain sense co-creators of its attributes."[27]

Has Bell Gone Bats?

Herbert is a follower of Irish physicist John Stewart Bell. Bell in 1964 began working on a mathematical proof that has supposedly solved some of the major problems of quantum theory. Herbert argues that unless we adopt Bell's theory, quantum theory's world of subatomic "stuff" will remain incoherent and without dynamic attributes except when observed.

To introduce Bell's breakthrough, Herbert begins with David Bohm. Bohm in 1952 offered a theory that brought objective reality back to the subatomic universe by arguing that the attributes of the quanta are contextual; they influence each other, and thus in a sense hold each other together. There was one flaw in his reasoning: to

---

25. *Ibid.*, pp. 45-46.
26. *Ibid.*, p. 47.
27. *Ibid.*, pp. 134-35.

"hold each other together" in a context, subatomic particles and waves had to connect to each other at speeds faster than the speed of light, Einstein's one universal constant. Without supposing such trans-luminary connections, there is no way to restore coherence to the quantum world. "Without faster-than-light connections, an ordinary object model of reality simply cannot explain the facts."[28]

Consider what he is saying. The speed of light and gravitation have been the modern world's only constants. It is the speed of light that supposedly proves that the universe is over ten billion years old. It is the speed of light that has shoved creation back into the mists of forgotten time, and shoved God out of the universe entirely. Yet now that God is conveniently distant, science is now ready to scrap the speed of light as a constant. God is now psychologically removed from modern science, so the precise scientific instrument that was used to shove Him out of His domain can now be restructured to fit man's latest speculative theories of matter.

God no longer provides coherence to the quantum world. Scientists desperately wanted to find coherence in the universe apart from God. His Bible was not to be made into the standard of coherence. The speed of light was their agreed-upon choice as the source of cosmic measurement. But this once-inflexible speed of light can no longer provide it, at least in the world of the quanta, or so David Bohm's theory indicates. Herbert says that Bell's theorem provides the needed coherence, but only if the concept of space-time relations is scrapped—*just as it is scrapped in the biblical account of creation.* The mutual influencing process of the world of the quanta must involve the entire universe, Bell says. There must be instantaneous communication across the entire universe. He calls these influences "non-local influences." Three centuries ago, they were called the voice of God.

Non-local influences do not diminish with distance. They are as potent at a million miles as at a millimeter.

Non-local influences act simultaneously. The speed of their transmission is not limited by the velocity of light.

A non-local interaction links up one location with another without crossing space, without decay, and without delay. A non-local interaction is, in short, *unmediated, unmitigated,* and *immediate.*[29]

---

28. *Ibid.*, p. 51.
29. *Ibid.*, p. 214.

In 1972, a test was conducted by physicist John Clauser of the University of California, Berkeley. This test demonstrated that two photons traveling at the speed of light in different directions influenced one another at a distance instantaneously. He had set out to disprove Bell, which makes the experiment that much more curious. Another test was conducted by physicist Alain Aspect of the University of Paris in 1982. It also confirmed Bell's thesis of non-local reality. The universe is no longer governed by the universal constant of the speed of light. What happens at one "end" of the universe may very well influence something at the other end, without waiting 20 billion light years.

What Bell has offered is a mathematical proof of an interconnected *yet still impersonal* universe. There is no personal God holding it together. Herbert's song, "Bell's Theorem Blues," indicates the problem:

> Doctor Bell say we connected.
> He call me on the phone.
> Doctor Bell say we united.
> He call me on the phone.
> But if we really together, baby
> How come I feel so all alone?[30]

Think of what Colossians says about Jesus Christ: "By him were all things created, that are in heaven, and that are in earth, visible and invisible. . . . And he is before all things, and by him all things consist" (Col. 1: 16a, 17). God's administration of cause and effect is not constrained by the speed of light.

But if the speed of light is no longer a limiting constant, what about the 20-billion-year-old universe, a calculation based on the speed of light?

Schrödinger's Cat

The British Broadcasting Corporation (BBC) asked physicist John Gribbin to explain to the viewers what science now teaches about subatomic "particles-waves." Gribbin was the scientist who co-authored a book in 1974 about the biggest non-event of the 1980's: the 1982 "grand alignment" of the planet Jupiter and several other planets, which supposedly might set off earthquakes around the

---

30. *Ibid.*, Appendix II.

world.[31] Nothing happened. Nevertheless, Isaac Asimov wrote the forward to the book, so Gribbin was at least within the "pop science" fraternity in 1974, and was not cast out after 1982.

Gribbin is a defender of Copenhagen's version of quantum theory: nothing is real at bottom, and so it is the observation that imparts reality to the subatomic world. He discusses the fact that Einstein found the conclusions of quantum mechanics unacceptable; so did physicist Erwin Schrödinger. The two men wanted desperately to believe in the inherent orderliness of autonomous nature. But such a view is scientifically old fashioned, Gribbin's book demonstrates. Modern quantum mechanics rests on the presupposition that the subatomic world is governed by equations, and there is no underlying physical reality corresponding to the equations. The equations, not physical reality, are primary in modern quantum mechanics. As he forthrightly says, *nothing is real*. "For what quantum mechanics says is that nothing is real and that we cannot say anything about what things are doing when we are not looking at them."[32]

Schrödinger resisted this implication of modern physics, which, after all, is supposed to deal with what the Greeks called *phusis*, the independent, eternal laws of nature. The subatomic world, modern physics tells us, is a world in which light is both wave and particle. It is a world governed by equations, not physical reality. So Schrödinger designed a hypothetical experiment which he believed would refute the worldview of quantum mechanics. Place a cat in a box, he said. In the box is a hammer suspended over a glass container of poisonous gas. The hammer is connected to a triggering device that in turn is connected to another device that registers the decay of a radioactive substance. If a particular atom decays, the recording device signals the triggering device that holds the hammer. This second device releases the hammer, which falls on top of the glass container, releasing the gas. The cat dies.

Say that there is a 50-50 chance that in any period of time, the particular controlling atom will decay. The cat therefore has a 50-50 chance of surviving. Thus, *the survival of the cat is based on a statistical probability*, the decay or non-decay of an atom.

---

31. John Gribbin and Stephen Plagemann, *The Jupiter Effect* (New York: Walker, 1974).

32. John Gribbin, *In Search of Schrödinger's Cat: Quantum Physics and Reality* (New York: Bantam, 1984), p. 2.

Place the lid on the box. The experimenter can no longer see the cat. Now, Schrödinger asked, is the cat dead or alive? Has the radioactive material produced the decay of the atom that will trigger the hammer, break the glass container, release the gas, and kill the cat? According to quantum mechanics, Schrödinger fully understood, *an atomic particle is simply a statistical wave function.* It is in an undefinable state in between decay and non-decay. If this is true about atomic particles, Schrödinger was saying, *then the cat is also only a statistical wave function:* it is neither dead nor alive; it remains simply a statistical wave function until such time as someone opens the box and sees whether it is dead or alive. But doesn't this prove that the world of quantum theory is preposterous? Schrödinger thought that it did.

Obviously, the experiment really deals with radioactive waveparticles, not cats. But Schrödinger thought that by describing the quantum theory in terms of a common object such as a cat, he would show the preposterous nature of quantum mechanics' theory regarding the non-substance of unobserved atoms. Einstein agreed with him. But instead of persuading their professional colleagues of the reality of subatomic physical particles, this hypothetical experiment convinced a generation of quantum theorists of the truth of the preposterous. *They came to believe that the cat really would occupy a statistical no-man's land between existence and non-existence.* The only way to give actual status to the cat, either dead or alive, is to open the box and look. Gribbin writes:

> But now we encounter the strangeness of the quantum world. According to the theory, *neither* of the two possibilities open to the radioactive material, and therefore to the cat, has any reality unless it is observed. The atomic decay has neither happened nor not happened, the cat has neither been killed nor not killed, until we look inside the box to see what has happened. Theorists who accept the pure version of quantum mechanics say that the cat exists in some indeterminate state, neither dead nor alive, until an observer looks into the box to see how things are getting on. Nothing is real unless it is observed.[33]

All this stems from "the fundamental axiom of quantum theory, that no elementary phenomenon is a phenomenon until it is a recorded phenomenon. And the process of recording can play strange tricks with our everyday concept of reality."[34]

---

33. *Ibid.*, pp. 2-3.
34. *Ibid.*, pp. 209-10.

What about electrons? What about radioactive decay? Does a physical process of cause and effect govern them? Is there a physical explanation for the decay of a particular atom at a particular time? No, says quantum mechanics. Gribbin writes that "no 'underlying reason' for radioactive decay or atomic-energy transitions to occur when they do has ever been found. It really does seem that these changes occur entirely by chance, on a statistical basis, and that already begins to raise fundamental philosophical questions. In the classical world, everything has its cause. . . . But in the world of the quantum, such direct causality begins to disappear as soon as we look at radioactive decay and atomic transitions. An electron doesn't move down from one energy level to another at a particular time for any particular reason. . . . No outside agency pushes the electron, and no internal clockwork times the jump. It just happens, for no particular reason, now rather than later."[35]

Things happen *for no particular reason*. This sounds crazy to the average person. It sounded crazy to Schrödinger and Einstein, too. In later years, Schrödinger said of his hypothetical experiment, "I don't like it, and I'm sorry I ever had anything to do with it."[36] Nevertheless, this nonsense is today the foundation of modern physical science, from chemistry to genetic engineering. *The idea of physical cause and effect has disappeared in the discipline of subatomic physics.* The idea of statistical randomness has triumphed to such an extent that scientists really believe that all there really is in the unobserved world is statistical randomness, until they or one of their instruments measures an effect. In short, "no observer—no reality."

Lest Gribbin's speculations regarding the lack of causality be dismissed as the ramblings of an unrepresentative physicist, consider the words of John von Neumann, one of the most respected mathematicians of this century. He wrote what Herbert has called the quantum bible.[37] Neumann said that "there is at present no occasion and no reason to speak of causality in nature—because no experiment indicates its presence, since macroscopic experiments are unsuitable in principle, and the only known theory which is compatible with our experiences relative to elementary processes, quantum mechanics, contradicts it."[38] Historian of science Stanley Jaki

---

35. *Ibid.*, p. 66.
36. *Ibid.*, introductory page.
37. Herbert, *Quantum Reality*, p. 47.
38. J. von Neumann, *Mathematical Foundations of Quantum Mechanics*, trans. R. T. Beyer (Princeton, New Jersey: Princeton University Press, 1955), p. 327; cited by Stanley Jaki, *The Relevance of Physics* (University of Chicago Press, 1966), p. 362.

traces this line of reasoning back to a 1927 scholarly paper by physicist Werner Heisenberg.[39] Jaki, a Benedictine scholar and a philosophical realist, rejects such speculation as "careless," but he admits that Neumann's book "is still regarded as perhaps the deepest and most rigorous probing into the mathematical foundations of quantum mechanics."[40]

The physicists have done with physical cause and effect what they have also done with God: first, they have denied that *anyone can know* the process of physical causation in subatomic physics, and therefore the concept of physical causation is irrelevant to subatomic physics; second, they jump (and not randomly!) to the conclusion that a cause-and-effect relationship *does not exist* in the realm of subatomic physics. Substitute "God" for "cause and effect," and you can see the transition from official agnosticism to atheism.

If this view of quantum mechanics is assumed by a significant minority of modern physicists, then what does the quantum physicist do with subatomic reality when that reality has no God to observe it? Does it disappear? Gribbin struggles with the unsatisfying intellectual alternatives left to man. He begins with *atheism* as the only scientifically acceptable presupposition: *no outside observer exists.* "By definition, the universe is self-contained. It includes everything, so there is no outside observer who notices the existence of the universe and thereby collapses its complex web of interacting alternative realities into one wave function."[41] In other words, there is no God who observes what is going on inside the closed box of the universe, precisely because it *is* a closed box.

Problem: Who gives reality to the universe by reducing the statistically possible wave functions to a single wave function? Who makes the world real? Gribbin is willing to consider even Bishop Berkeley's eighteenth-century philosophy, *solipsism*: the idea that I know that I exist, but that it is impossible to prove that anyone else exists. "I would prefer even the solipsist argument, that there is only one observer in the universe, myself, and that my observations are the all-important factor that crystallizes reality out of the web of quantum possibilities—but extreme solipsism is a deeply unsatisfactory philosophy for someone whose own contribution to the world is

---

39. *Idem.*
40. *Ibid.*, p. 363.
41. Gribbin, *Schrödinger's Cat*, p. 236.

writing books to be read by other people."[42] Nevertheless, better this "deeply unsatisfactory philosophy" than faith in the providential God of the Bible, Gribbin is saying.

We see the truth of the psalmist: "The fool hath said in his heart, There is no God" (Ps. 14:1a). Modern science has adopted foolishness rather than adopt the doctrine of the creation of the world by God. Today's scientists are unwilling to accept as the basis of the world of subatomic physics, or even of Schrödinger's cat, the words of Moses: "The secret things belong unto the Lord our God: but those things which are revealed belong unto us and to our children for ever, that we may do all the words of this law" (Deut. 29:29). If scientific man cannot know the secret things of the universe, then scientists are prepared to argue that *chaos is lord*. If man's statements about the unseen universe are limited to making statistical correlations, then the unseen universe itself is nothing more than statistical correlations. Humanist man attempts to create the universe in his own image.

The Christian replies that God knows everything, God observes everything, and God holds the universe together: "And he is before all things, and by him all things consist" (Col. 1:17). The atheist scientist would rather live in a world whose substance is nothing more than statistical models than to admit that this world is God's.

The Disintegration of the West's Worldview

Why this digression on quantum mechanics? Because twentieth-century science must be recognized for what it is: a system self-consciously upheld by the irrational. Modern physics is beginning to resemble Eastern mysticism, as we see in books such as Fritjof Capra's *The Tao of Physics* (1975) and Gary Zukav's *The Dancing Wu Li Masters* (1980), both of which appear in Gribbin's recommended bibliography, despite his disclaimer that in *his* book, we would find no Eastern mysticism.[43]

As atheistic scientists become more consistent in their atheism, they find that the subatomic world is disintegrating, if not before their very eyes, then at least whenever they close them or turn off their measuring devices. But this disintegration of the unobserved realm of subatomic physics has not taken place because the actual

---

42. *Ibid.*, pp. 236-37.
43. *Ibid.*, p. xvi.

realm of subatomic physics is really a statistical wave function whenever no one is observing it. No, it is because the Christian worldview of the West has been abandoned. The West's vision of reality is disintegrating, not the realm of matter. To sustain that original scientific vision of an integrated, coherent universe, men need a biblical doctrine of God.

From the days of Isaac Newton, there have been major unanswered (and seemingly unanswerable) questions associated with modern physics. Gravity is a big question. How do stars and planets influence each other, as Newton claimed, "at a distance"? If there is no substance linking them, then how does one produce an effect on the other, or both on each other? This question baffled scientists right up until the end of the nineteenth century, when they finally agreed to stop asking. They had first proclaimed that a substance called the *ether* fills interstellar space, and then they spent almost two centuries trying to find any evidence of its existence. They failed, and after Einstein and other modern physical theorists began writing in the first decade of this century, scientists finally abandoned belief in the ether. They now face a major question: "ether/or?" Or what?

They could answer, as Newton did, that it is God who holds the mass of the universe together, not the ether. They could say that an invisible, yet undiscovered physical force holds it together, "but we will not call it the ether." They could say that nothing holds it together, but somehow it displays incredibly predictable regularities. They are so hostile to the idea that a personal force (God) holds it together that they would prefer to believe that nothing does. Or they could say that it is held together by statistical formulas. More and more, they are drifting toward the last solution. Until they agree, however, they just repeat endlessly, "Gravity holds it together," for want of a better magical incantation.

What I am arguing is simple enough: the concept of natural physical law is acceptable intellectually only to those who are Christians, or at least those whose worldview has been heavily influenced by the conclusions of theism. To the extent that men abandon biblical Christianity, they abandon the foundation of rational discourse. In this century, scientists have become more consistent with their anti-God presuppositions. They have therefore begun to destroy the intellectual foundation of science. They would rather abandon natural law than retain faith in a God-sustained universe. Step by step, from the realm of unobserved subatomic physics to Schrödinger's cat in the box, irrationalism is invading Western science. Twentieth-century scientists have steadily abandoned faith in natural law. And in some ways, what they have adopted resembles magic. Physicist John Wheeler has written: "There may be no such thing as the 'glittering central mechanism of the universe' to be seen behind a glass wall at the end of the trail. Not machinery but magic may be the better description of the treasure that is waiting."[44]

The Quest for Natural Law

From the day that men began to observe the external realm around them, they have faced the problem of sorting out the "meaningful" regularities from the "irrelevant" events of any aspect of reality. We know, for example, that biological species reproduce in certain ways. "And God said, Let the earth bring forth the living creature after his kind . . ." (Gen. 1:24a). Discovering what a "kind" is, or discovering the essential nature of each "kind," is not as easy as it sounds. Discovering the biological mechanism (and "mechanism" is probably a misleading word) of transmitting and maintaining a "kind" is exceedingly difficult. Why is a sheep not a goat?[45] Why is a donkey not a horse? Why is a mule neither a donkey nor a horse, but the offspring of a donkey and a horse? And why can't a mule reproduce? These are legitimate scientific questions. Scientists require "models" to help them sort out the relevant from the irrelevant. They need to know the "essence" of some feature of the world they are investigating, meaning *fixed relationships*.

What is fixed about any relationship, and what is flexible? What is necessary, and what is irrelevant? (Necessary for what purpose? Irrelevant for what purpose?) Are the observed regularities that we have regarded as crucial truly fixed? Or are they simply statistical averages? Are they fixed, "unless. . . ."? Do men always die *unless* God intervenes? Does clothing always wear out *unless* God intervenes? How can we define "God intervenes" without simultaneously tampering with the doctrine of the providence (the sustaining hand) of God? Does God control the world in two essentially different

---

44. Cited by Herbert, *Quantum Reality*, p. 29.
45. In 1984 British scientists used genetic manipulation techniques to produce a new species which is a combination of sheep and goat. Jeremy Rifkin, *Declaration of a Heretic* (London: Routledge and Kegan Paul, 1985), p. 42. The resulting sterile hybrid animal has been called a "geep." See a photograph in *Newsweek* (May 4, 1987), p. 64.

ways: By predictable law, but also by occasional violations of this supposedly fixed natural order?

In short, what is a "law of nature"? How can we measure it or put it to productive use? What is a random deviation from a law of nature? What, for that matter, is randomness? What is a miracle? Can we legitimately speak of absolutely fixed natural laws without denying miracles? Can we speak of miracles without in some way compromising the definition of natural law? More important, can we legitimately speak of God's providence without calling into question the naturalness (independence, or self-contained lawfulness) of natural law? Can we speak of natural law without adopting humanist presuppositions concerning the *autonomy* of nature, the *simplicity* of nature,[46] and the *impersonalism* of nature?

In the past, discussions of the laws of nature have led to humanist conclusions, which is one reason why Darwinism triumphed historically.[47] These kinds of questions were important in the transition from "Christian" Newtonian science to modern evolutionism during the nineteenth century. Christians had already given up too much ground to the humanist scientists by the time *Origin of Species* was published in 1859.[48]

Christian scholars still have yet to deal systematically with these

---

46. Henry Morris refers to the operation of nature's "Principle of Least Action" and the theological principle of "the Economy of Miracles": *The Genesis Record: A Scientific and Devotional Commentary on the Book of Beginnings* (San Diego, California: Creation-Life Publishers, 1976), p. 195. For a theological critique of the fallacy of simplicity, see R. J. Rushdoony, *Foundations of Social Order: Studies in the Creeds and Councils of the Early Church* (Fairfax, Virginia: Thoburn Press, [1969] 1978), ch. 9.

47. Gary North, *The Dominion Covenant: Genesis*, Appendix C: "Cosmologies in Conflict: Creation vs. Evolution." For a detailed study of the debate over the operations of nature in historical geology, see R. Hooykaas, *Natural Law and Divine Miracle: A Historical-Critical Study of the Principle of Uniformity in Geology, Biology and Theology* (Leiden, Netherlands: E. J. Brill, 1959).

48. Writes evolutionist Michael Ruse: "However, by 1859, even in Victorian Britain, nearly all intelligent and informed people realized that one could no longer hold to a traditional, Biblically inspired picture of the world: a world created by God in six days (of twenty-four hours each); a world of very, very recent origin (4004 B.C. was the favored date of creation, based on genealogies of the Bible); and, a world which at some subsequent point had been totally covered and devastated by a monstrous flood. Through the first half of the nineteenth century, scientific discovery after scientific discovery had modified these traditional beliefs." Michael Ruse, *Darwinism Defended: A Guide to the Evolution Controversies* (Reading, Massachusetts: Addison-Wesley, 1982), pp. 285-86. He cites as an additional reference his earlier book, *The Darwinian Revolution: Science Red in Tooth and Claw* (Chicago: University of Chicago Press, 1979).

issues, which is one reason why the humanists have been so successful in eliminating Christians from scientific debate. For the most part, they still agree with the humanists with respect to the observed regularities of "nature in general"; they debate only about the "once in a while" deviations from natural law — miracles, demonic occurrences, God's direct revelation to man, and so forth.[49] The humanist scientists have seen fit to ignore a scientific world-and-life view based on "once in a while" deviations from "nearly autonomous" natural law.

Covenantal Regularities

The Christians have not framed their explanations of the external world in terms of a biblical doctrine of the covenant. As James Jordan remarks: "Why doesn't God do miracles all the time? Well, the answer to this is so we can fulfill the cultural mandate of Genesis 1:26-28, 2:15. If God were always changing His ways of doing things, we could not count on the world's going along the same way from day to day. God, however, has *covenanted* to keep the world on a predictable course (Gen. 8:20-22). What we have here is not some natural law which we may take for granted, but God's covenantal faithfulness which must lead us to worship. Science is possible only on the basis of faith in God's word, His promise to keep things going in a predictable way. We can count on God, depend on Him." In short, "What we call 'natural laws' are simply summary statements of what God *usually* does. There are no 'natural laws' which God has infused into the universe to run the universe automatically. God is wholly Personal, and He personally runs all things."[50]

In the eyes of a conventional non-Christian scientist, any violation of the perceived autonomous order (or disorder) of the universe must be rejected. Above all, *nature must be explained as autonomous from God*, whether nature is inherently orderly or disorderly. The humanist says categorically that such unexplained events cannot possibly be the direct or indirect interventions of the God of the Bible.

---

49. "Many of the Bible miracles (though not all, by any means) are similar miracles of creation, requiring the suspension of one or both [of] the two laws of thermodynamics, and testifying to the direct power of God the Creator." Henry Morris, "Thermodynamics and Biblical Theology," in Emmett L. Williams (ed.), *Thermodynamics and the Development of Order* (Norcross, Georgia: Creation Research Books, 1981), p. 137.

50. James B. Jordan, "The Bible and Modern Science," *The Biblical Educator*, II (Nov. 1980), [p. 3], published by the Institute for Christian Economics.

Laws of nature are only the beginning of the intellectual-theological problem. What about laws of human behavior? What about laws of social development? Are these laws really laws? Are they fixed? Can we make accurate predictions if we know them? Do they even exist?

This raises another very important and difficult intellectual problem: the relationship between *physical regularities* and *social regularities*. Can we legitimately apply physical laws (regularities) to social relationships? I argue in this book against such a connection, but others have long argued the opposite.

Then there is an additional question: How will defenders of various world-and-life viewpoints interpret the regularities that they discover? It is never simply a question of "raw data," "brute facts," and "inescapable law." It is always a question of *how these perceived facts are interpreted*. People are not neutral, not even scientists. So, we must also bear in mind that the various discoveries of science will be used by scholars to prove different things. This is why we need to understand the major competing worldviews, even before we begin to discuss the primary topic of the book, the second law of thermodynamics and its legitimate uses (if any) in social theory.

Conclusion

The search for regularities is legitimate. It is an inescapable aspect of all rational and scientific investigation. Nevertheless, we must beware of any proposed system of regularities that relies on any supposed autonomous "law" of nature. Nature is orderly, just as God is orderly, but nature is not autonomous, and nature's laws are not autonomous. *Nature is not simple*, which is why we have to devise mental "shorthand" models of reality to assist us in our search for order, and to help us to predict future events. We are simple-minded; nature is not simple.[51] The more that physicists study nature, the more complex and baffling it becomes for them. The nice stable mathematical universe described by Newton is accurate, up to a point, but not a subatomic point. Our knowledge of Newtonian regularities enables us to achieve tremendous progress.[52] But the

---

51. Physicist Eugene Wigner writes: "The world around us is of baffling complexity and the most obvious fact about it is that we cannot predict the future. . . . It is, as Schrödinger has remarked, a miracle that in spite of the baffling complexity of the world, certain regularities in the events could be discovered." Wigner, "The Unreasonable Effectiveness of Mathematics," *op. cit., p. 4.*

52. *Ibid.*, pp. 8-9.

more deeply that scientists look into the workings of nature, the more complex nature seems to be, and the more overwhelmed the scientists become. Their own equations become the only true reality for them.

In this sense, nature is like the Bible. It is simple enough for retarded people to understand and be converted; it is also difficult enough to baffle teams of scholars. Both nature and the Bible reflect God. He is both simple (one) and complex (three). We should beware of any exclusive reliance on such shorthand theories as Occam's famous fourteenth-century razor: that the simplest explanation is always best. The simplest explanation, from Occam to Darwin to modern physics, always excludes God as an unnecessary and overly complex hypothesis.[53] It may not be harmful to use a modified version of Occam's explanatory razor, as Henry Morris does,[54] but taking it too seriously is dangerous. If we adopt it as a universal rule, the humanists will use it to erase God from the universe.

Regularities are covenantal. They are created by God. God uses them for His purposes, and we can use them for ours. But the farther away we get from God ethically, the less effective our knowledge of "universal laws" will be. Furthermore, the world around us will begin to display the annoying aspects of wear and tear that Jeremy Rifkin and Henry Morris call entropy. God's curses, day by day, will manifest themselves more plainly. These manifestations of God's judgment will not be random, however. In this sense, they will be far more threatening than mere impersonal entropy.

This covenantal cause-and-effect relationship between ethical rebellion and external curses from God also points to its opposite: the *closer* we get to God ethically, the *less* our social world and even the natural world will be subject to the cursed aspects of entropy. Our wives and animals will not suffer miscarriages (Ex. 23:26). Our

---

53. This statement may appear extreme, since there are no doubt Christian physicists. But in their textbooks and professional papers, physicists do not refer to God as their operating presupposition, or at least not the God of the Bible, nor do they cite the Bible as the foundation of their own understanding of the way the world works. This is implicitly epistemological atheism, as Cornelius Van Til argued throughout his career, and *in the profession as a whole*, this has not been simply atheism by default.

54. "It would be helpful to keep in mind Occam's Razor (the simplest hypothesis which explains all the data is the most likely to be correct). . . ." *The Genesis Record*, p. 195. We can safely say "most likely to be correct," which means that we use it when we like the conclusions, but it is not an absolute law of nature or interpretation. It is simply a handy mental tool.

genetic pool will improve. This cannot be explained in terms of the atheistic version of the Newtonian science of the nineteenth century. Entropy, therefore, is an *interpretive* category. Men interpret science in terms of their presuppositions concerning the nature of God, man, time, and law.

In summary:

1. The humanist has no answer for the question: How does the mind of man understand the universe?
2. The humanist has no answer for the question: Why does mathematics (a product of the mind) successfully describe the operations of the external universe?
3. The biblical answer is simple: God created the world, and He created man in His image.
4. Christians have three doctrines that make science possible: creation, providence, and linear time.
5. When Christians refer to "natural law," they have in mind a God-created order.
6. As humanists have abandoned the biblical outlook, they have lost faith in natural law.
7. Modern humanistic philosophy replaces God with autonomous man.
8. Modern philosophy therefore makes the operations of the world dependent on the mind of man.
9. Modern science has begun to reflect modern philosophy.
10. Some scientists have resisted this conclusion: e.g., Einstein, Schrödinger.
11. Modern quantum mechanics abandons the views of the older, "independent world" physicists.
12. Quantum mechanics teaches that without a human observer, the universe is merely statistical wave functions. ("Smile! Wave!")
13. The concept of physical cause and effect has been increasingly abandoned by modern physics in the realm of subatomic physics.
14. Modern physics is based on the idea that chaos is lord, governed only by mathematical formulae.
15. Irrationalism now rules the world of science.
16. Men seek regularities in the world around them in order to make sense of the world and to control it.
17. They seek "laws of nature."
18. Prior to the twentieth century, the idea of the universal laws of nature was based on the belief that a) there is no God, and b) the universe is self-sustained (autonomous).

19. How can we explain God's miracles in a world controlled completely by impersonal natural law?
20. The biblical answer is the covenant.
21. All facts are God-created facts and God-interpreted facts.
22. There is no neutrality.
23. Facts don't "speak for themselves."
24. The search for regularities is legitimate.
25. If these regularities are not seen as covenantal, they are eventually denied in favor of irrationalism, tyranny, or both.

2

THE PESSIMISM OF THE SCIENTISTS

Physics tells the same story as astronomy. For, independently of all astronomical considerations, the general physical principle known as the second law of thermo-dynamics predicts that there can be but one end to the universe — a "heat-death" in which the total energy of the universe is uniformly distributed, and all the substance of the universe is at the same temperature. This temperature will be so low as to make life impossible. It matters little by what particular road this final state is reached; all roads lead to Rome, and the end of the journey cannot be other than universal death.

Sir James Jeans[1]

What I argue in this chapter is simple enough: the second law of thermodynamics has become an important intellectual foundation justifying radical pessimism. Those intellectuals and natural scientists who are in the habit of drawing social and philosophical conclusions from natural science have been unable to escape the pessimistic implications of the second law. This growing pessimism now threatens Western civilization.

Admittedly, those scientists who devise grand cosmological schemes are always a minority in the profession. Obviously, most scientists are specialists who spend their lives doing very carefully circumscribed experiments in laboratories. They are seldom called upon to make pronouncements concerning the meaning of life or the long-term implications of their implicit worldview. The prominent astronomer Edwin Hubble recognized that scientists are not normally called into the public arena to set forth grand principles and schemes, but he insisted that on major questions (such as nuclear

---

1. James Jeans, *The Mysterious Universe* (New York: Macmillan, 1944), p. 15. Jeans was one of the world's most famous astronomers during the first half of the twentieth century.

war), they must begin to speak out. They can no longer legitimately hide in the shadows of their laboratories. "Scientists in general are not very articulate; they work in comparative seclusion and they do not cultivate the art of persuasion. But now a new era has emerged, and reticence is no longer a virtue."[2]

Hubble understood that scientists' efforts have had major consequences outside the laboratory. Science is more than a game or a curiosity; it is one of the major religions of modern life. People rely on scientists. Science has produced more and better consumer products, as well as more and better weapons. Science has "delivered the goods." People are going to pay attention to any technique or way of looking at the world which has affected their lives to the extent that modern science has. Thus, when a scientist speaks authoritatively in the name of science, many people will listen, especially nonscientific intellectuals, at least if he speaks in a language even remotely like the vernacular.

Three Religious Worldviews

There are three major outlooks that prevail today. They are ancient rivals. The debate among the various proponents of these outlooks has effects in the consideration of entropy and its social, economic, and political implications.[3] Jeremy Rifkin and most Scientific Creationists represent the second outlook.

1. *Power Religion*

This is a religious viewpoint which affirms that the most important goal for a man, group, or species, is the capture and maintenance of power. Power is seen as the chief attribute of God, or if the religion is officially atheistic, then the chief attribute of man. This perspective is a satanic perversion of God's command to man to exercise dominion over all the creation (Gen. 1:26-28).[4] It is the attempt to exercise dominion apart from covenantal subordination to the true Creator God.

---

2. Edwin Hubble, *The Nature of Science and Other Lectures* (San Marino, California: Huntington Library, 1954), p. 3.

3. The following section on the three types of religious thought is included in several of my books. It is clearly basic to my understanding of how men think about the role of man in this world.

4. Gary North, *The Dominion Covenant: Genesis* (2nd ed.; Tyler, Texas: Institute for Christian Economics, 1987).

What distinguishes biblical *dominion religion* from satanic *power religion* is ethics. Is the person who seeks power doing so primarily for the glory of God, and secondarily for himself, and only to the extent that he is God's lawful and covenantally faithful representative? If so, he will act in terms of God's ethical standards and in terms of a profession of faith in God. The church has recognized this two-fold requirement historically, and has established a dual requirement for membership: profession of faith and a godly life.

In contrast, power religion is a religion of *autonomy*. It affirms that "My power and the might of mine hand hath gotten me this wealth" (Deut. 8:17). It seeks power or wealth in order to make credible this very claim.

Wealth and power are aspects of both religions. Wealth and power are covenantal manifestations of the success of rival religious views. This is why God warns His people not to believe that their autonomous actions gained them their blessings: "But thou shalt remember the LORD thy God: for it is he that giveth thee power to get wealth, that he may establish his covenant which he sware unto thy fathers, as it is this day" (Deut. 8:18). It must be recognized that God's opponents also want visible confirmation of the validity of their covenant with death, but God warns them that "the wealth of the sinner is laid up for the just" (Prov. 13:22b). The entry of the Hebrews into Canaan was supposed to remind them of this fact: the Canaanites had built homes and vineyards to no avail; their enemies, the Hebrews, inherited them (Joshua 24:13).

Those who believe in power religion have refused to see that long-term wealth in any society is the product of ethical conformity to God's law. They have sought the blessings of God's covenant while denying the validity and eternally binding ethical standards of that covenant. In short, they have confused the fruits of Christianity with the roots. They have attempted to chop away the roots but preserve the fruits.

2. *Escapist Religion*

This is the second great tradition of anti-Christian religion. Seeing that the exercise of autonomous power is a snare and a delusion, the proponents of escapist religion have sought to insulate themselves from the general culture—a culture maintained by power. They have fled the responsibilities of worldwide dominion, or even regional dominion, in the hope that God will excuse them from the general dominion covenant.

The Christian version of the escapist religion is sometimes called "pietism," but its theological roots can be traced back to the ancient heresy of *mysticism*. Rather than proclaiming the requirement of *ethical union* with Jesus Christ, the perfect man, the mystic calls for *metaphysical union* with a monistic, unified god. In the early church, there were many types of mysticism, but the most feared rival religion which continually infiltrated the church was *gnosticism*. It proclaimed many doctrines, but the essence of gnostic faith was radical individualism. It involved a self-conscious retreat from the material realm and escape to a higher, purer, spiritual realm through techniques of self-manipulation: asceticism, higher consciousness, and initiation into secret mysteries. Gnosticism survives as a way of thinking and acting (or failing to act) even today, as R. J. Rushdoony has pointed out. The essence of this faith is its *antinomianism* — anti (against) nomos (law). Gnostics despise the law of God. But their hatred for the law of God leads them to accept the laws of the State.

Rushdoony has commented on the persistance of gnosticism throughout Western history right up to the present. A major feature of gnosticism is the gnostics' contempt for time, their unwillingness to try to change external events. Their exclusive concern was salvation of the individual and escape from the external world. In some cases, they even had contempt for the material world, as well as for morality, as Rushdoony notes:

> Gnosticism survives today in theosophy, Jewish Kabbalism, occultism, existentialism, masonry, and like faiths. Because Gnosticism made the individual, rather than a dualism of mind and matter, ultimate, it was essentially hostile to morality and law, requiring often that believers live beyond good and evil by denying the validity of all moral law. Gnostic groups which did not openly avow such doctrines affirmed an ethic of love as against law, negating law and morality in terms of the "higher" law and morality of love. Their contempt of law and of time manifested itself also by a willingness to comply with the state. . . . The usual attitude was one of contempt for the material world, which included the state, and an outward compliance and indifference. A philosophy calling for an escape from time is not likely to involve itself in the battles of time.[5]

The basic idea lying behind escapist religion is the denial of the dominion covenant. The escape religionist believes that the tech-

---

5. Rousas John Rushdoony, *The One and the Many: Studies in the Philosophy of Order and Ultimacy* (Fairfax, Virginia: Thoburn Press, [1971] 1978), p. 129.

niques of self-discipline, whether under God or apart from God (Buddhism), offer power over only limited areas of life. They attempt to conserve their power by focusing their ethical concern on progressively (regressively) narrower areas of personal responsibility. The "true believer" thinks that he will gain more control over himself and his narrow environment by restricting his self-imposed zones of responsibility. His concern is self, from start to finish; his attempt to escape from responsibilities beyond the narrow confines of self is a program for gaining power over self. It is a religion of works, of *self-salvation*. A man "humbles" himself—admits that there are limits to his power, and therefore limits to the range of his responsibilities—only to elevate self to a position of hypothetically God-like spirituality.

Escapist religion proclaims institutional peace—"peace at any price." Ezekiel responded to such an assertion in the name of God: ". . . they have seduced my people, saying, Peace; and there was no peace" (Ezek. 13:10a). Patrick Henry's inflammatory words in 1775 were taken from Jeremiah: "They have healed also the hurt of the daughter of my people slightly, saying, Peace, peace; when there is no peace" (Jer. 6:14). This rival religion proclaims peace because it has little interest in the systematic efforts that are always required to purify institutions as a prelude to social reconstruction.

In short, escapist religion calls for flight from the world, and because man is in this world, it calls for *a flight from humanity*.[6] Its advocates may hide their real concern—the systematic abandonment of a world supposedly so corrupt that nothing can be done to overcome widespread cultural evil—by appealing to their moral responsibility of "sharing Christ to the world" or "building up the Church" rather than rebuilding civilization, but their ultimate concern is *personal flight from responsibility*. It is a revolt against maturity.[7]

3. *Dominion Religion*

This is the orthodox Christian faith. It proclaims the sovereignty of God, the reliability of the historic creeds, the necessity of standing up for principle, and the requirement that faithful men take risks for God's sake. It proclaims that through the exercise of saving faith, and through ethical conformity to God's revealed law, regenerate

---

6. R. J. Rushdoony, *The Flight from Humanity: A Study of the Effect of Neoplatonism on Christianity* (Fairfax, Virginia: Thoburn Press, [1973] 1978).

7. R. J. Rushdoony, *Revolt Against Maturity: A Biblical Psychology of Man* (Fairfax, Virginia: Thoburn Press, 1977).

men will increase the extent of their dominion over the earth. It is a religion of conquest—*conquest through ethics*. The goal is ethical conformity to God, but the results of this conformity involve dominion—over lawful subordinates, over ethical rebels, and over nature. This is the message of Deuteronomy 28:1-14. It is also the message of Jesus Christ, who walked perfectly in God's statutes and in God's Spirit, and who then was granted total power over all creation by the Father (Matt. 28:18). I am not speaking here of Christ as the Second Person of the Trinity, who always had total power; I am speaking of the Incarnated Christ, who as the perfect man *gained* total power through ethical conformity to God and through His death and resurrection.

Dominion religion recognizes the relationship between *righteousness* and *authority*, between covenantal faithfulness and covenantal blessings. Those who are faithful in little things are given more. This is the meaning of Christ's parable of the talents. The process of dominion is a function of *progressive sanctification*, both personal-individual and institutional (family, church, business, school, civil government, etc.: Deuteronomy 28:1-14).

Covenantal religion is always *openly, forthrightly creedal;* it has a public theology. Power religion and escapist religion may or may not be openly creedal. Nevertheless, every worldview has a creed, even if that permanent creed states only that "there is no valid creed." *Creeds are inescapable concepts*. It is never a question of "creed vs. no creed"; it is a question of *which* creed.[8] We must understand, however, that power religion seldom announces itself as an inescapably creedal religion, although Communism and Nazism have been exceptions to this general rule. In the historic environment of the "liberal" West, power religion's advocates have seldom announced their intentions openly until the final phases of their capture of institutional power.

In contrast to covenantal, creedal religion is gnosticism, both old and new. Rushdoony has pointed out that gnosticism has generally been hostile to creeds. "Creeds too obviously revealed its departure from and hostility to the faith. It was much more effective to affirm the Apostles' Creed, and then re-interpret it in terms of Gnosticism. This, from Gnosticism on through neo-orthodoxy, has been a favored method of heresy." Gnosticism is a rival religion. Rushdoony

---

8. R. J. Rushdoony, *Foundations of Social Order* (Fairfax, Virginia: Thoburn Press, [1969] 1978), pp. 1-2. Cf. Rushdoony, *Infallibility: An Inescapable Concept* (Vallecito, California: Ross House, 1978).

continues: "Gnosticism was in essence *humanism*, the glorification of man. In humanism, man makes himself ultimate by undercutting the ultimacy of God. The vaguer the doctrines of the Father, Son, and Holy Ghost were made, the more clearly man emerged as the sovereign, and man's order as the ultimate order."[9]

Religious Worldviews Govern Scientific Interpretation

These three outlooks still divide men. In this book, I primarily deal with two rival versions of the escapist religion, and then I offer an alternative, the dominion (ethics) religion. I operate with this presupposition: men are either self-consciously under God and over nature, or else they are self-consciously in rebellion against God and under nature.

The modern power religionist wants to place most men under the control of a scientific elite (which is a part of nature),[10] while the humanist escapist religionist (very often a mystic) wants to see all men living in harmony with nature and each other without the element of human power anywhere in the society. The history of man can be understood in terms of the increasing epistemological and ethical self-consciousness of man. Therefore, in our day the conflict between these two worldviews—power vs. escape—has become sharper and less easily deferred.

Historically, Christianity has been influenced by all three outlooks: power religion, dominion religion, and escape religion. The medieval quest for power over civil government by the institutional church was in part an aspect of power religion. In reaction, European pietism—the Mennonites and Amish—have been characterized by their withdrawal from politics and culture: escape religion. These two isolated pietist groups have also been pacifist in outlook.

Mainstream Christian escapists (pietists, mystics) want only to defer the "power vs. escape" confrontation until Jesus comes back again and solves it by means of His power. This theology of deferral has become visibly bankrupt in the 1980's. Christians of all eschatological views have begun to abandon it, some more consistently than others.

The power religion in our day is humanistic elitism (including Communism), which has as its goal autonomous man's conquest of

---

9. Rushdoony, *Foundations of Social Order*, p. 11.
10. C. S. Lewis, *The Abolition of Man* (New York: Macmillan, [1947] 1969), ch. 3.

nature (including mankind). It often misuses the intellectual discipline of science in this effort. It is opposed by the escapist religion, as well as by the ethics-based dominion religion. The two forms of the escapist religion that are most prominent in the United States today are modern Christian pietism and some (though not all) forms of the New Age movement — the bliss-seeking mystics and miracle-seeking magicians,[11] not the political activists.[12] Implicitly, both are opposed to the idea that legitimate long-term progress is possible prior to the coming of Christ in power (fundamentalism) or the coming of "Christ-consciousness" within humanity (New Age).

Christian Reconstruction offers as an alternative a dominion concept of long-term scientific, economic, and intellectual progress which can overcome most (though not all) of the limits placed by God on His creation as aspects of His curse. It offers hope through covenantal faithfulness to God's law.[13]

Nick Herbert argues that the scientific community's view of reality eventually seeps out and down to the common man. This view of physical reality will eventually influence the way we view social and political reality. "For better or worse, humans have tended to pattern their domestic, social, and political arrangements according to the dominant vision of physical reality. Inevitably the cosmic view trickles down to the most mundane details of everyday life."[14] I would argue, on the contrary, that this is what scientists prefer to believe, but that the reality is far different: *the dominant religious worldview establishes what cosmic vision is acceptable for scientists to believe.* There is always interaction, but the primary motivation comes from the pulpit, the "old boy network," the newspaper staff assignment room, and Party headquarters, not the laboratory.

It is Jeremy Rifkin's tactic to pretend that Herbert's view is correct, that what scientists believe about the universe will soon reshape our social and political world. He is a dedicated propagandist, and

---

11. Gary North, *Unholy Spirits: Occultism and New Age Humanism* (Ft. Worth, Texas: Dominion Press, 1986), chaps. 4, 6, 7.
12. *Ibid.*, ch. 10.
13. Gary North, *Dominion and Common Grace: The Biblical Basis of Progress* (Tyler, Texas: Institute for Christian Economics, 1987); Ray R. Sutton, *That You May Prosper: Dominion By Covenant* (Tyler, Texas: Institute for Christian Economics, 1987).
14. Nick Herbert, *Quantum Reality: Beyond the New Physics* (Garden City, New York: Anchor Press/Doubleday, 1985), p. xi.

he seeks to cover his implicitly political program with a scientist's white smock.

Pessimism

What I argue in this book is that some (though not all) members of both the Scientific Creation movement and the more mystical proponents of the New Age movement have promoted an *explicit pessimism* concerning human progress. New Age mystics conceal this pessimism because they usually focus on short-term evolutionary "leaps of being." But one man, Jeremy Rifkin, is quite open in his presentation of the case for "entropic pessimism," and I focus on his arguments in this book.

I also argue that modern rationalistic, humanistic power-seekers and profit-seekers also ultimately share in this pessimism, but their innate pessimism is suppressed because of their faith in either scientific planning or free market productivity. The power religionists have no long-term cosmological hope, and the more consistent ones admit this. The Christian escapist religionists profess no short-term cosmological hope, and they appeal only to the long-term hope of cosmological redemption and total transformation. The New Age mystics have no long-term hope, not much short-term hope, and refuse to admit either.

Rifkin has argued that our view of nature gives us our sense of meaning. When we search for understanding concerning our personal final end, we turn to nature. "The fact is, we human beings cannot live without some agreed-upon idea of what nature and life are all about. When we ponder what our own personal fate might be after the last breath of life is extracted, or when we try to imagine what existed before existence itself, we are likely to become paralyzed with doubt. Our concept of nature allows us to overcome these ultimate anxieties. It provides us with some of the answers, enough to get along. A concept of nature, then, is more than just an explanation of how living things interact with one another. It also serves as a reference point for deciphering the meaning of existence itself."[15]

What I argue is exactly the opposite: *our view of our final end is what gives us our view of nature.* Despite his long-winded critique of modern

---

15. Jeremy Rifkin and Nicanor Perlas, *Algeny: A New Word — A New World* (New York: Viking, 1983), p. 28.

natural science, especially Darwinism, Rifkin assumes the Darwinian time scale and the Darwinian theory of origins. He assumes a vision of "last things" (eschatology) which he claims is provided by modern science. What he does not mention is that this view of modern science was derived from men who had a religious impulse: *to escape God's final judgment.*[16]

The Textbook Version of Thermodynamics

What have scientists said about the second law of thermodynamics? They have said a great deal, but most of what they have said is confined to textbooks, with scholarly articles thrown in as an extra bonus. The standard thermodynamics textbook is filled with elegant mathematical equations and suggested experiments. The authors of these college-level textbooks seldom digress into discussions of the cosmic implications of the science of thermodynamics. They just present the technical material, usually within the context of mechanical engineering or statistical mechanics. Here is a standard description of the second law of thermodynamics:

> When a system containing a large number of particles is left to itself, it assumes a state with maximum entropy, that is, it becomes as disordered as possible.[17]

We must understand that this disordered state — "maximum entropy" — is always structured by certain fixed limits. It is randomness within an ordered physical environment.

Another textbook statement is important because it presents the view of the second law that Jeremy Rifkin accepts as the agreed-upon foundation of Western science. What I will argue later in this book is that *Rifkin has not misled us with respect to what physical scientists have taught*, but he has misapplied a fundamental doctrine of science. Here is the definition:

> Closely associated with the concept of changes in entropy is **the second law of thermodynamics**. One statement of the second law is: *The total amount of entropy in nature is increasing.* Although we can pick out many natural processes that may involve increases in the degree of ordering (for example, the precipitation of salts in salt lakes or the growth of living

---

16. Gary North, *The Dominion Covenant: Genesis*, pp. 375-86.
17. K. R. Atkins, *Physics* (New York: Wiley, 1966), p. 206.

organisms), other processes are taking place that decrease the order of nature (for example, the evaporation of water or the decay of organisms). The overall effects of the latter processes appear greater than of the former in the part of the universe we observe.

Another way in which the second law is stated is: *In any spontaneous change the amount of free energy available decreases.* This is one way of saying that natural processes go downhill. A familiar example of the second law is that heat cannot pass from a colder to a hotter body without the action of some external agency.[18] (Emphases in original.)

The authors have covered their academic backsides with the qualification, "in the part of the universe we observe." They do not explicitly argue that for every local decrease in disorder (decrease in entropy) there must be an even greater increase in disorder *for the universe as a whole*. They just state that in any part of the universe we observe, this is what we find. Rifkin universalizes the process; so, for that matter, do most other scientists. They have done so ever since Rudolph Clausius first formulated the second law in 1850.

A textbook account informs the student that when a gas is in equilibrium, with its molecules randomly bouncing against the walls of a container—a container through which energy does not flow (a hypothetical condition that is never achieved in the real world)[19]—the experimenter can draw some rigorously scientific conclusions. The second law officially applies only to this hypothetical *and impossible* condition: a perfectly closed system in equilibrium. This is why the main branch of the science of thermodynamics is called *equilibrium* thermodynamics. This is the thermodynamics of the textbooks.

A gas is capable of producing work under certain conditions, meaning that it can lift a weight or move an object in a particular direction or heat a room. To get a container of gas that is in equilibrium to do this, a spark or some other external catalyst is introduced. This destroys the original equilibrium condition of the gas. After this energy-releasing change has taken place, the new equilibrium condition of the gas or its resulting chemical products will be capable of less work. While scientists can state this principle of physics in many

---

18. Charles W. Keenan and Jesse H. Wood, *General College Chemistry* (3rd ed.; New York: Harper & Row, 1966), p. 420.
19. The technical term for such a container is an adiabatic wall. On the usefulness of the concept, despite the fact that such a condition is impossible to achieve, see Don C. Kelly, *Thermodynamics and Statistical Physics* (New York: Academic Press, 1973), p. 6.

different ways, this is the meaning of the second law of thermodynamics.

This law was discovered early in the nineteenth century as a result of observations of pumps. It was observed that heat transfers only in one direction: from a warmer object to a cooler object. This heat transfer can perform work, but once performed, the heat will not flow from the cooler object back to the warmer object, so the work cannot be done again. In short, there is *directionality in heat loss*.

Consider a textbook example of a weight suspended by a rope on a pulley. The man holding the other end of the rope grows tired, and he lets go of the rope. The weight drops to the floor, and its impact briefly spreads heat (speeded-up molecules) throughout the floor. The weight is now sitting on the floor. A constant temperature for the weight, air, and floor is achieved when the overall temperature is in equilibrium—a condition of *randomness*, meaning a random distribution of heat within the confines of the room.

If the temperature of the room, floor, and weight is now in equilibrium, the second law of thermodynamics states that the weight will not suddenly rise to the ceiling because of the energy supplied by the room, with the room somehow spontaneously growing colder, and with the decrease in room heat taking the form of a gust of wind that suddenly lifts the weight, warming it in the process.[20] In short, heat is spontaneously transferred only from the warmer object to the cooler. "Henry A. Bent, a chemist at the University of Minnesota, has made calculations which show that it is *more likely* for a tribe of wild monkeys, punching randomly on a set of typewriters, to turn out Shakespeare's complete works fifteen quadrillion times in succession without error than is the conversion at room temperature of one calorie of thermal energy to work."[21]

So far, the second law of thermodynamics does not appear to be the foundation of a new worldview. But it is. It is the foundation of a powerful, intellectually compelling worldview, one which is radically pessimistic.

---

20. Cf. Stanley W. Angrist and Loren G. Helper, *Order and Chaos: Laws of Energy and Entropy* (New York: Basic Books, 1967), pp. 149-50.

21. *Ibid.*, pp. 150-51. I think Prof. Bent invented this off the top of his head; in reading his comment in the original, I find no discussion of his actual calculations. But it does give the reader some indication of just how universal in scope scientists believe the second law of thermodynamics to be. See Harry A. Bent, *The Second Law* (New York: Oxford University Press, 1965).

The Heat Death of the Universe

If heat is transferred only from the warmer to the cooler, then eventually the temperature of the universe will be equalized, *if the universe is a closed system*. Virtually all modern scientists operate on the assumption that it is a closed system, although they cannot prove this.[22] When the temperature of all objects at last is equal, no more work will be possible. This, in fact, is the scientific definition of "at last." It is the modern scientific definition of the end of time. Heat flows one way only. When the fires of the suns of the universe have been extinguished, and no more heat energy flows into the "cosmic heat sink" of space, the randomness of bouncing molecules will then overwhelm every sense of directionality in the universe. Time will end, for time is directional. This is the legendary future condition called the heat death of the universe.

We now have gone from tightly defined laboratory experiments to a theory of the extinction of the universe. Is this intellectual jump legitimate? The non-scientist intuitively accepts the jump, but this may be because he has been told endlessly by scientists that it is not only legitimate, it is inescapable. If heat really goes from warmer to cooler, then eventually everything in the universe will be at the same temperature. Work will then cease. This seems to follow from the initial statement of the second law, even though the second law *officially* applies *only* to closed systems in equilibrium. The layman accepts this conceptual leap, for he assumes that the universe is a closed system which is headed for equilibrium, meaning a world of random, directionless, and therefore timeless change. But is the layman's understanding correct? Have serious, competent scientists in the field of thermodynamics made this leap of faith? The answer is yes. In fact, one of the founders of thermodynamics came to this conclusion in 1865: Rudolph Clausius.

---

22. "The only candidate for a truly isolated system is the universe." Kelly, *Thermodynamics and Statistical Physics*, p. 5. "The universe is certainly isolated. . . ." *Ibid.*, p. 120. "Conceiving the universe as an isolated system, we may then say. . . ." Leonard K. Nash, *Elements of Classical and Statistical Thermodynamics* (Reading, Massachusetts: Addison-Wesley, 1970), p. 74. "Since the entire universe is itself an isolated system and therefore cannot exchange energy and matter with any outside system (by definition of the universe there can be nothing outside it), the second law of thermodynamics applies to it." Lloyd Motz, *The Universe: Its Beginning and End* (New York: Scribner's, 1975), pp. 305-6. "Indeed, we cannot be certain that we are dealing with a truly closed system unless we take for our system nothing less than the entire universe." Isaac Asimov, *Understanding Physics: Motion, Sound, and Heat* (New York: New American Library, 1966), p. 233.

Clausius' Theory

Rudolph Clausius formulated an early statement of the second law in 1850, and he specifically called it the second law of thermodynamics.[23] He also invented the word *entropy*.[24] He argued that whenever there is a closed system, it is either in a random equilibrium state, or else it becomes increasingly random. He called this equilibrium state *entropy*. Entropy is therefore a *characteristic* of a physical system. The lower the entropy of a closed system, the greater the order. A textbook puts Clausius' law in bold face: "**The entropy of an isolated system never decreases**. This statement is generally referred to as the *entropy principle*."[25] Another physicist states that "**the entropy of a closed system tends to remain constant or to increase**."[26] In short, the road to universal randomness is a one-way street.

Maybe. Why maybe? Because of the outside possibility that at some point in the future, the universe may begin to contract. That would decrease entropy by decreasing the number of possible states for matter. Like a collection of marbles in a shrinking box, the number of different locations possible for any given marble would be reduced. The system as a whole would become less random. Thus, a cautious physicist writes: "Fifty years ago it was common to say that the entropy of the universe is increasing, which may very well be true. This is a cosmological question. The 'Big Bang' models of the expansion of the universe imply an increase in the entropy at the present epoch. If the universe contracts at a later epoch, the entropy will probably decrease."[27] Popular writer (and chemist) Isaac Asimov warns: "On the basis of our observations and experiments we can say exactly nothing about the relationship between entropy and a contracting universe."[28] We are free to suppose that entropy will decrease during contraction, he says; but this implies that we are equally free to suppose that it does not.

In any case, today it seems unlikely that there is sufficient matter in the universe to enable it to contract in the future. But why does it

---

23. Isaac Asimov, *Understanding Physics: Motion, Sound, and Heat*, p. 230.
24. *Ibid.*, p. 231.
25. Kelly, *Thermodynamics and Statistical Physics*, p. 119.
26. Charles Kittel, *Thermal Physics* (New York: Wiley, 1969), p. 61.
27. *Ibid.*, p. 65.
28. Isaac Asimov, *A Choice of Catastrophes: The Disasters That Threaten Our World* (New York: Simon & Schuster, 1979), p. 57.

matter what happens to matter? Asimov speculates that if the contraction takes place, it may take 500 billion years for the universe to "come to a halt about halfway to heat death," and then another 500 billion years to the creation of a new compressed cosmic egg.[29] Who cares? Yet even in a textbook, a scientist thinks that men (including scientists) *do* care: "Life in a forever expanding universe seems less attractive than in one which is 'closed.' For this and other (less psychologically motivated) reasons, astronomers are still looking for additional matter in the vast expanses of the universe."[30]

It's About Time

The reason why people care what happens to the universe is difficult to explain, but I think it is closely related to *the psychic need in man for eternal life*. If man's work survives, then a part of man survives. Like the schoolboy who carves his initials on a desk, like the juvenile delinquent who spray paints his first name on a wall, and like authors who write books, the scientist wants to leave traces that his work is not in vain. "History will judge," a man believes. But what if history dies? Who or what will then judge man? A sovereign God? That thought is just not acceptable. Something more *impersonal* is sought after by rebellious man to serve as cosmic judge. That impersonal cosmic judge is time. But if the increase in entropy is time's arrow, then what happens to time if entropy finally reaches its theoretical limit in cosmic randomness? The judge dies.

Judgment is intimately bound up with the question of *meaning*. The British humanist and mathematician-philosopher Bertrand Russell put it this way in 1903: ". . . all the labours of the ages, all the devotion, all the inspiration, all the noonday brightness of human genius, are destined to extinction in the vast death of the solar system, and that the whole temple of Man's achievement must inevitably be buried beneath the debris of a universe in ruins—all these things, if not quite beyond dispute, are yet so nearly certain, that no philosophy which rejects them can hope to stand. Only within the scaffolding of these truths, only on the firm foundation of unyielding despair, can the soul's habitation henceforth be safely built."[31] Mankind has only a firm foundation of ultimate despair to

---

29. *Ibid.*, p. 59.
30. Kelly, *Thermodynamics and Statistical Physics*, p. 122.
31. Bertrand Russell, "A Free Man's Religion" (1903), in *Mysticism and Logic* (Garden City, New York: Anchor, n.d.), pp. 45-46.

build upon. Heat death will snuff out all his efforts and all his self-generated, autonomous meaning.

This was Clausius' legacy. He was the first to argue for the inevitable heat death of the universe. Few scientists have dared to challenge him; instead, they generally ignore the issue. They write textbooks that judiciously avoid raising it. Another great physicist, Ludwig Boltzmann, who eventually did challenge Clausius' theory, initially refused to disagree with him in public. Boltzmann addressed Austria's Imperial Academy of Science in 1886: "All attempts at saving the universe from this thermal death have been unsuccessful, and to avoid raising hopes I cannot fulfil, let me say at once that I too shall here refrain from making such attempts."[32]

At this point, I need to cover some technical material.[33] I do not expect every reader to follow these arguments closely. I am including this section so that students and scholars will recognize how important the concept of cosmic time is in the worldview of modern science, and how important to science's concept of cosmic time the concept of entropy has become. Science textbooks seldom consider such questions in detail. Christian textbooks had better consider them in the future in much greater detail. We are now approaching the soft underbelly of modern science: its despair concerning the future.

Linear Time vs. Cyclical Time

I know of no more brilliant and incisive historian of science than Stanley Jaki. His book, *Science and Creation* (1974), is nothing short of a classic. He discusses in considerable detail the impact that the second law of thermodynamics had on the premier scientists of the late nineteenth century. There was no escape from the cosmological implications of Sadi Cournot's observations of heat pumps and his long-neglected 1824 conclusion concerning heat loss:

The cosmological implication of the loss of a part of the utilizable energy in every physical process was spelled out by [Lord] Kelvin [William Thompson—G.N.] as early as 1852. Two years later Helmholtz himself appraised Carnot's principle "as a universal law of nature" which radiated

---

32. Ludwig Boltzmann, "The Second Law of Thermodynamics" (1886), in *Theoretical Physics and Philosophical Problems*, edited by Brian McGuinness (Boston: D. Reidel, 1974), p. 19.

33. Providentially, I was pushed into this because of continuing harassment by Arthur Robinson.

light "into the distant nights of the beginning and the end of the history of the universe." In 1865 Clausius summed up the Second Law of thermodynamics in the now famous statement, "The entropy of the universe tends towards a maximum." After that only a few years passed before two theologically minded Scottish physicists, B. Stewart and P. G. Tait, concluded that the law of entropy proved it absolutely certain that the minimum and maximum entropy of the universe represented its beginning and end.[34]

Jaki makes the very important point that every attempt to overcome the logic of Clausius' position has "implied the notion of a universe capable of restoring in endless cycles the energy dissipated across the endless expanse of space." Jaki cites the argument of W. J. M. Rankine, one of the founders of thermodynamics, that the dissipated energy might create new stars and planetary systems. "According to Rankine's conception, the universe consisted of cosmic compartments in any of which either the reconcentration or the dissipation of energy was going on at any given time. . . ." This does not make better sense a century later. Nevertheless, Jaki writes, "Whatever one may think of Rankine's speculations, he at least faced with frankness a real problem instead of trying to talk it away or give it the silent treatment."[35] A lot of scientists still play the academic game called "sweep this implication under the rug."

Boltzmann's Subsequent Attempt

Jaki recognizes the similarities between Rankine's view and the one articulated by Boltzmann two years before he committed suicide, and eighteen years after his lecture in which he had decided not to challenge Clausius' theory of the heat death of the universe. In 1904, Boltzmann argued that within the framework of a universe that is already in equilibrium, there can be pockets of randomly appearing order.[36] This theory was an extension of his theory first articulated in his *Lectures on Gas Theory*, published in two sections in 1896 and 1898. In that work, he had abandoned the idea that time is

---

34. Stanley Jaki, *Science and Creation: From eternal cycles to an oscillating universe* (Edinburgh: Scottish Academic Press, [1974] 1980), p. 294.

35. *Ibid.*, p. 295.

36. "The laws of probability calculus imply that, if only we imagine the world to be large enough, there will always occur here and there regions of dimensions of the visible sky with a highly improbable state of distribution." "Über statistische Mechanik" (1904) in *Populäre Schriften* (Leipzig: J. A. Barth, 1905), p. 362; cited by Jaki, *ibid.*, p. 297.

linear: "In any case, we would rather consider the unique directionality of time given to us by experience as a mere illusion arising from our specially restricted viewpoint."[37]

Here was the founder of statistical mechanics formulating a theory of gigantic fluctuations within a universe already in equilibrium, a theory which required him to give up the idea of linear time. Why did he do this? Because so powerful and threatening was Clausius' hypothesis of the heat death of the universe that Boltzmann was desperate to find an alternative, no matter how incoherent and implausible. This is science at its worst. He had no evidence to point to — nothing. He had only some mathematical expressions of the theory and a desire to escape the rule of the second law. Jaki's assessment is on target: "The saving grace of the Boltzmann cosmology was that its most special features were relegated to the realm of the unobservable, to the realm of the infinitely distant."[38] In other words, no one could test his hypothesis.

Today, we find few supporters of Boltzmann's theory. Not that scientists wouldn't like to support it. It does offer a possible solution to a difficult problem: an explanation of biological life, a clearly "anti-entropic" aspect of the universe.[39] Life seems to violate the prediction of increasing cosmic disorder and randomness. But Boltzmann's theory breaks down, or so argues physicist Don Kelly:

> Boltzmann's fluctuation hypothesis suggests that the universe is in equilibrium but that the portion which we observe is part of a gigantic fluctuation — the granddaddy of all accidents. At first sight, the argument for such a hypothesis seems to be a strong one. Some sort of fluctuation is required to ensure the existence of observers (you and me!), that is, biological development requires special conditions — conditions of a distinctly nonequilibrium nature. Thus the very fact that such biological development has occurred — that I write and you read — seems to be strong evidence for the

---

37. Boltzmann, *Lectures on Gas Theory*, translated by S. G. Brush (Berkeley: University of California Press, 1964), p. 446; cited in *ibid.*, p. 300.

38. *Ibid.*, p. 299.

39. "It is by avoiding the rapid decay into the inert state of 'equilibrium' that an organism appears so enigmatic. . . ." Erwin Schrödinger, *What Is Life? The Physical Aspect of the Living Cell* (Cambridge University Press, [1944] 1967), p. 75. "What I wish to make clear in this last chapter is, in short, that from all we have learnt about the structure of living matter, we must be prepared to find it working in a manner that cannot be reduced to the ordinary laws of physics." *Ibid.*, p. 81. Cf. Emmett L. Williams, "Resistance Of Living Organisms To The Second Law Of Thermodynamics," in Williams (ed.), *Thermodynamics and the Development of Order* (Norcross, Georgia: Creation Research Books, 1981), ch. 5.

fluctuation hypothesis. However, the argument is unsound. It is enormously more likely that such a fluctuation would occur over a small volume, say the size of our solar system, and leave the rest of the immediate universe in equilibrium. To pursue the traffic analogy, being involved in an accident is not unusual, but we would generally be able to see beyond the wreckage and discern the equilibrium flow of traffic. The chance that the fluctuation hypothesis is true is less than the likelihood of an accident involving every car on the road today. Such states of chaos seem most unlikely.[40]

Nevertheless, scientists are playing with explanations of the universe that are far more unlikely than anything Boltzmann proposed. Modern science has until very recently been unalterably opposed to the biblical idea of God's creation of the universe out of nothing. Modern science has therefore been pagan in its orientation, as dedicated as Aristotle was to the idea of the eternality of matter.[41] No longer. The doctrine of creation out of nothing has reappeared, accompanied by a concept of de-creation into nothing. John Gribbin summarizes:

> Perhaps cosmology really is a branch of particle physics. For, according to one idea that has progressed over the past ten years or so all the way from being thought of as completely crazy to the near-respectability of being regarded merely as outrageous, the universe and everything in it may be no more, and no less, than one of those vacuum fluctuations that allow collections of particles to burst forth out of nothing, live for a while, and then be reabsorbed into the vacuum. The idea ties in very closely with the possibility that the universe may be gravitationally closed. A universe that is born in the fireball of a Big Bang, expands for a time and then contracts back into a fireball and disappears, *is* a vacuum fluctuation, but on a very grand scale.[42]

As he says, this idea can be traced back to Ludwig Boltzmann. Now it has begun to catch on.

Catch on to *what*? To what is this theory hanging on? It is a vacuum theory for periodic vacuum worlds spun in the minds of scholars who do not want to face the biblical cosmology of the creation of the universe by God. They want to avoid linear history to such an extent that they are willing to fuse pagan cyclical theories of

---

40. Kelly, *Thermodynamics and Statistical Physics*, p. 121.
41. Aristotle, *Physics*, Part VIII.
42. John Gribbin, *In Search of Schrödinger's Cat: Quantum Physics and Reality* (New York: Bantam, 1984), p. 271.

time with endless, impersonal, purposeless creations out of nothing and destructions into nothing. But then what happens to the first law of thermodynamics, that matter-energy is neither created nor destroyed?

Atheism's universe is coming unglued, along with atheism.

The Communist Position: Cyclical History

One scientist adamantly rejects Clausius' theory of heat death: Soviet scientist I. P. Bazarov. This is understandable. To say a good word for Clausius in the Soviet Union is the first step in a trip to the Gulag archipelago. Frederick Engels, the co-founder of Communism, was a bitter foe of Clausius' theory. As I have argued elsewhere, Marx's conception of time seems on the surface to be linear, and therefore Western, but at bottom, it is a cyclical view. There is nothing in Marx's system to explain why the future Communist society will not fall into alienation again, and begin another cycle of historical development from communism to slavery to feudalism to capitalism to socialism, and finally to yet a higher state of communism.[43]

With Engels, the commitment to cosmic cycles was explicit. It was the foundation of his book, *Dialectics of Nature*, which Bazarov feels compelled to cite in his textbook as if it were a serious work of science. In the Introduction, Engels summarizes his view of the Darwinian revolution: "The new conception of nature was complete in its main features; all rigidity was dissolved, all fixity dissipated, all particularity that had been regarded as eternal became transient, the whole of nature shown as moving in eternal flux and cyclical course."[44] But Clausius' theory of the heat death of the universe pointed to a one-time-only historical development. Engels rejected any such view in the name of *cosmic historical cycles:*

. . . we arrive at the conclusion that in some way, which it will later be the task of scientific research to demonstrate, the heat radiated into space must be able to become transformed into another form of motion, in which it can once more be stored up and rendered active. Thereby the chief difficulty in the way of the reconversion of extinct suns into incandescent vapour disappears.

---

43. Gary North, *Marx's Religion of Revolution: The Doctrine of Creative Destruction* (Nutley, New Jersey: Craig Press, 1968), pp. 100-1.
44. Engels, *Dialectics of Nature* (New York: International Publishers, 1940), p. 13. This book was extracted posthumously from his notebooks.

For the rest, the eternally repeated succession of worlds in infinite time is only the logical complement to the co-existence of innumerable worlds in infinite space. . . . It is an eternal cycle in which matter moves, a cycle that certainly only completes its orbit in periods of time for which our terrestrial year is no adequate measure, a cycle in which the time of highest development, the time of organic life and still more that of the life of beings conscious of nature and of themselves, is just as narrowly restricted as the space in which life and self-consciousness come into operation; a cycle in which every finite mode of existence of matter, whether it be sun or nebular vapour, single animal or genus of animals, chemical combination or dissociation, is equally transient, and wherein nothing is eternal but eternally changing, eternally moving matter and the laws according to which it moves and changes.[45]

Thus, the laws of nature are somehow eternally fixed, yet the total flux of material cycles is equally eternal. So, he concludes the Introduction, "we have the certainty that matter remains eternally the same in all its transformations, that none of its attributes can ever be lost, and therefore, also, that with the same iron necessity that it will exterminate on the earth its highest creation, the thinking mind, it must somewhere else at another time again produce it."[46]

In short, there is no end of time. More to the point, *there is no inescapable physical process that points to the end of time, and which therefore points also to the destruction of mankind, the god of communism.*

The debate over the proper application of the second law of thermodynamics is not simply a neutral scientific debate, for there is no such thing as a neutral scientific debate. It is a debate over cosmology. It is a debate over the origin and final fate of the universe. It is therefore a debate about the existence of God. Engels recognized this, though modern physicists prefer to ignore the obvious. Referring to Clausius, Engels asks what becomes of the "apparently" lost heat. He is confident in his cyclical theory as he is in his atheism. "No wonder that it has not yet been solved; it may still be a long time before we arrive at a solution with our small means. But it will be solved, just as surely as it is certain that there are no miracles in nature and that the original heat of the nebular ball is not communicated to it miraculously from outside the universe."[47] No miracles,

---

45. *Ibid.*, pp. 23-24.
46. *Ibid.*, p. 25.
47. *Ibid.*, p. 202.

please. The universe is a closed system. By humanist definition, it *must* be a closed system.

Jaki has identified the source of Engels' animosity to Clausius. "Clausius, entropy, and the heat-death of the universe meant one and the same thing for Engels. They represented the most palpable threat to the materialistic pantheism of the Hegelian left for which the *material* universe was and still is the ultimate, ever active reality. Engels made no secret about the fact that the idea of a universe returning cyclically to the same configuration was a pivotal proposition within the conceptual framework of Marxist dialectic. He saw the whole course of science reaching in Darwin's theory of evolution the final vindication of the perennial recurrence of all, as first advocated by the founders of Greek philosophy."[48]

So we find that poor Professor Bazarov must reject Clausius' theory of heat death, and worse, that he must cite Engels as his justification. He notes that "the reactionary views of Clausius have been the subject of Engels' crushing criticism."[49] He then cites "materialist" Boltzmann's theory of fluctuations as a possible alternative to Clausius, reproducing a section from *Lectures on Gas Theory*.[50] But he then rejects the heart of Boltzmann's theory, namely, the existing equilibrium of the universe.[51] He offers no resolution to the problem. He uses two arguments that have gone nowhere in this century: 1) that the thermodynamic principles that apply to a laboratory experiment do not apply to the universe as a whole (an approach taken by the physicist Ernst Mach in the late nineteenth century, in contradiction to his own theory of the gravitational influence of the whole universe on all parts)[52] and 2) the appeal to some sort of statistical formula escape hatch, without a description of the physical processes that would make the statistical solution possible (Boltzmann's approach). It is an oddity of history that Boltzmann killed himself in 1906 because other physicists kept clinging to Mach's soon to be outmoded anti-atomism theory,[53] yet they both unsuccessfully opposed Clausius.

---

48. Jaki, *Science and Creation*, p. 312.
49. I. P. Bazarov, *Thermodynamics* (New York: Macmillan, 1964), p. 76. The typeface of this book is the familiar style used only by the English-language division of Moscow's publishing operation. It is obvious that Macmillan simply photocopied the book and published it in the United States.
50. *Ibid.*, p. 77.
51. *Ibid.*, p. 78.
52. Jaki, pp. 297-98.
53. John T. Blackmore, *Ernst Mach: His Work, Life, and Influence* (Berkeley: University of California Press, 1972), ch. 13.

Humanist Versions of Death and Resurrection

The second law of thermodynamics teaches that *if* the universe is a closed system, then the world is wearing out. It is going to die. It is headed for an inescapable heat death. Only if it contracts, and becomes a "cosmic egg," as Asimov calls it,[54] playfully reviving the imagery of the creation accounts of primitive paganism,[55] to explode in another Big Bang, can the heat death of the universe be avoided. Man either dies from heat death or dies from the crushing weight of being squeezed into the cosmic egg. In short, man is doomed . . . *if the universe is a closed system.*

What began as an observation of heat pumps in 1824 became after its rediscovery in 1850 a debate over the nature of the universe. It also become a debate over the nature of time. As Angrist and Helper remark: "All other variables with which science is concerned can be increased or decreased—but entropy and time always increase. Entropy can only be decreased temporarily and then only in a localized region at the expense of a greater increase elsewhere. It is a one-way variable that marks the universe as older today than it was yesterday. Entropy, as Arthur Eddington expressed it, is 'Time's Arrow.' "[56]

At the beginning of this chapter, I cited astronomer Sir James Jeans' observations concerning the heat death of the universe. He recognized clearly that the debate is between those who believe in linear time and those who believe in cyclical time. He also recognized the religious impulse of this continuing debate:

> The science of thermodynamics explains how everything in nature passes to its final state by a process which is designated the "increase of entropy." Entropy must forever increase: it cannot stand still until it has increased so far that it can increase no further. When this stage is reached, further progress will be impossible, and the universe will be dead. Thus, unless this whole branch of science is wrong, nature permits herself, quite literally, only two alternatives, progress and death: the only standing still she permits is in the stillness of the grave.
>
> Some scientists, although not, I think, very many, would dissent from this last view. While they do not dispute that the present stars are melting

---

54. *A Choice of Catastrophes*, p. 59.
55. Mircea Eliade, *Patterns in Comparative Religion* (New York: Sheed & Ward, 1958), pp. 413-16: "The Cosmogonic Egg."
56. Angrist and Helper, *Order and Chaos*, p. 160.

away into radiation, they maintain that, somewhere out in the remote depths of space, this radiation may be reconsolidating itself again into matter. A new heaven and a new earth may, they suggest, be in process of being built, not out of the ashes of the old, but out of the radiation set free by the combustion of the old. In this way they advocate what may be described as a cyclic universe; while it dies in one place the products of its death are busy producing new life in others.

This concept of a cyclic universe is entirely at variance with the well-established principle of the second law of thermodynamics, which teaches that entropy must for ever increase, and that cyclic universes are impossible in the same way, and for much the same reason, as perpetual motion machines are impossible. That this law may fail under astronomical conditions of which we have no knowledge is certainly conceivable, although I imagine the majority of serious scientists consider it very improbable. There is of course no denying that the concept of a cyclic universe is far the more popular of the two. Most men find the final dissolution of the universe as distasteful a thought as the dissolution of their own personality, and man's strivings after personal immortality have their macroscopic counterpart in these more sophisticated strivings after an imperishable universe.[57]

Re-read that last sentence. It comes to the heart of the matter concerning the fate of matter. *The death of the universe is the psychological equivalent of the death of God, for it points to the death of man, humanism's god.* Man's environment will have long since disappeared. Nothing will carry on man's work, man's story, or man's meaning. Man will not be the judge of himself and the universe around him. The universe dies, and man must die with it. Man, the king of humanism, is in fact nothing more than a *cosmic parasite*, and his host is dying. This is bad news for all those men whose dream of autonomy from God has led them to proclaim an autonomous universe, closed to God.

God alone could sustain the dreams of man by regenerating the universe, even as He regenerates man. But regeneration points to the final judgment, and autonomous man above all wants to avoid the eternal judgment. Better the ultimate despair of the heat death of the universe or the pseudo-hope of a cyclical universe which will destroy today's man, but which will open the possibility of eternally recurring cycles of Big Bangs, thermodynamic dissipation, contractions, and Big Bangs. Better eternal cycles than an eternity in hell, says modern man. And for God-denying, God-defying men, this conclusion is correct. It is not an available option, but it cer-

---

57. Jeans, *The Mysterious Universe*, pp. 179-81.

tainly would be better than hell. But it is not better than resurrection and eternal life for those people whom God chose before the foundation of the world to regenerate (Eph. 1:4-7).

Columbia University's astronomer Lloyd Motz gives us science's two options: heat death or cosmic crushing. He favors the latter, by the way. "While it appears that the earth is safe from galactic catastrophes, it is not safe from the various overall cosmological events that can, and ultimately will, bring things to an end. *An end* here does not mean that all matter will disappear but rather that a situation will occur where the orderly evolution and change that a man sees going on all around him will cease. This will happen either because the universe has run down, like the spring of a watch, or because it has contracted down to a tiny, but highly concentrated, bit of matter."[58]

He favors the oscillating universe, as did all the pagans of the ancient world. Somehow, being crushed to death gives man hope, for "man's existence implies that life will occur over and over again, but not precisely as it evolved in the present universe, for the normal fluctuations that occur in all physical systems will change the initial conditions of each new expansion phase of the universe, so that no two such phases will be identical. Thus, men have (in their own existence) not only the promise of life renewed but also the promise of almost infinite variety in such life."[59] This is humanistic science's version of hope in the resurrection. This is how he hopes to escape the curse of God, "ashes to ashes, dust to dust." Cosmic dust will revive itself, and it will again bring forth life.

Who knows, maybe you will someday become a dinosaur with a high IQ! Such is the logic of the humanist who combines Darwin and ancient man's cyclical cosmology in order to escape the logic of Rudolph Clausius. This is reincarnation without a belief in the human soul. This is madness.

Conclusion

The only thermodynamics textbook I have seen that at least points to the underlying cosmological issues is Gordon J. Van Wylen's. He is at least willing to ask the inevitable questions that are raised by the equations for the second law of thermodynamics and its

---

58. Motz, *The Universe: Its Beginning and End*, p. 305.
59. *Ibid.*, p. 317.

physical state, entropy. He is willing to do what the other textbook writers judiciously avoid: come to grips with God.

A final point to be made is that the second law of thermodynamics and the principle of increase in entropy have great philosophical implications. The question that arises is how did the universe get into the state of reduced entropy in the first place, since all natural processes known to us tend to increase entropy? Are there processes unknown to us, such as "continual creation," which tend to decrease entropy, and thus offset the increase in entropy associated with the natural processes known to us? On the other end of the scale the question that arises is what is the future of the universe? Will it come to a uniform temperature and maximum entropy, at which time life will be impossible? Quite obviously we cannot give conclusive answers to these questions on the basis of the second law only, but they are certainly topics that illustrate its philosophical implications. The author has found that the second law tends to increase his conviction that there is a Creator who has the answer for the future destiny of man and the universe.[60]

Next, consider his comments in the 1973 edition. He and his coauthor ask some new questions: "Does the second law of thermodynamics apply to the universe as a whole? . . . If the second law is valid for the universe (we of course do not know if the universe can be considered as an isolated system) how did it get in the state of low entropy?" Then they repeat his original affirmation of a Creator, although they do not capitalize the word in the later edition.[61] They raise the relevant question: *Is the universe really a closed system?* As believers in God, obviously they know that it isn't, but they do raise the question. It is *the* question that must be raised.

Modern physics and modern astronomy leave mankind without hope. Bertrand Russell saw its implications clearly. He wrote in 1935: "Some day, the sun will grow cold, and life on the earth will cease. The whole epoch of animals and plants is only an interlude between ages that were too hot and ages that will be too cold. There is no law of cosmic progress, but only an oscillation upward and downward, with a slow trend downward on a balance owing to the diffusion of energy. This, at least, is what science at present regards

---

60. Gordon J. Van Wylen, *Thermodynamics* (New York: Wiley, [1959] 1961), p. 169. Three comments are in order. First, Van Wylen was Chairman of the Department of mechanical engineering at the University of Michigan. Second, Wiley is a conventional publisher of scientific books. Third, the book was in its third printing.

61. Gordon J. Van Wylen and Richard Sontag, *Fundamentals of Classical Thermodynamics* (2nd ed.; New York: Wiley, 1973), p. 248.

as most probable, and in our disillusioned generation it is easy to believe. From evolution, so far as our present knowledge shows, no ultimately optimistic philosophy can be validly inferred."[62]

To overcome this inherent, inescapable pessimism of modern Western science, Jeremy Rifkin offers what he says is new hope for the future, but without adopting the Christian doctrines of creation, redemption, and resurrection. The quality of such hope we will explore in detail in subsequent chapters.

In summary:

1. The second law of thermodynamics has become a major scientific foundation of modern pessimism.
2. Most scientists fail to speak out on major philosophical issues.
3. Three major views of the world govern all interpretations: power religion, escape religion, and dominion religion.
4. Pessimism concerning the future is common to the escape religion.
5. Humanistic pessimism is acknowledged in principle but ignored as much as possible by the power religion.
6. Pessimism is denied by the dominion religion.
7. The pessimists want to escape God's judgment, either in history (through the "Rapture") or at the end of time (atheism, mysticism).
8. Those who write on the second law seldom mention its implications.
9. The second law teaches that the universe is becoming more random, wearing out.
10. The universe is therefore headed for extinction.
11. This has been taught by the physicists who pioneered the laws of thermodynamics.
12. The debate over the second law of thermodynamics is important because of its effect on man's concept of time and final judgment.
13. Some physicists have created incoherent explanations of the universe in order to escape the implications of the second law.
14. The only atheistic alternative to the linear history of entropy is cyclical history.
15. Cyclical history was the outlook of the pagan ancient world.
16. Rebellious men do not want to think about the end of time, for it points to the final judgment.
17. If the universe dies, then man dies.
18. If man dies, there can be no meaning to the humanist's world.
19. The humanist is today without hope.

---

62. Bertrand Russell, "Evolution," in *Religion and Science* (New York: Oxford University Press, [1935] 1972), p. 81.

3

ENTROPY AND SOCIAL THEORY

Now, however, a new world view is about to emerge, one that will eventually replace the Newtonian world machine as the organizing frame of history: the Entropy Law will preside as the ruling paradigm over the next period of history. Albert Einstein said that it is the premier law of all science; Sir Arthur Eddington referred to it as the supreme metaphysical law of the entire universe. The Entropy Law is the second law of thermodynamics. The first law states that all matter and energy in the universe is constant, that it cannot be created or destroyed. Only its forms can change but never its essence. The second law, the Entropy Law, states that matter and energy can only be changed in one direction, that is, from usable to unusable, or from available to unavailable, or from ordered to disordered.

Jeremy Rifkin[1]

Is there any relationship between men's worldviews and the kind of science they adopt? Probably there is. Henry M. Morris suggests that one reason why today's younger defenders of evolution have begun to abandon the neo-Darwinian synthesis of slow, organic changes is that they were educated during the "radical 'sixties." Revolutionary Marxism had been a quiet but effective intellectual force throughout the 1960's on many campuses.[2] His chapter title is "Evolution and Revolution."

It therefore seems fair to ask this question of the Creation Scientists: Is there any relationship between the kind of defense offered by one generation of six-day creationists and the overall worldview that they hold? I suggest that there are such relationships. A more important question is this one: Is there any relationship between the

---

1. Jeremy Rifkin (with Ted Howard), *Entropy: A New World View* (New York: Bantam, [1980] 1981), p. 6.
2. Henry Morris, *Evolution in Turmoil* (San Diego, California: Creation-Life Publishers, 1982), pp. 91-93.

eschatological views of one group of creationists and the type of intellectual defense they adopt? I think there is. Finally, is there a relationship between one's eschatology and one's overall social outlook? I think there is. That is the topic of this chapter.

Natural Science and Social Theory

The question inevitably arises: Can the so-called "law of entropy" be applied in social theory? Such attempts are questionable.[3] Those who rely heavily on the entropy theory in their cosmological explanations also tend to produce pessimistic social theories. It is my contention that: 1) their pessimism is their presupposition; and 2) pessimists sometimes adopt certain "entropic" cosmologies in order to support their pessimistic theories. Thus, what appears to be a conclusion — social pessimism — is in fact an original presupposition.

For over six years, the evangelical world has remained silent in the face of Rifkin's books, except when the response has been somewhat favorable. I believe that this silence has prevailed in large part because evangelical scholars share Rifkin's interpretation of entropy, his use of natural science in developing social theory, and his underlying pessimism regarding history and man's part in it. Evangelicals may not be comfortable with his economic and political conclusions, but they are even more uncomfortable in challenging them, given their own shared frame of reference: his pessimistic worldview.

The Resurrection

What the evangelical world has failed to emphasize is that the doctrine of Christ's resurrection is the unique New Testament doctrine that should be the starting point in Christian social theory. Creation, rebellion, resurrection, and restoration: here is the Bible's message of hope and transformation *in history* — not just for individuals, but also for societies — that must become the basis of Christian social theory.

---

3. One attempt to apply certain aspects of the entropy theory to economics is a difficult book by a brilliant economist, Nicholas Georgescu-Roegen, *The Entropy Law and Economic Process* (Cambridge, Massachusetts: Harvard University Press, 1971). The problem is that it is not clear that the entropy process of physical science is really similar to the processes of ignorance and waste in economic planning. The author uses the same word to describe both realms, but this does not prove the case for social and economic entropy. In any case, the book has not exercised visible influence within the economics profession.

The New Testament has given us a new understanding of the plan of God for history, and the doctrine of Christ's resurrection is at the heart of this perspective. Without this doctrine, Christians have nothing. Paul is adamant; he even repeats his argument, which he rarely does in his letters, concerning the resurrection and the validity of Christian faith: "But if there be no resurrection of the dead, then is Christ not risen: and if Christ be not risen, then is our preaching vain, and your faith is also vain. Yea, and we are found false witnesses of God; because we have testified of God that he raised up Christ: whom he raised not up, if so be that the dead rise not. For if the dead rise not, then is not Christ raised: and if Christ be not raised, your faith is vain; ye are yet in your sins" (I Cor. 15:13-17). Christian faith without the resurrection of Christ in history is vain faith.

Our apologetic methodology inevitably influences our general outlook. Should we begin with the Bible or with a nineteenth-century version of classical Newtonian physics? I contend that we should begin with the Bible, and specifically with the resurrection, rather than with the Fall of man in the garden. It is Christ's resurrection, not Adam's Fall, that is the dominant theme of the New Testament. To use the second law of thermodynamics against the evolutionists as the bedrock doctrine of Christian apologetics is to weaken the case for Christianity.

The Second Law of Thermodynamics

The second law has been used by Creation Scientists to argue that evolutionists have not been consistent in their devotion to the second law, which they virtually equate with science as perhaps science's most universal law. There are several problems with this strategy. First, many modern scientists have begun to abandon the universality of the second law or to apply it in radically unorthodox ways. Boltzmann's example (Chapter Two) is just one among many. Second, Darwinists constantly appeal to the "open system" character of life on earth, and they remind the Creation Scientists that the law applies only to closed systems. They never admit the validity of the Creation Scientists' use of the second law, and they accuse the Creation Scientists of not being scientific because they ignore "open systems."[4]

---

4. Evolutionist Michael Ruse responds to the Scientific Creationists' appeal to the second law, but he responds judiciously, for he does not admit that entropy is *always* increasing in the universe, only that it *may* be increasing: "The second law obviously applies only to closed systems. But, argue evolutionists, given the influx of usable

The debate goes on and on, like two endless loop cassette tapes playing at each other.

At best, to appeal to the second law as anything more than a convenient way to expose the possible scientific inconsistency of the evolutionists, and thereby to help strengthen Christians' confidence in creationism, is to grant too much authority to modern science. The problem is that this seemingly convenient argument (which somehow never convinces our evolutionist opponents) has in some cases been taken so seriously by Christians that they have followed Rifkin's example, and have begun to construct Christian social theory in terms of the second law of thermodynamics. When we see where Rifkin's approach is taking us, we should reconsider this application of classical physics to society. It is far better to rely on the Bible to provide us with our foundations of social theory.

Whenever anyone uses "neutral" physical science to support any social theory, he faces the problem that a radically unneutral humanist worldview undergirds modern physical science. An alien worldview can too easily be quietly imported into Christian social theory when Christians use modern science as a supposedly common-ground basis for the construction of social theories. Christians give away too much to the enemy when they begin with humanism's science to construct their worldview.

I. Creation Science's Social Pessimism

I am arguing in this book that there is a serious danger to Christianity when Christians try to use the second law of thermodynamics to justify a particular social theory. Let me cite an example from the world of Scientific Creationism. In a flyer produced by the Bible-Science Association and the Genesis Institute (same address), we read the following: "The creationist realizes that the world is growing old around him. He understands that things tend to run down, to age, to die. The creationist does not look for the world to improve,

---

energy from the sun, the organic world is an open system. Hence evolution is possible. Entropy may be increasing through the universe, taken as a whole, but it does not mean that, in small localized areas, entropy cannot decrease. The world of organic evolution is one such area. The sun shines down on the Earth. This makes the plants grow. Animals live and feed on the plants. And thus life goes forward." Michael Ruse, *Darwinism Defended: A Guide to the Evolution Controversies* (Reading, Massachusetts: Addison-Wesley, 1982), p. 296. Cf. pp. 306-7. This is a theory of "sunshine evolution"; see pp. 192ff. below.

but to crumble slowly—as in erosion, decay, and aging."[5] This is a philosophy of self-conscious defeat, a cry of despair. It is also not the kind of philosophy that anyone would normally choose to use to challenge the Marxists in Latin America.

The whole idea is wrong-headed. First, the entropic process of cosmic physical decay takes place in humanist time scales of billions of years. Such a time scale is irrelevant for social theory, Christian or pagan. Societies do not survive for billions of years—not so far, anyway. I shall return to this theme when I deal with Rifkin's writings.

Second, what does it mean to say "the world will [or will not] improve"? What world? The geophysical world? What does an ethical or aesthetic term such as "improve" have to do with the physical world? Scientific evolutionists have been careful to avoid such value-laden adjectives with respect to historical geology or biology, at least until man appears on the historical scene and begins to affect his environment. Without a moral evaluator, there can be no meaning for the word "improve."

Christians should be equally careful in their use of language. The Christian should argue that *God evaluates* any improvements or declines of the external world, and therefore men, acting as God's subordinates, also make such evaluations. But there is no autonomous *impersonal* standard of "world improvement," as any evolutionist readily admits. So the flyer apparently had as its point of reference not the geophysical world but rather *man's social world*. This immediately raises a crucial question: How do the operating standards of man's social world relate to the physical process of entropy? This is the question that Scientific Creationists have generally avoided, and when they have on occasion said something about it, they have sounded like Jeremy Rifkin.

Rifkin's Tactic

Rifkin has fully understood this. He uses it against his fundamentalist Christian reader. He appeals directly to premillennial eschatology in creating the case for social pessimism. He also appeals to the Creation Scientists' use of the first and second laws of thermodynamics. In fact, he sounds as though he is paraphrasing Henry Morris: "Interestingly enough, the creation story directly parallels the two basic laws of thermodynamics. According to Gen-

---

5. *What's the Difference? Creation/Evolution?* (no date), p. 2.

esis, God's order is fixed. He created everything that exists at one moment in time. Similarly, the first law of thermodynamics states that all matter and energy in the world are constant and fixed. That is, they can neither be created nor destroyed."[6] Then he goes on to link his pessimistic worldview to premillennial or amillennial pessimism regarding human history and also to the second law of thermodynamics:

> Evil is synonymous with the forces of chaos and disorder. History, in theological terms, is seen as a long and protracted war in which the forces of evil continually attempt to enlist the help of fallen individuals in their battle to spread chaos in God's world. The forces of evil win most of the battles, but ultimately lose the war. That is, with the help of sinful people, they succeed in creating more and more disorder in the world, until Christ's return once again to earth. God then triumphs over evil at this climactic moment of history, and the world, which the evil forces have turned into complete and utter chaos, is transformed back into God's kingdom.
> The second law of thermodynamics posits a similar view of history. It states that all matter and energy were created, in this original state, with an order and value to them. That ordered state is continually being eroded by an irreversible natural process. According to the law of entropy, all matter and energy are constantly and without exception moving from an ordered to a disordered state.[7]

This is a clever technique. First, appeal to the familiar pessimistic eschatologies of the readers. Second, use the familiar language of the Creation Scientists regarding the laws of thermodynamics. Third, remind them of the futility of seeing God's kingdom operating in history, thereby removing any hope of a *progressive removal of entropy's curses*. Throw back at them their traditional pessimism: "The evangelicals would argue that while only God can usher in the kingdom—reverse the process of entropy and remake the world—each person still has a responsibility during his lifetime to serve as a witness to the coming of that kingdom. Serving witness means respecting and protecting God's created order to the fullest, even while knowing that all of one's efforts are ultimately insufficient to the task."[8] Rifkin's "witness" is a person who struggles against the inevitable forces of decay. He is doomed to failure in history. Here also is the heart of amillennial and premillennial social pessimism.

---

6. Jeremy Rifkin (with Ted Howard), *The Emerging Order: God in the Age of Scarcity* (New York: Ballantine, [1979] 1983), pp. 232-33.
7. *Ibid.*, p. 233.
8. *Ibid.*, p. 234.

Yet Rifkin chides premillennialists for giving up on the world. "The premillennialists view history in much the same way as the second law of thermodynamics. However, their overriding preoccupation with arriving as quickly as possible at the end of history—God's return—precludes any serious service as stewards over God's created order. Their attention has become so riveted on anticipation of the coming of the kingdom and saving as many souls as possible in the remaining time, that they have left God's created order unguarded and unprotected. In not honoring their covenant to God to serve as stewards, the premillennialists are acting in direct rebellion."[9] He challenges them to become stewards. How can they do this? By adopting his philosophy of anti-growth and anti-science. How do we slow down this universal evil, meaning the entropy process? By abandoning most Western technologies. "Technologies, after all, are designed to speed up the entropy process by more progressively using up the stock of available matter and energy in the world."[10]

Rifkin is attempting to reduce Christians' resistance to his theories by making them feel guilty. He chides them for becoming consistent with their eschatological pessimism. He calls them to a life of sacrifice, despite guaranteed failure. This strategy of guilt-manipulation is an effective means of producing a program for your enemies' cultural paralysis.

Simple to Complex?

The creationist quite properly challenges the evolutionist to explain how it is that an increasingly complex and increasingly orderly world could have evolved from a random, "noisy," *Creator-less*, lifeless world. Evolutionists feel the heat of this question. (Someday, they will be subjected to a lot more heat.) Isaac Asimov has gone so far as to say in a footnote response to an essay written by Scientific Creationist Duane Gish: "Astronomers do not believe the Universe began in a disordered, chaotic state. It began, in fact, in a condition of high order. A departure from this order, an inhomogeneity, led to the formation of stars and galaxies *in accordance* with the second law."

This is an astounding statement. He is saying that the "cosmic stuff" of the legendary Big Bang was highly ordered. No molecules yet, but more highly ordered than molecules! No organic life yet,

---

9. *Ibid.*, p. 236.
10. *Ibid.*, p. 233.

but more highly ordered than organic life! This boggles the mind of the average person who, unlike Asimov, is unable to write two books a month. Asimov does not tell us which astronomers have said this. He also does not mention how this highly ordered system started, or what it was. He does not because he cannot. But this is supposedly irrelevant. In the standard false humility side of modern two-faced science, he adds: "Scientists do not know how the condition of high order began, but scientists are accustomed to lack of knowledge."[11] They are always ready to feign humility when they get caught on the horns of an obvious intellectual dilemma.

Eschatology and the Second Law

But creationists erroneously believe that they have achieved more of a victory than the idea of entropy entitles them to. The previously cited flyer asserts: "Evolution demands that things 'wind up' even as we see them run down. Therefore the evolutionist looks for things to improve." Again, what do we mean, "improve"? What "things"? For that matter, what does the evolutionist mean by "improve"?

Pastor Tommy Reid has written an intelligent essay from a premillennial perspective, one which relies in part on the postmillennial optimism of David Chilton's book, *Paradise Restored*. Reid has also read Jeremy Rifkin. His observations are very significant for the thesis of this book, namely, that the use of the entropy concept in social theory leads to anti-Christian, socially paralyzing conclusions (as Rifkin understands so well):

Recent concepts have contributed to either a fatalistic or monastic attitude among other evangelicals, not the least of which is our modern emphasis on science. The rather recent discovery of the law of thermodynamics has shaped the philosophical view of the world held by some evangelicals. The second law of thermodynamics states that all matter and energy were created in this original state with an order and value to them. [This is

---

11. "The Genesis War," *Science Digest* (Oct. 1981), p. 82. Six pages later, when he concludes his own essay against Gish, he becomes absolutely confident, in contrast to his earlier "scientific" humility: "In fact, the strongest of all indications as to the fact of evolution and the truth of the theory of natural selection is that all the independent findings of scientists in every branch of science, when they have anything to do with biological evolution at all, *always* strengthen the case and *never* weaken it." (Emphasis in the original.) Always strengthen? Never weaken? This is humble science? No, this is just sloppy philosophy masquerading as science.

not a good statement of the second law, as held by conventional scientists; it does reflect the language of Creation Scientists—G.N.] That ordered state is continually being eroded by an irreversible natural process. According to this law of entropy, all matter and energy are constantly and without exception moving from an ordered to a disordered state.

Many evangelicals have basically embraced this scientific view of matter and have applied it to society, with an attendant fatalism.[12]

The key word is *fatalism*. This is the heart of my critique of the use of the second law to construct social theory. What I argue is that this fatalism has in fact been imported from two sources: 1) a popular (though fading) version of premillennial eschatology—one which Reid's article rejects—and 2) an inapplicable version of nineteenth-century physical science, one which evolutionists had been unwilling to apply to social theory until Rifkin appeared on the scene.

"Winding Down"

Let us pursue this "wind up" and "run down" analogy. Clocks (like galaxies) unquestionably run down over time, but this has nothing to do with the purposes, good or evil, to which clocks can be put. Furthermore, men can rewind clocks. Similarly, God can also "rewind" the universe or any aspect of the universe. He has done so in the past. If we feel compelled to use mechanistic analogies, we can call such a "rewinding event" a *miracle*. When Jesus healed sick people, multiplied fishes and loaves, turned water into wine, resurrected Lazarus from the dead, rose from the dead Himself, and ascended into heaven, He overcame the "entropy process" (assuming that we equate the "entropy process" with the curse of Genesis 3:17-19, as Creation Science usually does). He "rewound" certain aspects of the unwinding cosmic clock.

Why, then, should Christians cling frantically and fanatically to the doctrine of entropy as immutable? It clearly is *not* immutable. It is only a "most of the time" backdrop to life. One reason for this adherence to the second law by Christians is that most modern scientists today still hold such a view of the universe as a whole—the "closed system" of the supposedly uncreated universe. Since educated Christians want to be thought of as scientific, they adopt this commonly held entropic view of the long-term fate of the universe. In

---

12. Tommy Reid, "Understanding 'Kingdom Now' Teaching," *Ministries* (Summer 1986), p. 76.

their attempt to defend the Christian faith scientifically, they give away too much of the case to their opponents.

Another reason is this: *they are really trying to defend their pessimistic eschatological views regarding the fate of the world prior to the return of Christ.* They are what we might call "pessimillennialists," and their emphasis on the scientific doctrine of entropy—the running down of the universe—has come as a result of their views of the timing of Christ's second coming. Science is not neutral; the emphases of scientists are not neutral. Eschatology matters in a theory of matter.

A third reason is this: they have failed to think through the implications of the "entropy process." But Rifkin has done so, and he is developing these implications as weapons to be used against Western civilization in general, and against Christian conservatives in particular.

Whether or not a creationist believes that God overcomes many of the effects of God's curse in the realm of human society depends on his view of ethics and eschatology, not on the scientific phenomenon called entropy. To de-emphasize the priority of ethics in explaining "social entropy"—in my view, a misapplication of a concept taken from classical physics (thermodynamics)—is simultaneously to de-emphasize the gospel and its positive effects in relation to the Fall of man and the resulting curses. In short, some dispensational fundamentalists and traditional amillennialists who happen to be six-day creationists are (probably unconsciously) introducing their pessimistic eschatologies through the back door of the church in the name of "irrefutable scientific law." This is not a legitimate intellectual procedure. It is also highly dangerous, as Pastor Reid recognizes:

> Most evangelicals grew up within the confines of small, anemic, minority churches that were largely impotent insofar as changing the world was concerned. Now evangelicals have awakened to a world in which they have power, prestige and ability to bring about sociological change.
>
> Those who teach kingdom-now hold that evangelicals must develop a theology of sociological responsibility or we will again permit the liberals in Protestantism and the liberation theologians in Catholicism to shape our world—while we go merrily along awaiting the rapture. We need to remember how the church in Russia found itself "arguing about the color of the drapes in the cathedral" while the atheists were building a newly reformed society around them.[13]

---

13. *Ibid.*, pp. 76-77.

Henry Morris has remarked that the "punctuated evolution" theory of the younger Darwinians may well be the product of their graduate school experiences during the 1960's, and that the older evolutionists held to a gradual evolution view because they were educated during the era of the older "gradualistic" political liberalism.[14] Tommy Reid has pointed to a similar relationship between the older fundamentalism's eschatological and social pessimism, as well as an attitude hostile to social reform, and the tiny and culturally impotent churches that served as the spiritual environment of that older movement. I would go one step farther. I think this pessimistic attitude strongly influenced their selection of the second law of thermodynamics as their primary scientific defense of creationism. These connections are not perfect, but I think they do exist in a loose sense — at least as tight as the relationship between the radicalism of the 1960's and the acceptance of "punctuated" evolutionism.

Let us return to the previously mentioned flyer from the Bible-Science Association. It also says that *things tend to run down*. What does this mean? If things only *tend* to run down, this implies that sometimes things *don't* run down. If so, there must be offsetting progressive forces in operation. What might these be? The main one is the *gospel of salvation*. Regeneration restores ethical wholeness to men. Another offsetting factor is *obedience to the law of God*. God's law enables men to rebuild a cursed world. In other words, *ethics is fundamental; entropy isn't*. This is why entropy, to the extent that any such phenomenon applies to the universe as a whole, is only a tendency.

The reason why I keep referring to this small document (tract) is because it is the one creationist document I have seen that even mentions social theory, and even then only vaguely. I would have been happy to consider other documents from Creation Scientists that deal with entropy in relation to social theory, but I have been unable to find any. I searched the complete set of the *Creation Social Sciences and Humanities Quarterly* and found nothing on the topic. Why this silence on social theory? It may be that the entropy paradigm is so powerful that six-day creationists have become pessimistic about the possibility of constructing the foundations of a self-consciously biblical social science. Perhaps they have been baffled by the question: "If entropy is the dominant factor in life, how can there be progress in social institutions, including the church?" The answer that I offer is simple enough:

---

14. Morris, *Evolution in Turmoil*, ch. 4.

> The resurrection has made possible the historical overcoming of the *cursed aspects* of entropy in the physical universe, and to whatever extent that entropy-related curses affect social institutions, these effects can be offset even more rapidly than in the physical realm, because the three main institutions of society—family, church, and State—are covenantal. The closer we get to man, the more the covenant's sanctions of blessings and cursings become visible.

The development of these ideas in Ray Sutton's book, *That You May Prosper*, gives a detailed defense of God's judgments in history, which are two-fold: curses and blessings.[15] The Creation Science movement and premillennialists in general have paid too little attention to God's covenantal blessings in history. They have focused their attention exclusively on the cursings.

Ethics and Entropy

This emphasis on entropy in the apologetic methodology of six-day creationists has clouded their thinking. The members of this movement in the past have generally been committed to the doctrine of the premillennial return of Christ. (Most of the others have been amillennialists, either Lutherans or Calvinists, and they are even more committed to pessimism, for they do not acknowledge the possibility of the physical return of Jesus to rule prior to the final judgment.)[16] Dispensationalists see our present dispensation of the "Church Age" as under God's curse. They believe in *continuing ethical decline* and therefore *continuing social decline* before Jesus returns personally to set up a visible kingdom.

They have a problem. They have great difficulty in explaining how modern man has reached today's pinnacle of economic, scientific, and technological glory. Even if social decline lies ahead, it is decline from *something*. Why are we so far ahead scientifically compared to where the founders of the faith were in Jesus' day? For that matter, why are we so far ahead of Moses? We possess mass-produced inexpensive Bibles, satellite TV networks, radio stations, and other technological miracles, which in fact are not miracles, but repeatable technologies in a world characterized by entropy. How can Chris-

---

15. Ray R. Sutton, *That You May Prosper: Dominion By Covenant* (Tyler, Texas: Institute for Christian Economics, 1987), ch. 4.

16. An exception was R. J. Rushdoony, who helped Morris and Whitcomb to get *The Genesis Flood* published in 1961. He is a postmillennialist.

tians account for the growing complexity of social life, any more than evolutionists can account for the growing complexity of biological life? The biblical answer is *ethics:* God has blessed His holy word as it has been extended across the West. It is *the abandonment of the gospel* which now threatens the West, not the "process of physical entropy" as such. Scientific Creationists have another problem if they are premillennialists. Will the return of Christ overcome the entropy process? Will the effects of entropy be in some way suspended, at least with respect to biology? Will people live longer and healthier? What about reducing "social entropy"? Will communications improve (i.e., will "noise" be reduced)? Will order begin to overcome randomness? If so, how? If not . . . what kind of millennium will *that* be?

But if the effects of entropy can and will be overcome after Jesus returns bodily to reign, but before the final judgment and the transformation of the universe, then why can't we also argue that if men voluntarily begin to conform themselves to God's laws *before* Jesus returns physically, the *cursed* effects of entropy will be progressively overcome just as surely as after Jesus' premillennial return? Premillennialists argue that men will not repent in this fashion, but this begs the question. The question is: Does God promise that the effects of His curse on man and nature can progressively be overcome (though not absolutely) in response to ethical regeneration? The biblical answer is clear: *yes* (Deut. 28:1-14).

Entropy is, at most, a backdrop—a kind of measurable down payment on the death that awaits all life apart from regeneration and ethical restoration. Entropy's effects can (and have been) overcome by righteousness. Miracles are real. So is regeneration. So is human progress.

II. Jeremy Rifkin's Social Pessimism

The same sorts of questions should be directed against Rifkin's social speculations. Rifkin has written two widely read and enthusiastically reviewed books that popularize a theory of static society, *The Emerging Order: God in the Age of Scarcity* (1979) and *Entropy: A New World View* (1980). These books are clear, well-written, and present a consistent, profoundly anti-Christian view of the world. Because of the consistency of his arguments, and because of his anti-Christian conclusions—conclusions presented in the name of a "new Christianity"—Rifkin's books deserve considerable attention.

These are not scholarly books or immortal books. One cynical reviewer has gone so far as to say that "What Rifkin offers in this book is a pop version of a world view: *Entropy* is to Vico, Toynbee, Hegel and even Teilhard what a McDonald's hamburger is to *haute cuisine*."[17] But let us not forget that McDonald's restructured the restaurant industry in the United States. McDonald's also changed people's tastes. Let us also not forget that Christians in our day are "McDonald's people," not *"haute cuisine* people." So we need to consider Rifkin's books, not because they are profoundly original books, but because educated Christians and others have taken him seriously enough to buy lots of paperback copies. Even television evangelist Pat Robertson was lured into promoting Rifkin's *Entropy* in a pre-publication review of the book which appeared in *Pat Robertson's Perspective* (June/July 1980), for which Constance Cumbey has quite properly criticized him.[18] Rifkin's books are very useful for contrasting the teachings of the Bible with those of an alien faith. Even more important, the alien nature of his faith has not been widely recognized by Christian reviewers, indicating a startling blindness, intellectually and theologically, on the part of the reviewers. I believe that this blindness results from shared presuppositions.

Blaming Christianity

Rifkin imports Eastern mysticism's view of social reality in the name of modern physical science. Predictably, he is hostile to Christian orthodoxy. "The fact is, we made a mistake. Our parents made a mistake and so did theirs. It began a long time ago when God said to the first of our kind, 'You shall have dominion over the fish of the sea and over the birds of the air and over every living thing that moves upon the earth.' We thought God meant for us to subdue the

---

17. John C. Caiazza, "Pop Intellectuality," *Chronicles of Culture* (March/April 1981), p. 26.

18. Constance E. Cumbey, *A Planned Deception: The Staging of a New Age "Messiah"* (East Detroit, Michigan: Pointe Publishers, 1986), pp. 161-62. I think Pat Robertson's error was mainly intellectual, or perhaps bureaucratic (maybe a staff writer wrote the review), not religious and philosophical. I do not believe that he is a conscious New Age promoter. He is certainly a promoter of the idea of Christian dominion, and his book, *The Secret Kingdom*, is a defense of "kingdom now" dominion theology. As we shall see, Rifkin is totally hostile to dominion theology. So, for that matter, is Constance Cumbey. It should be mentioned that Mrs. Cumbey was forced to self-publish this book because her original publisher, William Keith of Huntington House, did not approve of her excessively harsh criticisms of Mr. Robertson. She has escalated these criticisms since 1986.

earth, to become its master."[19] That, as he well knows, is precisely what God intended for man: *to subdue the earth*. This is the meaning of dominion. Two verses later in Genesis we read: "And God blessed them, and God said unto them, Be fruitful, and multiply, and replenish the earth, and subdue it: and have dominion over the fish of the sea, and over the fowl of the air, and over every living thing that moveth upon the earth" (Gen. 1:28). Rifkin carefully avoids citing this verse. *Rifkin knows exactly what he is doing.* He is deliberately misleading his readers.

His view of the historical relationship between the teachings of Christianity and the advent of pollution is conventional within the ranks of the zero-growth community, and I have commented negatively on this thesis elsewhere.[20] This line of argument goes as follows: in the past, especially since the Protestant Reformation, Christianity taught dominion over nature; the attempt to exercise dominion over nature led to the exploitation of nature; therefore, in order to avoid the exploitation of nature, Christians must abandon the theology of dominion over nature.[21]

Christianity Didn't Do It

I need to point out that this interpretation of the historical cause of ecological disruptions has also been called into question by René Dubos, a world-famous microbiologist and prominent leader in the ecology movement. In his book, *A God Within* (1972), he points to the history of man's relationship with nature, and he concludes that ecological devastation has not been a monopoly of Christian civilization. "Erosion of the land, destruction of animal and plant species, excessive exploitation of natural resources, and ecological disasters are not peculiar to the Judeo-Christian tradition and to scientific technology. At all times, and all over the world, man's thoughtless interventions into nature have had a variety of disastrous consequences or at least have changed profoundly the complexion of nature."[22]

Dubos comes as close as any non-theist can to calling these disasters judgments of God. "History is replete with ecological disasters:

---

19. Jeremy Rifkin, *Declaration of a Heretic* (London: Routledge and Kegan Paul, 1985), p. 107.
20. Gary North, *The Dominion Covenant: Genesis*, pp. 31-36; cf. R. V. Young, Jr., "Christianity and Ecology," *National Review* (Dec. 20, 1974).
21. Rifkin, *Entropy*, pp. 232-33.
22. René Dubos, *A God Within* (New York: Scribner's, 1972), pp. 158-59.

the most flourishing lands of antiquity seem to have been under a malediction."[23] (A malediction—evil speaking—is an *oath of cursing*, calling down evil on someone or something. The self-maledictory oath is the legal basis of the three biblical covenantal institutions: church, State, and family.)[24] He also lists the civilizations of Mesopotamia, Persia, Egypt, West Pakistan, and much of India, China, Southeast Asia, and Latin America. We could also list classical Greece, and numerous primitive cultures. "All over the globe and at all times in the past, men have pillaged nature and disturbed the ecological equilibrium. . . ."[25] More than this: "In fact, the Judeo-Christian peoples were probably the first to develop on a large scale a pervasive concern for land management and an ethic of nature."[26]

When a dedicated humanist and professional ecologist of Dubos' stature dismisses Rifkin's accusations against Christianity, we have to ask ourselves a key question: Is Rifkin being honest with the reader?

Denying Progress

Rifkin never mentions Dubos' summary. This is understandable, given his own commitment to Eastern mysticism. Rifkin's interpretation of what a reworked theology of dominion ought to teach would introduce to the West an Eastern *static cosmology* in the name of Christianity. He teaches an Eastern view of the fixed order of the creation, a view which does not grasp the implications of *progressive cultural sanctification*, meaning the building up, development, or recreation of the garden's image, in time and on earth.[27]

Incredibly, he claims that he bases his new interpretation of the Book of Genesis on the writings of several Protestant theologians, including Francis Schaeffer. (It is unlikely that Schaeffer would have acknowledged the legitimacy of the following application of his work.) "The new interpretation of Genesis," writes Rifkin, "begins with the idea that since God created the heavens and the earth and everything in this world, that all his creations take on importance and an intrinsic worth because they are of his making. Since the creation of God's has a purpose and order to it, that purpose and order

---

23. *Ibid.*, p. 153.
24. Ray R. Sutton, *That You May Prosper*, ch. 4.
25. Dubos, *A God Within*, p. 161.
26. *Idem.*
27. David Chilton, *Paradise Restored: A Biblical Theology of Dominion* (Ft. Worth, Texas: Dominion Press, 1985).

is [sic] to be revered just as God's creations are to be revered. Finally, what God has created is fixed. The Lord created the world and *everything* in it and then he rested, according to the Creation story. It follows from this, argue the new theologians, that anything that exploits or harms God's creations is sinful and an act of rebellion against God himself. Likewise, anything that undermines the fixed purpose and order that God has given to the natural world is also sinful and an act of rebellion."[28]

Ethics and Nature

Here we see a fundamental theological error: confusing the fixed order of *ethics* with the fixed order of *nature*. This may not seem like a serious error, but it is at the heart of the division between true and false religion. Is the uniformitarian[29] principle ethical or is it biological? Should men honor the ethical laws of God or the status quo of nature? Are men subordinate to God or nature?

Perhaps we can see the implications of Rifkin's theology by asking this question: Should the scientists in Britain who presently have in a laboratory the last known specimens of smallpox destroy these smallpox germs? The disease has been one of man's great scourges in history. It is transmitted only from man to man, and therefore it is one of the few known diseases that can be eradicated if it is separated from its host, man, for any length of time. The World Health Organization reports that since the late 1970's, there have been no known outbreaks of the disease. The World Health Organization takes much of the credit for this victory over smallpox. (Its officials prudently refuse to mention the damaging evidence that its years of inoculating Africans may have been the source of the initial spread of AIDS.[30] Trading the minimal threat of smallpox for what may become the most deadly scourge in man's history is too great an embarrassment for messianic humanists.) This means that the few organisms being artificially maintained in that laboratory in Britain are the last ones left alive on earth, if the epidemiology of smallpox is correct, and if there really have been no outbreaks of the disease. Should they be killed?

---

28. Rifkin, *Entropy*, p. 233.
29. Uniformitarianism in physical science asserts that the processes in nature that we observe today are the same as those that operated countless ages ago. Uniformitarianism in ethics argues that God and His law are the same, yesterday, today, and tomorrow.
30. *London Times* (May 11, 1987).

It is obvious that a literal application of Rifkin's version of Genesis would prohibit the extermination of one of God's biological creations. Rifkin is straightforward: "Every species must be preserved simply because it has an inherent and inalienable right to life by virtue of its existence."[31] It is equally obvious that a literal application of the Protestant version of the dominion covenant would encourage this particular "exploitation of nature." Kill the creatures! Smallpox would be eradicated from the earth.

There is, sadly, still a third view, neither Eastern nor Christian: the *scientific* view. "Keep the organisms alive, so that scientists can conduct more research, even if there is a risk that the disease will get out of the laboratory and back into society at large." (This may already have happened once. In 1978, a medical photographer for Birmingham University died of smallpox. She had been working one floor above the virology research department which had been involved in smallpox research.)[32] The autonomy of scientific research is placed above the welfare of society.

What the Bible never teaches is the preservation of all life or all species, irrespective of the legitimate—though we can argue about what constitutes "legitimate"—needs of mankind. Care with nature, yes. Caution in introducing new species (through genetic manipulation), yes.[33] Care in moving one species to a new environment where it has few biological enemies, of course. But it is the *needs of man*—specifically, the needs of a growing number of regenerate and morally sanctified people who act as God's lawfully delegated agents—*as revealed in the Bible and through Bible-governed human wisdom* that must govern the dominion covenant. In other words, because there is a *fixed moral order* there can be a *progressive development of the creation* under the auspices of man. As men begin to conform themselves to the terms of biblical law, they will exercise greater power, meaning long-term, God-honoring, man-satisfying power, over the creation. This is what Genesis 1:26-28 is all about.

Dubos, a non-Christian, has an inkling of this necessity of progress, although men will debate over the proper definition of progress.

---

31. *Ibid.*, p. 210.
32. Associated Press story, *Durham Morning Herald* (Sept. 17, 1978).
33. Rifkin, *Who Shall Play God?* (New York: Dell, 1977). For a more optimistic and less apocalyptic view of genetic engineering, see William Tucker, *Progress and Privilege: America in the Age of Environmentalism* (Garden City, New York: Anchor Press/Doubleday, 1982), ch. 11.

"The solution to the environmental crisis will not be found in a retreat from the Judeo-Christian tradition or from technological civilization. Rather it will require a new definition of progress, based on better knowledge of nature and on a willingness to change our ways of life accordingly."[34] To abandon science and technology at this point in man's history would be suicidal and irresponsible.

Rifkin vs. Private Ownership

Rifkin at least understands the deeply theological nature of the competing world-and-life views. He understands it far better than most of his humanist peers and most of his Christian readers. He understands the importance of the attempt by non-orthodox theologians to reinterpret the dominion covenant in the name of a "new reformation," which is in fact a revival of a non-Christian cosmology in the name of Christ.

By radically redefining humanity's relationship to the rest of God's creation, contemporary Christian scholars are thrusting a theological dagger directly into the heart of the expansionist epoch. The new concept of dominion as stewardship and conservation rather than ownership and exploitation is at loggerheads with both traditional Christian theology and the mechanical world view of the past several hundred years. By refocusing the story of Creation and humanity's purpose in the world, Christian theologians have committed an act of open rebellion against their own doctrinal past. The Christian individual who for hundreds of years sought salvation through productivity and subduing of nature is now being challenged by a new Christian person who seeks salvation by conserving and protecting God's creation. *The Christian work ethic is being replaced by the Christian conservation ethic.* This new emphasis on stewardship is providing the foundation for the emergence of a new Christian Reformation and a New Covenant vision for society.[35]

Notice how Rifkin defines "dominion" as "stewardship and conservation," in contrast to "ownership and exploitation," by which he means *private* ownership. This is the language of all socialist theory, although he does not openly call for the socialization of the means of production. But he does call for State ownership of land and other "non-renewable resources." In the "ideal steady state" society—*a zero-*

---
34. Dubos, *A God Within*, p. 172.
35. *Entropy*, pp. 236-37.

growth society—which Rifkin advocates, "The concept of private property will apply to consumer goods and services, but not land and other renewable and non-renewable resources. The long-accepted practice of private exploitation of 'natural' resources will be replaced with the notion of public stewardship for the common good."[36] In *Entropy*, he says the same thing, except here he refers to "public guardianship."[37]

Rifkin explicitly rejects the idea that the competitive, open, free market is a means of dovetailing people's varying economic plans—a Christian concept which was secularized in the eighteenth and nineteenth centuries. "The orthodox economic view that each person's individual self-interest when added up together always serves the common good of the community is regarded with suspicion or, more appropriately, with outright derision."[38] He deliberately creates a "stick man" to overcome: no prominent defender of traditional classical liberalism ever argued that individual self-interest *always* serves the common good. But more to the point, how is the preservation of the common good guaranteed by the control of land by tenured bureaucrats who operate officially under the overall authority of politicians —politicians who cannot control much of what the bureaucrats do in the name of the common good?

Implicit Faith in Bureaucracy

The Rifkins of the world seem to believe that their class—the articulate, formally educated class—will wind up in the positions of power in a bureaucratic society. They do not recognize the central skill of bureaucratic administration: the shuffling of papers rather than the writing of books. Bureaucrats are seldom noted for their intellectual abilities. They are seldom articulate people. On the contrary, they are noted for their ability to adopt confusing language which communicates very little useful information to those outside the bureaucracy, or even inside.[39] Intellectuals seldom understand the process by which bureaucracies overwhelm the political institutions of democracy.

---

36. Rifkin, *The Emerging Order*, p. 84.
37. Rifkin, *Entropy*, p. 209.
38. *Idem*.
39. Every month, *Washington Monthly* reprints a "Memo of the Month," the most outrageous departmental announcement from a Washington bureaucracy. A collection of these memos is *The Hazards of Walking and Other Memos from Your Bureaucrats*, edited by Carol Trueblood and Donna Fenn (Boston, Massachusetts: Houghton Mifflin, 1982).

Max Weber, the great German sociologist, did understand, but his warnings have generally gone unheeded by the professional scholars. The democratization of society in its totality, Weber wrote, "is an especially favorable basis of bureaucratization, but by no means the only possible one." We cannot say that this increase in the power of bureaucracies is automatic, he said, but there are reasons to believe that modern political conditions are especially favorable for bureaucratic expansion. "The power position of a fully developed bureaucracy is always great, under normal conditions overtowering. The political 'master' always finds himself, vis-à-vis the trained official, in the position of a dilettante facing the expert."[40] Politicians lose control.

The profit management system of capitalism at least keeps the "experts" in check by means of price competition, innovation, and the legal ability of consumers to say "no."[41] But this aspect of the market has not been understood by the vast majority of intellectuals in the twentieth century. Rifkin is no exception.

Waste Is Expensive

As we have already seen, he contrasts "productivity" with "conservation." This is the language of the ecology movement, as well as most versions of Eastern religion that are popular in the West. I elsewhere discuss at some length the relationship between private ownership and the incentive to conserve assets, and the relationship between socialist ownership and the incentive to waste or consume "free" resources.[42] Productivity in a free market must take into consideration all known costs of operation, and the free market encourages owners to discover formerly hidden costs, in order to reduce them through greater efficiency. One of these costs is the cost of the *reduced future value of capital assets that are being used up in any given production process*. Waste is a cost to owners of capital assets. If owners can find a way to reduce waste or extend the productive life of their capi-

---

40. Max Weber [pronounced Mawx VAYber], *Economy and Society: An Outline of Interpretive Sociology*, edited by Guenther Roth and Claus Wittich (New York: Bedminster Press, 1968), III, p. 991. This chapter on bureaucracy was published posthumously in the early 1920's in Weber's *Wirtschaft und Gesellschaft*.

41. Ludwig von Mises, *Bureaucracy* (Cedar Falls, Iowa: Center for Futures Education, [1944] 1983). This book is now distributed by the Libertarian Press, Spring Mills, Pennsylvania.

42. Gary North, *Tools of Dominion: The Case Laws of Exodus* (Tyler, Texas: Institute for Christian Economics, 1988), ch. 14: "Pollution, Ownership, and Responsibility."

tal, they will do so if the possible changes cost less than the expected loss of capital value.

There is always waste in every production process, for men are not omniscient and omnipotent. In short, they make mistakes. But in capitalist economies, it often pays owners to alter production processes in order to reduce waste. What capitalism does is to pressure profit-seeking owners of productive resources to put a *price tag on waste*. Owners determine which wasteful process should be borne for the sake of higher output, and which should be reduced for the sake of long-term preservation of capital asset value. It is therefore utterly misleading, both historically and in terms of economic theory, for Rifkin to complain that "Up to now, there has been little public outcry over the exploitative and wasteful ways of the capitalist system."[43] That such anti-capitalist propaganda is being taken seriously in the evangelical world points to the present intellectual bankruptcy of evangelicalism.

Conclusion

Because the Scientific Creationists rely so heavily on the doctrine of entropy in building their case against the Darwinists, some of them have adopted a pessimistic view of human history that is remarkably similar to the view set forth by New Age theorist Jeremy Rifkin. Instead of simply using the entropy doctrine as a foil to embarrass the Darwinists—showing that their opponents are not really consistent in their proclamation of uniformitarianism—the Scientific Creationists actually adopt the theory in an attempt to develop a Christian alternative to scientific Darwinism.

Rifkin's misuse of the entropy process to create a vision of social pessimism and the defeat of optimistic man has been imitated by those six-day creationists who have adopted the social entropy doctrine by way of Scientific Creationism. They, too, hold out no hope for society's progress prior to the second coming of Christ. Thus, we find that fundamentalists, charismatics, and neo-evangelicals have been unable or at least unwilling to challenge either Rifkin's Eastern theology or his third-rate social science. Their eschatological pessimism has played into his grasping hands. It has aided Rifkin in his self-conscious attempt to capture the minds of the charismatics and neo-evangelical leadership during a period which he recognizes as

---

43. Rifkin, *The Emerging Order*, p. 80.

being potentially a second Protestant Reformation.[44]

In summary:

1. Men's religious views of the world influence the kinds of science they do.
2. The theology of the Creation Science movement influences their selection of arguments.
3. Their pessimistic eschatology has shaped their use of the second law of thermodynamics.
4. Jeremy Rifkin has attempted to apply natural science to social theory.
5. He has also selected the second law as the key idea in his system.
6. The evangelical world has failed to place Christ's resurrection at the center of its view of time, judgment, and society.
7. Creation Scientists emphasize Adam's Fall, God's curse, and the decay of the universe.
8. Their reliance on the entropy concept has placed them at the mercy of Rifkin.
9. The pessimism of Creation Science is based on its eschatology and its reliance on the second law.
10. They see no long-term improvement for the world.
11. They cannot explain the improvement we have seen without calling into question their apologetic methodology: the second law.
12. Rifkin exploits this weakness.
13. He appeals to the pessimistic eschatologies of his targeted audience, evangelical Christians.
14. A kind of fatalism concerning the world has overwhelmed Christian social thinkers.
15. The world is "wound back up" by miracles.
16. Obviously, entropy is not universally binding.
17. Christians have not paid sufficient attention to the healing effects of righteousness.
18. Ethics is fundamental; entropy isn't.
19. How can we explain Western history without a concept of progress?
20. What threatens the West is its abandonment of the gospel, not entropy.
21. The cursed effects of entropy can and have been overcome.
22. Rifkin blames Christianity for the crises of the West.
23. He rejects the biblical idea of dominion by covenant.
24. He ignores the evidence presented by other scientists that Christianity isn't to blame.

---

44. *Ibid.*, Introduction.

25. Rifkin denies that scientific progress is truly progress.
26. He confuses the fixed order of ethics with the supposedly fixed order of physical nature.
27. Rifkin also rejects the free market economy.
28. He denies the desirability of economic growth.
29. He has an implicit faith in bureaucracy.
30. The Scientific Creationists have adopted a similar view of society: one that cannot be healed by Christ in history.

4

THE ENTROPY DEBATE
WITHIN HUMANISTIC SCIENCE

From the biblical perspective, the triumph of man under God involves the conquest of time and history, its redemption in terms of covenantal purpose, by timetable, schedule and clock among many other things. . . . This concept undergirded the exuberant conquest of time and nature by Western man as scientist. The world of the clock, timetable and schedule was seen as the liberation of man in terms of his purposive mastery of time and nature. But, as scientific man moved steadily from his Christian origin and perspective into a philosophy of process [evolutionism — G.N.], he perversely saw the timetable, clock and schedule as, first, a means of de-humanizing man as against God's insistence that man is primarily covenant man, and, second, as a tyranny to be rebelled against in the name of freedom. Thus, at the moment of science's triumph, science began to be viewed as demonic by its very sons, who sought vain refuge from the clock of history in "time lived."

R. J. Rushdoony[1]

Jeremy Rifkin has taken the long-term pessimistic implications of the second law of thermodynamics and has used them to attack the Western concept of short-term progress, especially scientific progress. He is using the ultimate implications of Western science to call into question the benefits of Western technology. He is using the linear time concept involved in entropy — the modern scientific basis of linear time ("time's arrow," Sir Arthur Eddington called it) — to destroy Western humanist man's admittedly naive faith in history. He is using Western science to justify the acceptance of Eastern mysticism. He has seen a vulnerable spot in the soft underbelly of

---

1. R. J. Rushdoony, *The Mythology of Science* (Nutley, New Jersey: Craig Press, 1967), pp. 76-77.

self-proclaimed autonomous science—the proclamation of a closed universe that denies God—and he has pierced it. He has understood the implicit pessimism of the entropy concept, and he has used it to attack scientists' more familiar short-run optimism concerning the benefits of modern technology.

His work was preceded by about fifteen years of propaganda from other social entropists. They rose to prominence during the counter-culture movement which began around 1964 or 1965.[2] This anti-technology perspective accelerated almost overnight with the orchestrated appearance of the ecology movement in 1967. As Harvard economist Marshall Goldman remarked in 1967, "Today's news media devote almost as much attention to air and water pollution as to the problems of poverty. Virtually overnight pollution seems to have become one of America's major issues."[3] It turned out to be a fad, and half a decade later ecological concerns had been transmuted politically into a massive Federal bureaucracy, the Environmental Protection Agency. Once this bureaucracy was in place, public manifestations of "ecology fever" subsided.

Nevertheless, a breach had appeared in the mind-set of Western intellectuals. The technophobia of the intellectuals of the late 1960's has not been completely abandoned. Doubts were raised that have not been laid to rest. Rifkin, in 1980, attempted to construct a new worldview out of the smoldering ashes of these doubts.

There have been attempts from the scientific community to refute the world-and-life view of the social entropists. John Maddox, the editor of the British journal, *Nature*, wrote a book, *The Doomsday Syndrome* (1972), which presents the case for the possibility of a series of scientific solutions to problems of pollution, starvation, energy shortages, and other man-made catastrophes. Maddox's book is a defense of controlled science and technology, although Maddox is not clear about just who should do the controlling.[4]

---

2. Perhaps the most eloquent though loquacious defense of technophobia was theologian-social theorist Jacques Ellul's book, *The Technological Society* (New York: Vintage, [1954] 1964). The American publication date is significant, not the earlier French publication date. A more popularly written presentation was Eugene S. Schwartz, *Overskill: The Decline of Technology in Modern Civilization* (New York: Ballantine, 1971). There were hundreds of similar books, 1967-74. I deal with the counter-culture in my study of the coming of age of modern occultism, *Unholy Spirits: Occultism and New Age Humanism* (Ft. Worth, Texas: Dominion Press, 1986), Introduction.

3. Marshall I. Goldman, "Introduction," in Goldman (ed.), *Controlling Pollution: The Economics of a Cleaner America* (Englewood Cliffs, New Jersey: Prentice-Hall, 1967), p. 3.

4. John Maddox, *The Doomsday Syndrome* (New York: McGraw-Hill, 1972), p. 11.

Maddox asks (but does not ever really answer), "Why has the environmental movement flourished in the past few years?"[5] He does not recognize the theological impulses of today's social world. First, there is the Darwinian view of man, which makes man the master of his fate, the only known source of meaning and purpose in the universe. Maddox, as a Darwinian, should understand the religious nature of this impulse, but he doesn't. The defenders of central economic planning, from Karl Marx to Lester Frank Ward, and from Ward to the modern social engineers, have understood Darwin this way.[6] Second, Maddox does not recognize the intellectual impact on the West of an essentially Eastern and mystical view of reality. In short, he does not understand the nature of the theological warfare in the West.

I. Is Man Responsible?

There is always an ambivalence in the minds of humanists concerning the ecological role and responsibility of man. Man is a product of the universe and the laws of evolution, yet he is also apparently sovereign over this process, at least to some degree. He is "of the world" and "in the world," yet he is also in some sense "over the world." He is the product of impersonal natural forces, yet through scientific planning, he supposedly can become progressively a master of these forces, personalizing an otherwise impersonal universe.[7]

The Christian affirms something similar about man's being in the world, but the Christian argues that man is not *of* this world; his origin ultimately lies outside the creation. Man is of the world in terms of his body: from dust to dust (Gen. 3:19), but this is not the heart and soul of man. God breathed life into him, and he is God's own image. Man knowingly operates under the sovereignty of God, even if he rebelliously suppresses this knowledge (Rom. 1:18-22).[8] But the humanist cannot consistently appeal to a Creator God in order to undergird his concept of man's sovereignty over nature. So he sometimes sees man's responsibility as "living in harmony with nature," yet sometimes he wants man to be the caretaker over nature who improves upon the operations of nature.

---

5. *Ibid.*, p. 24.
6. Gary North, *The Dominion Covenant: Genesis* (2nd ed.; Tyler, Texas: Institute for Christian Economics, 1987), Appendix A.
7. *Idem.*
8. Gary North, *Unconditional Surrender: God's Program for Victory* (3rd ed.; Ft. Worth, Texas: Dominion Press, 1987), Pt. I.

Is Man in Charge?

We can see this ambivalence in the thinking of René Dubos, whose book, *A God Within*, I cited in the previous chapter. Dubos has been one of the important intellectual leaders of the ecology movement since the 1960's. He has expressed humanism's dualism between man and nature very well. In an interview in the popular news magazine, *U.S. News & World Report* (Feb. 23, 1981), he stated the case for "man over nature": "Humans can improve on nature. We can transform the earth and bring to light potentialities of nature that are not expressed in the state of wilderness."

Does this mean that we should exploit the environment? Not at all. But we should not be overwhelmed by it, either: "We really have to rethink what it is we like about nature. Certainly, we must maintain as much wilderness as possible — in the Rockies and Sierras, the Adirondacks and in the few other parts of the country where it still exists. But I think that, in general, people think of nature not as wilderness but as something adapted to them on a human scale that they can appreciate with the totality of their being. They like to be able to feel that they can walk through it rather than be overwhelmed by it."

Is man really destroying the environment? No, says Dubos. "Nature is very resilient, and so I am optimistic about the ability of the environment to recover from the damage people inflict on it. . . . There is a phenomenal resiliency in the mechanisms of the earth." So man ultimately can be in harmony with the earth: "When we deal gently with the earth — even when we have thoughtlessly damaged it — we can repair our friendship with it." He sounds a lot like Maddox: "In the case of both nature and human beings, we can improve them by developing their potentialities and taking advantage of their resiliency. But there is a point beyond which such activities can become dangerous." What we need is for science to anticipate the dangers of any given process or development — precisely what Maddox recommends.[9] (Neither of them spells out how this might be accomplished by scientists.) Yet Dubos is one of the scientists who is criticized by Maddox in his book.

The debate among scientists over ecology has been conducted within the framework of Darwinism, and has therefore been caught

---

9. Maddox, *Doomsday Syndrome*, p. 11.

in the Darwinian dualism between "man, the product of purposeless evolution," and "Man, the purposeful master of evolution." Confusion only increased when proponents of another religious perspective entered the debate on the side of ecology and environmentalism, namely, mystics who see no hope in the humanist rhetoric of progress, science, and economic growth. Accompanying these Eastern mystics were representatives of Christian pietism, who also see no long-term hope in the rhetoric of earthly progress.[10] Having no hope in the future, they reject science and technology as valid means of bringing long-term improvement to society or nature. It is this perspective which baffles Maddox. Yet as a Darwinian, he is caught in entropy's logical trap. His universe is running down, just as Rifkin's is. The only question is the time frame in which the entropy process is socially significant.

Ignoring the Long Run

As an evolutionary scientist, Maddox is aware of entropy, but he also knows that it is an exceedingly long-range problem. "In the long run, as Lord Keynes put it, we shall all be dead. The catalogue of natural disasters includes equally unpredictable natural phenomena which will eventually be more damaging. . . . The ultimate disaster, remote though it may be, will come within the transformation due eventually to take place in the sun."[11] The sun will become exhausted and expand to up to a hundred million miles in diameter. The earth is 93 million miles away from today's sun. But this event is "certain" to be a thousand million years in the future. "These are horrendous prospects, but they provide a kind of yardstick with which to assess the durability of spaceship earth. On this scale, the self-destructive potential of terrestrial technology will be puny for a long time to come. The analogy of the spaceship is false simply because the scale of the earth is so different from that of any spaceship that could be constructed artificially."[12]

The response of the believer in conventional science and technology is straightforward. The human race has plenty of time remaining. Even though humans are increasing the dissipation of the universe's

---

10. Rifkin cites some of these authors, and certain anabaptist radicals, in turn, cite him.
11. *Ibid.*, p. 27.
12. *Ibid.*, p. 28.

energy and order, the universe is very, very large; it can sustain the loss. Maddox accepts the overall worldview of the entropists, but he is not overwhelmed by it. Mankind will be long gone by the time the last star flickers out. Though the world is running down, our puny efforts in dissipating the universe's order will hardly be noticed, especially since man is the only known species in the universe who might notice. The Darwinian evolutionists proclaim a doctrine of entropy which allows for the development of *zones of order* that reverse the "entropy process" regionally. They want an "open box" for mankind and his environment, at least for a few billion more years or so.

How Big a Closed Box?

On this point, the Darwinians and the social entropists disagree. The social entropist agrees with the Scientific Creationists (and disagrees with conventional Darwinists) on this one issue: the earth is an "entropically closed box." Rifkin emphasizes this point: ". . . the earth is a closed system in relation to the universe; . . . [O]ur planet remains a closed subsystem of the universe. . . . The point is, the sun, by itself, does not generate life. You can let the sun flow into an empty glass jar from now until the final heat death of the solar system and still no life will come forth. For life to unfold, the sun must interact with the closed system of matter, minerals and metals on the planet earth converting these materials to life and the utilities of life. This interaction facilitates the dissipation of this fixed endowment of terrestrial matter that makes up the earth's crust."[13] Thus, there is no universe-wide storehouse of unused and usable energy to extend the life span of the earth. The social entropist wants Western man to deal institutionally with this entropy factor immediately, for time is truly running out. The smaller the "closed box," the more rapidly entropy disrupts the environment.

The social entropist's argument is simple: we live on a tiny ball; the earth is not an open box. Yes, it was an open box when life first appeared. The sun's energy did create life, not a Creator God. The earth was sufficiently open to get God out of the picture as a necessary explanation. But now we are trapped on earth, and we are running out of resources. We do not have much time remaining to us. We must act fast—preferably, before the end of the twentieth century.

The fact that the sun probably will not run down for several bil-

---

13. *Entropy*, p. 37.

lion years is irrelevant to Rifkin. So, for that matter, is science. Rifkin is not arguing about science, which is why Maddox has such trouble dealing scientifically with people who possess Rifkin's outlook. They use the language of science as an ideological weapon against those who have only a smattering of scientific knowledge.

The Meaning of Life

Maddox does not understand the motivation behind "the doomsday syndrome." He looks at the issues from the point of view of science, of Newtonian cause and effect. Why all the fuss about pollution, catastrophes, and running out of resources? If man has time, capital, ingenuity, and scientific techniques at his disposal, most of these problems can be solved *at some price*. We can debate about the price, of course, for there will always be trade-offs in life, but why throw up our hands in despair, as if men were incapable of discovering acceptable solutions to these problems? Maddox looks to the success we have had as a species in using science to come up with solutions over the past two centuries, and he appeals to reason: we can do it over the next two centuries, if we have faith, intelligence, and capital investment. But his arguments do not convince the doomsday prophets. Why not? Because Maddox misses the point: *the debate is really about the meaning of life, not the time framework of the entropy process.* It is an eschatological debate, not scientific.

Entropy vs. Meaning

What is the proper biblical analysis of this "family quarrel" between the two factions of entropists? To answer this, we must understand entropy. If entropy is a universal law, then it will inescapably swallow up the works of man. If man is bounded by history rather than the Creator—if our universe is a "closed box" ethically, historically, and cosmically—then man's works have no ultimate meaning or significance. But this means that mankind has no ultimate meaning or significance. What does the amount of time remaining matter: a century, a millennium, or ten thousand millennia? *If entropy is god, then mankind eventually becomes a sacrificial victim to that god.*

I cited in Chapter Two the pessimistic conclusions of British mathematician and philosopher Bertrand Russell, who faced up to the implications of the heat death of the universe. He wrote: ". . . all the labours of the ages, all the devotion, all the inspiration, all the noonday brightness of human genius, are destined to extinction in the vast death of the solar system, and that the whole temple of Man's achievement must inevitably be buried beneath the debris of a universe in ruins—all these things, if not quite beyond dispute, are yet so nearly certain, that no philosophy which rejects them can hope to stand. Only within the scaffolding of these truths, only on the firm foundation of unyielding despair, can the soul's habitation henceforth be safely built."[14]

The proponents of zero economic growth are simply trying to adapt today's way of thought and life to what science assumes will probably be incomparably long-term implications of the entropy process. They are doing this *as a religious commitment*. They refuse to allow themselves to be deluded by the *illusion of meaning* provided by an inevitably "short-run" period of economic growth—say, a few million years. Growth is a product of *future-orientation*. The debate over the legitimacy or desirability of growth—any kind of growth—is necessarily a debate about mankind's legitimate orientation toward the future.

If mankind has no ultimate earthly future, which is what scientist-philosophers-speculators have argued, whether Darwinists or Eastern mystics, then what is our proper response as a species? Both sides of this humanist debate call on mankind to keep a stiff upper lip, and persevere as best we can. The Darwinian entropists add that while we are at it, let us continue to eat, drink, and be merry—at a compound growth rate of 6% per annum, if we can—for eventually the human species dies.

The social entropists reply that this would produce a fool's paradise, that man must find inner meaning, or union with the (dying) cosmos, or metaphysical union with an impersonal god who will somehow survive entropy. They want to restructure man's immediate institutions, thought patterns, and reproduction rate in order to acknowledge *ritually* the trillion-year meaning of entropy. *Theirs is a religious commitment*. They believe that the works of man's hands—of all men's hands—should testify *immediately* to the cosmic reality of entropy, even if mankind might conceivably eke out another century or two of growth through improved technology and capital accumulation. The fact that the earth could easily have 10 million centuries ahead does not impress the social entropists.

---

14. Bertrand Russell, "A Free Man's Religion" (1903), in *Mysticism and Logic* (Garden City, New York: Anchor, n.d.), pp. 45-46.

II. Entropy and Guilt

Rifkin's book is a call to the West to experience a religious conversion. He wants all men, but especially residents of the industrial West who rely on the West's energy-dissipating technology, to stop aiding and abetting the entropy process. We must stop using so much energy. "Addiction! There is simply no other way to accurately describe America's energy habit."[15] In other words, he wants us to take steps to *avoid guilt* in what must be regarded as man's cosmic rebellion against nature. The social entropists are unconcerned about man's *ethical rebellion against the Creator*; they worry about Western man's supposed rebellion against the very *mode of being of the creation* (including man himself), which they believe is an entropy-bound evolutionary process. In short, *they worship the creation rather than the Creator* (Rom. 1:18-22).

These are guilt-ridden men, or at least they are politicians who are trying to make guilt-ridden people out of their readers. They are residents of the industrial (and originally Christian) West, and they see themselves as accomplices in a kind of gang rape of the cosmos, or at least of the "fragile, defenseless" earth. They are seeking religious atonement by crying out against the supposed metaphysical sin of the West, which ultimately is the sin of life itself. *All living beings are an affront to entropy.* Life dissipates the energy and order of the cosmos, speeding up the entropy process by at least a few milliseconds (or picoseconds) in a 100 or 500 billion-year process of the universe. What a sin! We must atone! Life must therefore be limited.

The question is: Whose life?

Life and Death

Rifkin is caught in a theological dilemma: he worships all life, as a good Eastern mystic always does,[16] yet he also believes that the entropy process must be honored. On the one hand, he writes: "Every species must be preserved simply because it has an inherent and inalienable right to life by virtue of its existence."[17] On the other hand, he writes, "even the tiniest plant maintains its own order at the expense of creating greater disorder in the overall environment."[18]

---

15. Rifkin, *Entropy*, p. 99.
16. Cf. R. J. Rushdoony, *Politics of Guilt and Pity* (Fairfax, Virginia: Thoburn Press, [1970] 1978), ch. 2.
17. *Entropy*, p. 210.
18. *Ibid.*, p. 53.

But if life inescapably dissipates energy, how can man live and also avoid rebellion against other living beings in nature? How can he sustain his life or the life of any of his "chosen" species, thereby increasing the "burden" sustained by his environment, and still avoid guilt? If life must be honored, then which form of life? If plant or animal life interferes with man's life, who decides which life is to be sacrificed?

These may sound like preposterous questions. Nevertheless, they are valid Christians responses to a preposterous worldview. Men "owe" no allegiance to an impersonal, murderous process of nature called entropy. Death is the last enemy to be overcome by Christ at the day of resurrection (I Cor. 15:26). We labor against death and sickness, for death is an enemy to be overcome progressively. Ethical conformity to God's law brings us a progressive victory over sources of death. The scientists in England who have the last remaining smallpox germs in their laboratory should take the final step to wipe out smallpox, for the germs are agents of death. To keep them alive "for the sake of further scientific experimentation" is not sensible. This scourge can be wiped from the face of the earth in an afternoon.

Life Accelerates Entropy

If the West's production system were destroyed, and its "energy-dissipating processes" swept from history, the social entropists would rejoice (though not in mass-produced paperback books), at least until they began starving, as they almost certainly would, along with a few hundred million of their neighbors. Logically, they would have to see mass starvation as a benefit for the environment. Rival species could survive for an extra few hundred or few thousand years. But if the sin of man is his sin against the environment, then why not "go all the way" and call for the death of man? Why not go even farther and call for the destruction of all life? If the "energy addiction" of the West is evil, then all man-made dissipation of energy is evil. *If man-made energy dissipation is evil, then all living creatures are inherently guilty of this sin.* Life itself is a form of "energy addiction." It is only a matter of degree, species by species.

Rifkin attacks technology as life-destroying and exploitative. "Technologies, by their very nature, are expropriating; they extract, they distill, they process, they organize, they convert, they consume, they regiment."[19] This sounds evil. But then he softens the blow:

---

19. Jeremy Rifkin, *Declaration of a Heretic* (London: Routledge and Kegan Paul, 1985), p. 92.

"There is an acknowledgement that some form of expropriation is always necessary. All things desire to live, and it is a law of nature that for something to live, something else must die."[20]

This creates an ethical dilemma, the kind of ethical dilemma that the pantheist physician Albert Schweitzer faced: How can we affirm life, if all life survives by imposing death? Can we set forth guidelines of ethical living in such a universe? Rifkin does not even try. He hides behind the vague undefined words, "too much": "But it is also true that too much expropriation can result in destroying the very life support systems we rely on for our future survival."[21] Whose life support systems? *Ours*. Who must survive? *We must*. We are back to the original presupposition of all humanism: *man must prevail*.

The consistent entropist should call for an end to all life. Only inconsistency prevents this. But if the social entropist is unwilling to be consistent and call a halt to the energy drain associated with all living things, then why should he expect residents of the West to pay any attention to him and cut back on their lifestyles? After all, it is only a matter of degree, of comparative rates of "energy addiction." The lifestyle of the urban Westerner is only relatively more guilty before the god of entropy than the lifestyle of the savage, or for that matter, of the amoeba.

The philosophy of social entropy is innately *a philosophy of death*, despite the fact that it officially affirms all life. It worships a physical "law of entropy" as its governing (uniformitarian) principle. It worships an impersonal god of destruction. But this is equally true of scientific, Darwinian entropy. Its uniformitarian principle is also an impersonal consuming god. God is correct: ". . . all those who hate me love death" (Prov. 8:36b).

Conclusion

John Maddox has come face to face with a religious impulse that he does not understand. It makes no sense to him. His old fashioned secular humanism blinds him to the reasons for the intellectual power and appeal of a rival form of humanism. He is dealing with people who virtually worship entropy the way that savages worship a god of death. They want to sacrifice human progress on entropy's altar, in order to avoid a direct confrontation with the entropy pro-

---

20. *Ibid.*, p. 95.
21. *Idem.*

cess. They want to placate entropy, as savages want to placate their god of death. They want a peace treaty with entropy; Maddox wants mankind to fight against unconquerable entropy until the very end.

Maddox wants temporary dominion; Rifkin wants a stalemate, so that he can escape into "higher consciousness." In mankind's Darwinian war against entropy, Rifkin is a Quisling; Maddox is a kamikaze.

In summary:

1. Humanists are at war with time.
2. Rifkin uses the second law of thermodynamics to call into question all progress.
3. Rifkin therefore uses science to challenge science.
4. He is promoting Eastern mysticism by means of Western science.
5. The counter-culture of the late 1960's was also anti-technological.
6. Confidence in science began to wane within certain intellectual circles.
7. John Maddox tried to refute these pessimists in 1972.
8. He did not understand the deeply religious commitment of his opponents.
9. The humanist cannot explain man.
10. Is man responsible? To whom? Or what?
11. Is man over nature, even though he is supposedly the product of purposeless nature?
12. Is man the cosmic destroyer?
13. Is man the source of healing?
14. Eastern mystics and Christian pietists reject the idea of man as a healer, whose job is to exercise dominion over nature.
15. Maddox's universe is doomed; it is only a question of time.
16. Maddox ignores the long-run consequences of entropy.
17. His opponents are guided by the long run, despite any short-run gains.
18. He does not understand their religion-based outlook.
19. Rifkin and his followers are pessimists about the short run because they are blinded by the pessimism of the long run.
20. The debate is over the meaning of life, not pollution.
21. Rifkin uses entropy to create a sense of guilt.
22. He worries about man's technological revolt against nature, not man's ethical revolt against God.
23. For Rifkin, all life is an affront to the universe, for life accelerates entropy.

24. Rifkin's is a philosophy of death.
25. Maddox, as a Darwinian, is unable to deal with the underlying religious issues.

5

CHRISTIANITY VS. SOCIAL ENTROPY

Man, being in rebellion against law and causality as infringements on his ***becoming*** *and on his ultimacy in process [evolution—G.N.], must therefore be also in rebellion against clock time as the epitome of his slavery. Clock time is a bondage whose ticking always and monotonously moves in terms of an eternal decree external to and transcending man. Man's rebellion against eternity therefore must be followed by a rebellion against time. Time always beats to and echoes the stroke of eternity. . . . Thus the rejection of God inevitably requires as its logical concomitant the rejection of time. Man seeks either to arrest time, as from the days of the Tower of Babel to Hitler's "thousand year" Reich and the United Nations, by his own decree, or to flee from time by the clock, from history, into* ***mysticism****, time lived. In either case, man as god is saying, "Time shall be no more."*

R. J. Rushdoony[1]

All parties to the debate understand the appeal of optimism. The Scientific Creationists, because they are Christians, offer the hope of individual salvation to man. The premillennialists implicitly (though never explicitly) offer the hope of partially overcoming entropy during Christ's millennial reign. The amillennialists offer hope at least beyond the grave, though not before.[2] Postmillennialists alone are the Christian theologians of hope for history.

Rifkin has no true eschatological hope to offer. He is a believer in evolution,[3] and he is also a believer in the entropy law. He claims

---

1. R. J. Rushdoony, *The Mythology of Science* (Nutley, New Jersey: Craig Press, 1967), pp. 77-78.
2. Gary North, *Dominion and Common Grace: The Biblical Basis of Progress* (Tyler, Texas: Institute for Christian Economics, 1987), ch. 4.
3. ". . . it took nearly three billion years of natural evolution to create this tremendous stock of energy." *The Emerging Order*, p. 45.

that the universe is running down to the timeless oblivion of heat death. Nevertheless, only Bertrand Russell and a few hard-core evolutionists have fearlessly discussed the grim implications of this pessimistic claim. Thus, Rifkin adopts a very clever tactic: to promote optimism by means of a system which guarantees mankind the ultimate defeat of meaninglessness, impotence, and death. To this extent, Rifkin is epistemologically schizophrenic: he cannot decide whether to adopt Western entropy-based pessimism or the escapist bliss of anti-rational, anti-scientific Eastern mysticism.

False Optimism

Rifkin's language is unquestionably religious in tone. "This book is about hope: the hope that comes from shattering false illusions and replacing them with new truths."[4] But where is this hope? In what does it consist? The sober analysis of Bertrand Russell was more honest: "The same laws which produce growth also produce decay. Some day, the sun will grow cold, and life on the earth will cease. The whole epoch of animals and plants is only an interlude between ages that were too hot and ages that will be too cold. There is no law of cosmic progress, but only an oscillation upward and downward, with a slow trend downward on the balance owing to the diffusion of energy. This, at least, is what science at present regards as most probable, and in our disillusioned generation it is easy to believe. From evolution, so far as our present knowledge shows, no ultimately optimistic philosophy can be validly inferred."[5]

Russell's viewpoint is consistent. Its innate pessimism is straightforward. Whenever we encounter a philosophy that emphasizes the entropy process, we will find a dead end at the end of history — ultimately, the destruction of history. The universe grows cold. All directional movement ceases. There is no way to measure change over time, because there is no longer any non-random change to measure, nor any living being to measure it. The concept of time itself becomes meaningless. Time ends.

Intellectual Schizophrenia

Rifkin's book evades the obvious implications of his entropy process. He cannot decide which philosophy he wishes his readers to

---

4. Rifkin, "Author's Note," *Entropy.*
5. Bertrand Russell, "Evolution," in *Religion and Science* (New York: Oxford University [1935] 1972), p. 81.

accept: static Eastern mysticism or Western materialism. Western materialism acknowledges the reality of science, and therefore the reality of the second law of thermodynamics. Eastern mysticism, in the final analysis, denies the reality of matter. Matter is *maya*, an illusion. Meaning is found only in metaphysical union with god. Such a god is totally beyond matter, and therefore is unable to affect history. God is the monistic, impersonal One, the undifferentiated Being into which all being is absorbed. Life is swallowed up in changeless, meaningless, undifferentiated oneness. In such a cosmology, the second law of thermodynamics is ultimately irrelevant to anything, as are history, ethics, death, and everything else. It is only within this matter-denying cosmology that the "higher consciousness" techniques of Eastern mysticism are personally relevant, that is, materially irrelevant.

Rifkin proclaims both: 1) Eastern mysticism, with its promise of escape from meaningless matter and history into meaningless union with the One, and 2) Western science, with its promise of ultimate meaninglessness and timelessness when the entropy process has run its course. But what is even more astounding, he proclaims this fusion (or confusion) of cosmologies in the name of hope. He thinks this philosophy will provide hope for the world in terms of the processes of the material world.

A New Worldview?

Rifkin is convinced that this philosophy is about to sweep over Western civilization. "For our grandchildren's generation the entropic world view will be like second nature: they will not think about it, they will merely live by it, unconscious of its hold over them, as we have for so long been unconscious of the hold Newtonian mechanics has had over us. Already the outline of the new entropy paradigm is being filled in by scholars around the world. Within a few years every academic discipline will be turned inside out by the new entropy conception."[6] He believes that this new philosophy will lead to the reconstruction of Western culture.

He sees only three possible responses to this philosophy. *First*, "After finishing this book some will remain unconvinced that there are physical limits that place restraints on human action in the world." This is overstating the case; almost everyone in the modern,

---

6. Rifkin, *Entropy*, p. 7.

secularized, Darwinian West knows that there are limits in this world. "Man, the purposeful master of evolution" cannot forever succeed in his battle against the effects of entropy. The debate centers over the time framework. The question raised by modern science is simply, "How long, O lord of entropy, how long?"

Second, Rifkin goes on: "Others will be convinced but will conclude with despair that the Entropy Law is a giant cosmic prison from which there is no escape." *Third*, he writes: "Finally, there will be those who will see the Entropy Law as the truth that can set us free. The first group will continue to uphold the existing world paradigm. The second group will be without a world view. The third group will be the harbingers of the New Age."[7] This is unmistakably a religious appeal. He is the herald of a "New Age."

The New Age philosophy is mystical and frequently occult. There are many promoters of variants of this philosophy, but "higher consciousness" is certainly a universal New Age theme. It is the call to self-transcendence, a kind of *metaphysical "leap of being."*[8] It is not a call to ethical regeneration.

Rifkin's mystical social entropy theory leaves unanswered some obvious questions. He writes as though he does not want men to despair, as Bertrand Russell despaired. But how do his answers leave man with legitimate hope concerning his cosmic condition? Supposedly, man has hope in *a coming metaphysical union with a monistic god*. But what does this have to do with a systematic social theory based on insights from the second law of thermodynamics? Nothing.

Furthermore, how will man, who is presently physical and who, Rifkin claims, exists in terms of a universal law of physical entropy, be able to survive the entropic death of the universe, when this monistic god is indistinguishable from the universe? How can this pantheistic god survive entropy's death-dealing blow, any more than man can survive or the cosmos can survive? *A god of this world dies when this world dies.*

Stalemate Religion

Rifkin is a man without legitimate hope. His proposed utopian static society, even if it could somehow be achieved—and Rifkin offers no program for achieving it—it is not a society that offers

---

7. Rifkin, "Author's Note," *Entropy*.
8. Gary North, *Unholy Spirits: Occultism and New Age Humanism* (Ft. Worth, Texas: Dominion Press, 1986), ch. 9.

hope. Such a zero-growth society is the antithesis of the God-blessed society of Deuteronomy 28:1-14. Rifkin has accepted the false premise that our universe is an ethically "closed box," that there is no Creator above, no week of creation behind, no sustaining providence underneath, no resurrection of Christ, no long-run material progress in the future, and no escape from entropy. Why do men believe such ideas? *Because they refuse to acknowledge the historical fact of the ethical rebellion of Adam, in time and on earth.* They therefore deny the inescapable result of this event: a final judgment in the future.

Social entropy's remedy is useless in the long run. Rifkin proclaims a zero-growth philosophy as a solution for an entropy-bound world. He proclaims a status-quo economics in a dissipating, disintegrating universe. The status quo can never be maintained. *There is no status quo in history.* History progresses chronologically toward a final resolution. The ethical warfare which characterizes history continues. This warfare is not static. There are victors and losers, civilization by civilization. These battles have consequences for the external world.

What we must reject is *the myth of the status quo.* This myth is for history what the myth of neutrality is for philosophy. The source of both myths is the same: Satan. Satan is involved in a titanic struggle against God. It is an ethical struggle. He proclaims a rival world-and-life view — numerous views, in fact, but all premised on a rejection of the Creator-creature distinction. He promotes ethical rebellion in the name of neutrality; he promotes his temporal victory in the name of the status quo. He calls for a *stalemate.* Just give him the territory he already possesses. Just give him the neutral "laws of nature" by which to operate his kingdom. Just give him limited autonomy. That is really all he asks. God only needs to deny a little of His own sovereignty. This was Pharaoh's underlying argument to Moses against the "unreasonable" demands of the God of Israel.[9] It was Satan's underlying argument to Eve. It is an argument that denies the being and character of God.

Satan cannot achieve a stalemate. He is headed for external defeat. He has already experienced *definitive* defeat at Calvary. He can only look forward to *final* defeat on judgment day. Meanwhile, he is experiencing *progressive* defeat in history. He wins battles; he

---

9. Gary North, *Moses and Pharaoh: Dominion Religion vs. Power Religion* (Tyler, Texas: Institute for Christian Economics, 1985), ch. 10: "Total Sacrifice, Total Sovereignty."

will not win the war. His followers win battles; they will not win the war. Herbert Schlossberg is correct: "The Bible can be interpreted as a string of God's triumphs disguised as disasters."[10] The cross is the best example: Christ's death, which was followed by His resurrection. On the day of judgment, no prisoners will be taken. What Israel was told by God to do to the Canaanites, so will God do to all those who have rebelled and who have not repented. There can be no stalemate. Christians must abandon the stalemate mentality.[11]

Zero growth is one aspect of the stalemate religion. It offers mankind no hope, for in a world governed by entropy, there can be no stalemate. Entropy is a sure winner in the "closed box" universe of humanism. Stalemate is a myth here, too. Mankind will lose to the forces of cosmic heat death. Even the increase of entropy must end, when the final dissipation of energy has taken place. History is bounded even for the humanists: from the "Big Bang" origin to the final dissipation of energy. While scientists seek frantically to locate sufficient mass in the universe to make theoretically plausible endless cycles of expansion and contraction, they have not found this much-needed matter. History is linear, and it leads to the death of man. And even a cyclical universe will guarantee the death of man, for the universe will be crushed into a point (or even a vanishing point) that might produce the next Big Bang. Humanist science can offer only extinction to man. To that degree, *humanist science is demonic*. The death of man is Satan's goal. His religion of stalemate teaches ultimate defeat for man, the image of God. Satan would prefer this sort of universal defeat for all mankind to the victory of God's people over Satan's followers. "Better the death of all men than the triumph of God's men."

III. Biblical Optimism: Progressive Sanctification

Rifkin does not want Western humanist man's theology of power.[12] He also does not want Western man's vision of ultimate defeat in the heat death of the universe. He proclaims a third way: the monistic absorption of man in mystical escape from the realm of

---

10. Herbert Schlossberg, *Idols for Destruction: Christian Faith and Its Confrontation with American Society* (Nashville, Tennessee: Thomas Nelson, 1983), p. 304.

11. Gary North, *Backward, Christian Soldiers?* (Tyler, Texas: Institute for Christian Economics, 1984), ch. 11: "The Stalemate Mentality."

12. Rifkin concentrates his attack on Western power religion in *Declaration of a Heretic* (London: Routledge and Kegan Paul, 1985).

matter. What Rifkin ignores is a fourth possible response to his book, a self-consciously biblical response.

The Christian accepts the reality of a time-bound, sin-filled, and God-cursed universe. He understands that God's curse is also a blessing for mankind, for economic scarcity makes profitable voluntary human cooperation.[13] The Christian also argues that various degradative processes are governed by man's ethical response to the gospel of Jesus Christ. When men respond in obedient faith to God, God lifts many aspects of the curse. He promises even to extend drastically the average lifetime of mankind (Isa. 65:20). In short, *ethics is primary, not some entropy process*. The tendency of all things to wear out is progressively overcome, just as surely as miracles reverse this tendency. Thus, degradative processes are not uniformitarian sentences of doom; they are *covenantal curses* that can be (and have often been) reversed in human history.

The Christian can therefore accept and promote some of the scientific conclusions of the present scientific world-and-life view, to the extent that this view is future-oriented, rational, and based on the concept of cause and effect. The Christian believes in the possibility of ethics-based dominion, for God promises to bless covenant-keeping man, and to remove His curse progressively, if men obey Him. Covenant-keeping man does not seek power as a religious impulse; he seeks first the kingdom of God and His righteousness, and all things, including power, are then given to him (Matt. 6:33).

The Christian must not accept Darwinism, or pure materialism, or the idea of the autonomous progress of man, but he can accept the basic optimism of the Western view of man, for this Western view was originally Christian. That this cursed world has a temporal end is specifically a Christian idea. In fact, its end can be expected several billion years before evolutionists expect the sun to flame out or explode in a nova. But the end of *this* world is not the end of *the* world in the Christian worldview, unlike the pessimism of the entropists' view.

Christians must reject the conclusion of the social entropists, namely, that because this present age is governed by physical entropy, man's social institutions cannot experience long-term growth. What the Christian must affirm is that there is always a possibility of long-term ethical improvement, both for individuals and collectives

---

13. Gary North, *The Dominion Covenant: Genesis* (2nd ed.; Tyler, Texas: Institute for Christian Economics, 1987), ch. 10: "Scarcity: Curse and Blessing."

(voluntary associations, civil governments, cultural groups, nations, and even the whole world order). In other words, the Christian must affirm the possibility of *progressive ethical sanctification*. He must not limit the sanctification process to the souls of men or to the internal life of the spirit.[14] Ethics has consequences for human action; human action influences the external world; and the external world responds. There is a long-term relationship between ethics and cultural progress (Deut. 28:1-14). Man's economic environment, like his numbers, can continue to grow until the day of final judgment.

Earthly Blessings

Because the Christian knows that there is hope beyond the last-day resurrection, both for man and his environment, he can have legitimate hope concerning the world's future.[15] We know that men's ethical decisions have heavenly consequences for both the unregenerate (Luke 12:47-48) and the regenerate (I Cor. 3:8, 12-15). We also know that God gives regenerate men an "earnest" (down payment) on their future spiritual victory (Eph. 1:14). How, then, should we regard the promises of external blessings in Deuteronomy 28:1-14? We must see them as down payments on the future physical triumph over the curse of the creation (Rom. 8:18-23). The Christian needs to be optimistic about our present world, for this world testifies to a God who judges, and this God is the rewarder of those who diligently search for Him (Heb. 11:6). To repeat: we are to seek first the kingdom of God *and His righteousness*, and all these things shall be added to us (Matt. 6:33). The issue is *ethics*, not entropy.

Victory in history is not going to be a discontinuous, unexpected event for God's people. Each Christian's victory over spiritual death at the day of resurrection is to be preceded by a partial, imperfect spiritual victory, in time and on earth, through personal self-discipline in terms of God's law. Similarly, victory over physical death also will not be a discontinuous event: we are told by God that we should expect health, long life, and an end to miscarriages. This is what Exodus 23:25-26 promises. This means that we should expect a population

---

14. Gary North, "Comprehensive Redemption: A Theology for Social Action," *Journal of Christian Reconstruction*, VIII (Summer 1981). Reprinted in this book as Appendix C.
15. David Chilton, *Paradise Restored: A Biblical Theology of Dominion* (Ft. Worth, Texas: Dominion Press, 1985).

explosion. The Christian West has experienced such events. Now humanism threatens to overturn these blessings.

Final Judgment: Biblical or Humanistic?

Christianity is not a zero-growth religion. From God's promise to fallen Eve of a future seed (Gen. 3:15), to His promise of a nation to Abraham (Gen. 15), to Christ's announcement of His total power and His instructions for His followers to disciple all nations (Matt. 28:18-19), the testimony of God is clear: we must expect growth. *Growth is an ethical imperative.*

Zero-growth philosophy is not a neutral philosophy. It is a counsel of despair, even when wrapped in words of optimism. Such a philosophy must be rejected by Christians. They must purge from their own social analysis all traces of this philosophy. If a growing number of people should respond in faith to God's offer of salvation, and if they begin to follow God's precepts that govern every area of life, then we should expect economic development, visible progress, and long-term population growth as God's visible response to widespread covenantal faithfulness. Christians argue about the Bible's teachings concerning such a future manifestation on earth of God's kingdom by means of the preaching of the gospel, but *in principle*, God offers to mankind the hope of salvation, which means He offers the possibility of the transformation of man's social environment and even his biological lifespan through covenantal obedience. *God offers an escape from social entropy.*

A spiritual battle is in progress. Our ethical warfare is not a straight-line phenomenon, either personally (as the Psalms teach us) or socially (as Deuteronomy 28:15-68 teaches us). But the historical framework in which we operate *is* a straight-line phenomenon, and it points to the final judgment by God, not judgment by impersonal cosmic heat death. A zero-growth philosophy ultimately is mythical. By its own terms, it points to the frozen death of energy dissipation. No Christian can adopt a zero-growth philosophy and still remain orthodox.

What we find, then, is that *evolutionism has a doctrine of a final judgment*. This judgment is based on the postulate of entropy. The entropists proclaim a fixed order of entropy, not a fixed ethics. There is no way to reconcile social entropy with Christianity, or to reconcile science's doctrine of impersonal final judgment with Christianity's doctrine of final ethical judgment.

The war between evolutionism and Christianity must not be minimized. We see the conflict between rival religions. This war manifests itself in the debate over the nature of the final judgment. As Rushdoony says,

> The details differ, but every world-view and every faith has its version of judgment, heaven, and hell. For some, hell is existence, and heaven is nirvana and nothingness. But the basic categories remain. The relativists, nihilists, and existentialists who deny all absolute values and laws demand judgment on God, law, and morality; hell for them is a world of absolute values, which they wage war against, and heaven is a world beyond good and evil.
>
> But to transfer final judgment, heaven, and hell from the eternal order to time is to absolutize history and to enthrone man as god. It means the destruction of liberty, because history ceases to be the realm of liberty and testing but becomes the place of final trial. Having made the final judgment temporal, the humanist cannot permit liberty, because liberty is hostile to finality; liberty presupposes trial and error and the possibility of serious waywardness when and where man is sinful and imperfect. History cannot tolerate both trial and error and [also] insist on finality and the end of trial and error. The humanistic utopias are all prisons, because they insist on a finality which man does not possess. Accordingly, the socialist utopias demand the "re-education" of man in the post-revolutionary world, in the era beyond judgment. The "new era" is the new heaven on earth. . . .
>
> But history refuses to terminate on man's orders, because it runs on God's time, and not in terms of man's myths. As a result, the final orders which men build have an inevitable habit of decay, and the order which claims to be final ensures its own destruction as the movement of history crushes it underfoot in its unrelenting march to epistemological self-consciousness.[16]

Conclusion

The appeal of optimism is a kind of "uniformitarian ideological constant." Every group that seeks a large audience understands that it must offer hope. Premillennialists and amillennialists offer hope beyond the grave; premillennialists also offer hope during the millennium, when Christ returns physically to rule in power. These are appeals *beyond the declining historical present*. They are appeals to discontinuity in the midst of cultural and historical despair—a despair

---

16. R. J. Rushdoony, *The Foundations of Social Order: Studies in the Creeds and Councils of the Early Church* (Fairfax, Virginia: Thoburn Press, [1968] 1978), pp. 176-77.

toward history that supposedly cannot be overcome by the efforts of Christians who faithfully preach and obey the gospel, given the principles of interpretation of these two eschatological systems.

What is needed is postmillennialism's vision of victory in history, not simply victory outside history. Christians need to believe that their personal efforts in history do have world-transforming effects in history, before Jesus Christ returns physically to judge men at the last day. They need the self-confidence that faith in the future brings. They need to know that God's external covenantal blessings will be showered on His church before the "Church Age" ends — blessings experienced by Christians throughout the promised millennial era of peace and prosperity that the faithful preaching of the gospel by the church inevitably leads to. Christians need faith in *the world-healing power of the gospel*. Christ's resurrection is behind us. Satan's defeat was in principle established at Calvary. He was cast down to earth at that time.

And the great dragon was cast out, that old serpent, called the Devil, and Satan, which deceiveth the whole world: he was cast out into the earth, and his angels were cast out with him. And I heard a loud voice saying in heaven, Now is come salvation, and strength, and the kingdom of our God, and the power of Christ: for the accuser of our brethren is cast down, which accused them before our God day and night. And they overcame him by the blood of the Lamb, and by the word of his testimony; and they loved not their lives unto the death (Rev. 12:9-11).

We now have the Holy Spirit and the law of God. What more do we need? Postmillennialism offers true earthly hope. It asks rhetorically: "O entropy, where is thy sting?"

Rifkin also uses the language of hope. He appeals to the hope of achieving a decent lifestyle in the midst of decline. This hope is limited to men's internal, psychological lives: becoming "one with nature," etc. But man's potential hope is offset eternally by cosmic pessimism, and immediately by social pessimism. Rifkin says that not only is the universe inescapably declining, but human society is about to decline, when it runs out of resources, including the resource of a clean environment. The hope he offers is strictly temporal; he makes no legitimate appeal to a world beyond the grave, a regenerated world beyond the curse of degeneration.

How can Christians challenge Rifkin's view of the present world order? How can they make a convincing challenge to his despairing view of the present drift of events? Obviously, they can appeal to a heavenly escape: internal and psychological (church membership, happy Christian family life, etc.), and also a discontinuous miraculous event, the physical return of Christ in power. But unless they utterly abandon their eschatologies of temporal defeat, they will remain unable to challenge Rifkin's earthly pessimism regarding mankind's temporal prospects. Those who hold pessimistic eschatologies already agree with him concerning the futility of social reform. (See Appendix D.) They share his pessimistic short-term eschatology. Remember the flyer cited on page 70, above: "The creationist realizes that the world is growing old around him. He understands that things tend to run down, to age, to die. The creationist does not look for the world to improve, but to crumble slowly — as in erosion, decay, and aging."[17]

Christianity teaches that there is a covenantal curse, but that it is nevertheless possible to overcome many of the effects of this curse, in time and on earth, through covenantal faithfulness. *God's covenant is man's primary constant.*[18] Thus, to the extent that Christians understand their faith, and have confidence in the covenantal promises of God, they remain immune to Rifkin's theory of inescapable social pessimism. If they do not understand the ethical terms of the covenant and the promises of the covenant, then they remain vulnerable to his conclusions, or at least incapable of challenging him forthrightly.

In summary:

1. Humanists are at war with time.
2. Christianity offers hope to individuals.
3. Rifkin has no legitimate hope to offer.
4. He adopts false optimism to gain converts.
5. He wavers between Eastern mysticism and the logic of science.
6. He says the West is about to be transformed by a new worldview.
7. He calls men to transcend themselves as humans.
8. In this appeal, he is clearly a New Age thinker.
9. Rifkin calls for metaphysical union with a monistic, impersonal god.
10. But how can man escape the death of nature?
11. Rifkin calls for zero growth.

---

17. *What's the Difference? Creation/Evolution?* (no date).
18. Ray R. Sutton, *That You May Prosper: Dominion By Covenant* (Tyler, Texas: Institute for Christian Economics, 1987).

12. He never mentions Christ's victory at Calvary.
13. There is no hope in the status quo if entropy governs the world.
14. He calls for a stalemate: Satan's old lie.
15. History is linear.
16. Scientists cannot find a way for mankind to escape oblivion.
17. Biblical optimism is based on God's progressive sanctification of the world.
18. Ethics is primary, not entropy.
19. God brings covenantal blessings on those who are faithful to Him.
20. Christianity must reject humanism's pessimism.
21. We can see real progress in history.
22. Victory is supposed to be a continuous process in history.
23. Growth is a Christian imperative.
24. All systems have a doctrine of final judgment.
25. Humanism's is the heat death of the universe.
26. This absolutizes history and the creation.
27. History will end on God's orders, not man's, and not entropy's.

6

THE QUESTION OF ETHICS

*Man is thus a temporal creature in rebellion against time and hence against his own being. Because he sees his problem as not ethical but metaphysical, time is, in terms of his philosophy of process, a disease in man to be overcome. Man's **becoming** is thus a process of overcoming the limitations of death, time, and history. It is no wonder, therefore, that the historical and bodily resurrection of Jesus Christ is an offense to modern man. After all, his own temporal and bodily existence is increasingly also an offense to him because he refuses to be a creature and strives in his heart "to be as God."*

R. J. Rushdoony[1]

This chapter focuses on the war of the worldviews: humanism's cosmological and economic entropy vs. *consistent* biblical creationism and economic growth.

First, as is true in the debate over cosmology, both sides have their respective principles of *uniformitarianism*. Christian social theory — at least the social theory undergirding my books — is based on a belief in a fixed ethical order.[2] This fixed ethical order is above history, yet within history. God is transcendent, yet He is also present.[3] So is God's law.

In contrast to this view, "entropic" social theory is based on the idea that what should be regarded as static and unchanging is not God's revealed law, but "nature's processes," meaning man and

---

1. R. J. Rushdoony, *The Mythology of Science* (Nutley, New Jersey: Craig Press, 1967), p. 78.
2. Greg L. Bahnsen, *Theonomy in Christian Ethics* (2nd ed.; Phillipsburg, New Jersey: Presbyterian & Reformed, 1984); *By This Standard: The Authority of God's Law Today* (Tyler, Texas: Institute for Christian Economics, 1985).
3. Ray R. Sutton, *That You May Prosper: Dominion By Covenant* (Tyler, Texas: Institute for Christian Economics, 1987), ch. 1.

nature, an integrated whole. Ethical principles change ("evolve") as nature changes. Rifkin wants to use "man in the natural world" as *the* operating principle in constructing an ethical base for mankind: "A low-entropy culture emphasizes man and woman as a part of nature, not apart from it. Nature becomes not a tool for manipulation, but the source of life that must be preserved in its entire workings. Once it is understood that human beings are 'one' with nature, then an ethical base is established by which the appropriateness of all human activity can be judged."[4]

Second, each side has a theory of *open and closed ethical boxes*. Christian social theory proclaims that this universe is open upward ethically. Men can appeal to God for justice. God is sovereign over the affairs of men, bringing to perfect fruition His purposes for history.[5] The Bible teaches that there is no such thing as social entropy. Civilizations prosper or fail, advance or disappear, in terms of their adherence to biblical law (Deut. 28).

Darwinism's universe is an ethically closed box, and no appeal beyond the universe is feasible. Thus, the State, as the most powerful agency of sovereign man, becomes the god of the age. Rushdoony has summarized the political, ethical, and legal implications of Darwinian humanism quite well:

> Humanistic law, moreover, is inescapably totalitarian law. Humanism, as a logical development of evolutionary theory, holds fundamentally to a concept of an evolving universe. This is held to be an "open universe," whereas Biblical Christianity, because of its faith in the triune God and His eternal decree, is said to be a faith in a "closed universe." This terminology not only intends to prejudice the case; it reverses reality. The universe of evolutionism and humanism is a closed universe. There is no law, no appeal, no higher order, beyond and above the universe. Instead of an open window upwards, there is a closed cosmos. There is thus no ultimate law and decree beyond man and the universe. Man's law is therefore beyond criticism except by man. In practice, this means that the positive law of the state is absolute law. The state is the most powerful and most highly organized expression of humanistic man, and the state is the form and expression of humanistic law. Because there is no higher law of God as judge over the universe, over every human order, the law of the state is a closed system of law. There is no appeal beyond it. Man has no "right," no realm of justice,

---

4. Rifkin, *Entropy*, pp. 209-10.
5. R. J. Rushdoony, *The Biblical Philosophy of History* (Nutley, New Jersey: Presbyterian & Reformed, 1969).

no source of law beyond the state, to which man can appeal against the state. Humanism therefore imprisons man within the closed world of the state and the closed universe of the evolutionary scheme.[6]

Defenders of both Darwinian and New Age social entropy believe that man dwells in an *ethically* "closed box." Man has no appeal beyond the cosmos.

Third, both sides have a theory of entropy. The creationist sees the universe as under a curse and headed for destruction, except for one mitigating factor: *the grace of God*. There certainly appear to be degradative factors in our cursed immediate environment, but these factors can be mitigated and partially overcome through the creation of God-honoring institutions. Furthermore, all Christians believe that degradative processes, assuming that they are aspects of the curse, will be overcome after the final resurrection, for the curse will be overcome.

Both the scientific Darwinians and the social entropists believe in the ultimate material effects of entropy. There is no escape. Where there is directional movement, there is an increase in entropy. But the conventional Darwinians still think that it pays man to seek to overcome the effects of entropy temporarily through scientific experimentation, technological progress, and planning. They proclaim a temporary optimism based on the autonomous ethics of scientific dominion. The social entropists reject this view. The new ethics of man, they argue, must be based on a static society in a universe which is steadily moving downhill. But both interpretations elevate the constancy of entropy over the creationists' concept of fixed ethical order. *The only ultimate order for the humanist is the long-run movement toward disorder and death*. The ethical debate among humanists centers around the question of what mankind needs to do to withstand temporarily the effects of "inescapable entropy," and how long those effects can be withstood.

False Hope

The social entropist may appear to be offering mankind a more consistent ethical vision of "the life of entropy," but this recommended lifestyle is really not very consistent. "Entropic man" really cannot

---

6. Rushdoony, Introduction to E. L. Hebden Taylor, *The New Legality* (Nutley, New Jersey: Craig Press, 1967), pp. vi-vii; the text of this citation was incorrectly printed in Taylor's book and was later corrected by Mr. Rushdoony.

legitimately believe in long-term static stability; the entropy of the universe must eventually overcome all of man's efforts to preserve himself or nature. Furthermore, life increases entropy, so a static society will require technological advances, if only to "stay even," since civilization will have to run faster and faster "just to stay in the same place," as the Queen said to Alice in *Alice in Wonderland*. A theory of a static society which relies on a reduction of technology to maintain its changeless order is an exercise in mythology. Stand still in a universe governed by entropy, and you inevitably fall behind.

All Rifkin can offer mankind is a kind of grim "holding action" which does not even hold out the hope of temporary victory through technological innovation and capitalization. Thus, he says, "In an entropic sense, the only way to 'save' time is to keep a society's energy flow as close as possible to that which naturally takes place in our environment. In this way, the end of time and life will approach as slowly as possible. But the pragmatist will try to 'save' time by attempting to streamline the existing energy flow. This will only escalate the entropy process and, along with it, decrease the amount of time available to sustain life for generations yet to come."[7] In short, *we cannot legitimately speak of "growth."* Why not? Because growth is really contraction. More is really less: ". . .'growth' is really a decrease in the world's wealth, nothing more than a process to take usable energy and transform it into an unusable state."[8] The question arises: "Usable by whom?" If men are not supposed to use it, who should be allowed to use it? For whom are we to save the world's wealth, as it inevitably erodes? Impersonal nature?

All living things are *parasites* that feed off of the available energy around them: ". . . even the tiniest plant maintains its own order at the expense of creating greater disorder in the overall environment."[9] He quotes from Harold Blum's book, *Time's Arrow and Evolution*: "The small local decrease in entropy represented in the building of the organism is coupled with a much larger increase in the entropy of the universe."[10] Life speeds up the entropy process. The best way to reduce the overall "rate of entropy" of the universe is clear enough, but Rifkin never admits it: *put an end to all life.*

---

7. Rifkin, *Entropy*, p. 246.
8. *Idem.*
9. *Ibid.*, p. 53.
10. *Ibid.*, p. 52.

The Hatred of Economic Growth

We can now understand Rifkin's hostility to economic growth. In his view, economic growth "is really a decrease in the world's wealth, nothing more than a process to take usable energy and transform it into an unusable state. Entropy shows us that the more an economy grows, the more it digs itself into a hole."[11] There is no real hope for a reversal of this process of social decay—a *microcosm of disaster* packed into a few generations which parallels the ultimate macrocosmic disaster of universal entropy a hundred billion years (or more) down time's increasingly random road. We must make the shift to new "energy environments" by the end of the twentieth century.[12] "There is no way to escape the Entropy Law. This supreme physical rule of the universe pervades every facet of our existence."[13] In short, "The second law of thermodynamics, therefore, contradicts the modern notion of progress. The world is moving inextricably from a state of more order to less order, from more value to less value."[14]

But what answer does the social entropist give to the men who proclaim, "let us eat and drink, for tomorrow we shall die" (Isa. 22:13)? Why not "live it up," if life has no future, if death has no meaning, and if ethics is natural but nature is dying, too? Why not "go out in a blaze of glory," or at least a blaze of wasted resources? Why restrict our consumption of goods today for the sake of generations yet unborn, but ultimately equally doomed? Why not legislate compulsory birth control for everyone and experience a final fireworks display of mass consumption? In short, why not do exactly what twentieth-century hedonistic humanists are in the process of doing?

The social entropist, like the stoic philosopher of Rome who also believed that he was facing a dying civilization, must find his "joy" in keeping a "stiff upper lip," and not expecting too much. His hedonistic humanist cousin prefers to use up all the assets at his disposal in one final burst of glory and mirth. Neither of them can reverse the process of social death, any more than he can reverse personal death or the death of the devolving cosmos. Neither the entropist nor the hedonist has long-term hope.

---

11. *Ibid.*, p. 246.
12. *Ibid.*, p. 250.
13. *Ibid.*, p. 238.
14. Rifkin, *Emerging Order*, p. 63.

The Christian Alternative

The Christian, on the other hand, *does* have hope in life after death: for the cosmos and for himself. He also has faith in the law-order revealed to him in the Bible. He knows that *the process of social decay can be reversed through repentance and humility before God.* The physical universe is an open cosmos—open to God and His grace. God sustains it. The social world is also an open cosmos. God sustains it, too. We live in an *ethically open box,* not a closed box marked by long-term disintegration with only moments of short-term growth. Therefore, God tells ethically rebellious men to agonize over their sins, not over the cosmos. "And in that day did the LORD God of hosts call to weeping, and to mourning, and to baldness, and to girding with sackcloth" (Isa. 22:12). But hedonists prefer not to listen to God's call: "And behold joy and gladness, slaying oxen, and killing sheep, eating flesh, and drinking wine: let us eat and drink; for to morrow we shall die" (Isa. 22:13).

Rifkin wants us to put on perpetual sackcloth and ashes, to mourn the fate of ourselves and our social cosmos, which has no more hope than the entropy-bound universe. But his sackcloth offers no future. It is *metaphysical* sackcloth, not ethical sackcloth. It is not to be worn as a sign of repentance and distress over sin. It is to be worn as a permanent cloak, *a symbol of man's submission to inevitable cosmic destruction.*

Rifkin's world is a closed universe. This universe cannot save itself or save us, either. In fact, we must do our best to conserve the environment—why, he does not say, for there is no one over us to condemn us or reward us. We cannot save it from destruction; we can at best delay the demise of our little corner of the cosmos, but only by dissipating energy out of the rest of it. Man cannot save man or his environment, nor can the environment save man. Entropy swallows everything. Ours is supposedly a world devoid of long-term positive feedback, and what little growth there is, Rifkin regards as a threat to long-term survival (meaning an extra few generations).

Restoration

What is the biblical alternative to this philosophy of ultimate destruction? *God's promise of ultimate restoration.* The problem is, Christians have too often preached that this restoration can come only after the final judgment (amillennialism) or after Christ's return to rule bodily during the millennium (traditional premillennialism). The possibility of progressive restoration as God's historical down payment on full restoration beyond the grave and the resurrection has not been taken seriously in the twentieth century. Thus, with respect to the period of history prior to Christ's bodily return, Christians have tended to agree with a vision of the future that parallels Rifkin's: a future without serious potential for peace, prosperity, growth, and the beating of swords into ploughshares. In fact, some Christians have argued that anyone who comes in the name of God with such a message of earthly optimism has adopted the social and economic outlook of the Antichrist.[15]

What we need to argue as Christians is that the gospel possesses power to transform men, and if it can transform men, then it can also transform men's social and economic relationships. The economic and technological conditions that Rifkin describes—a social world governed by entropy—is a clear denial of the power of the gospel. The resurrection of Christ points to the overcoming of entropy's curses.

But what about history? Scientific Creationists have argued from the beginning that physical entropy is a universal phenomenon—*the* law of physical science. If they are correct, then how can Rifkin be incorrect, for he bases his worldview on the second law of thermodynamics?

Now, the main argument Rifkin uses—that entropy points to the heat death of the universe—has nothing to do with mankind's social arrangements. By the time the heat death of the universe arrives, man will not be around to shiver. Social arrangements are concerned with life, not death.

What about the theology of entropy? The point made by the Creation Scientists is that the origin of life itself is a contradiction of entropy. Life must have come before the second law of thermodynamics appeared. In fact, the whole universe must have been in place. What we have experienced since then is a reduction in order, not an increase. Thus, there could never have been evolution.

The problem for Christians who adopt this argument is that the language of decline is so powerful. What about social institutions? What about the extension of longevity through science? What about

---

15. Dave Hunt, *Peace Prosperity and the Coming Holocaust* (Eugene, Oregon: Harvest House, 1983). Mr. Hunt apparently dislikes commas in his book titles.

the promised extension of life spans in the future? After all, Isaiah taught that "There shall be no more thence an infant of days, nor an old man that hath not filled his days: for the child shall die an hundred years old; but the sinner being an hundred years old shall be accursed" (Isa. 65:20). Note: sinners are still in the picture. He was not speaking of the world after the final judgment.

Entropy in the Garden of Eden

Animals died in the garden. This was not a curse as such. Man exercised dominion over curse-free nature before the Fall. The blessing of God was seen in the subordination of the world to man's dominion. Kline comments: "Similarly, the curse on man consists in the reverse of this relationship—not in the mere presence of things like death but in man's falling victim to them. . . . When the subhuman realm is consecrated to man, a state of beatitude exists; when man is made subservient to or victim of the sub-human, a state of curse exists."[16]

The Bible does not require us, therefore, to think of the character and working of man's natural environment before the Fall as radically different than is presently the case. To be sure, the garden God prepared as man's immediate dwelling was a place eminently expressive of divine goodness and favor. Nevertheless, the elements that could be turned against man were already there in nature. Man's state of blessedness is thus seen to be primarily a matter of God's providential authority over creation, controlling and directing every circumstance so that everything works together for man's good and nothing transpires for his hurt or the frustration of his efforts. God gives his angels charge over the one who stands in his favor lest he should dash his foot against a stone (Ps. 91:12). Blessing consists not in the absence of the potentially harmful stone, but in the presence of God's providential care over the foot. Adam's world before the Fall was not a world without stones, thorns, dark watery depths, or death. But it was a world where the angels of God were given a charge over man to protect his every step and to prosper all the labor of his hand.[17]

The resurrection of Christ in principle put an end to *cursed* entropy, just as it put an end in principle to Satan. I say cursed entropy because entropy—the normal, "natural" transition toward physical randomness—existed prior to the Fall of man, just as the death of

---

16. Meredith G. Kline, *Kingdom Prologue*, 3 vols. (By the Author, 1981), I, p. 80.
17. *Ibid.*, p. 81.

The Question of Ethics 125

plants and animals existed. This is what the terminology of Creation Scientists denies. They have argued that the second law became a reality only after the Fall of man. Henry Morris writes that "the Second Law is a sort of intruder into the divine economy, not a part of either the original creation or God's plan for His eternal kingdom."[18] But this leads the reader to a misunderstanding of science. Like human work, which existed in the garden, but later was cursed by God, so entropy also existed. It was not originally a curse to man.

Let us take a believable example. Let us imagine that Adam and Eve strolled through the garden. They smelled the delightful fragrance of wonderful, uncursed flowers and other plants. But how could they have smelled them? The same way we do: because the pollen or other microscopic bits of material that produced the fragrances were carried into the air and mixed randomly, just as they mix today. The sense of smell is dependent on the ability of the nose to identify minute traces of floating material. This floating material is randomly distributed through the air. This is the scientific definition of entropy: physical processes move toward equilibrium, meaning a random distribution. Remember the textbook definition of the second law: "When a system containing a large number of particles is left to itself, it assumes a state with maximum entropy, that is, it becomes as disordered as possible."[19] Remember also that this disorder always occurs within the ordered limits of the environment.

For the purpose of our ability to smell roses, *the disorder of the material* floating in the air is in fact an example of *God's orderly creation*. Some processes have been specifically designed by God to drift toward a random distribution. This is why the second law of thermodynamics was part of Adam's world. It was not a threat to mankind then, and for progressively faithful societies, it is supposed to be progressively less of a threat over time. It will not be a threat in the restored world beyond the final judgment, either.

Or consider this example. Say that Adam had decided to play a friendly game of solitaire. He picked up a deck of playing cards. The cards were arranged in an orderly manner because he failed to shuffle them at the end of the last game. So he shuffled them. What

---

18. Henry M. Morris, *A Biblical Manual on Science and Creation* (San Diego, California: Institute for Creation Research, 1972), p. 14. The same passage appears in his book, *The Remarkable Birth of Planet Earth* (Institute for Creation Research, 1972), pp. 17-18.

19. K. R. Atkins, *Physics* (New York: Wiley, 1966), p. 206.

did this mean? He deliberately rearranged the cards into a random assortment that would not predictably affect the outcome of the game. The act of shuffling cards calls upon the second law of thermodynamics: the movement of the world toward a random distribution.

Entropy guarantees that if someone shuffles a deck's 52 cards a million times, they will not "rearrange themselves" into four suits of thirteen consecutive cards. If entropy were not a fact of life, shuffling a deck of cards would not produce the effect we want: an arrangement that no player can use to predict the outcome of any deal.

How could Adam have discovered chemistry, or the internal combustion engine, or any other mechanical wonder that relies on a random mixing of gasses, liquids, and solids? The idea that this natural move toward disorder (randomness) appeared only after the Fall of man is simply not acceptable. What *is* acceptable is to view the second law of thermodynamics as a background to man's actions — a background that has been cursed by God. Instead of a world in which man could safely operate with entropy, using it to achieve his goals, and not worrying about its effects on his genes, environment, and so forth, we now find ourselves battling the *cursed effects* of entropy, just as we battle the other cursed aspects of the creation.

Did the sun shine in the garden? Of course! Did the atomic explosions that make a star possible operate then? We have no reason to suspect that they didn't. How God intended to sustain the sun as an energy source the Bible does not say. No doubt because of the curse, some aspect of God's providential sustaining of this energy source was removed. But this does not mean that atomic energy did not operate in terms of the second law, with the sun's randomly distributed energy cascading into the garden. It means that after the universe was cursed, what had been a helpful law of nature became, along with all other aspects of nature, a potential threat to man. Gardens now produce weeds (a weed is best defined as an unwanted plant); our plans produce unwanted side effects (a side effect is an effect we did not plan for, and usually one that we do not like); the sun is dying; and so are we. It is God's curse on our environment that is our burden, not the second law of thermodynamics.

Why the Silence?

All of this is obvious, isn't it? *Then why have Creation Scientists refused to discuss what is obvious for over a quarter century?* I believe that the answer is that they have become wedded to a particular defense of creationism that is tied too closely to their pessimistic eschatological presuppositions. Pessimism colors their every discussion of entropy. They find it nearly impossible to say a good word about entropy. They cannot discuss entropy without returning to the Fall of man. They are hypnotized by the curse of God on nature. They are blinded to the world-transforming effects of the resurrection, and also to the existence of entropy in the pre-Fall garden of Eden. They also do not discuss the implication that entropy will also be a feature of the world beyond the final judgment.

Science is necessarily colored by one's presuppositions. If these presuppositions are incorrect, there will be blind spots and major errors in one's scientific conclusions.

How do we battle these unwanted effects of God's curse in history? By conforming ourselves to the requirements of God. When we do this as a society, God promises that our social world will not randomly oppose us, but that things will go well for us most of the time (Deut. 28:1-14). On the other hand, if we rebel, then things will go badly for us most of the time (Deut. 28:15-68). What is never stated in the Bible is that things will go randomly for us in God's covenanted world. They will not drift along toward an equilibrium state (steady state). It is not a drift toward randomness (entropy) that is inescapable; what is inescapable is *mankind's march toward God's judgment,* either toward His blessings or cursings.

How could Henry Morris have made such a serious mistake for over thirty years in identifying the origin of the second law as the Fall of man? On one occasion, he vaguely hinted that he knew better. In an essay addressed primarily to scientists rather than the general Christian public, he presents a properly modified statement: "The formal announcement of the second law in its post-Fall form is found in Genesis 3:17-20. . . . Thus, as best we can understand both Scripture and science, we must date the establishment of the second law of thermodynamics, in its present form at least, from the tragic day on which Adam sinned. . . ."[20] To speak of the "second law in its post-Fall form" and "in its present form at least" is an unobjectionable way to discuss the second law. Why didn't he pursue this line of reasoning in his popular writings? Why did he leave his readers in the dark? The average Christian reader of Scientific Crea-

---

20. Morris, "Thermodynamics and Biblical Theology," in Emmett L. Williams (ed.), *Thermodynamics and the Development of Order* (Norcross, Georgia: Creation Research Books, 1981), pp. 129-30.

tionist literature never saw this technical book, which went out of print quite rapidly. It is the average Christian reader who is Rifkin's target.

Why quibble over when we should date the origin of entropy? Because a philosophy that is based on the idea of entropy as an inescapable threat to man produces *a social philosophy of earthly, historical despair.* It leads to social theories like Rifkin's. It says that entropy cannot be harnessed to benefit man, the way God harnessed it in the garden. It says that a supposedly fixed law of nature is a threat to God's redeemed people. But entropy needn't always be a threat. When I drive to the market, it is not a major threat to me that air and gasoline molecules mix on a randomly distributed basis once my car's carburetor arranges the appropriate mixture. True, if I light a match close to a gasoline tank, entropy becomes a threat. But the Bible tells us that men can learn, and one of the things we learn is not to light matches around gasoline.

When the Bible says that the truth shall set us free, it gives us hope: knowledge allows us to overcome the limits of our cursed environment.

Conclusion

The Bible teaches that economic growth is God's gift to societies that obey His covenantal laws. There is no escape from economic growth. "And all these blessings shall come on thee, and overtake thee, if thou shalt hearken unto the voice of the LORD thy God" (Deut. 28:2). God's blessings *overtake* a society. This is the biblical account of the relationship between ethics and prosperity.

Clearly, Rifkin resents such a relationship. He would have Western societies *hold back* the blessings of God, for He does not believe in the God of the Bible. Like the sinners who *hold back* the knowledge of God (Rom. 1:18), so would Rifkin hold back God's blessings.

I am not arguing that a Scientific Creationist would self-consciously hold back God's blessings. Nevertheless, I am unaware of any economics literature produced as a product of the Scientific Creation movement that explains how and why Christian principles of growth and development can be conformed to a vision of a world under the burden of the second law of thermodynamics. Their scientific materials imply that any advancement in slowing the rate of decay must be taken out of the environment's hide. Henry Morris' range of application of the two laws sounds very much like Rifkin's theory of "life increases entropy" thesis: "To a local 'open' system, directly applicable in most situations and always applicable as a *normal tendency* in the system, with exceptions possible only under certain special conditions as described elsewhere, and then only at the cost of offsetting external conditions which maintain the integrity of the two laws in the universe as a whole."[21] Thus, it is easy for unsuspecting Christians who have been influenced by the Scientific Creationists' apologetic to be almost hypnotized by Rifkin's rhetoric. They may take seriously his zero-growth economy in the name of a moral imperative to reduce the "entropic" impact of God's curse.

The biblical response is to call mankind to a self-conscious overcoming of the effects of entropy through technology, science, freedom, and self-government under God and God's law. Paraphrasing Patrick Henry, "If this be premeditated assault on the dying cosmos, make the best of it!"

In summary:

1. Humanists are in rebellion against time.
2. Man's problem is ethical.
3. Christian social theory is based on the idea of a fixed ethical order above yet within history.
4. The entropists argue that the only fixed aspect of the historical process is the second law of thermodynamics.
5. Humanists say that ethical principles evolve with nature itself.
6. Christians say that the universe is open upward to God, since we can appeal to God for justice within history.
7. Darwin's universe is an ethically closed box: no appeal to anything outside nature and history.
8. The Christian sees the curses of entropy as temporary, capable of being overcome partially in history and totally after the final judgment.
9. The Darwinists see no escape from entropy's destructive effects.
10. Thus, Darwinism's vision is one without long-run hope.
11. Life for Rifkin becomes a grim holding action in the face of cosmic disintegration.
12. Rifkin hates all signs of growth, for he believes that mankind's growth and order come at the expense of increased entropy elsewhere in the environment.
13. The microcosm (human civilization) reflects the macrocosm (entropy's destruction).

---

21. *Ibid.*, p. 122.

14. Christianity teaches that social decay can be overcome and reversed through faith in Christ.

15. We live in an ethically open environment that can receive the external blessings of God.

16. Rifkin wants men to wear sackcloth and ashes to acknowledge our participation in a world that is perishing without hope of restoration.

17. The heat death of the universe will not happen; the world will be burned up by God, not frozen by entropy.

18. Even if heat death were inevitable, that would have nothing to do with man's responsibilities.

19. Entropy is not a curse, for it existed in the garden of Eden.

20. Entropy has been cursed, just as everything else has.

21. Randomness is not always a curse: shuffling cards, smelling flowers, carburetion.

22. We partially overcome the cursed aspects of entropy by obeying God's law.

23. Entropy—the movement toward randomness—is not always a threat to people.

24. Economic growth is a legitimate way to overcome the cursed effects of entropy.

7

MYSTICISM VS. CHRISTIANITY

On the one hand, **the days**, *times present, are evil; on the other hand, these days must be eagerly redeemed as a season of great value and meaning. The contrast is a dramatic one. Instead of flight from evil days, there is an eager purchase or redemption of them as a time or season of great profit and advantage under God. . . . For this reason, because the godly man's concern is to redeem the time, Christians, especially Puritans, have been highly conscious of time and the clock. As a valuable commodity, time cannot be wasted. This horror of wasting time is alien to those outside the world of Biblical faith. Consciousness of time is for the ungodly a consciousness of decay and death. . . .*

R. J. Rushdoony[1]

Christianity is a religion of ethical restoration. It preaches Christ and Him crucified. The perfect humanity of Christ is declared by God to be the possession of the redeemed person. Instead of looking at the sins of each Christian, God looks at Christ's perfection. Christ's perfect humanity is *imputed* to redeemed men, just as Adam's sin is imputed to all men until they become regenerated through God's grace (Rom. 5:19).[2] It is this alone which enables man to escape from the curse of God's final judgment.

Understand that it is Christ's perfect humanity which is imputed (judicially transferred) to man by God at the point of the person's regeneration. The divinity of Christ remains His possession alone. God does not share His divinity with man. *Man does not become God*, either by science, or techniques of meditation, or magic, or self-discipline. Christ was both God and man from the beginning. He

---

1. R. J. Rushdoony, *Revolt Against Maturity: A Biblical Psychology of Man* (Fairfax, Virginia: Thoburn Press, 1977), p. 230.
2. John Murray, *The Imputation of Adam's Sin* (Nutley, New Jersey: Presbyterian & Reformed, 1977).

alone is God incarnate. Man does not become God through magical or metaphysical union with God. It is the age-old heresy of Satan that man can become God.

Because man is restored ethically before God, he has become a new creation, Paul says. "Therefore, if any man be in Christ, he is a new creature [creation]: old things have passed away; behold, all things have become new" (II Cor. 5:17). *All things*: Christians are supposed to take this seriously. God grants *comprehensive redemption* to His people.[3] Every aspect of their lives is transformed. God sends the Holy Spirit that they might be comforted and led into all truth (John 14:16-17). The dominion covenant can be fulfilled through the efforts of His redeemed people.

The Bible teaches redemption, not mysticism. It teaches dominion, not retreat. It teaches reconstruction, not conformity to this world. It teaches growth, not stagnation and a steady-state economy. It teaches conquest through time, not mystical transcendence beyond time.

Rifkin's Mysticism

Rifkin's theology is mystical, not Christian. Christianity explains man's history in terms of *ethics*: the rebellion against God which led to the curse of creation. Rifkin cites the "small is beautiful" guru, E. F. Schumacher, author of *Buddhist Economics*: "The most urgent need of our time is and remains the need for metaphysical reconstruction. . . ."[4] But Christianity teaches that it is not metaphysical reconstruction that is needed; it is *ethical reconstruction*. The Christian philosopher Cornelius Van Til has warned against any confusing of the ethical theology of Christianity with the metaphysical theology of humanism:

> We know that sin is an attempt on the part of man to cut himself loose from God. But this breaking loose from God could, in the nature of the case, not be metaphysical; if it were, man himself would be destroyed and God's purpose with man would be frustrated. Sin is therefore a breaking loose from God ethically and not metaphysically. Sin is the creature's enmity and rebellion against God but is not an escape from creaturehood.

---

3. Gary North, "Comprehensive Redemption: A Theology for Social Action," *Journal of Christian Reconstruction*, VIII (Summer 1981). Reprinted in this book as Appendix C.

4. *Entropy*, p. 205.

When we say that sin is ethical we do not mean, however, that sin involved only the will of man and not also his intellect. Sin involved every aspect of man's personality. All of man's reactions in every relation in which God had set him were ethical and not merely intellectual; the intellectual itself is ethical.[5]

Rifkin is therefore incorrect when he lumps Christianity into the following summary: "The traditional wisdom, as embodied in all the great world religions, has long taught that the ultimate purpose of human life is not the satisfaction of all material desires, but rather the experience of liberation that comes from becoming one with the metaphysical unity of the universe."[6] On the contrary, Christianity calls men to become ethically conformed to Christ in His perfect humanity, not His Godhead. *Union with Christ is to be ethical, not metaphysical.*

Men are never called by God to become metaphysically united to Him or the creation. Men do not evolve into the Godhead. We do not possess "sparks of divinity" within our souls. Even Jesus Christ, in His perfect humanity, did not possess "sparks of divinity" within his perfect human nature. He was fully divine in His nature as God, and fully human in His nature as man. He was one person, but with two natures that were in union but not intermixed. This has been the testimony of the orthodox church since the fifth century. Rushdoony comments on the Council of Ephesus in A.D. 431. He says that "the Council made it clear that only God could be worshipped; not even Christ's humanity could be worshipped but only His deity. The humanity of Christ is not nor ever can be deified. The two natures are without confusion, even in the unique incarnation."[7] We are not called to become God; we are called to exercise dominion over the creation, *under* God. This is the essence of the intellectual conflict between the "New Age" humanism and orthodox Christianity.

Rifkin wants us to follow the mystics, such as the late-medieval heretic, Meister Eckhart,[8] and calls us to a "New Age" philosophy[9]

---

5. Cornelius Van Til, *The Defense of the Faith* (2nd ed.; Philadelphia: Presbyterian & Reformed, 1963), p. 46.
6. Rifkin, *Entropy*, p. 205.
7. R. J. Rushdoony, *Foundations of Social Order: Studies in the Creeds and Counsels of the Early Church* (Fairfax, Virginia: Thoburn Press, [1968] 1978), p. 47.
8. Rifkin, *Entropy*, p. 206.
9. *Ibid.*, pp. 211-20. Several criticisms of the "New Age" humanism have appeared since 1980, most notably Constance Cumbey's *The Hidden Dangers of the Rainbow* (Shreveport, Louisiana: Harvest House, 1983). The literature published by "New

—the religion of "higher consciousness,"[10] self-transcendence, and (though he may not know it) occultism.[11] As a mystic, Rifkin sounds the trumpet to retreat. "It should also be recognized that we often mistakenly associate new human ideas for organizing the physical world we live in with higher forms of consciousness. The two are not the same. In fact, social development and spiritual development have, for the most part, followed opposite trajectories throughout much of human history. They can only begin to converge once again when humanity surrenders its will to dominate and begins to adjust to a world not of our making but for which we were made."[12] In other words, we were not made by a God who created a fixed ethical order. For Rifkin, the creation, including mankind, is not governed by an ethically fixed order; it is a "becoming process."[13] Accordingly, we must adjust to our environment. This is *environmentalism*, not Christianity.

Absorption vs. Dominion

God's law is our tool of dominion; by abandoning the concept of an ethically fixed universe, and by substituting entropy as the uniformitarian principle, Rifkin turns our attention from the Christian goal of dominion over nature, under God, to the mystic's goal of *absorption by the cosmos through "higher consciousness."* He wants us to adopt the Hindu goal of becoming one with nature (though how this will enable us to escape the inescapable increase of entropy, he does not say). "Our goal is to join with, to become one with all of the rest of creation."[14] This monism of "creation" is Rifkin's impersonal god, similar to the impersonal god of Buddhism.

We are not to exercise dominion over nature; instead, we are to subordinate ourselves to nature's laws in order to live in harmony

---

Age" organizations is vast. Probably the most influential of these books is Marilyn Ferguson's *The Aquarian Conspiracy: Personal and Social Transformation in the 1980's* (Los Angeles: J. P. Tarcher, 1980). I suppose that my book, *None Dare Call It Witchcraft* (New Rochelle, New York: Arlington House, 1976), offered the first specifically Christian analysis of this movement's political goals, in Chapter Nine: "Escape From Creaturehood." This has been reprinted in the updated version of *None Dare* which is titled *Unholy Spirits: Occultism and New Age Humanism* (Ft. Worth, Texas: Dominion Press, 1986), ch. 10.

10. *Ibid.*, p. 253.
11. Gary North, *Unholy Spirits*.
12. Rifkin, *Entropy*, p. 254.
13. *Ibid.*, p. 255.
14. Jeremy Rifkin, *Declaration of a Heretic* (London: Routledge and Kegan Paul, 1985), p. 84.

with nature. We are to integrate ourselves into the web of nature. "In the new scheme of consciousness, security is achieved by becoming an integral participant in the larger communities of life that make-up [sic] the single organism we call earth. Security is no longer to be found in self-contained isolation but rather in shared partnership with the creation. Security is not to be found in dominating and manipulating, but rather in reweaving ourselves back into the web of relationships that make up the earthly and cosmic ecosystems."[15]

We see here the truth of the statement that men either become subordinate to the God of the Bible and dominant over nature, or else they rebel against God and become subordinate to nature. Rifkin goes so far as to revive the idea that the universe is itself purposeful, "a mind pulsating with purpose and intention. . . . In this way one eventually ends up with the idea of the universe as a mind that oversees, orchestrates, and gives order and structure to all things."[16] Only Christianity, which preaches God as the purposeful source of history and meaning, is more hated by Darwinian scientists than this idea of purposeful nature. It represents a revival of pantheism. It also represents a revival of the outlook of ancient paganism: nature, not man, as an autonomous source of decisions.

> To end our long, self-imposed exile; to rejoin the community of life. This is the task before us. It will require that we renounce our drive for sovereignty over everything that lives; that we restore the rest of creation to a place of dignity and respect. The resacralization of nature stands before us as the great mission of the coming age.[17]

He calls for the *re-sacralization* of nature. But nature is not sacred, nor was it ever intended by God to be sacred. Only those who worship the creature rather than the Creator would argue for re-sacralization. Rifkin wants us to adopt the cosmology of Eastern mysticism, but in the name of a "new" Christianity. He sees that a revival of Christianity in the latter days of the twentieth century seems likely, and he knows that the widespread adoption of Eastern religion is unlikely.[18] As a non-Christian who sees that the statist, expansionist, and above all, rationalist world is losing its adherents,[19]

---

15. *Ibid.*, p. 90.
16. Rifkin and Perlas, *Algeny*, p. 195.
17. *Ibid.*, p. 252.
18. Rifkin, *Emerging Order*, p. 89.
19. *Ibid.*, ch. 1: "An Establishment in Crisis."

he wants to transform traditional humanism as well as traditional fundamentalism into a new, anti-biblical religious ideology.[20] (What he *really* wants, as do almost all revolutionaries throughout history — religious and secular — is *sexual license* freed from the restraint of biblical morality!)[21]

There is nothing even remotely Christian about Rifkin's social theory, for there is nothing remotely Christian about his cosmology. Social theorists who take seriously the social entropy theory, but who also regard themselves as Christians, are either deluded about the humanistic origins of the theory, or else they do not understand (or accept) Christianity's implications for social theory.

New Left, New Age

The conservative American sociologist, Robert Nisbet, has described the political and intellectual changes that preceded the higher consciousness or "New Age" politics. When he wrote this analysis, the "New Age" political movement was barely discernible. Its fundamental principles, however, were already present in the New Left political movement which appeared during the Vietnam War era after 1965. The conflict between the rationalist Old Left and the subjectivist New Left continues, though not with the same visible confrontations that shook the university campuses in the late 1960's. Nisbet wrote in 1972:

I think it can be said accurately that the Old Left's hatred of the New Left was, and is, based on two fundamental points. The first is obvious enough. It is the New Left's seeming disdain for the nice, bureaucratic-humanitarian society the Old Left helped to build, that had, so to speak, liberalism-and-six-per-cent as its motto, and that now seemed to be going down the drain as a result of the antics of the New Left. The universities in America, from Harvard across the country to Berkeley, had become cherished, increasingly luxurious homes for Old Radicals, exhilarating settings for the permanent politics to which the Old Left was consecrated. When the New Left turned with such ferocity upon these monasteries of

---

20. *Ibid.*, Section II: "The Religious Response."
21. "The sexual revolution of the past twenty years has done a great deal to liberate men and women from the unnatural inhibitions imposed by the Puritanism of orthodox Christian dogma." *Ibid.*, p. 246. On the perpetual call for unregulated sexual activity in revolutionary circles, especially the idea of the communality of wives, see Igor Shafarevich, *The Socialist Phenomenon* (New York: Harper & Row, 1982), pp. 12, 23-24, 36-38, 47-48, 63-64, 214, 236.

privileged affluence, seeking to destroy them along with [the] Pentagon and General Motors, this was more than the Old Left could bear. . . .

The second point is hardly less fundamental in the Old Left's hatred of the New Left. It lies in the New Left's ever more articulate disdain for the whole rhetoric of rationalism—of objectivism—that for so long had made the Kingdom of Heaven a simple matter of annihilating enough external institutions and pursuing enough ends through the rationalist techniques of politics. From the Old Left's point of view, the increasing references in the New Left to consciousness, to identity, to reflexive states of mind, and to awareness seemed nothing short of a failure of nerve—a recrudescence of the kind of society Gilbert Murray's *Four Phases of Greek Religion* describes in the ancient Athens of the post-Alexandrian period when bizarre beliefs and cults abounded, when the external world seemed nothing more than varied projections of consciousness, when objectivism passed into subjectivism and solipsism.[22]

The fears of the Old Left were fully justified. The intellectual and spiritual revolution that shook the West after 1963 unleashed the forces of irrationalism, mysticism, and occultism. It did indeed create a "failure of nerve" in the West. It did produce a rapid growth of cultic and occult groups. The West increasingly does resemble the classical civilization of Hellenic and Roman times—a civilization that collapsed intellectually and spiritually centuries before it fell to barbarian invaders.[23] The familiar intellectual and institutional foundations that rationalist humanism preached and then constructed after the Darwinian revolution no longer are accepted by the proponents of "New Age" humanism.

Jeremy Rifkin is one of those New Left political revolutionaries who has made the transition to "New Age" politics. He maintains his old hostility to Establishment liberalism, and he therefore can serve as a recruiting officer for "New Age" politics among the evangelicals. The theology of the neo-evangelicals is already in tune with much of Rifkin's "New Age" religion: mystical rather than biblical law-oriented, disenchanted with the institutional results of the old political liberalism-statism, and hoping for some sort of emotional revival of faith which will restore a lost sense of community. They,

---

22. Robert Nisbet, "Radicalism as Therapy," *Encounter* (March 1972), p. 56. Murray's book was updated in 1925 and published under the title, *Five Stages of Greek Religion*.
23. Charles Norris Cochrane, *Christianity and Classical Culture: A Study in Thought and Action from Augustus to Augustine* (New York: Oxford University Press, [1944] 1957).

like Rifkin, are hostile to biblical law, with its promises of growth and its vision of responsible progressive dominion. They cannot refute him, nor even recognize the totality of his underlying hostility to Christian orthodoxy, because they have themselves abandoned too many of the fundamental tenets of the Christian faith.

Misrepresenting Christianity

Rifkin seeks to overcome the opposition of potential Christian critics by misrepresenting their views. He may even think that he can confuse them into silence. First, he offers his total misrepresentation of the biblical view of dominion: " 'Dominion,' which Christian theology has for so long used to justify people's unrestrained pillage and exploitation of the natural world, has suddenly and dramatically been reinterpreted." This summary of the theology of dominion is, as we have seen, a total fabrication. Then he continues: "Now, according to the new definition of dominion, God's first instruction to the human race is to serve as a steward and protector over all his creation." This means *zero growth*: the triumph of the steady-state society, the victory of the status quo.

Finally, Rifkin brags about the victory of this perverse misrepresentation of Christian theology: "It is interesting to observe that this most fundamental reconception of God's first order to his children on earth has been accepted by Protestant scholars, ministers and practitioners in just a few short years without any significant opposition being voiced. In fact, one would be hard pressed to find a leading Protestant scholar anywhere today who would openly question this new interpretation of dominion in the Book of Genesis."[24] (Quite clearly, my economic commentary on the Book of Genesis, *The Dominion Covenant*, openly questions "this new interpretation of dominion.")

Rifkin will be forgotten soon enough. (So, for that matter, will the neo-evangelicals.) But his mass-produced paperback books received a wide hearing in neo-evangelical circles in the early 1980's, which indicates just how confused the intellectual leadership of late-twentieth-century Christianity really is. The inability of Christian intellectuals to recognize the profoundly anti-Christian nature of Rifkin's explicitly and defiantly anti-dominion ideology testifies to the extent to which Christian intellectuals have themselves adopted the presuppositions and outlook of the new humanism.

---

24. Rifkin, *Emerging Order*, p. xi.

One Christian scholar who has understood the man-denying aspects of this revival of Eastern religion posing as "concerned ecology" is Otto Scott. I am reproducing his short essay, "Science vs. Man," in its entirety because I regard it as basic to understanding the theological war we are in.

* * * * *

Recently the airwaves were clotted with reports of "Humphrey the Wayward Whale," which was said to have accidentally wandered into the Sacramento river. "Scientists" were quite concerned over Humphrey, who weighed 40 tons, was humpbacked, and who appeared to enjoy cleansing the Sacramento of fish. They said that immersion in fresh water would certainly kill Humphrey, and it was clear that they—and the media—regarded this as a great potential tragedy.

While bystanders collected on the banks of the river, and others took to their boats, aiming binoculars and cameras, Humphrey wandered about in typical whale fashion, surfacing from time to time to exhale, emerging in great leaps and diving down with loud slaps of his tail.

Meanwhile, it became evident that the scientists who specialize in marine activities considered themselves responsible for Humphrey's life. They tried hammering underwater on metal pipes in an effort to drive Humphrey back to sea; eventually they resorted to playing underwater tapes of other humpbacked whales feeding. These tapes were apparently made in the normal course of scientific monitoring of other forms of life in, around, and over these United States.

In due course the scientists claimed a great success: Humphrey swam out of the river and back into the ocean, showing none of the debility from fresh water that the scientists had predicted. The scientists said nothing about the failure of this prediction, but called attention to what they claimed was their success in luring Humphrey back to sea with their tapes. They also said their efforts had cost the State of California $60,000, and they requested donations to one fund or another to replace this money, to enable science to proceed to other necessary, "scientific" efforts.

Reports of these scientists paralleled earlier reports of other scientists, who are obsessed about the condors of California. Tens of thousands of condors exist on the west coast of South America, but California, it seems, has only dwindling bands. Therefore some scientists roosted in high places for weeks, filming and watching condors, and recording their every wing flutter. One such team described how a male and female condor, having produced their season's one egg, fell into an aerial fight over which would next sit on the egg. Apparently condors rotate this duty, and this particular pair had lost count. Their fight was waged in the air, with much pecking, raucous screams and clawing. In the struggle, they dislodged the egg, which rolled out of the nest and crashed. The scientists were appalled, and discussed ways to steal future eggs, to save future condors from such irresponsible parents.

Other tales could be told of the obsessive belief of modern American scientists that it is their duty to prevent the extinction of any and all species of life, to monitor each and every sparrow, and to be responsible for all that moves or lives on this planet . . . except human beings.

This flight from reality—for this is what it is—represents a new, modern form of Animism, in which all manifestations of life—except the human—are considered sacred. The ancient belief in Animism was, of course, that every living creature and object had a spirit of its own. Ancient Animists, generally associated with primitive cultures but actually active in Greece and Rome as well (to say nothing of Egypt and Babylon), attached supernatural qualities to trees, certain species of animals, the sky, some marine life and even insects.

Modern scientists do not recognize "soul." They express no religious belief about non-human forms of life; they simply take it for granted that all non-human forms must be protected against Man at all costs. Their indifference to Man comes, in fact, close to hatred.

The pursuit of this animus has cost America immense sums, curtailed industrial progress, and has led to millions of acres of land being declared off-limits to the American people and their enterprises. Rushdoony has compared these sequestered acres to the Crown lands set aside in England, beginning with William the Conqueror, reserving the right to hunt deer. Since that distant time, property rights in England have been especially detailed regarding the right to hunt game or to fish, and poachers are still held in abhorrence by the British gentry. The American gentry has taken an even loftier approach: the land is to be held sacrosanct for its unsullied beauty, and for the exclusive use of non-humans.

Until modern times, no government in the West has ever gone so far in its disdain for all its citizens. The prevailing "ecological" view appears to be based on the premise that Man is an excrescence in the Universe. This is a mirror-reversal of the traditional Christian belief that Man was created in the image of God for a special purpose, and was given dominion on earth over all other creatures and forms of life.

The governmentally sponsored "scientific" position has led to amazing developments. A great dam project was first delayed and then ruled out of existence because, the scientists said, the snail-darter—a small, nearly unknown fish—would be rendered extinct by the creation of the dam. Since then, snail-darters have been discovered in embarrassing numbers in various locations, but so far as I know the dam remains unbuilt.

Arguments against offshore drilling for oil center on presumed ecological damage to the sea and the shore. But fish thrive on oil spills, for oil is a natural substance. The ocean tides wash away oil residues on shore. Some birds have, it is true, suffered from oil spills. But so far, not to the extent that the seabird population has been significantly affected. On the other hand, the loss of the oil obtainable from our shores has cost the American people and industry untold billions in jobs, products and quality of human life.

Some years back a debate arose over DDT. This insecticide, made from coal-tar derivatives, is credited with eradicating malaria in many parts of the world and with preventing the spread of typhus at the close of World War II. Since typhus has killed more people than battles, DDT was responsible for saving millions of lives. But some said that DDT was deleterious because it builds up in the system and resulted in creating thinner egg-shells in some species of birds. This, it was claimed, would reduce the bird population to dangerous levels.

Rachel Carson, a writer on biological subjects, afflicted with terminal cancer, read such arguments and was overcome with dread. In 1962 she wrote *Silent Spring*, which depicted a grim, lifeless world without birds. *Silent Spring* helped spawn an environmental movement that saw Man as a menace to all living things. A campaign was launched against DDT. Despite a scientific report that said DDT was beneficial, the U.S. Court of Appeals, in response to environmental arguments, ordered an end to its use. Since then, the infestations and damage created by insects upon crops and humans alike have spurted.

A few years after the DDT action came a scare about mercury in fish. This scare led to a drop in the sale and consumption of fish, greatly damaging fishermen, canneries, restaurants and allied industries. It was later discovered that mercury has been present in fish since prehistoric times, and presents no harm.

To detail all the follies attendant upon the blind worship of what is called "Nature," and sometimes "Mother Nature," would, of course, soon grow encyclopedic. Suffice to say that there is no such entity as "Nature," let alone its "Mother." There is only God, who created this marvelous world within which we dwell.

What is truly macabre about the scientific attempt to monitor all forms of life, however, is the indifference of the "environmental" lobbies and the scientists regarding the destruction of human beings in various part of Asia (Cambodia, Vietnam, Tibet, Communist China), Syria, Africa (Libya, Ethiopia, Uganda, Zimbabwe, etc.), Latin America (Guatemala, El Salvador, Nicaragua, etc.). There have been eighteen million abortions in the United States since the U.S. Supreme Court ruled that abortion is a constitutional right. Abortions in Communist China now range into the hundreds of millions.

None of these terrible human deaths—by murder, by deliberate starvation, by abortions forced and voluntary—have enlisted judicial, political or media support on a level equal to that achieved on behalf of condors (a scavenger bird), of whales, or snail-darters, or insects.

To say that this weird disparity represents a loss of proportion is to understate. One is reminded of Hemingway's response to a question about his beliefs. He said that, if he had his dearest dream, he would have been "a shark, cutting cleanly through the water, in a world without Man."

This anti-human remark, made by one of our most loudly modern successes, proved that Hemingway was a true man of his civilization, his time. For Hemingway, having no faith, after a life spent in pursuit of self-indulgence, committed suicide. A similar goal is being pursued by our scientists. Our environmentalists' concern for non-human life forms is merely the reflection of their self-hatred, and their enmity to all other humans—and to God.

Fortunately, those of us who believe in God know that such modern heretics, such enemies of mankind, will fall—as did Hemingway and all his ilk—by their own hands, through their own excesses.[25]

---

25. Otto Scott, "Science vs. Man," *Chalcedon Report*, #246 (Jan. 1986). Address: P.O. Box 158, Vallecito, California 95251.

* * * * *

Conclusion

Traditional statist humanism has come under attack by new, "revolutionary" humanists—humanists who proclaim the need and imminent likelihood of the self-transcendence of mankind in a new evolutionary leap of being.[26] Sadly, members of the evangelical leadership feel compelled to take sides with these humanistic "revolutionaries." The evangelicals do not recognize the irreconcilable nature of all forms of humanism with Christianity. Perhaps they feel guilty because they have promoted in the past a baptized version of a now-waning type of humanism—the humanism of central planning and intervention into the free market—and they now want to atone for their former ideological sins by washing themselves in the cleansing waters of anti-dominion, zero-growth, mystical humanism. They are substituting one form of baptized humanism for another—a socially pessimistic version which is far more consistent with their premillennial and amillennial eschatologies. And even those evangelicals who do not share Rifkin's vision of the steady state entropic society have remained silent, unable or unwilling to challenge Rifkin's vision in the name of Christian orthodoxy. Is it because their version of Christian social theory is impotent to deal with the social issues that Rifkin has raised?

In summary:

1. Christians are supposed to respect time, for it is no threat to them.
2. Christianity is a religion proclaiming ethical restoration with God.
3. Christ's perfect humanity is imputed to redeemed people.
4. Christ's divinity is not imputed to anyone.
5. God grants comprehensive redemption to His people.
6. Rifkin's theology is mystical.
7. He calls for metaphysical reconstruction, not ethical reconstruction.
8. Union with Christ is ethical, not metaphysical.
9. Even in Christ's perfect humanity, He did not possess "sparks of divinity."

---

26. Gary North, *Unholy Spirits*, ch. 10.

10. Rifkin calls for surrender to the world, not dominion over it.

11. He calls for "higher consciousness," a New Age doctrine.

12. Men who are not subordinate to God become subordinate to nature.

13. Rifkin seeks to transform traditional fundamentalism into New Age Eastern mysticism.

14. This New Age movement shares the outlook of the New Left politics of the late 1960's: hatred of bureaucracy and hatred of rationalism.

15. The neo-evangelicals are near-mystics, hostile to biblical law, just as Rifkin is.

16. Rifkin redefines Christian dominion to mean anti-dominion: zero growth.

17. Otto Scott recognizes the anti-humanity perspective of humanism's ecology movement.

18. Humanistic ecologists consider all life sacred, except man's.

19. Man is seen as an excrescence of the universe.

20. Humanists are worshipping nature rather than God.

21. They are more worried about condors than aborted babies.

22. The evangelicals have not seen that these humanistic New Age mystics are enemies of the Christian faith, and also enemies of the West that was produced by Christian faith.

8

DOMINION AND SANCTIFICATION

The state of grace is, as we have seen, a state of growth. It leads to a growing person and a progressing society. The society of fallen man can be marked by revolutions in certain phases of its history, but its basic purpose is to establish an unchanging order; whether it was ancient Chinese society, the Incas of Peru, or modern Marxist theory, its hope is a static order, in brief, the **graveyard society** *to which freedom is a "threat" and growth has no place. . . . The graveyard society of science, sociology, and humanism is inescapable unless men are in a state of grace. Men in the state of grace reign with Christ (Eph. 2:4-6); Christ, who rules all things in time and eternity, empowers His people to establish that reign in history (Matt. 28:18-20). Men in the state of grace will do more than grow; they shall conquer and reign.*

R. J. Rushdoony[1]

As slaves in Egypt, the Hebrews had experienced what has to be the most rapid population growth on record. Using Donovan Courville's estimate of 215 years from Joseph to the exodus, a single family, plus bondservants, had grown in two centuries to as many as two million people (Ex. 12:37). Mathematically speaking, such an increase can be explained only by assuming that during the first century of Israel's residence in Egypt, other tribes and even Egyptians had voluntarily joined themselves with the Hebrews through conversion and circumcision during the era of prosperity in the land of Goshen.[2] Thus, a mathematically possible but historically unprecedented rate of reproduction and survival had demonstrated God's

---

1. R. J. Rushdoony, *Revolt Against Maturity: A Biblical Psychology of Man* (Fairfax, Virginia: Thoburn Press, 1977), p. 183.
2. Gary North, *Moses and Pharaoh: Dominion Religion vs. Power Religion* (Tyler, Texas: Institute for Christian Economics, 1985), ch. 1.

presence with His people—a slave population growing so rapidly that it made the Pharaoh of the enslavement tremble (Ex. 1:7-10).

Even after the exodus, God told them that their numbers were insufficient to enable them to subdue the land of Canaan all at once. Speaking of the pagan cultures still in the land, God said: "I will not drive them out from before thee in one year; lest the land become desolate, and the beast of the field multiply against thee. By little and little I will drive them out from before thee, until thou be increased, and inherit the land" (Ex. 23:29-30).

This is an extremely important passage. *First*, it affirms man's authority over land and animals. Even the morally perverse Canaanite tribes possessed God-given authority over the works of nature. Men, not the beasts, are supposed to subdue the earth. *Second*, this passage warns God's covenant people against attempting to achieve instant dominion. They must first build up their numbers, their skills, and their capital before they can expect to reign over the creation.

Pagans possess skills and capital that are important to the continuity of human dominion. Pagans can be competent administrators. Their labor can be used by God and society until an era comes when God's people are ready to exercise primary leadership in terms of God's law. At that point, ethical rebels will either be regenerated through God's grace, or else steadily replaced by the new rulers of the land.[3] Until then, God's people must be content to wait patiently, improving their own administrative abilities and increasing their numbers. *Dominion is an ethical process*, a process of *self-government under God's law*.

God promised His people a specific reward for covenantal faithfulness: "And ye shall serve the LORD your God, and he shall bless thy bread, and thy water; and I will take sickness away from the midst of thee. There shall nothing cast their young, nor be barren, in thy land: the number of thy days I will fulfil" (Ex. 23:25-26). He promised them *health*, including an absence of miscarriages among both humans and domesticated animals. This means that He promised them an escape from miscarriage-producing genetic defects. In short, He promised them an escape from an important aspect of the curse. (Perhaps we can regard genetic "misinformation" part of the

---

3. Gary North, *Dominion and Common Grace: The Biblical Basis of Progress* (Tyler, Texas: Institute for Christian Economics, 1987).

curse of the entropy process.) This *conditional promise* would have enabled the Hebrews, had they remained faithful as a nation, to have achieved cultural dominion more rapidly. Ultimately, it would have led to the subduing of the whole earth, had the same rate of population growth which they had experienced in Egypt been sustained for a few more centuries.

Obedience and Biology

Is dominion essentially biological? Could their growth of population have been even more rapid than in Egypt? In Egypt there had been no guarantee against miscarriages. In short, that which is *biologically abnormal*—no miscarriages—is declared by God to be *culturally and historically normative* for His redeemed people. Did God expect them to fill the earth in only a few centuries?

The rate of conception could have been reduced by God, either directly or, as in the modern world, through the development of the technology of contraception. Thus, the birth rate might have dropped in response to the increasing pressures of population growth. It is possible that God would have delayed the external fulfillment of the population aspect of the dominion covenant. We are not told, however, that any such delay was normative. There is no indication in the revelation of God to His Old Covenant people that they would experience anything except large families, zero miscarriages, and high rates of population growth, *if* they would conform themselves to His law. Certainly, the *biological option* of rapid population growth was offered to them by God.

How can we say, then, that entropy is normative?

History: Cyclical or Linear?

Nature is not normative; it is under the curse as a result of man's ethical rebellion (Gen. 3:17-19). The so-called "balance of nature" hypothesis assumes either an autonomous process of temporary linear developments within an overall framework of decay (Darwinism) or else an eternal alternating process of development and decay (cycles). Both perspectives regarding nature are completely antithetical to the biblical viewpoint. The growth of human population, if directed by God in response to the widespread honoring of God's law, is normative. So is economic growth (Deut. 8). Not cycles of nature or culture, but *linear development*, is God's response in history to men's ethical conformity to His law-order.

God's law-order is designed to promote the *rapid* fulfilling of the terms of the dominion covenant. God does not desire nature to remain governed by the law of the jungle, the desert, or the frozen wastes. He wants the *ethical obedience of mankind*. When people give Him obedience, He promises to extend their rule over nature. The extension of man's rule over nature is delayed primarily by ethics, not by innate "limits to growth" in nature. Individual limits can be overcome in a few generations, though not at zero cost.

It was sin and rebellion that thwarted the Hebrews in the attainment of their assigned tasks. They turned to the gods of Canaan — gods of the chaos festivals, the eternal cycles, and the abolition of time.[4] It was not the hypothetical autonomous restraint of biological "negative feedback" which kept the Hebrews from multiplying and filling the earth; it was instead their adoption of Canaanitic religions of cyclical growth and decay. They began to work out the implications of these rival religions, and God permitted them to sink their culture into the paralyzing pessimism of pagan faiths. He gave them their request, but sent leanness into their souls (Ps. 106:15). Then He scattered them: by the Assyrians, the Babylonians, the Greeks, and the Romans.

History is directional. It is headed toward final judgment. This has always been the message of biblical religion. Jewish scholar and legal theorist Harold J. Berman of Harvard writes:

> In contrast to the other Indo-European peoples, including the Greeks, who believed that time moved in ever recurring cycles, the Hebrew people conceived of time as continuous, irreversible, and historical, leading to ultimate redemption at the end. They also believed, however, that time has periods within it. It is not cyclical but may be interrupted or accelerated. It develops. The Old Testament is a story not merely of change but of development, of growth, of movement toward the messianic age — very uneven movement, to be sure, with much backsliding but nevertheless a movement *toward*. Christianity, however, added an important element to the Judaic concept of time: that of transformation of the old into the new. The Hebrew Bible became the Old Testament, its meaning transformed by its fulfillment in the New Testament. In the story of the Resurrection, death was transformed into a new beginning. The times were not only accelerated but regenerated. This introduced a new structure of history, in which there was a fundamental transformation of one age into another. This transformation, it was believed, could only happen once: the life, death, and resur-

---

4. Gary North, *Moses and Pharaoh*, ch. 17.

rection of Christ was thought to be the only major interruption in the course of linear time from the creation of the world until it ends altogether.[5]

The judgments of God are revealed in history, and they are twofold: cursings and blessings.[6] Because Christians have been heavily influenced by humanism's pessimism and by pessimistic doctrines of the future, they have overemphasized the cursings of God in history and underemphasized the blessings of God in history.

Sanctification in History

Is it possible for the church of Jesus Christ to purify itself ethically? The Bible says yes. But if it does steadily cleanse itself ethically, won't this manifest itself in history? Won't God honor His covenantal promises in Deuteronomy 28:1-14? In short, can the effects of moral purification be bottled up inside the institutional church? Satan wishes this were the case, but it cannot be true. Unfortunately for the church, Satan's wish has become the dominant Christian theology in our day—a theology of eschatological pessimism.

Sanctification involves moral cleansing. The Bible says that this cleansing of the church will be achieved before the end of time. Paul's words are clear on this point:

> Husbands, love your wives, even as Christ also loved the church, and gave himself for it; that he might sanctify and cleanse it with the washing of water by the word, that he might present it to himself a glorious church, not having spot, or wrinkle, or any such thing; but that it should be holy and without blemish (Eph. 5:25-27).

Paul's language leaves no doubt concerning Christ's intention to cleanse His church. It also leaves no doubt that Paul was writing for the so-called "Church Age." No dispensational group, even including the groups classified as "ultradispensationalists" (anti-baptism followers of C. R. Stam,[7] and zero-Lord's Supper followers of E. W. Bullinger), has classified Ephesians as anything except a "Church Age" document.

---

5. Harold J. Berman, *Law and Revolution: The Formation of the Western Legal Tradition* (Cambridge, Massachusetts: Harvard University Press, 1983), pp. 26-27.
6. Ray R. Sutton, *That You May Prosper: Dominion By Covenant* (Tyler, Texas: Institute for Christian Economics, 1987), ch. 4.
7. Cornelius R. Stam, *Things That Differ: The Fundamentals of Dispensationalism* (Chicago: Berean Bible Society, 1959).

Christ intends to sanctify the church *in history*, before time ends. He intends to make it holy. These two words mean the same thing: *to set apart*. Christ sets apart His people from the world—not geographically, but ethically. He does this through the power of His Word. Christ's remarkable public prayer in John 17 spells this out clearly:

> I pray not that thou shouldest take them out of the world, but that thou shouldest keep them from the evil. They are not of the world, even as I am not of the world. Sanctify them through thy truth: thy word is truth. As thou hast sent me into the world, even so have I also sent them into the world. And for their sakes I sanctify myself, that they also might be sanctified through the truth (John 17:15-19).

Both in English and in Hebrew, the word for *sanctify* has the same root as the word for *sanctuary*. To clean something morally (*kaw-dash*) means to sanctify it, to make it holy. The sanctuary (Ex. 36:1, 3-4, 6) is the *ko-desh*, a holy place. The sanctuary of God is a place that is set aside *for* worshipping Him. The sanctified person is the one who has been set aside by God *to* worship Him. The English word *saint* means the one who has access to the *sanctuary*. The same is true in New Testament Greek. The Greek word for *saint* is *hagios*. The Greek word *hagiadzo* means to purify, consecrate, set apart, make holy, and sanctify.

So much for word studies. Two questions remain. First, how is something or someone sanctified? Second, is it an instantaneous condition or it is something developed over time?

Christ's Perfection in History

Jesus Christ was born the Son of God. He did not earn this office; He was born to it. He was not a perfect man who somehow became God; He was a perfect man who was also the incarnate God, one person (for God is a Trinity: Father, Son, and Holy Ghost) with two natures: human and divine. This has been the testimony of the orthodox faith since at least the Council of Ephesus in A.D. 431. To cite Rushdoony's comments on this council once again: ". . . the Council made it clear that only God could be worshipped; not even Christ's humanity could be worshipped but only His deity. The humanity of Christ is not nor ever can be deified. The two natures are without confusion, even in the unique incarnation."[8] There is no

---

8. R. J. Rushdoony, *Foundations of Social Order: Studies in the Creeds and Counsels of the Early Church* (Fairfax, Virginia: Thoburn Press, [1968] 1978), p. 47.

need here to defend this theology in detail. God is God; man is not.

But if Christ was born a perfect human being, why did He have to suffer and die? Because He was our office-bearer. He suffered the punishment that sinful men deserve, so that they can escape it.

He lived a perfect life. While He began perfect, unstained by Adam's original sin, He nevertheless had to work out His perfection in fear and trembling: praying, shedding tears, and doing His Father's will in history. His perfection was a *demonstrated perfection* in history. It was not a perfection beyond history; it was *perfection within the confines of history.* It was perfection that left evidence behind.

And many other signs truly did Jesus in the presence of his disciples, which are not written in this book: But these are written, that ye might believe that Jesus is the Christ, the Son of God; and that believing ye might have life through his name (John 20:30-31).

So, Jesus *began* perfect, and He *matured* this perfection. He was not more perfect ethically at His death than at His birth, yet He was required by God to walk the highways of Palestine, performing miracles, confronting His opponents, training His disciples, and then dying on the cross. We dare not say that He was more perfect ethically at His death than at His birth, for perfection is perfection; it cannot be added to. Yet we also dare not deny that His perfection matured in history, giving evidence of what a righteous walk before God should be. Thus, Paul wrote: "Be ye followers of me, even as I also am of Christ" (I Cor. 11:1). Christ, as revealed in the Bible, is the only appropriate model for men to imitate.

For whom he did foreknow, he also did predestinate to be conformed to the image of his Son, that he might be the firstborn among many brethren (Rom. 8:29).

And be not conformed to this world: but be ye transformed by the renewing of your mind, that ye may prove what is the good, and acceptable, and perfect, will of God (Rom. 12:2).

So, Jesus went from perfection to perfection. This is a variation of what Cornelius Van Til calls the "full-bucket problem." God was perfect before He created the world. He did not need the world, as heretical mystics have proclaimed for millennia. A perfect Being has no needs that men can satisfy. Such a Being has no needs other than self-communion. Nevertheless, He created the world for His glory.

History pleases God. It does not add anything to Him, but it pleases Him. Thus, Van Til says that we must content ourselves with saying that to the glory of a perfect God (a "full bucket" of glory) is added glory from history ("filling"), yet this historical process of glorification does not add anything to His original glory. God was no less glorious before time began.

We see a similar problem for Creation Science. History to them is necessarily a process of degeneration. The idea of progressive sanctification in history is opposed to their system, as it also is to Rifkin's. Even before the Fall, if we take them seriously, there could have been no historical progress. Adam's world was as advanced as it could be. History, had Adam not sinned, would have been without improvement—a negative outworking of the "can't fill up a full bucket" problem. We can see this pessimism with respect to history in the book by Henry Morris and Gary Parker *What Is Creation Science?* (1982). It contains a lengthy section on entropy. They write:

> The creation model, on the other hand, shows the universe created in perfect organization. Particles, chemicals, planets, stars, organisms, and people were all created, so that long ages were not required for their development.
>
> Although the universe was thereafter to be maintained by the continuing processes of conservation, it is conceivable that its "degree of organization" would change. If so, however, the organization could not increase (having begun in perfection); it could only decrease.[9]

They do not mention Adam's Fall, so I must assume that they have in mind development within a hypothetical sin-free world when they write that "the organization could not increase (having begun in perfection); it could only decrease." If so, they have not understood the doctrine of progressive sanctification in history. There *can* be progress historically, even beginning with perfection, just as there can be glory added in history to a God who began perfectly glorious. Adam was told by God to dress the garden (Gen. 2:15), despite its original perfection. Even if Adam had not sinned, there would have been added knowledge and improvements in organization in the world. There will also be advancements beyond the final resurrection in the sin-free era of the New Heaven and New Earth. *History*

---

9. Henry M. Morris and Gary E. Parker, *What Is Creation Science?* (San Diego, California: Master Books, 1982), pp. 158, 161.

has meaning. We must be content with this apparent contradiction between original perfection and historical development.

We must respect the limitations of our own minds when we encounter any variation of the "full bucket" problem. We know that God is perfectly glorious. We also know that history has meaning. We dare not say that the creation, and especially man, adds something to God (Western mysticism, e.g., Meister Eckhart), yet we also dare not say that history is irrelevant to God and man (Eastern mysticism, e.g., the concept of *maya*, or the illusion of the material). God is glorious, and history has meaning and pleases God. God does everything perfectly, yet man has legitimate work to do. We must affirm both.

Sanctification: Both Definitive and Progressive

So it is with Christ's ethical perfection. He was perfect man and fully God at birth, yet His life, death, resurrection, and ascension were not meaningless. Christ possessed an *original perfection*, yet He also experienced a *historically maturing perfection*. He began with perfection appropriate to an infant; he matured to perfection appropriate to an adult.

We all are born in sin, and we all die in sin. Yet some people are saved, while others are lost. How can we make sense of this?

All regenerate people are made perfect in the sight of God through the perfection of Christ which is imputed ("declared") to them. Yet all regenerate people continue to sin.

> If we say that we have no sin, we deceive ourselves, and the truth is not in us. If we confess our sins, he is faithful and just to forgive us our sins, and to cleanse us from all unrighteousness (I John 1:8-9).

Here it is again: *cleansing*. We never escape the taint of sin, yet God provides a way for us to cleanse ourselves ethically before Him. Christ's perfection is imputed to us. God declares us "Not guilty!" at the time of our regeneration. Yet He also offers us a way to receive confirmation of that same declaration, day by day, as we sin, confess our sin, and go back to work.

Our limited goal, obviously, is the *steady reduction of sin* in our lives. The ultimate goal is *moral perfection*. Yet we never achieve this in history. All we can do is *mature* in righteousness. We do not evolve into perfection. We certainly do not evolve into God. But we are supposed to mature ethically in history.

This ethical process is two-fold: definitive ("declared by God from outside history into history") and progressive ("maturing by the grace of God inside history"). The definitive declaration of God—"Not guilty!"—is based on Christ's perfect work in history; God transfers Christ's moral perfection to us at conversion. Without this, we could not enter into God's presence in the heavenly sanctuary, any more than men (except for the high priest once a year) could enter into the holy of holies and live. Yet we are not to "rest on His laurels." We are to *work* on His laurels:

For by grace are ye saved through faith; and that not of yourselves: it is the gift of God: Not of works, lest any man should boast. For we are his workmanship, created in Christ Jesus unto good works, which God hath before ordained that we should walk in them (Eph. 2:8-10).

Visible Cleansing in History

We now return to the original theme concerning the progressive sanctification of the church in history: "That he might sanctify and cleanse it with the washing of water by the word, that he might present it to himself a glorious church, not having spot, or wrinkle, or any such thing; but that it should be holy and without blemish" (Eph. 5:26-27). What can this possibly mean?

What it *cannot* possibly mean is that the church of Jesus Christ will not mature ethically in history. There is progress for the church. In fact, there can be no long-term progress in the world ("common grace") without progress for the church ("special grace"). The world eats the crumbs that fall from the table of the saints.[10]

While God in all ages has imputed to the church the perfection of Christ—the only basis of its standing before God—it nevertheless matures: ethically, creedally, intellectually, and in every other way. It begins *in principle* without wrinkles, yet it also *develops toward* a condition of no wrinkles. Meanwhile, it has wrinkles.

Will the church *as a collective, covenantal organization* mature unto perfection? Paul says that it will. Will this be sin-free perfection before the return of Christ? John's first epistle says not: there will always be sin and the need for confession. But Paul insists: there will be ethical maturation in history.

What this means is that *Christ's ethical perfection* is imputed to *a col-*

---

10. Gary North, *Dominion and Common Grace*.

lective organization, the church. The church is *definitively sanctified*, as well as *progressively sanctified*. What happens to each Christian as he matures in the faith also happens to the church as an international collective unit. The basis of both kinds of sanctification is Christ's perfect life, death, resurrection, and ascension.

The church is being progressively sanctified (set apart) and cleansed ethically. Christians must not despair. Though in certain periods of history it seems as though there is no ethical progress, and sometimes even retrogression, in the life of the church, this historic process is not fundamentally different from backsliding in the lives of the saints. David's example is ours: the end result of confession is rebounding. The goals are ethical maturity and victory over sin.

Sanctification and Dominion: Progressive

But with victory over sin comes dominion. As Christians bring themselves progressively under the rule of God's law, they increase their influence. The positive feedback process of the biblical covenant brings them the external blessings of God. These blessings then serve as capital to be used in the subduing of the earth.

The kingdom of God has manifestations on earth. The salvation of people is only one such manifestation. We know people's hearts by their lives. Christ said by their fruits shall we know other men (Matt. 7:16). This means that *by men's outward lives* shall we know them, as well as by their verbal professions of faith. This means that there will be visible transformations from wrath to grace in the lives of individuals. But if this is true, then we will see changes in those areas of life in which God has placed these regenerate people—military, business, education, politics, and so forth. *The kingdom of God is to be manifested in the lives of regenerate people.* Therefore, institutions that are under the influence of these people will also be visibly transformed.[11]

Thus, the concept of progressive sanctification encompasses every area of life. Only if we argue that God will never convert large numbers of people can we legitimately conclude that the kingdom of God will not have earthly manifestations in history. If large numbers of people are eventually converted to faith in Christ, then there *will* be visible manifestations of the kingdom of God.

To argue that the kingdom of God is exclusively spiritual, invisi-

---

11. Gary North, *Liberating Planet Earth: An Introduction to Biblical Blueprints* (Ft. Worth, Texas: Dominion Press, 1987).

ble, and heavenly is to deny the legitimacy of church discipline for visible, public sins. It means the destruction of the integrity of the institutional church. It therefore means the impotence of Christ's church. When Dave Hunt tells us, "The Bible doesn't teach us to build society but instructs us to preach the gospel, for one's citizenship is in Heaven,"[12] he is implying that the church is not part of society, for he knows that the Bible *does* teach us to build the church. But the church *is* part of society. In fact, it is the primary institution that Christ came to establish. It is a training ground of dominion. It is a visible manifestation of God's heavenly kingdom. Hunt and all defeat-preaching premillennialists — though not all premillennialists preach defeat — are telling us that we can have only one set of citizenship papers, and that anything earthly cannot claim our allegiance. But the church is on earth, and it does claim our allegiance. So do our families. Shouldn't they be brought under Christ's dominion? Shouldn't they also reflect God's kingdom principles? And if the church and family are to reflect them, *where in the Bible does it say that all other human institutions are not to reflect these principles?*

It doesn't say this. This is why the preachers of visible defeat for Christians in history cannot do justice to the Bible. This is why Hunt rejects the idea of visible cleansing — progressive sanctification — in history, when he rejects Christian Reconstructionism because its "major focus is upon cleaning up the earth ecologically, politically, economically, sociologically, etc."[13] Ethical cleansing in history means *cultural responsibility for Christians in history*, and it is this, above all, that the defeat-preachers are desperate to avoid. They want to take the easy way out, figuratively (or even literally) standing on street corners passing out tracts, and doing it poorly, mindful of the fact that how well they pass out tracts is irrelevant to history, for the gospel will not save most of the recipients of the tracts anyway.

The only way to bring righteousness on earth is through the establishment by Christ of a visible international totalitarian bureaucracy, we are told. "During His thousand-year reign, Christ will visibly rule the world in perfect righteousness from Jerusalem and will impose peace on all nations."[14] Why is this the only way to estab-

---

12. *CIB Bulletin* (Feb. 1987), fourth page.
13. *Ibid.*, first page.
14. Dave Hunt, *Beyond Seduction: A Return to Biblical Christianity* (Eugene, Oregon: Harvest House, 1987), p. 250.

lish external peace? Because the church cannot do it. "How could the church be expected to establish the kingdom by taking over the world when even God cannot accomplish that without violating man's freedom of choice?"[15] Well, God can accomplish this the same way He presumably converted Mr. Hunt: *by regenerating people*. Certainly, if Mr. Hunt can be converted to Christ, others can, too. It is up to God how many He will bring to Himself through Christ.

> The king's heart is in the hand of the LORD, as the rivers of water: he turneth it whithersoever he will (Prov. 21:1)

> For whom he did foreknow, he also did predestinate to be conformed to the image of his Son, that he might be the firstborn among many brethren (Rom. 8:29).

> According as he hath chosen us in him before the foundation of the world, that we should be holy and without blame before him in love: Having predestinated us unto the adoption of children by Jesus Christ to himself, according to the good pleasure of his will (Eph. 1:4-5).

It does not take a top-down bureaucratic State run by Jesus in person in order to establish peace on earth. God can change people's hearts, send them His Spirit, and give them His law as a tool of government—self-government, family government, church government, and civil government. Mr. Hunt worries about the free will of men, yet he also admits (as every dispensationalist must admit) that Jesus will allow no freedom to sin without punishment in the millennial reign. Jesus will rule sinners with a rod of iron, they say. Yet dispensationalists tell us categorically that He will never rule the world in love through the hearts of a majority of people in the future.

Why not? Where is the power of the gospel?

Stagnation as Judgment

God's covenant governs the family, as well as the church. The family is a covenantal institution.[16] The same system of blessings and cursings that governs the church also governs the family. We read of such blessings in the fifth commandment: long life for honoring parents (Ex. 20:12), health (Ex. 23:25), and large families (Ps. 127:5).

Long-term stagnation—economically, demographically, intellectually—is a sign of God's displeasure. Growth must not be seen as inherently destructive. More than this: *a static culture cannot survive*. It

---

15. *Idem*.
16. Sutton, *That You May Prosper*, ch. 8.

has to change in order to survive. Population growth, like any kind of social growth, can be either a blessing or a curse (a prelude to disaster), depending on the *character of the people* who are experiencing the expansion. It is *ethics*, not growth as such, that determines the legitimacy of any given social growth process.

Greater numbers of people can and often do result in more efficient ways to fulfill the dominion covenant. The increasing division of labor permits greater specialization and greater output per unit of resource input.[17] Population growth is specifically stated to be a response of God to covenantal faithfulness, but it is also a tool of dominion. God's ethical universe is one of *positive feedback*: from victory unto victory. This ethical standard has visible effects in history. Ethical development, meaning progressive sanctification ("set-apartness") in terms of God's law, is eventually accompanied by the compound growth process, i.e., positive feedback, in human affairs.

Negative Feedback

Negative feedback is a limiting factor in a cursed world. The animals are not allowed to multiply and overcome the land. They are restrained by man or by "the forces of nature," meaning the environment's built-in limitations on the compound growth process. Negative feedback is the product of God's curse. There are indeed limits to growth. Growth is not automatic. Growth is not a zero-price process. But negative feedback is not the characteristic feature of the universe. The grace of God through faith in Jesus Christ is the characteristic feature of the universe: *resurrection, redemption, and restoration*.

When Rifkin's entropy postulate or any similar postulate characterizes the faith of a particular civilization, that civilization is under the curse of God. It was this lack of faith in the future which brought down the ancient city-states, including Rome. When classical civilization finally capitulated to the inherent pessimism of all cyclical history, nothing could save it.[18] Rome fell: to Christianity in the East (Byzantium), and to the barbarians in the West.

---

17. This does not mean that a growing population is always an economic blessing. Again, it is the ethical character of the people, not rates of biological reproduction, which determines the character of the growth process, either curse or blessing.

18. Charles Norris Cochrane, *Christianity and Classical Culture: A Study of Thought and Action from Augustus to Augustine* (New York: Oxford University Press, [1944] 1957).

Negative feedback is a sign of God's curse, even for individuals at the final judgment. Positive feedback is a sign of God's grace. It depends on one's ethical standing before God: "For whosoever hath, to him shall be given, and he shall have more abundance: but whosoever hath not, from him shall be taken away even that [which] he hath" (Matt. 13:12). There is growth for the godly and contraction for the ungodly. In neither case is there the status quo.

Humanism, Paganism, and the Status Quo

A zero-growth philosophy is the product of humanism, both secular and occult. It is a philosophy of the status quo—the preservation of the society of Satan. The universe is cursed; its resources are limited; but this reality is not evidence that favors a no-growth philosophy. The biblical doctrine of fallen man does not teach men to believe in a world that is cursed forever. Judgment and final restoration are coming. Time is bounded. Redeemed mankind must accomplish most of the dominion assignment in history. (Because of sin, mankind's historical fulfillment of the dominion assignment will never be perfectly complete.)

Humanists and satanists wish to deny the sovereignty of God, and therefore they affirm the sovereignty of the entropy process. They wish to escape the eternal judgment of God, so they affirm an impersonal finality for all biological life. Men have sometimes turned to a philosophy of historical cycles to help them avoid the testimony of God concerning linear history. Others have turned to the entropy process when they have adopted a Western version of linear history. They settle for slow decay rather than cycles. The goal in both cases is to escape the judgment of God. All of them prefer to avoid the truth: for covenant-breakers, the growth process will be cut short. A new downward cycle will triumph. Entropy will triumph. Anyway, *something* will triumph, but not the God of the Bible.

Rushdoony's comments on pagan antiquity's hostility to change is applicable to the zero-growth movement of the modern humanist world:

> The pagan hatred of *change* was also a form of asceticism [asceticism— G.N.], and it is present in virtually all anti-Christianity. The hatred of change leads to attempts to stop change, to stop history, and to create an end-of-history civilization, a final order which will end mutability and give man an unchanging world. Part of this order involves also the scientific efforts to abolish death. This hatred of change is a hatred of creation, and of

its movement in terms of God's purpose. Unlike the pagan and the humanist, the orthodox Christian is committed to a respect for creation. This respect for creation gave roots to science in the Christian west. It is not an accident of history that science in other cultures has had a limited growth and a quick withering. . . . The pagan perspective is one of a fundamental disrespect for creation, for the universe. The central problems for the Hellenic mind were *change* and *decay*. . . .[19]

The religion of zero growth is a religion of *decay* and *delay*. It proclaims inescapable decay, and it offers a short-term social program of delaying the effects on society of this supposedly inescapable decay. The proper response to this religion is to point to God, whose law-order, through grace, offers redeemed man an escape hatch from decay. The godly response is to promote long-term growth by means of a proclamation and enforcement of biblical law. We must proclaim *dominion through long-term growth* — a growth process which is the product of *progressive ethical sanctification*.

Conclusion

Christianity is not a religion of decay, but of life and progress. It is not a religion of delay, but of the speedy return of Christ in judgment (Rev. 22:20), after Christ has delivered up a developed earthly kingdom to God (I Cor. 15:24), and He has put all His enemies under His feet (I Cor. 15:25). Christianity is not a religion of entropy, either cosmic or social; it is a religion of progress, both cosmic and social.

We must not promote growth for its own sake. "Growth for the sake of growth is the ideology of the cancer cell," Edward Abbey once remarked. We are not to pursue the fruits of Christian faith; we are to pursue the roots. We are to conform ourselves and our institutions to the requirements of biblical law. The result will be long-term growth. Growth is a reward for righteous living, not a goal to pursue at the expense of righteous living. But we must not be deluded into believing that the fruit of righteousness is zero growth. Far less are we to pursue zero growth as a way of life. Our obligation is to seek first the kingdom of God; all these other things will be added unto us (Matt. 6:33). *Added* — not subtracted, and not kept the same.

---

19. R. J. Rushdoony, *Foundations of Social Order*, pp. 208-9.

Dominion requires the mastery of every area of life in terms of God's revealed laws. This in turn requires faithful preaching of the comprehensive effects of God's redemption. Christ bought back everything when He sacrificed Himself. What dominion produces is order and growth, as well as orderly growth.

When God brings judgment on rebellious societies, He brings disorder and stagnation. The modern no-growth humanists are proclaiming a gospel of stagnation. They want order—a top-down, centrally planned order—but they do not want growth. The very complexity of a modern growing economy threatens their ability to promote State-directed order. Thus, their ideology is hostile to growth of most kinds.

God says that such a view of His kingdom is evil, although it is appropriate to view Satan's kingdom in this way. To promote a zero-growth philosophy is to promote historical stalemate—a stalemate between God's kingdom and Satan's, between growth and decay, between good and evil. Satan wants a stalemate if he cannot get a victory. God will not allow Satan a stalemate.

Long-term economic growth is a product of God's grace in response to covenantal faithfulness, itself a gift from God. Long-term economic growth is therefore a denial of stalemated kingdoms. It is a demonstration of God's victory over Satan, creativity over destruction, ethics over power.

In summary:

1. The state of grace is a state of growth.
2. Humanism offers a graveyard society in place of Christianity.
3. The Hebrews in Egypt experienced population growth.
4. God drove the Canaanites out of Canaan slowly, so the animals would not take over Canaan in the meantime.
5. Better rule by God's enemies than dominion by animals.
6. God's people must be patient.
7. They are to establish their rule by their faithfulness to biblical law: dominion through ethics.
8. God promises external blessings to covenantally faithful societies.
9. Ethics, not entropy, is normative.
10. Nature is not normative; the Bible is.
11. History is linear.
12. The Hebrews failed ethically; therefore, they did not experience world-transforming growth.

13. Christians should recognize that God's judgments involve blessings as well as cursings.

14. Modern Christian pessimism has ignored this fact.

15. There is supposed to be ethical sanctification in history.

16. Christ's perfection matured in history.

17. Ethical sanctification is definitive (imputed perfection) and also progressive (ethical maturing).

18. God wants spiritual cleansing in the lives of His people.

19. Christians are declared "Not guilty!" to enable them to work faithfully.

20. The institutional church is to be cleansed progressively in history.

21. With victory over sin comes historical dominion.

22. Growth is a blessing of God.

23. Stagnation is a curse of God.

24. The universe is supposed to reflect the grace of God: resurrection, redemption, and restoration.

25. Humanists are now beginning to adopt a philosophy of the status quo—an anti-biblical outlook.

26. They prefer long entropic decay to the final judgment of God.

27. They want stagnation as a way to slow down decay.

28. Pagans hated change in the ancient world.

29. The zero-growth religion is a religion of decay and delay.

30. Christianity is a religion of dominion and growth.

9

RESURRECTION AND RECONSTRUCTION

Even as God the Son came and, by His incarnation, made history the area of victory, so by His continued work, history shall see the further implications of His kingship. Christ, as the perfect man, did not thereby **end** *history in fulfilling all righteousness, but rather opened up the "last days," the great era of the kingdom of God. His resurrection was not a surrender of history and the material world to the devil, but a declaration of His Lordship over creation and the promise, as the first-fruits of them that sleep, of His victory within it. By His virgin birth, His perfect obedience to the law, and His resurrection, He became the last Adam, the fountainhead of the new humanity, and hence the fulfilment of time and history,* **not** *the means to escape from it. . . . The death of Jesus was thus* **the true exodus** *of the people of God from slavery to freedom, from sin and death to life and righteousness in Him. Hebrews 9:15-23 made clear that "the death of the testator," Jesus Christ, made His testament law and opened up that inheritance promised and shadowed in the old covenant for the people of the new. The material and spiritual blessings promised therefore in the old covenant begin to come into true force by means of the death of Jesus Christ.*

R. J. Rushdoony[1]

The doctrine of Christ's resurrection in history is fundamental to a proper understanding of the progressive conquest of the effects of evil and the curses of God over nature. If we ignore this crucial biblical doctrine, we will be easily misled. It becomes too easy for Christians who focus on the effects of Adam's Fall and God's curse of nature to believe that the world is inevitably running down. Such a

---

1. R. J. Rushdoony, *Thy Kingdom Come: Studies in Daniel and Revelation* (Fairfax, Virginia: Thoburn Press, [1971] 1978), pp. 90-91.

worldview plays into the hands of zero-growth humanists like Jeremy Rifkin. But Rifkin is more dangerous than simply another zero-growth humanist, for he is self-conscious in his attempt to undermine Christians' faith in the earthly future. He is self-conscious in his attempt to call the dominion covenant into question. He is self-conscious in his denial of future historical progress. In this sense, he is radically anti-Christian.

The Idea of Historical Progress

The origin of the idea of progress in history was exclusively Western; it was originally a Christian idea. Only with the widespread acceptance of the biblical concept of linear time did men begin to believe that there could be earthly progress. They began to act in terms of a view of life that says that whatever a man does lives after him, and that future generations will be different to some degree because he lived, worked, and died exactly when he did.

Nevertheless, linear history is not, in and of itself, progressive history. Something more is needed: the idea of compound growth, or *positive feedback*. It is not simply that history is linear; it is that it is also *progressive*. Such a view of history rests squarely on Deuteronomy 28:1-14. It also rests on the notion of *covenantal reinforcement*, as described in Deuteronomy 8:18:

> But thou shalt remember the LORD thy God: for it is he that giveth thee power to get wealth, that he may establish his covenant which he sware unto thy fathers, as it is this day.

This is positive feedback: covenantal faithfulness brings external blessings from God, which in turn are supposed to reinforce people's confidence in the covenant, leading them to greater faithfulness, bringing them added blessings, and so forth. It was the postmillennial optimism of early Calvinism and Puritanism that first introduced this worldview of culture-wide, compounding, covenantal growth to Western civilization.[2] The vision of Deuteronomy 28:1-14 captivated the Puritans: the external cultural blessings that accompany covenantal faithfulness.

The development of the Calvinistic and Puritan doctrine of both

---

2. *The Journal of Christian Reconstruction* , VI (Summer 1979): "Symposium on Puritanism and Progress."

spiritual and cultural progress reshaped the West. For the first time in human history, men were given a full-blown idea of progress, which was above all a doctrine of ethical progress. This vision was secularized by the *philosophes* of the Enlightenment, but that secularized version of progress is rapidly fading from the humanist West.[3] Belief in the universality of entropy (meaning inevitable decay) is only one of the causes of this growing pessimism, but it is a powerful one.

In the twentieth century, "pessimillennialism" — premillennialism and amillennialism — have been the dominant eschatologies. Those who hold such views have self-consciously rejected the idea of visible, institutional, social progress. They insist that the Bible does not teach such a hope with respect to the world prior to Christ's personal, physical return in judgment.

I realize that there are premillennialists who will take offense at this statement. They will cite their obligations under Luke 19:13: "Occupy till I come." (The original Greek actually says, "do business," not "occupy": New American Standard Bible; also translated as, "trade with this": New English Bible.) But the leaders of the *traditional* premillennial movement are quite self-conscious about their eschatology, and we need to take them seriously as spokesmen. For example, John Walvoord, author of many books on eschatology, and the long-time president of Dallas Theological Seminary, the premier dispensational institution, has not minced any words in this regard. In an interview with *Christianity Today* (Feb. 6, 1987), Kenneth Kantzer asked:

Kantzer: For all of you who are not postmils, is it worth your efforts to improve the physical, social, political situation on earth?

Walvoord: The answer is yes and no. We know that our efforts to make society Christianized is futile because the Bible doesn't teach it. On the other hand, the Bible certainly doesn't teach that we should be indifferent to injustice and famine and to all sorts of things that are wrong in our current civilization. Even though we know our efforts aren't going to bring a utopia, we should do what we can to have honest government and moral laws. It's very difficult from Scripture to advocate massive social improvement efforts, because certainly Paul didn't start any, and neither did Peter. They assumed that civilization as a whole is hopeless and subject to God's judgment (pp. 5-I, 6-I).

---

3. Robert A. Nisbet, *History of the Idea of Progress* (New York: Basic Books, 1980), ch. 9.

He then went on to observe that premillennialists run most of the rescue missions. "Premillennialists have a pretty good record in meeting the physical needs of people." This is quite true, but there is no doubt from his words that he does not believe it is possible for Christians to influence the creation of a world in which there will be freedom, righteousness, and productivity — a world in which fewer rescue missions will be necessary. His vision of social action is to get people out of the gutter. This is because his view of the gospel is to take people out of this world — first mentally and then physically, at the Rapture.

Now, let me say that I believe in the Rapture of the saints into the sky at the return of Christ in judgment. As far as I know, every Bible-believing group believes this. What most Christian groups have denied throughout church history is that this gathering of the saints takes place before the final judgment. The Rapture of the saints inaugurates the final judgment. There is a tendency for dispensationalists to argue that their opponents have denied the Rapture just because they date the Rapture at the end of history rather than at the beginning of the seven-year tribulation period or at the beginning of the millennium. The debate within Christianity is not over the reality of the so-called Rapture, but only over its dating in history. The non-premillennialists expect the Rapture at the close of history.

Before the Rapture, we will see the public triumph of God's people in history, in every area of life. Jesus said in His Great Commission: "All power is given unto me in heaven *and in earth*" (Matt. 28:18). The positive effects of this covenantal progress of Christ's people in history will be manifested in man's physical environment.

Overcoming Decay

Physical decay will be completely overcome at the final judgment. All Christians believe this. Henry Morris has commented on this aspect of the final judgment in his exposition of Revelation 22:3: "The agelong curse is gone. There is no more death and no more sin. The earth and its inhabitants, indeed the entire creation, are henceforth to thrive in fullest vigor forever. None will ever age, nothing will ever be lost, all work will be productive and enduring. The entropy law, the so-called second law of thermodynamics, will be repealed. Information will nevermore become confused, ordered systems will not deteriorate into disorder, and no longer will energy have to be expended merely to overcome friction and dissipation into nonrecoverable heat."[4]

Implicitly, premillennialist scientists have to assume that entropy will be partially overcome during the millennium. Christ returns in His perfect humanity. He rules with perfect knowledge, perfect ethics, and perfect power. All people will obey His perfect words. Their rebellion will be cut short. Thus, I presume that premillennialists would say that there will be "a net decrease in the rate of entropy" on earth. Unfortunately, premillennial Creation Scientists have not discussed the implications of this for their theory of universal, uniformitarian entropy.

The postmillennial creationist must take a similar but nevertheless different approach. The millennium will not be inaugurated by the physical return of Christ. The kingdom now operates. It will be steadily manifested by the spread of the gospel and by the progressive sanctification of men and institutions.[5] It will not be a mixed economy of eternally living and sin-free people who work alongside death-cursed, pre-resurrection people. Men will find ways of using God's gifts — better knowledge, less expensive and less polluting energy sources, better medical techniques, etc. — to overcome the "natural" effects of degeneration processes. Whether the universe's total of entropy will be increased or reduced is impossible to say. Who knows for sure that the universe is a closed system, or what the total of entropy is or will be? How can such a process be measured? The whole question is irrelevant for human action.

On this point, we agree with the *implicit* position of premillennialists: the reduction of entropy's effects during an earthly millennium. As men conform themselves ethically to God, their ability to overcome the *cursed effects* of the entropy process will increase, just as it increased in the West after the West adopted Christianity. There will be less confusion, less lost information, better techniques of conserving energy and obtaining more of it inexpensively. The cursed effects of entropy — which are what count, not simply the presence of entropy itself in the universe as a whole — will be progressively overcome, in time and on earth.

Sadly, Christians have failed to understand the cosmological im-

---

4. Henry M. Morris, *The Revelation Record: A Scientific and Devotional Commentary on the Book of Revelation* (Wheaton, Illinois: Tyndale House, 1983), p. 467.

5. David Chilton, *Paradise Restored: A Biblical Theology of Dominion* (Ft. Worth, Texas: Dominion Press, 1985).

plications of Christ's death and resurrection. The resurrection of Christ was the *definitive* overcoming of the cursed aspects of the entropy process, announced in history. It points to the final resurrection (final judgment), the *final* overcoming of the cursed entropy process. In the meantime, we experience the *progressive* overcoming of entropy's cursed effects. We are promised an extension of human life spans (Isa. 65:20), a reduction in sickness (Ex. 23:25-26), and therefore a population explosion. Christianity is a *religion of resurrection*.

Miracles and Providence

The Creation Science movement divides nature into two segments: a scientific realm governed by entropy and a miraculous realm which is governed directly by God. Science applies only to the entropy-bound realm of nature, where "natural laws" rule. They admit, of course, that this entropy-bound realm is under God's control, for they argue that entropy exists because of God's curse. Nevertheless, they use entropy as a constant—a supposedly mutually agreed-upon constant—in their debates with Darwinians.

Clearly, the Bible teaches that God performs miracles. Obviously, these miracles are not governed by the law of entropy. They are comparable to "free goods." In a world under God's curse, there are very few free goods. There is scarcity. But even before Adam's Fall, there was always some kind of scarcity: it always takes time to accomplish anything. We walk only one step at a time. Adam did before the Fall, and redeemed people will also walk this way after the resurrection.

Nevertheless, in a capitalist society, we normally see falling prices. If there were no counterfeiting of money, either by private individuals or commercial banks, the increase in the output of goods would tend to force prices lower.[6] This steady increase in production testifies to the ability of men to overcome the effects of scarcity, though not perfectly—not at zero price.

Rifkin is outraged by the productivity of capitalism. He says that capitalism is destroying the environment, that we are using up our natural resources. Yet the price of raw materials keeps falling, especially in economies (such as Switzerland) that do not pour fiat money into the economy. We continue to discover new natural

---

6. Gary North, *An Introduction to Christian Economics* (Nutley, New Jersey: Craig Press, 1973), ch. 9: "Downward Price Flexibility and Economic Growth."

resources all the time; this discovery process has been accelerating for two centuries.[7] Per capita wealth continues to rise, *exactly as God promised the Hebrews.*

What we are seeing in economic life is a reduction in the effects of many degradative processes. This indicates that men can overcome these effects through covenantal faithfulness to God, which means obedience to God's economic laws.[8] Western capitalism stands as a historic testimony against Eastern mysticism, and also against any social theory which asserts the dominion of entropy over covenant-keeping man.

In short, God's grace to covenant-keeping societies comes through their obedience to revealed covenant law (Deut. 28:1-14). It is not simply that God promises a miracle now and then, in order to break "the steady downward pressure of entropy." It is that God promises to lift the cursed effects of entropy in response to covenantal faithfulness. The "miracle" of zero miscarriages — a genetic reduction in entropy — is to become the continuing standard for the whole society, God promised Israel (Ex. 23:26).

God is not some Eastern karmic force. For every benefit, He does not impose a loss. Two people can trade voluntarily, and both people involved can come out winners. There is no Eastern "balance of karma," any more than there is some sort of autonomous "balance of nature." We live in a world of covenantal law. *The environment responds positively or negatively to mankind in terms of a society's covenantal faithfulness.*[9] God promised that the hornets would go before the Hebrews and drive out the perverse Canaanites. God sent plagues on Israel's enemies from time to time, and in response to the evil of the Hebrews, He sometimes sent plagues on them.

What this should teach us is that the so-called "natural law" is covenantal in the same way that miracles are. Natural law is governed by God; better put, natural law is in fact the very process of God's government over nature. God responds in His ordinary government of the universe to covenant-keepers and covenant-breakers: their

---

7. Julian Simon, *The Ultimate Resource* (Princeton: Princeton University Press, 1981), ch. 3. For a somewhat revised application of Simon's thesis, see Gary North, *Moses and Pharaoh: Dominion Religion vs. Power Religion* (Tyler, Texas: Institute for Christian Economics, 1985), pp. 328-33.

8. Gary North, *The Sinai Strategy: Economics and the Ten Commandments* (Tyler, Texas: Institute for Christian Economics, 1986).

9. Ray R. Sutton, *That You May Prosper: Dominion By Covenant* (Tyler, Texas: Institute for Christian Economics, 1987).

"natural" environment either rebels against them or becomes progressively less threatening. What we learn from God's miraculous interventions into the affairs of men, blessings and cursings, is supposed to teach us a principle of God's continuing providential but "non-miraculous" governing of His creation.

Reducing the Curse's Degradative Processes

The Darwinians see no link between man's ethics and nature's laws. This includes New Age mystics such as Rifkin, at least when they are pretending to be scientific. Unfortunately, I see no evidence in the writings of the Scientific Creationists that they have recognized this link between ethics and nature. They know that the curse will be lifted from nature after the final judgment, but they see this as a totally discontinuous event. They see the arrival of a supposedly zero-entropy world only after history ends, but by the time that day arrives, the cosmic effects of entropy will have created even more noise and confusion in the world than we see today. Creation Scientists do not speak of the possibility of a *continuous, progressive reduction in the rate of man-threatening decay.* They do not discuss the possibility that God promises to reduce His curse of the earth progressively in response to the progressive ethical sanctification of individuals and societies.

I contend that at least some of them have refused to discuss this possibility for three reasons: 1) they have adopted something like Rifkin's understanding of entropy; 2) they are eschatological pessimists who have rejected the idea that there can be progressive sanctification in human history; and 3) they are antinomians who have rejected the doctrine of the covenant, which implies the continuing validity of God's revealed covenantal law. In short, they share too many presuppositions with the Darwinians with respect to their doctrine of God, man, and law.

There is a legitimate though unfortunate reason for their silence: they have not read Rifkin. This may be due to a fourth cause for their silence: they are not really interested in social theory. But they should recognize, first, that physical science at any point in time is shaped by prevailing social theory, including presuppositions about the proper role of science. Second, physical science in turn shapes social theory. Science is not conducted in a social and intellectual vacuum.

We need to distinguish cosmological speculation that parades as science from the kind of science that goes on in the laboratory. Obviously, the prevailing cosmology will be restructured when men begin to adopt the biblical view of covenantal blessings and covenantal cursings. Men will be less tempted to elevate a phenomenon such as entropy to a position of supposedly crucial importance for mankind's view of time and space. Science will also be affected. When their theological presuppositions shift, men's scientific and cosmological presuppositions will also shift. Science, like all areas of the human intellect, is a very religious endeavor; there is zero neutrality involved.

When Christians who have not adopted an eschatology of defeat, but who also maintain belief in the Bible as the only source of valid cosmological speculation, begin to apply themselves to the discipline of natural science, the modern humanistic (and mystical) version of uniformitarian entropy will no longer be taken seriously in the social sciences. Even today, it can hardly be taken seriously for social science, but a lot of people who bought and read Rifkin's books may not understand this.

One of the remarkable ironies about modern cosmological speculation is that all three of the present-day cosmologies — the "big bang theory," the steady-state theory (few scientists still hold this view), and the oscillating universe theory — were present in early Greek philosophical speculation.[10] The cosmological outlines remain the same; only the footnotes change.

What is central to these cosmological theories is the idea of an *autonomous universe*. God did not create it, He does not sustain it, and He will not judge it. Science is conducted today on the presupposition that men can ignore God in their scientific endeavors. The result is a mental world in which the best minds of science believe that without a human observer, the world of subatomic physics (and perhaps even the reality that the subatomic world supports) is nothing more than statistical wave functions, statistical probabilities. This is highly sophisticated madness. God will not be mocked.

To take the theoretical speculations of modern physical science and apply bits and pieces of these intellectual constructs to social theory is to court disaster, personal and intellectual, and possibly even social. If intellectuals begin to take seriously the idea of entropy as the basis of a reconstruction of the world's economy into a steady

---

10. Stephen Toulmin and June Goodfield, *The Discovery of Time* (New York: Harper Torchbook, [1965] 1966), pp. 254-57.

state economy, and then they begin to preach such nonsense, we will find the philosophical basis of Western liberty and Western prosperity under attack. If voters take such speculation seriously, we will see the collapse of the world economy. That might make Jeremy Rifkin happy. It should not make Christians happy.

Christians should begin to think about social theory. They need to think about the implications of such biblical doctrines as the Fall, the curse of the ground, and the resurrection of Christ. They need to think carefully about the relationships between obedience to God's covenantal law and external prosperity, including biological transformations. They need to take seriously the biblical imperative of self-government under law.

When they do, they will no longer take seriously Jeremy Rifkin.

Conclusion

Orthodox Christianity preaches the triumph of Jesus at Calvary. But this triumph must be seen as three-fold: definitive, progressive, and final. To deny the progressive nature of sanctification for the individual is to deny the possibility of personal spiritual maturity and progress. To deny the progressive nature of sanctification for the church is to deny the improvement of the creeds and to deny the healing of society by the preaching of the gospel. To deny progressive sanctification socially is to deny the power of the gospel in history. It is to affirm the progressive power of Satan's followers in history. It is to preach the historic defeat of Christians, the gospel, and the Holy Spirit. *This is the ultimate form of pessimism.* It is the pessimism that Satan wants Christians to believe above all other kinds of pessimism.

This pessimism has deeply crippled the social vision of six-day creationists, who should have been the pioneers of a new, anti-humanistic worldview. Because their pessimism regarding the future has dominated their approach to science, they have focused their attention on the Fall of Adam rather than the resurrection of Christ. They have made the second law of thermodynamics their key argument, rather than the much better argument that the evolutionists do not have sufficient time available to have made possible the evolution of the universe or the species through natural selection.

What we should expect, as creationists, is that God intends to remove the cursed effects of the Fall as Christians mature in history.

The cause-and-effect relationship between man's ethics and nature that brought on God's curse—by cursing the second law of thermodynamics—still exists. The progressive overcoming of sin in the lives of a growing number of converts will have its effects in nature: a progressive overcoming of the cursed aspects of the universe, including the second law of thermodynamics.

When six-day creationists at last admit their mistake and begin to rethink their apologetic strategy, they will begin to produce first-rate social theorists from among their ranks.

In summary:

1. Christ did not surrender history at His resurrection.
2. The death of Christ opened up the inheritance of the world to Christians.
3. The idea of progress is a biblical idea.
4. It affirms progressive linear history.
5. Covenantal faithfulness of Christians brings forth God's external blessings in history.
6. This positive vision of the future has been stolen by various humanist groups since the early 1700's.
7. Dallas Seminary's John Walvoord says that our efforts to reform society are futile.
8. Christ has been given all power on earth (Matt. 28:18).
9. One of the visible effects of this power will be the triumph of the gospel in history: the postmillennial faith.
10. The victory of Christ in history involves a progressive conquest over the physical effects of God's curse.
11. Creation Scientists admit this with respect to the world beyond the final judgment.
12. They implicitly assume this partial triumph during the millennial reign of Christ, but they never talk about it.
13. The postmillennialist sees this conquest over the curse as progressive.
14. This is a consequence of Christ's resurrection and His empowering of the church in history.
15. Miracles testify to the incomplete reign of entropy.
16. Capitalism's economic growth also testifies to the ability of men to overcome entropy's cursed effects.
17. Rifkin hates capitalism.
18. In voluntary trade, entropy's cursed effects are overcome: both people win.
19. Man's total environment responds positively to a society's covenantal faithfulness.

20. Darwinists deny any link between ethics and the operations of nature.

21. Creation Scientists have not publicly challenged the Darwinists on this point.

22. They seem to have adopted Rifkin's views concerning entropy.

23. They are also eschatological pessimists, as Rifkin is.

24. They agree with Rifkin that obeying biblical law cannot restore the fallen world.

25. Science is never neutral.

26. Scientists are heavily influenced by the prevailing world view of scientific culture.

27. If Creation Scientists were self-consciously covenantal and optimistic, this would be reflected in their attitudes toward the thesis of the universal reign of entropy.

28. The universe is not autonomous.

29. We must not transfer to social theory humanist theories of autonomous nature.

30. Christians must begin to think seriously about social theory.

31. They must abandon Jeremy Rifkin's pagan social theory.

32. Christians must begin to have faith in God and in history.

33. Pessimism toward the success of the gospel in history paralyzes Christians in their efforts to rethink social theory.

34. Pessimism regarding the triumph of the gospel in history is the worst sort of pessimism possible.

35. It is just this pessimism that has crippled the worldview of Creation Scientists.

CONCLUSION

The fact is, the assumptions upon which modern man and woman base their sense of meaning, purpose and direction in the world is false. Not just partially false, but 100 percent false. Progress, science, and technology have not resulted in greater order and value in the world, but their opposite. This is not a purely philosophical or sociological observation. . . . The modern world completely and utterly contradicts the second major law of thermodynamics — a law which has guided the entire age of physics. Like a giant blind spot, we have refused to understand the profound implications of this law even as we have selectively applied it in order to create the modern technological society.

Jeremy Rifkin[1]

The "Entropy Law" is simply the latest and most scientific sounding of Satan's blueprints for Christ's defeat in history. It is indicative of the crisis in the Christian worldview today that so many Bible-believing, well-educated Christians have taken seriously a whole series of misuses of the legitimate concept of entropy. What is desperately needed today to restore Christians' confidence in the future of the church and also to reconstruct science in terms of a consistent Christian worldview is a new Reformation. This Reformation must be based on five principles: the doctrine of the absolute sovereignty of God,[2] God's hierarchical covenants,[3] biblical law,[4]

---

1. Jeremy Rifkin, *The Emerging Order*, pp. 61-62.
2. Gary North, *Unconditional Surrender: God's Program for Victory* (3rd ed.; Ft. Worth, Texas: Dominion Press, 1987), ch. 1.
3. Ray R. Sutton, *That You May Prosper: Dominion By Covenant* (Tyler, Texas: Institute for Christian Economics, 1987).
4. R. J. Rushdoony, *The Institutes of Biblical Law* (Nutley, New Jersey: Craig Press, 1973); Greg L. Bahnsen, *Theonomy in Christian Ethics* (2nd ed.; Phillipsburg, New Jersey: Presbyterian & Reformed, 1984).

Van Til's presuppositional apologetic method,[5] and optimism about the long-run earthly future.[6] What is also needed is a new scientific paradigm based on this new Reformation.

This new Reformation must be institutionally decentralized, confident about the church's role in history, orderly, and uncompromising. It must have its own agenda, its own blueprints for social reconstruction,[7] and its own financing. It must break with radical apocalypticism, whether fundamentalist apocalypticism or New Age apocalypticism. It must be based self-consciously on the biblical concept of continuity in history.[8] It must be based on the biblical idea of progress.[9] It must fight ideas that are incorrect with something much better: a consistent biblical worldview.

Any concept of science that is self-consciously Christian must begin with the Creator-creature distinction. Man is made in God's image, and therefore he can think God's thoughts after Him. Covenant-breaking man's mind is ethically fallen, but covenant-keeping people are given the mind of Christ (I Cor. 2:16). This increase in the orderliness of man's mind is the product of ethical transformation through God's grace. It has nothing to do with any scientific law of entropy. This increase in clarity of vision is not matched by some increase in confusion elsewhere in the universe.

The creation reflects the orderly character of God the Creator. The perceived disorder is in part the product of man's fallen mind and in part the product of God's curse of the world. But Christianity must proclaim the historical reality of Christ's resurrection and ascension. This resurrection leads in history to the progressive transformation and liberation of nature from God's curse, just as surely as the Fall of Adam led in history to a discontinuous transfor-

---

5. Cornelius Van Til, *The Defense of the Faith* (rev. ed.; Phillipsburg, New Jersey: Presbyterian & Reformed, 1963); *In Defense of Biblical Christianity*, 6 vols. (Presbyterian & Reformed, 1967-1976).

6. Roderick Campbell, *Israel and the New Covenant* (Tyler, Texas: Geneva Divinity School Press, [1954] 1981); David Chilton, *Paradise Restored: A Biblical Theology of Dominion* (Ft. Worth, Texas: Dominion Press, 1985); David Chilton, *The Days of Vengeance: An Exposition of the Book of Revelation* (Ft. Worth, Texas: Dominion Press, 1987).

7. See the Biblical Blueprints Series published by Dominion Press, Ft. Worth, Texas.

8. Gary North, *Moses and Pharaoh: Dominion Religion vs. Power Religion* (Tyler, Texas: Institute for Christian Economics, 1985), ch. 12.

9. Gary North, *Dominion and Common Grace: The Biblical Basis of Progress* (Tyler, Texas: Institute for Christian Economics, 1987).

mation and enslavement of nature. To preach the triumph of the curse is to deny the triumph of Christ at Calvary. To construct a methodology of science in terms of the historically irrevocable effects of the second law of thermodynamics is to ignore a fundamental doctrine of the Christian faith.

This is precisely what Rifkin has done: *denied the definitive, progressive, and final universe-transforming power of Christ's resurrection in history.* Creation Science has denied the definitive and progressive universe-transforming power of Christ's resurrection in history, although affirming the post-historic power of the resurrection. This denial of the power of the resurrection has rendered them intellectually incapable of successfully refuting Rifkin.

Rifkin's Appeal

Rifkin's appeal is to those Christians who have given up on the future, who have abandoned personal responsibility for working to bring the future under the covenantal reign of Christ. That appeal has been sporadically successful. There is a war on by the fundamentalist apocalyptists to defend their cherished cultural pessimism and their equally cherished apocalypticism. Rifkin is a self-conscious humanistic accomplice of Christian "pessimillennialists" in this work of cultural erosion. He has added his cry of despair to the growing chorus of Christian despair concerning the diminishing effects of the gospel in history. He looks for the steady-state stagnation of socialism to delay the judgment; "pessimillennialists" look for the physical return of Christ to speed up the judgment. They have all turned their backs on the idea of historical progress, one of Christianity's most valuable contributions to the West—in fact, one of the crucial foundations in the creation of the West.

Rifkin has offered a worldview in the name of Western science (the second law of thermodynamics) that breaks with modern Western science, and especially Western technology. He has also offered this worldview in the name of a new "Reformation Christianity" that breaks with Christianity. Rifkin argues that the coming changes in the world economy will produce a change in religion. "The first Protestant Reformation will not outlive the economic age it grew up with."[10] This argument is suspiciously similar to the old Marxist doctrine that religion is simply part of the ideological

---

10. Rifkin, *Emerging Order*, p. xv.

superstructure that is built on top of the true structure of society, the mode of production. Marx wrote in the *Communist Manifesto* (1848): "What else does the history of ideas prove, than that intellectual production changes its character in proportion as material production is changed? The ruling ideas of each age have ever been the ideas of its ruling class."[11] Again, "The mode of production in material life determines the general character of the social, political and spiritual processes of life."[12] Lo and behold, we find that *The Emerging Order* is divided into two sections. He titles Section I: "The Great Economic Transformation." He titles Section II, "The Religious Response."

Rifkin scores initial points with conservative Christians by attacking liberalism. Liberalism is a dying philosophy in our day, he says. But his reason for saying this is based on his philosophy of *economic determinism* (one of twentieth-century liberalism's most precious creeds, taken from Marx): "The twilight of liberalism is upon us because the basis for liberal society no longer exists. Liberalism is founded on one overriding precondition—the possibility of *unlimited economic growth*."[13]

Here it is again, *precondition*. It is specifically an *economic* precondition. You know, as in "economic substructure" or "mode of production." But historically, the argument is wrong. Classical liberalism preceded modern economic growth. It began to be formulated in the seventeenth century, especially by John Locke toward the end of the century. The Scottish Enlightenment—Adam Fergusson, David Hume, Adam Smith, etc.—developed the premises of classical liberalism during the first three-quarters of the eighteenth century. Then, around 1780—*after* the fundamental tenets of classical liberalism were in place—the Industrial Revolution in Britain began. There was feedback between the ideology and the growing economy, just as there will always be feedback between covenantal law, covenantal faithfulness, and covenantal blessings (Deut. 8:18). This hardly means that economic growth was dependent on the economic precondition of economic growth. If anything, *it was the growing acceptance of the economic recommendations of classical liberalism that made possible the West's economic growth.*

---

11. Karl Marx and Frederick Engels, "The Manifesto of the Communist Party" (1848), in *Selected Works*, 3 vols. (Moscow: Progress Publishers, [1969] 1977), I, p. 125.
12. Marx, "Preface," *A Contribution to the Critique of Political Economy* (New York: International Library, [1859] 1904), p. 11.
13. Rifkin, *Emerging Order*, p. 7.

What were the most important ideas of classical liberalism? They included these: the autonomy of the individual, the rule of law, the desirability of republican forms of government, and "life, liberty, and the pursuit of happiness." Twentieth-century liberalism abandoned the classical liberal's faith in the free market economy, and has added other doctrines supposedly more fundamental than the older ones: equality, the need for economic planning, the necessity of compulsory State education, secular humanism, the autonomy of the State from revealed religion, and the use of legislation as an instrument of social change ("salvation by law"). But to single out economic growth as *the* foundation of liberalism is to stack the intellectual deck.

To prove that he is no liberal—the heart of Rifkin's deception of conservative Christians—he calls liberalism into question by calling economic growth into question. He tries to separate himself from liberalism by writing a book against economic growth. Yet in calling Christians to follow him in this supposedly anti-liberal intellectual reformation, he is calling on Christians to throw out one of the fundamental conclusions of Christianity: the doctrine of progress.

Those Christians whose theological and especially eschatological presuppositions are implicitly or explicitly based on a rejection of the link between Christianity and historical progress (God's covenantal blessings in history) are intellectually hampered in challenging Rifkin.

Rifkin vs. Progress

Consider his class analysis of the history of liberalism. Does it differ in any major respect from Marx's? "In essence, what the modern liberal is attempting to do is to take principles which were first enunciated over 300 years ago as the doctrine of a single class, the bourgeoisie, and extend them to all members of society."[14] Why this accent on *class philosophy*? Why should such a concept be important in a book about the supposed "new Reformation"? Recall Marx's words introducing Part I of the *Communist Manifesto*: "The history of all hitherto existing society is the history of class struggles."[15] Four paragraphs later, Marx wrote: "Our epoch, the epoch of the bourgeoisie, possesses, however, this distinctive feature: it has simplified the class antagonisms."

---

14. *Ibid.*, p. 36.
15. Marx, *Selected Works*, I, p. 108.

Rifkin says that he is against progress, especially technological progress. "The second law of thermodynamics, therefore, contradicts the modern notion of progress."[16] He says that economic growth cannot go on much longer. He says that a new worldview will accompany this change in the economic substructure. There will be a new Reformation. This Reformation will bring with it ecological reform, land reform,[17] more government-enforced economic equality,[18] simpler lifestyles, and reduced per capita wealth. He says that men must realize at last that man is subject to nature, and not nature to man.[19] In short, what Rifkin is opposed to is Western civilization in general and the Protestant work ethic in particular. "The Calvinist individual who for hundreds of years sought salvation through productivity and the exploitation of nature is now being challenged by a Christian person who seeks salvation by conserving and protecting God's creation. *The Protestant 'work' ethic is being replaced by the Protestant 'conservation' ethic.*"[20]

Now we know who the enemy is. We are.

Jeremy Rifkin spotted his targets, and he was able to pick off many of them, especially in the neo-evangelical Christian world, a world in which liberal-sounding rhetoric and cast-off humanistic intellectual fads have immediate appeal. But he has also appealed to some literate fundamentalists. How can this be? How can a self-professed New Age social theorist gain support from Bible-believing Christians for his radically pessimistic conclusions?

First, he understood that their premillennial eschatology is inherently hostile to the idea of progress. His *official* worldview is also hostile to historical progress. (If he is as dedicated to a Marxist view of history as he appears to be dedicated to the rhetoric of Marxist revolutionaries, then his official worldview is a sham. But perhaps he really does believe all the nonsense he writes about entropy and the decline of Western civilization. In either case, he is both dangerous and wrong.) He recognized that he could appeal to an already existing mind-set.

Second, he recognized that the favorite intellectual defense of the creationist movement was based on the second law of thermodynam-

---

16. *Emerging Order*, p. 63.
17. *Ibid.*, p. 84.
18. *Ibid.*, p. 56.
19. *Ibid.*, p. 61.
20. *Ibid.*, p. 255.

ics. This provided him with a second tactical approach: the appeal to entropy. What could creationists say in response? That they really *do* believe in historical progress—progressive sanctification in history—despite their commitment to the second law as an intellectual weapon against the evolutionists? No, they have remained silent. They recognize that Rifkin's brand of socialism is wrong, but they have not been willing to scrap their own pessimistic eschatologies and their implicit acceptance of entropy as binding in social theory, as well as in physical theory. They are even willing to cite Rifkin's views on entropy as if he were a representative and respectable humanistic social theorist, simply because of his commitment to entropy as an inescapable concept.[21]

Rifkin and the West's Failure of Nerve

What we are witnessing in the final decades of the twentieth century is the social and religious phenomenon described by Gilbert Murray as *the failure of nerve*.[22] Murray was describing the final centuries of classical Greece, but the phrase applies just as well to Western Civilization today, in part because it is the spiritual and intellectual heir of humanistic Greek culture. By the time of Christ, this pessimism had combined with various apocalyptic visions of the imminent transformation of man and the cosmos. This vision of defeat affected members of the early church, not just the pagan Greeks and Romans. As David Chilton writes:

> The "apocalyptists" expressed themselves in unexplained and unintelligible symbols, and generally had no intention of making themselves really understood. Their writings abound in pessimism: no real progress is possible, nor will there be any victory for God and His people in history. We cannot even see God acting in history. All we know is that the world is getting worse and worse. The best we can do is hope for the End—soon.[23]

This happened again twelve centuries later. J. Huizinga's study,

---

21. Henry M. Morris and Gary E. Parker, *What Is Creation Science?* (San Diego, California: Master Books, 1982), p. 167.
22. Gilbert Murray, *Five Stages of Greek Religion* (Garden City, New York: Anchor, [1925]), ch. 4.
23. David Chilton, *The Days of Vengeance: An Exposition of the Book of Revelation,* p. 25. He refers the reader to Leon Morris, *Apocalyptic* (Grand Rapids, Michigan: Eerdmans, 1972).

The Waning of the Middle Ages (1924),[24] describes fourteenth-century Northern Europe in terms of radical pessimism and also a belief in apocalyptic deliverance. It was the end of an era, speeded along by the devastation of bubonic plague after 1347. Generation after generation, the plague returned. The era was also marked by apocalyptic religious and revolutionary violence.[25]

The decline of medieval Europe was accompanied by the rise of the Renaissance. The Renaissance was deeply magical in its worldview,[26] even though historians have long emphasized its rationalism and humanism. It was the product of a self-conscious imitation of classical civilization, which was also both rationalistic and occult.[27] The Renaissance was supremely confident, even as Western humanist culture was until 1964, until the return of Columbus from the New World. Columbus' expedition brought back more than tales of a New World in 1493; it brought back syphilis, and this killer disease spread across Europe within five years. It had struck China by 1506 or 1507, less than fifteen years after Columbus returned.[28] It shook the foundation of Renaissance confidence. In 1517, two dozen years after syphilis broke out in Europe, Luther nailed his 95 theses on the church door in Wittenberg. The Reformation began.

Today we face AIDS. The confidence of Western humanism has already shown signs of fading. What little confidence that remains will be destroyed unless there is a near-term cure for AIDS, which is unlikely, according to medical researchers. Apocalypticism — visions of the end of the world — is today a common feature within American fundamentalism. Any theory of hope in the earthly future is rejected by modern Christian apocalyptists as some sort of humanist remnant of an older optimism, or New Age speculation, meaning humanist

---

24. J. Huizinga, *The Waning of the Middle Ages: A Study of the Forms of Life, Thought and Art in France and the Netherlands in the Dawn of the Renaissance* (Garden City, New York: Doubleday Anchor, [1924]).

25. Norman Cohn, *The Pursuit of the Millennium: Revolutionary messianism in medieval and Reformation Europe and its bearing on modern totalitarian movements* (New York: Harper Torchbook, 1961).

26. Frances A. Yates, *Giordano Bruno and the Hermetic Tradition* (New York: Vintage, [1964] 1969).

27. Charles Norris Cochrane, *Christianity and Classical Culture: A Study in Thought and Action from Augustus to Augustine* (New York: Oxford University Press, [1944] 1957).

28. Fernand Braudel, *Civilization and Capitalism, 15th-18th Century*, 3 Vols., *The Structures of Everyday Life: The Limits of the Possible* (New York: Harper & Row, [1979] 1981), I, pp. 81-82.

apocalypticism: the creation of a man-made New World Order.[29] The "pessimillennialists," by adhering to a vision of defeat, are unable to challenge successfully the Rifkins of this world, so they pretend that pessimistic New Agers do not exist, pretend that optimism is *the* philosophy of the New Age movement. Why? By ignoring their own shared pessimism with Rifkin, they find it easier to impose "guilt by intellectual association" on orthodox Christians who proclaim victory in history in the name of the power of the bodily resurrection of Jesus Christ in history. By linking the eschatology of premillennial dispensationalism to the Bible, and then by linking Christian optimism about the future with New Age humanism, Dave Hunt and Constance Cumbey thereby have become self-conscious defenders of the New Agers' number-one cultural principle, namely, *the external defeat of Christ's people in history*. They have attempted to tar and feather Christian optimists with the charge of being naive "fellow travellers" with the New Age movement, when they themselves are equally vulnerable to the same accusation.

This should lead us to conclude that there are pessimists and optimists in both camps — New Age and Christianity — and that a person's eschatology is self-contained: *not* influenced by the New Age movement. But a person's consistent conclusions concerning the implications of his eschatology can be misused by certain humanist groups. The defense of one's eschatology and its conclusions should be based on what the Bible says, and not on what hypothetical links there may be between this or that New Age group. Prying open a can of "New Age paint" to splatter on one's eschatological opponents only succeeds in getting a face full of paint in return.

One thing is clear: Jeremy Rifkin is by far the most eloquent social philosopher of the New Age movement. No other figure has enjoyed anywhere near the number of book sales on as many different topics. For Mrs. Cumbey and Mr. Hunt to ignore Rifkin's self-conscious attempt to pick off the premillennialists by means of his and their shared pessimism about the future — a pessimism proclaimed by Mrs. Cumbey and especially Mr. Hunt — and then to try to link far more obscure New Age writers with the Christian Reconstruction movement's optimistic worldview, is not simply unfair; it shows startling unconcern with the primary sources of the New Age movement's impact in popular thought and culture. Jeremy Rifkin is

---

29. Dave Hunt, *Beyond Seduction* (Eugene, Oregon: Harvest House, 1987).

our problem, not Alice A. Bailey. (If you have never heard of Alice A. Bailey, don't feel too bad; neither has 99.999% of the U.S. book-buying population. Mrs. Cumbey believes that the theological writings of the late Mrs. Bailey are the key that unlocks the secrets of the New Age movement, and she lists Mrs. Bailey's Lucis Trust first in her appendix, "Selected New Age Organizations."[30] I think Mrs. Bailey's theological writings are more like a key into a lunatic asylum if you read too much of them. Rifkin's books have an air of coherence and sanity about them, which is why he, and not Mrs. Bailey, has had considerable success in the Christian intellectual community.)

Conclusion

Even conclusions need conclusions sometimes. I asked three questions at the end of my Introduction: 1) What is really fixed throughout world history: natural law, ethical law, or both? 2) How are these two forms of God-given law related? 3) Is there a relationship between how *mankind acts* and how the *world works*? I said that because Christians are divided over the answers to these three questions, we face a crisis in the Christian worldview. We have already seen what this crisis is: *a crisis in faith concerning the future.*

What are my answers to these three questions? First, it is the Bible-revealed law of God that is the constant in history, not physical laws. God providentially sustains His creation. He gives to mankind knowledge of the personal, social, and scientific laws necessary for mankind to exercise dominion. The moral laws—the ten commandments and the case laws—are constants in history. Laws of nature are also constants. But physical and biological laws can change.

Let me give an example. Smallpox is communicated only from human to human. Once someone gets smallpox and recovers, he ceases to be a carrier. If he has an innate immunity to smallpox, he does not transmit the disease after his exposure to it. Thus, scientists have stamped out the disease by locating outbreaks of smallpox and rushing in to quarantine the victims and immunizing everyone in the vicinity. The spread of the disease is halted, for the germs die in their hosts and fail to be transmitted. Region by region, the germs

---

30. Constance Cumbey, *The Hidden Dangers of the Rainbow: The New Age Movement and Our Coming Age of Barbarism* (Shreveport, Louisiana: Huntington House, 1983), Appendix A.

are exterminated. This scientific strategy has worked; except inside that one British laboratory, the smallpox species is gone. It is only because of the species' (presently) fixed epidemiological characteristics that it has been stamped out by science.

This raises a very curious question: What about Noah's family? For six months they were on the ark, alone. How did smallpox germs survive this isolation period? How did the disease ever get started again? We know that it did, but our knowledge of how the disease is transmitted tells us that it should have been wiped out in the "quarantine" period on the ark.

God has the power to preserve life or spread death by changing the way biological systems operate in any species. The "laws of biology" can change. We see an example of this in the Bible in the promise of God to eliminate biological miscarriages (Ex. 23:26).

Those physical regularities that are farthest away from man's control—gravity, the speed of light, radiation—seem to change least. They point to limits on man. The more universal a law is in galactic scope, the less it is likely to change. But it is obvious to a six-day creationist that the speed of light was not a constant during creation week, since billions of light-years were not available for light to travel from the newly created stars (day four) to the earth. Thus, at best, that most constant of scientific constants, the speed of light, is a very recent constant—more recent (day four) than the creation of the earth (day one).

Constants are in all cases *personal*. God personally sustains them. He provides these *covenantal regularities*. Physical constants are far less important than moral constants. Man's successful dominion efforts are not based primarily on his *knowledge of* physical constants, but on his *obedience to* biblical constants.

Second, God's personal covenant with mankind in general and with Christians in particular has established cause-and-effect relationships between the moral laws of God and so-called natural laws of the physical world. The cursed effects of entropy can be overcome by covenantal faithfulness to God, as revealed before men, angels, and God by means of personal obedience and Christian profession of faith. Man is given power to overcome the limitations of physical laws through knowledge, which in turn expands through covenantal faithfulness of a society. Ethics is closely related to knowledge. God grants the gift of knowledge to those who obey at least His external moral requirements.

Finally, there is a relationship between how mankind acts and how the world works—world in its broadest sense: social, physical, and historical. We see this clearly revealed in Deuteronomy 28. For faithful societies, the world works to bless men (vv. 1-14). In unfaithful societies, the reverse is true (vv. 15-68). There are covenantal blessings and cursings. God, who governs all things, uses His creation to bless and curse individuals and societies.

Thus, the emphasis on entropy as an inescapable, universal constant is misguided. Such an emphasis erroneously indicates that the processes of nature are in control of man and man's destiny, whereas the Bible clearly places man and the covenant above nature. Nature fights man or cooperates with man in terms of mankind's ethical battle against God or cooperation with God. This is the neglected lesson of Genesis 3. If mankind rebels against God, then nature will rebel against mankind. The covenantal relationship between man and God is primary; the covenantal relationship between man and nature is secondary; and the universal rule of physical entropy has meaning only in relation to the two prior covenantal relationships.

It is time for the Creation Science movement to rethink its present use of the second law of thermodynamics. There are so many solid scientific arguments that can be used to torpedo the Darwinists that the eschatology of entropy should be dropped or drastically modified. It has caught the attention of so many laymen in the creationist movement only because it fits their "pessimillennial" worldview. The appeal to entropy has not served to persuade the evolutionists, and it has done much to reaffirm the prevailing pessimistic, defensive, world-retreating outlook of six-day creationists. It has produced far more harm than good, and Rifkin's perception of its value to him is proof enough of its liability to creationism. To elevate the appeal to entropy as the key argument in the Scientific Creationist movement is to hide the creationist lamp under a basket. I think the younger Creation Scientists recognize this. It is time for the six-day creation movement to look to the resurrection as the foundation of its worldview, not the curse of God in the garden.

When this happens, we will also see a shift of eschatology. But that is as it should be. The Holy Spirit is alive and well on planet earth.

Appendix A

THE DISASTROUS QUEST FOR SCIENTIFIC COMMON GROUND

> *Together with thinking of the results of science as they are offered to us in various fields, we must think of the methodology of science. Perhaps there is greater agreement among scientists on the question of methodology than on the question of results. At any rate, it is quite commonly held that we cannot accept anything that is not consonant with the result of a sound scientific methodology. With this we can as Christians heartily agree. It is our contention, however, that it is only upon Christian presuppositions that we can have a sound scientific methodology. And when we recall that our main argument for Christianity will be that it is only upon Christian theistic presuppositions that a true notion of facts can be formed, we see at once that it is in the field of methodology that our major battle with modern science will have to be fought. Our contention will be that a true scientific procedure is impossible unless we hold to the presupposition of the triune God of Scripture. . . . The chief major battle between Christianity and modern science is not about a large number of individual facts, but about the principles that control science in its work. The battle today is largely that of the* philosophy *of science.*
>
> Cornelius Van Til[1]

What I argue in this appendix will alienate a lot of my readers. I argue that the methodologies of the Scientific Creationists and the modern Darwinian evolutionists are remarkably similar, and that this has compromised the Scientific Creation movement.

On the surface, this may seem preposterous, both to the Scientific Creationists and the Darwinians. Nevertheless, the similarities are there, and they should not be ignored, let alone deliberately concealed from the public. The *fundamental agreement* concerns the doc-

---

1. Cornelius Van Til, *Christian-Theistic Evidences* (Phillipsburg, New Jersey: Presbyterian and Reformed Pub. Co., [1961] 1978), pp. viii-ix.

trine of *uniformitarianism*: "Natural laws never change." Natural laws are seen as universal—the same in this region of the universe as in any other. The trouble is, neither side agrees with the other with respect to the scientifically legitimate applications of these natural laws.

The Creation Science movement uses certain arguments with respect to the second law of thermodynamics in its attempt to prove its case against evolutionists that the evolutionists also use against the creationists. Both groups use two basic approaches—closed systems vs. open systems—each mutually contradictory, with respect to that fundamental debating point, the meaning and proper use of the second law of thermodynamics. Both sides affirm that:

1. The second law of thermodynamics has only been shown scientifically to operate in closed equilibrium systems.
2. All local systems are ultimately open systems.
3. *Insofar as science is concerned*, the universe is a closed system.
4. The universe is therefore running down.

Whenever one side attacks the other by using a variation of the "closed system" argument, the other side responds with, "You can't say that because this particular system is an open system." So the arguments get nowhere. Neither side will allow itself to be pinned down in any given instance by the logic of the second law of thermodynamics.

I have argued in this book that Christian cosmologists' reliance on the entropy concept has placed them perilously close to the social theory of Jeremy Rifkin. In fact, this dependence on the concept of entropy has made the Creation Scientists virtually defenseless against the bulk of Rifkin's pessimistic conclusions.

The Terms of Discourse

As used in popular books (e.g., Jeremy Rifkin, Henry Morris), entropy is spoken of as a law that proves that all of nature is decaying, wearing out, and becoming increasingly random. The "noise" of the universe is overcoming its original coherence. The forces of life, growth, and heat are steadily losing to a purported counter-force, the second law of thermodynamics: death, decay, and randomness.

Such a heavy reliance on entropy has led to a paralyzing social pessimism within the creationist movement. In fact, it is this *unstated presupposition of eschatological pessimism* of the bulk of the Scientific Creationists that has been a major incentive in their adopting entropy as the linchpin of their argument against Darwinism. The appeal to entropy has become the key apologetic tactic in the movement.[2]

The social pessimism of the more consistent humanist defenders of this popularized version of entropy is matched by the equally consistent social pessimism of Christian defenders of entropy. It was not a coincidence that in his 1951 book, *The Bible and Modern Science*, Henry Morris begins with a chapter on "The Entropy Law"—"the physical universe is, beyond question, growing old, wearing out, and running down"[3]—and ends it with a chapter defending the Bible, an apologetic approach based on the fulfillment of Bible prophecy.[4]

It is fitting that a chapter on prophecy should be included in a book on the Bible and science. Prophecy is closely linked with a person's worldview. Eschatology sets the tone for consistent natural science. Eschatology also sets the tone for consistent social science.

Charges and Counter-Charges

Defenders of God's six-day creation have constantly appealed to the second law of thermodynamics[5] in order to demonstrate the absurdity of believing that the autonomous operations of an impersonal, increasingly random and disorderly universe could have led to an increase of order and coherence, meaning the conditions necessary for the supposed evolution of life.[6] They argue along these

---

2. The evolutionists recognize the importance of this argument for Scientific Creationism, and they go to considerable effort to refute the use of the second law: Philip Kitcher, *Abusing Science: The Case Against Creationism* (Cambridge, Massachusetts: MIT Press, 1982), pp. 89-96; Willard Young, *Fallacies of Creationism* (Calgary, Alberta: Detselig Enterprises, 1985), ch. 11.

3. Henry M. Morris, *The Bible and Modern Science* (rev. ed.; Chicago: Moody Press, [1951] 1956), p. 15.

4. "The greatest demonstrable evidence for the inspiration of the Scriptures, apart from the final, unanswerable proof of personal experience, lies in the fact that hundreds of prophecies contained in its pages have been remarkably fulfilled." *Ibid.*, p. 111.

5. J. Willard Gibbs and Rudolph Clausius were the two men whose names are generally closely associated with the second law. Clausius first used the term "entropy": Isaac Asimov, *The New Intelligent Man's Guide to Science* (New York: Basic Books, 1965), p. 328.

6. Henry M. Morris and John C. Whitcomb, *The Genesis Flood: The Biblical Record and Its Scientific Implications* (Philadelphia: Presbyterian & Reformed, 1961), pp. 222-27.

lines: "The Darwinian evolutionists claim to be scientists, but they ignore the operations of what is probably the most fundamental law of science, the second law of thermodynamics. They refuse to appeal to God to explain the origin of life — an order-producing, increasingly complex phenomenon — which must be regarded by consistent scientists as an unexplainable, impossible event in a truly autonomous universe that is governed as a whole by an invariable law of decay and increasing randomness. Thus, they are not truly scientific, for they refuse to apply this invariable scientific law to the study of origins. This shows that they apply scientific laws selectively. This illegitimate selectivity therefore shows that they are not really disciplined by a rigorously scientific methodology."

The Darwinians respond with arguments along these lines: "The creationists claim to be scientists, but they constantly appeal to God's miracles in order to explain historic events. They cannot prove the existence of God, and they cannot offer evidence that would enable us to explain how God interacts with the world. They even deny that His miracles are subject to the restraints of predictable scientific law. Nevertheless, they claim to be scientists. This is nonsense; they are only pseudo-scientists. They do not govern their scientific inquiries by the second law of thermodynamics or by any other scientific law. They apply scientific laws selectively. This illegitimate selectivity shows that they are not really disciplined by a rigorously scientific methodology."

I think these arguments are very similar. They both focus on the same issue: the opposition's failure to adhere to a methodology that applies absolutely fixed scientific laws to all the available empirical evidence. I intend to show that the arguments on both sides are so similar — and initially so compelling intellectually — that it should lead Christians to reconsider the whole approach of trying to apply absolutely fixed, impersonal laws to all available evidence. Both sides cannot be correct. Something must be wrong somewhere. Since neither side is willing to "stick to the rules," yet both claim to be rigorous ("scientific") in their approach to questions, perhaps there is a more acceptable (and more honest) methodology which allows us to be selective in the application of the familiar regularities of nature, yet still be truly scientific. Maybe absolutely fixed, impersonal laws do not really exist. In short, we need to ask ourselves: "What is the proper scientific methodology?" We also need to ask ourselves: "What does the Bible tell us concerning law?"

How Binding Is the Entropy Law?

What is entropy? Henry Morris writes: ". . . there are three basic vehicles of physical reality associated with the entropy concept. In the structure of all systems, entropy is a measure of *disorder*. In the maintenance of all processes, entropy is a measure of *wasted energy*. In the transmission of all information, entropy is a measure of *useless noise*. Each of these three concepts is basically equivalent to the other two, even though it expresses a distinct concept. Always, furthermore, entropy tends to increase. Everywhere in the physical universe there is an inexorable downhill trend toward ultimate complete randomness, utter meaninglessness, and absolute stillness."[7] In short, *entropy is a measure*.

The Scientific Creationists argue that because the world is naturally running down, becoming more and more disorderly, it follows that evolution through impersonal nature cannot be true. There has been an increase in order, not a decrease. Thus, the universal second law of thermodynamics testifies against the possibility of Darwinian evolution.

The Darwinists reply that the acknowledged fact of the second law of thermodynamics cannot legitimately be used to call into question the idea of biological evolution through natural selection. Yes, the universe as a whole may correctly be characterized by increasing entropy; nevertheless, a local region can sometimes escape the effects of an increase of entropy (at least temporarily) because of outside energy entering it, and therefore it can experience the "progress" of increasing complexity and order.[8] They usually argue that the

---

7. Henry Morris, *The Troubled Waters of Evolution* (San Diego, California: CLP Publishers, 1974), p. 121.

8. The standard attempted refutation is to argue that the second law of thermodynamics applies only to a "closed system," but that the development of some systems toward greater complexity and order indicates that they are "open." The earth receives energy from the sun, for example. Writes a critic of Morris: "Darwinian histories do presuppose that large amounts of energy remain available for work in large numbers of systems of living things. . . . Energy from the sun is constantly entering the system comprising the earth and its inhabitants. . . . Classical thermodynamics tells us that, within this vast closed system, entropy increases. It says absolutely nothing about entropy variation at the local level. . . . Let us recall our imaginary example of a closed system. I envisaged a perfectly insulated box within which bodies exchanged energy. Reality contains no such boxes. What we find are approximations to perfect insulation." Kitcher, *Abusing Science*, pp. 92, 93. The "local level" is the significant portion of the universe—the level in which evolutionary leaps are taking place, randomly. This level is an "open box," whereas the universe as a whole is a "closed box," meaning, above all, *closed to God*.

universe as a whole is "running down," although segments of it can postpone entropy's effects for a while.

I say "usually," but there are occasional exceptions. Evolutionist Michael Ruse responds to the Scientific Creationists' appeal to the second law, but he responds judiciously: "The second law obviously applies only to closed systems. But, argue evolutionists, given the influx of usable energy from the sun, the organic world is an open system. Hence evolution is possible. Entropy may be increasing through the universe, taken as a whole, but it does not mean that, in small localized areas, entropy cannot decrease. The world of organic evolution is one such area. The sun shines down on the Earth. This makes the plants grow. Animals live and feed on the plants. And thus life goes forward."[9] This is a theory of "sunshine evolution."

Note that Ruse does not assert that entropy *is* "increasing through the universe, taken as a whole," but only that it *may* be. He carefully guards his academic flanks with that seemingly harmless word, "may," a pre-attack defense so subtle that hardly anyone will notice what he is implicitly admitting, namely, that *modern science cannot prove that the universe as a whole is characterized by increasing entropy.* It is also interesting that he devotes only half a dozen brief paragraphs to this crucial but difficult topic, unlike Kitcher and Young. He displays considerable wisdom in this regard.

This Darwinian argument, based on "open regional systems," is denied by virtually all scientists who are six-day creationists,[10] but it is a necessary component of any scientifically rigorous Darwinian refutation of creationism. How seriously should we take "sunshine evolution"? Not very, says D. Russell Humphreys. He argues that the heat entering the earth's atmosphere *increases* entropy, just as heat applied to water raises its temperature and therefore increases the disorder among the water molecules. "Evolutionists want the sun's energy to produce greater and greater order upon the earth; this requires that entropy be decreasing in our open system. But solar energy does just the opposite; it *increases* the earth's entropy!"[11] In

---

9. Michael Ruse, *Darwinism Defended: A Guide to the Evolution Controversies* (Reading, Massachusetts: Addison-Wesley, 1982), p. 296. Cf. pp. 306-7.

10. See, for example, Emmett L. Williams, a physicist: "Resistance of Living Organisms to the Second Law of Thermodynamics," *Creation Research Society Quarterly*, VIII, No. 2 (1971).

11. "Using the Second Law More Effectively," *ibid.*, XIX, No. 4 (March 1978), p. 109.

short, "since there is such strong experimental evidence that the second law applies to all systems, open or closed, living or non-living, creationists do not need to grant the evolutionists the ground of possible exceptions to the second law of thermodynamics."[12] This is a representative response by a Scientific Creationist.

The point is, the Darwinians explain the operation of the second law of thermodynamics as exempting their most important theological point, namely, the possibility of organic evolution in a world of entropy. "Foul!" cry the Scientific Creationists. "Fair!" cry the Darwinian evolutionists.

It is not my task as a social theorist to go into great scientific detail beyond my competence. The apologetic problem (the philosophical defense of the faith) that faces the Scientific Creationists is that they have criticized the Darwinians for ignoring the second law of thermodynamics, but the Darwinians *sometimes* appear to be using it in a scientifically acceptable way in their search for an escape hatch: the argument against open systems. Classical thermodynamics *does* deal with closed systems, and *only* with closed systems (at equilibrium). Thus, the Darwinists seem to get the better of this phase of the argument. On the other hand, they sometimes abandon classical thermodynamics in order to solve problems raised by the Scientific Creationists, especially the key question of the world of biological change.[13]

If Scientific Creationists continue to insist on trying to expose their opponents by using their opponents' arguments against them, it would be wise to select a better example of Darwinian weakness. The creationists have pointed repeatedly to the impossibility for the

---

12. *Ibid.*, p. 110.
13. Willard Young insists quite correctly that the scientific concept of entropy applies only to closed systems in equilibrium: "What is especially interesting about entropy is that it provides a measure of the amount of energy which becomes *unavailable* to do work in an isolated (closed) system." *Fallacies of Creationism*, p. 169. "It is very important to realize that the Second Law is precisely defined for *closed* systems only" (p. 170). But a few pages later, he writes: "Classical thermodynamics dealt only with closed systems, and for this reason it could not accommodate phenomena of biological organization. . . . Since that time [the 1930's] thermodynamics has been developed and expanded to a much more general theory which includes both open and closed systems. The question of *how* entropy-decreasing processes may work in evolution is not fully understood, but this does not affect the conclusions so far. . ." (p. 180). He and his scientific colleagues therefore abandon classical thermodynamics when it appears convenient to do so. They do not regard the appeal to classical thermodynamics as a two-edged sword with no handle. They think of it as a one-edged sword with a handle, and one that can be legitimately used only by evolutionists.

cosmos to have had *enough time to evolve*, given presently observed rates of change. This does strike a major blow against the Darwinists. But to focus on the second law of thermodynamics, rather than on the Darwinists' overdrawn bank account of available time, has not persuaded many conventional scientists of the case for creationism. The two camps shout at each other endlessly over the proper use of the second law; it would be cheaper and waste less time for each group simply to buy an endless-loop cassette and play the recordings at each other. No one would listen, but it would give everyone more time to develop more effective arguments.

It would also get Jeremy Rifkin out of the picture.

Uniformitarianism: The Shared Faith

Why all this concern about the extent of entropy? Because the Darwinians base their case against the creationists on the logic of uniformitarianism, and the Scientific Creationists reply in kind (almost). Uniformitarianism is the scientific-religious doctrine that the laws of nature are fixed. Uniformitarianism asserts that *the laws that govern all historical change have been stable over time*. Without such fixed laws, both sides claim, there could be no science.

The Debate Begins

Scientific Creationist Henry Morris states that to the best of our knowledge, all the laws of nature have been in effect since the beginning of time.[14] At least he admits that this is to the best of our knowledge. He argues, however, that the evolutionist's presupposition of a world of constant change, of evolutionary flux, is a denial of these fixed laws of nature.

Evolutionist Willard Young counters this argument: "Evolution is a process which occurs under appropriate conditions *within the laws of nature* as they stand. Rather than suggesting that the laws of nature evolve, it assumes, on the contrary, that they have remained a constant. Except for this implicit assumption, the theory of evolution has nothing whatever to say about any of the fundamental laws of nature."[15] At least he admits that the fixed laws of nature are assumptions.

---

14. Henry M. Morris, *Scientific Creationism* (San Diego, California: Creation-Life Publishers, 1974), p. 18.
15. Young, *Fallacies of Creationism*, p. 168.

Morris could easily argue that this assumption is not warranted by the inherent presuppositions of Darwinian science regarding cosmic change. How does the flux of nature's processes produce fixed laws? How does anything remain fixed in a world of change? Therefore, Darwinian science really cannot assume what it needs in order to be scientific: fixed laws. But then Young could respond that Scientific Creationists are only part-time believers in fixed laws, for they believe in miracles—God's intrusions in history that temporarily overcome fixed laws, indicating that such laws are not actually fixed. They are fixed, "except when God interferes."

We are now dealing with that age-old philosophical problem of structure and change, of law and flux. Christian philosopher Cornelius Van Til argued throughout his career that the mind of self-proclaimed autonomous man cannot find an answer to this problem. Either stability is destroyed by change, or else change is really an illusion, and there is only the unity of stability. This is why Creation Scientists and Darwinian evolutionists go from one position to the other, from historical change to eternal law, to defend their respective systems, and ultimately each position is held by means of a logic-destroying dialectical tension. This is why the debate over evolution and creation cannot be solved by an appeal to the "brute facts" of "autonomous science."

This is also why the apologetic method (empiricism, the appeal to supposed common facts) of the Scientific Creationist movement is flawed. It appeals to a hypothetical common logic of man as if such a common ground existed. But men interpret all facts in terms of their religious presuppositions. The inability of either side to convince its opponents testifies to the futility of the search for common facts, common theories, or common anything else.[16] The futility of the attempt to get Creation Science into the public schools has not been recognized by these dedicated men, despite twenty years of failure in the courts and the state textbook committees, precisely because they still really believe in the myth of scientific neutrality: the appeal to a commonly shared body of scientific opinion. There is no shared body of opinion. There is only warfare over whose all-or-nothing system will be used in the classroom. The Darwinists, being more consistent, have triumphed. They will not tolerate equal time for God.

---

16. On this common ground aspect of the Creation Research Society, see Walter Lammerts' introduction to the first Annual (1964) of the CRS.

Rates of Change

The debate over uniformitarianism goes beyond the question of the fixed laws of nature. It also relates to rates of change in history. Pure uniformitarianism argues that rates of geological or biological change are always the same.[17] There are very few scientists who hold such a view; very few ever have. They always "fudge" when pressed. They qualify their claim. This is why the debate over uniformitarianism is so curious.

Historically, Darwinism grew out of the nineteenth-century concept of uniformitarian change. Historian-sociologist Robert Nisbet has identified the doctrine of uniformitarianism as the key doctrine in the attempt of nineteenth-century evolutionists to challenge Christianity. "It is hard today to realize the degree to which the attack on Christianity obsessed intellectuals of rationalist and utilitarian will. Christianity had much the same position that capitalism was to hold in the first half of the twentieth century. It was *the* enemy in the minds of most intellectuals. Uniformitarianism, above any other single element of the theory of evolution, was the perfect point of attack on a theory that made external manipulation its essence and a succession of 'catastrophes' its plot."[18]

Ironically, today's Scientific Creationists have presented their case against Darwinian evolution in terms of uniformitarianism: specifically, the doctrine of the unchanging entropy law, which they do not really and truly believe is unchanging (i.e., miracles). Both sides appeal to the same law in order to make their case. We therefore need to explore the implications of this debate — a debate based officially on entropy.

The Curse of Entropy

The Scientific Creationists build their case against Darwinian evolution in terms of the post-Fall curse: God's judgment on the cosmos, entropy. This is their version of *uniformitarianism*, meaning a process of change which is the same today as it was yesterday. Every science needs certain models, meaning fixed reference points that explain and measure change. The Scientific Creationists argue that

---

17. A good example is James Hutton, the late-eighteenth-century geologist, who argued that the rate of geological change has never varied.
18. Robert A. Nisbet, *Social Change and History: Aspects of the Western Theory of Development* (New York: Oxford University Press, 1969), p. 184.

all scientists must build the foundation of science on the inescapable, universal, irreversible law of entropy. Entropy is inescapable; it is the same yesterday, today, and tomorrow (well, not quite the same, as we shall see, but "usually" it is the same).

They then argue that the "closed box" aspect of the universe cannot possibly be true, given the assumptions of the Darwinists. The universe was not a self-created entity. It could not have evolved in the random way that the Darwinians claim. Such a development is not mathematically possible, according to the laws of probability.[19] God must have created the world, for there is no way to explain the coming of life in a world governed by the second law of thermodynamics. When man rebelled, God cursed the universe. This curse "from the outside" is the origin of the law of entropy, not nature itself: so runs the argument.

Henry Morris has openly praised the methodology of uniformitarianism: "But there is obviously no way of knowing that these processes and the laws which describe them have always been the same in the past or that they will always be the same in the future. It is possible to make an assumption of this kind, of course, and this is the well-known principle of *uniformitarianism*. The assumption is reasonable, in the light of our experience with present processes, and it is no doubt safe to extrapolate on this basis for a certain time into the future and back into the past. But to insist that uniformitarianism is the only scientific approach to the understanding of *all* past and future time is clearly nothing but a dogmatic tenet of a particular form of religion."[20]

He meant this last sentence to apply to modern Darwinists who reject miracles, but the best of the Darwinian scientists never held to such a rigid definition of the doctrine, since they, too, need ways to escape the limits of a fixed-rate system of geological and biological change,[21] and today we find a scientific revolution going on in the

---

19. See Edward Blick's estimates, in Henry M. Morris, *et al.* (eds.), *Creation: Acts, Facts, Impacts* (San Diego, California: Creation-Life Publishers, 1974), p. 175.

20. Henry M. Morris, "Science versus Scientism in Historical Geology," in *A Symposium on Creation* (Grand Rapids, Michigan: Baker Book House, 1968), pp. 12-13.

21. Harvard paleontologist George Gaylord Simpson writes: "Some processes (those of vulcanism or glaciation, for example) have evidently acted in the past with scales and rates that cannot by any stretch be called 'the same' or even 'approximately the same' as those of today." Simpson, *This View of Life: The World of an Evolutionist* (New York: Harcourt, Brace & World, 1964), p. 132.

Darwinian camp, primarily because of the "macroevolution" theories associated with Harvard's Stephen Jay Gould.[22] How, then, can the Scientific Creationists distinguish themselves methodologically— "uniformitarianism most of the time"—from the new "modified uniformitarian" Darwinian evolutionists who despise the Christian faith as much as the older ones did?[23]

The Darwinists Respond

Darwinian evolutionists are unimpressed by any Christian appeal to a "most of the time" version of the entropy law. In response to the creationists' view of the "open box"—a universe created by God and continually open to God and His miracles—the Darwinian uniformitarians still argue for the "closed box" theory of the universe. They deny the Christian doctrine of creation: no creator God of the Bible, no six-day creation, no perpetually binding ethics, and no final judgment (*especially* no final judgment). They defend themselves against the uniformitarian law of entropy by arguing that there are local or regional "open boxes" in which energy received from outside the region has sometimes been able to produce increasing complexity and order, thereby *temporarily* overcoming the universal "macro-evolutionary" tendency toward simplicity and randomness, which ultimately means "macro-devolution"—the final extinction of life and differentiation. It also means the extinction of man—his hopes, dreams, and meaning. Evolutionists cling religiously to a cosmology of death in preference to a cosmology of God-produced regeneration and cosmic renewal. This is as it should be. All those who hate God love death (Prov. 8:36b).

---

22. Cf. Steven N. Stanley, *The New Evolutionary Timetable* (New York: Basic Books, 1982). Rifkin recognizes that Gould has overturned the modern Darwinian synthesis: *Algeny*, Part 5: "The Darwinian Sunset: The Passing of a Paradigm."

23. Gould writes: "However, and ironically, the early 1980s have also witnessed an utterly different and perverse debate about evolution, often conflated in the public mind with these legitimate and exciting arguments about evolutionary mechanisms. I refer, of course, to the political resurgence of the pseudoscience known to its supporters as 'scientific creationism'—strict Genesis literalism masquerading as science in a cynical attempt to bypass the First Amendment and win legislatively mandated inclusion of particular (and minority) religious views into public school curricula. As in 1909, no scientist or thinking person doubts the basic fact that life evolves. Intense debates about *how* evolution occurs display science at its most exciting, but provide no solace (only phony ammunition by willful distortion) to strict fundamentalists." Stephen Jay Gould, *Hen's Teeth and Horse's Toes: Further Reflections in Natural History* (New York: Norton, 1983), p. 14.

Energy for the Darwinian evolutionist is substituted for the Creator God: an impersonal, purposeless force of nature which produces personal, purposeful living beings, and ultimately man, the only known agent capable of providing cosmic purposefulness for the universe.[24] Living beings, by means of energy transformation, can temporarily overcome some of the effects of entropy locally, though not for the universe as a whole.

Both sides in this debate agree that the *effects* of entropy can be overcome by such processes as photosynthesis in plants. Both sides believe that man, through purposeful planning and work, can create "pockets of order"—*at some price*—in a decreasingly orderly universe. Neither the Scientific Creationists nor the Darwinians believe that these "pockets of order" can perpetually withstand the entropy process. The Scientific Creationists believe that the intervention of God at the final judgment will overthrow the law of entropy—the curse of the cosmos.[25] Darwinians—at least those who write for the general public—believe that the entropy process will finally destroy all life in the final dissipation of energy.[26] In short, the universe ultimately faces either an absolute God, absolute destruction, or an endless series of meaningless cycles.[27]

The Biblical View

What is the biblical view of uniformitarianism? The Bible teaches the *uniformitarianism of God's being and character.* "For I am the Lord, I change not . . ." (Mal. 3:6). His law reflects His character. The principles of God's *ethical* law are fixed. We do not look to nature to find unchanging principles or laws, for nature is cursed; we look instead to God and His law.

Here is the grave error of the Scientific Creationists: they delib-

---

24. Gary North, *The Dominion Covenant: Genesis* (2nd ed.; Tyler, Texas: Institute for Christian Economics, 1987), Appendix A: "From Cosmic Purposelessness to Humanistic Sovereignty."

25. The premillennial Scientific Creationists believe that entropy is partially overcome during Christ's earthly millennium. The amillennialists do not believe in Christ's earthly millennium.

26. See Bertrand Russell's pessimistic description of the final fate of man and all his works: "A Free Man's Religion" (1903), in Russell, *Mysticism and Logic* (Garden City, New York: Doubleday Anchor, [1917] n.d.), pp. 45-46; "Evolution," in Russell, *Religion and Science* (New York: Oxford University Press, [1935] 1972), pp. 80-81.

27. Isaac Asimov, *A Choice of Catastrophes: The Disasters that Threaten Our World* (New York: Simon & Schuster, 1979), ch. 2: "The Closing of the Universe."

erately, self-consciously begin their scientific discussions without any reference to God and the Bible, let alone His fixed ethical law. This strategic error is the product of a self-conscious attempt to get creationist materials into the public schools. Henry Morris includes a section, "The Battle for the Public School," in his book, *Evolution in Turmoil*.[28] It is an approach based self-consciously on the presupposition, "equal time for Satan." Morris says forthrightly, "Creationists in no way wish to *control* public school curricula, of course, but they *have* been urging school administrators to be fair and to use a 'two-model' approach in the schools."[29] It is an attempt which has been unsuccessful (see Appendix B). Discussing scientific models without an appeal to the Bible may produce acceptable short-term results in short formal debates, but it has not convinced the courts or the teachers of evolution.[30] The public schools are not going to teach six-day creation, and any expenditure of resources to try to get them to do it is a waste of our very limited resources.

Our goal as self-conscious Christians and six-day creationists is not to sneak our highly religious perspective into the public schools by means of a cloak of supposed neutrality. There can be no neutrality. Thus, our goal is not to teach religion in the public schools; it is to shut down all tax money going to every school (except the military academies). We should not baptize the public schools by making them appear "sort of all right" to Christians who don't know any better. The proper Christian goal, "of course," should be to shut down the public schools and never again allow taxpayers' money to be used to educate children. Our cry should be, "No more socialism in education!"[31]

This "evidentialist" approach to science (and everything else) denies the fundamental starting point of all God-honoring intellectual investigations: God as the sovereign Creator of the universe, meaning the Creator-creature distinction.[32]

---

28. Henry Morris, *Evolution in Turmoil* (San Diego, California: Creation-Life Publishers, 1982), pp. 123-34. The best example of this strategy is Dr. John N. Moore's *How To Teach ORIGINS (Without ACLU Interference)* (Milford, Michigan: Mott Media, 1983).

29. Morris, *Evolution in Turmoil*, p. 123.

30. See, for example, the critique by the outspoken opponent of Scientific Creationism, Michael Ruse: *Darwinism Defended*, pp. 322-24.

31. Robert L. Thoburn, *The Children Trap* (Ft. Worth, Texas: Dominion Press, 1986).

32. In one sense, this error of apologetic methodology stems from their commitment to evidentialism and a late-eighteenth-century version of "natural religion." For a critique of this approach from a biblical philosophical standpoint, see Cornelius Van Til, *The Defense of the Faith* (2nd ed.; Phillipsburg, New Jersey: Presbyterian and Reformed, [1963]) and Van Til, *A Christian Theory of Knowledge* (Phillipsburg, New Jersey, Presbyterian and Reformed, [1932] 1969).

Continuity vs. Discontinuity

Each side appeals to a discontinuity to overcome the other side's supposed continuity. Each side also uses continuity to overcome the other side's supposed discontinuity.

The Debate Begins: Discontinuity

Let us begin with the arguments for discontinuity: exceptions to the universal reign of uniformitarianism. Both sides need exceptions to the uniformitarian principle of entropy. The Scientific Creationists allow for miracles, while the Darwinians allow for increasing order of evolutionary development—a temporary discontinuity in the entropy process.

The Scientific Creationists say that God overcomes entropy occasionally by intervening in history. A purposeful God created a purposeful universe, and He occasionally annuls entropy (a curse) for His own purposes. They admit that miracles are an exception to entropy, and therefore "unscientific," but they argue that the Darwinians have also been unscientific by affirming a temporary and unexplainable discontinuity called evolution: increasing order in an entropic world of decreasing order. But to argue this way, they have to equate the process of entropy with the second law of thermodynamics, and the second law with science itself. Writes Henry Morris: "As a matter of fact, thermodynamics could practically be considered as synonymous with science, since its concepts and laws embrace all scientific processes in all scientific disciplines."[33] (I should think that the same could be said of gravity or any number of other scientific laws.) Science is not everything there is, for God is the non-entropic Lord of the universe, but whatever *science* is, it *must* rest on entropy as its foundation. Therefore, they say, the Darwinists are not truly scientific. Darwinists want their exception to entropy—evolution—to remain within the framework of science, not outside it. This is cheating, say the Scientific Creationists.

The Darwinians reply that meaningless, zero-purpose, order-producing, unplanned and unplanning, entropy-reversing *energy* from outside a regional entropy-bound system can produce and has produced regional evolution. They say that this exception really is

---

33. Henry M. Morris, *The Biblical Basis for Modern Science* (Grand Rapids, Michigan: Baker Book House, 1984), p. 185.

not a true exception to the second law of thermodynamics. A temporary overcoming of entropy is legitimate, so long as we maintain that entropy wins out in the end (or at least just before the universe reverses itself and begins to contract). This seeming discontinuity really is not a true discontinuity. They say that they alone are truly scientific, since the discontinuities of Christian history are totally unscientific. They know that evolution must be a valid part of a world of entropy because God just cannot be.

Both sides want to stand on "solid scientific ground," meaning that both sides feel compelled to appeal to one "temporarily valid," anti-uniformitarian process in order to overcome the implications of the other side's system. Each side says, in effect, "my discontinuity is better than your discontinuity." So much for the exceptions—the discontinuities—to the continuity of uniformitarianism.

Continuity

Now let us look at the use of the argument from uniformitarian continuity against the other side's continuity. The Scientific Creationists use their temporary (post-Fall, pre-resurrection) universal law of entropy to prove that there could never have been uniformitarian, Darwinian, unplanned evolutionary development. They use one form of uniformitarianism (entropy) to refute another kind of uniformitarianism: "upward"-moving, increasingly ordered evolutionary progress within an increasingly random universe. They argue that the evolutionists' "discontinuity" of life's origins, above all, cannot be explained within the framework of the uniformity of entropy. They use the uniformity of entropy to refute the Darwinians' version of the discontinuity of life's origin, as well as to refute the supposed uniformity of upward evolutionary development.

The Darwinians also want a particular type of uniformitarianism, and they also must admit that it is temporary: the process of evolution. Someday, entropy's cold, dead hand will crush all regional, temporary evolutionary processes. (Most evolutionists are presently hesitant to throw out the concept of uniformitarian entropy, which is postulated today as being as old as the universe, but they may be willing to abandon or radically modify the idea in the future.) They want "regional escape hatches" from entropy's randomness in order to explain the process of evolution—regional "open boxes" that are temporarily (billions of years) sustained by energy sources outside the region. Darwinians use the idea of *uni-*

formitarian regional evolutionary processes — admittedly processes of limited duration — to modify the idea of uniformitarian, universal entropy. They want this form of uniformitarianism to refute the supposed "discontinuities" (anti-uniformitarianism) of the Christians: creation, miracles, and the Noachic Flood, and above all, the discontinuity of final judgment.

The Christians ultimately argue for a world of final discontinuity. The Christians proclaim cosmic restoration at the final judgment, a day that will inaugurate a new era of uniformitarianism peace without curses. The Darwinists ultimately argue for a world of continuity. They prefer the uniformitarian heat death of the universe, the result of triumphant entropy, to God's discontinuous day of triumphant final judgment.[34]

Stability vs. Change

It appears that while we all need fixed reference points in order to discuss historical change, none of us can tolerate the rule of such an inflexible monarch. We cannot seem to discover processes in nature that change at absolutely fixed rates over time. The Scientific Creationists want occasional miracles, the Darwinian evolutionists want occasional catastrophes, and the theonomists want Old Testament-New Testament changes in administration or application of God's fixed ethical law.[35]

Every philosophy has to come to grips with the problem of change within a framework of stability. The Bible teaches that God is

---

34. I do not want to go into a detailed discussion of the heat death of the universe, but there is a peculiarity of the heat death thesis. Entropy expands toward total randomness as time passes, although it is difficult to explain what it is that is passing when you define time in terms of entropy. If heat really dies, then the end result is a temperature of absolute zero. Now we must invoke the seldom-discussed third law of thermodynamics: at absolute zero, a system will have an entropy of zero. See Charles W. Keenan and Jesse Wood, *General College Chemistry* (New York: Harper & Row, 1966), p. 419. Here is a major antinomy (self-contradiction) of modern science: the entropy of the universe increases as it approaches perfect randomness and absolute zero as a limit. Then, discontinuously, it reaches its cosmic limit, and instantaneously (time's dying gasp) the closed system of the universe shifts from a state of maximum entropy to a state of zero entropy. Thus, even the universe of the evolutionists faces a great and final cosmic discontinuity. The world of perfect equilibrium — pure randomness without direction or hope of direction — is also the world of perfect death, absolute zero, and zero entropy. "The universe is dead. Long live the universe."

35. Greg L. Bahnsen, *Theonomy in Christian Ethics* (2nd ed.; Phillipsburg, New Jersey: Presbyterian & Reformed, 1984), Part IV.

the fixed reference point, that His law is the unchanging rule, and that both man and nature develop in history in terms of God's providential plan. It is the fundamental epistemological error of the entropists—Darwinian, New Age, and Scientific Creationists—that they look to nature rather than to God as their source of stable principles of understanding. They see entropy as the universally agreed-upon principle of scientific understanding, and sometimes also of historical understanding. Their religious and theological presuppositions govern their selection of a uniformitarian standard.

Open and Closed Boxes

The Darwinists and the Scientific Creationists have their own respective doctrines of *open and closed boxes*. Darwinians want *uncreated* open boxes (regions): *open outward*, meaning regions that are open to nearby sources of order-producing energy, but always within the ethically and metaphysically closed box of the universe. Modern humanism's universe is closed by definition to the God of the Bible. The Scientific Creationists want a *created* open box (universe): *open upward*, meaning a universe which gained its original order and energy from outside itself, but which is now dissipating both order and energy. The Darwinians want to deny the existence of a open box (universe) upward, while the creationists want to deny the evolutionary significance of the existence of open boxes (regions) outward.

The Darwinians want to extract order and social blessings from impersonal energy. This energy is transformed impersonally by chance and plants, and transformed personally by man into man-benefiting products. They now want to use biological science to create new life forms that will transform even more energy into man-benefiting products, a vision which horrifies New Age polemicist Jeremy Rifkin.[36]

The Scientific Creationists have generally remained silent about such world-transforming developments by modern science. (This silence makes them appear socially irrelevant.) However, since they are personally convinced that entropy rules life, and that evil will triumph before Christ returns to set up His kingdom, they do not expect scientific discoveries to change either the downward entropic drift of the universe or the downward moral drift of civilization.

---

36. Rifkin, *Algeny*.

They do not believe that the world's openness upward to God will have any permanent positive effects, at least not before a future millennium in which Christ appears physically to rule the nations, accompanied by resurrected saints who no longer are under the curse of entropy, even though everyone else on earth is.

Conclusion

What we find is that both sides appeal to entropy, and both sides also deny it. Both sides claim to be uniformitarians, and both sides deny it. The Scientific Creationists want entropy to rule unchallenged, except when miracles are involved. The Darwinians also want entropy to rule, but they also want an exception—"sunshine evolution." But how did the sun get here? In terms of the evolutionists' own presuppositions, we need to ask: How did a supposedly impersonal, undesigned cosmic order that is characterized by increasing randomness ever produce an orderly energy source (the sun) that in turn created pockets of increasing biological order? How long did this process take? What probability can be assigned that the sun's rays made life emerge from non-life? This is what Scientific Creationists keep asking? They do not get straight answers.

Discovering an explanation for getting order out of disorder is the top priority scientific problem for all evolutionary systems, whether physical science or social science. Discovering a program or process for preserving order is the second problem. How does society preserve order if the entropy law is valid? By an appeal to God and His miracles? By an appeal to sunlight and its temporary escape hatch? Or as the mystics would have it, by an appeal to a pantheistic god who is both totally immersed in and yet totally divorced from this world's reality, which they see as *maya*, or unreality?

Why all this technical discussion of cosmology? Because cosmologies have implications for every aspect of human thought and action. We find that the *doctrine of origins* has implications for our *doctrine of finality*, which in turn has implications for our *doctrine of immediate ethics*, not to mention our *doctrine of social reality*. We find that creationists and evolutionists debate questions of social theory by using arguments remarkably similar to the arguments that they use against each other in the field of cosmology. This book is concerned with social theory, so I was forced to devote part of it to cosmology.

Appendix B

THE END OF ILLUSIONS:
"CREATIONISM" IN THE PUBLIC SCHOOLS

The Establishment Clause forbids the enactment of any law "respecting an establishment of religion." The Court has applied a three-pronged test to determine whether legislation comports with the Establishment Clause. First, **the legislature must have adopted the law with a secular purpose**. *Second, the statute's principal or primary effect must be one that neither advances nor inhibits religion. Third, the statute must not result in an excessive entanglement of government with religion. (Emphasis added.)*

Justice William Brennan[1]

Shortly before I sent the manuscript of this book to the typesetter, the United States Supreme Court, by a 7 to 2 decision, declared unconstitutional a Louisiana law mandating the teaching of the "two-model view" of the origins of the universe whenever the topic was raised in a public school classroom. The case was *Edwards v. Aguillard* (June 19, 1987). The 1981 Louisiana state law had specified that whenever the origin of man or the universe was taught in public day schools (not in taxpayer-financed universities, however), the teacher had to present a two-model view of origins. The two required models were Darwinian evolution and a strange hybrid system that is essentially creationism without any mention of the Bible or God the Creator. The creation model had to be religiously neutral, for the state recognized that under federal law, it could not legally mandate the teaching of religion. The two-model view is, and always has been, built on a catastrophic mistake: the idea that the Bible's account of God the Creator can safely be ignored in all technical scientific discussions. This humanist presupposition has from the begin-

---

1. *Edwards v. Aguillard* (June 19, 1987), Syllabus, p. 3.

ning been the bedrock legal and also epistemological presupposition used by Scientific Creationists in their attempts to compel states to mandate the teaching of Creatorless creationism. What is not understood by the typical faithful believer in the pew is that most of those scientists who have defended the doctrine of creationism have done so as men who *deny* that science has anything to say about origins. In fact, they attempted to redefine science in order to maintain this position. Writes John N. Moore:

> In regard to *first* origins, certain questions must be raised. Can scientific research be applied? Is it possible to scientifically study the origin of the universe? Is it possible to scientifically study the origin of life on the earth? Is it possible to scientifically study the origin of humankind? According to the majority of the scientific community, the answer to each of these questions is "Yes." In actual fact, the most rigorous answer to each of these questions about first origins is a definite "No." It is the responsibility of the science teacher to fully examine, review and test all ideas.
>
> The science teacher should be especially able to help others to understand that *no* question about first origins can be answered scientifically. First origin questions involve events that are forever past. The very beginnings of the universe, of life on the earth, of humankind are *not* repeatable. Proper scientific research requires multiple, direct or indirect observations of repeatable events. From a rigorous metaphysical position, *all questions* of first origin should be considered more opportunely within the subject matter areas of philosophy and theology. Realistically, first origin questions — about ultimate cause — are within the purview of philosophers and theologians. Thus, they could more properly be included in humanities or social studies.[2]

Consider the logic of this position. First, science can deal only with repeatable events. The obvious response of virtually all scientists is simple: "Who says so?" Nobody takes such an argument seriously. For example, the science of historical geology deals with non-repeatable events. Alarm bells should sound in the ears of Scientific Creationists. If Dr. Moore's new definition of science is correct, then *it is scientifically illegitimate to discuss the origins of the geological effects of the event Christians refer to as the Noachic Flood.* Yet the Creation Science movement has always based the bulk of its geological case for creationism on a scientific study of the Noachic Flood. The movement's

---

2. John N. Moore, *How to Teach ORIGINS (Without ACLU Interference)* (Milford, Michigan: Mott Media, 1983), pp. xii-xiii.

premier "book of origins" is *The Genesis Flood* (1961).[3]

Second, all authority to deal with questions of origins must be transferred forever to theologians and philosophers. But this would solve nothing: modern philosophers appeal to scientific "facts" to create and defend their cosmologies. In fact, most of the major twentieth-century cosmologists have been trained scientists, though of course their theoretical speculations regarding origins are deeply philosophical. What Moore does not want to admit — and what the Scientific Creation movement has been unwilling to admit — is that *a worldview is necessarily of one piece*. If someone is a scientist, he can legitimately discuss origins precisely because *every science has a concept of origins*. Science is an outgrowth of a particular worldview. There is no such thing as science without a governing worldview.

Equal Time for Satan?

We cannot hope to solve our problem as Christians by attempting to redefine science as exclusively a study of repeatable events. Instead, we must become systematic in our scientific endeavors. We must self-consciously proclaim that every science can and does operate in terms of some particular philosophy and therefore some particular theology. We Christians must start with Christian theology and produce our own appropriate science, *just as Darwinists start with humanistic theology and produce their own appropriate science*.

The real scientific debate implicitly centers around the fundamental theological differences between true science and false science. True science must be defined as Bible-governed science; false science is therefore any science that denies Bible-governed science. True science must begin with the presupposition of God, the creation, and the Creator-creature distinction. It must begin with the doctrine of scientific regularities as an external manifestation of the providence of God. Any science that does not self-consciously begin with these presuppositions is simply another form of humanism. It may be baptized humanism, but it is nonetheless humanism.

It is impossible to separate theology and philosophy from science. Only a highly naive eighteenth-century view of science allows people to make such a mistake as to believe that such a separation is possible. This has always been the number-one problem with the Creation Science movement. Its apologetic method is based

---

[3]. By Henry Morris and John C. Whitcomb (Philadelphia: Presbyterian and Reformed).

The End of Illusions: "Creationism" in the Public Schools 209

on a late-eighteenth-century concept of philosophy, theology, and science. It is a vestige of Christianity's 1,800-year compromise with Greek paganism's natural law philosophy. Nobody takes natural law seriously any longer in the world of humanism, for Darwinism destroyed natural law.[4] That was Darwin's purpose: to destroy William Paley's natural law theology by substituting evolution through natural selection in place of medieval theology's argument for God by an appeal to cosmic order and also by an appeal to final causation (teleology).[5]

Instead of facing this issue squarely, Creation Scientists have naively gone about their work as if there were really a neutral scientific method of interpretation to which they could appeal their particular interpretations of hypothetically neutral scientific facts. This approach has never been successful, as I have argued throughout this book. It has led straight into the hands of people like Jeremy Rifkin. This approach has now been blown away by the U.S. Supreme Court's 1987 decision. The illusion of either legal or scientific neutrality should no longer bring any comfort whatsoever to a Creation Scientist who is serious about getting his ideas accepted. His ideas—though not his ideas concerning entropy—will be accepted only after Darwinian scientists are converted to Jesus Christ by God's grace, and they then begin to examine the truth or falsity of their scientific opinions by means of the Bible.

In short, the only hope for the widespread success of Scientific Creationism is in worldwide revival. That is the only hope for the success of every Christian's calling before God. Why should Creation Scientists think they are any less dependent on worldwide revival than the rest of us?

It means, quite simply, that all Christians must forever abandon any hope for the public schools. They can no longer hope to get "equal time for Jesus" in the classroom. The humanists, who half a century ago promised that they only wanted equal time for Darwinism, have made it plain ever since their overwhelming media victory at the Scopes trial in 1925 that they will settle for nothing less than full time for Darwinism. The fundamentalists have attempted to hold the fort

---

4. R. J. Rushdoony, *The Biblical Philosophy of History* (Phillipsburg, New Jersey: Craig Press, [1969] 1979), pp. 6-7.

5. Gary North, *The Dominion Covenant: Genesis* (2nd ed.; Tyler, Texas: Institute for Christian Economics, 1987), Appendix A: "From Cosmic Purposelessness to Humanistic Sovereignty."

for "equal time for Jesus" by offering the humanists "equal time for Satan." The humanists are no more ready to accept such a solution than the Pharaoh of the exodus was. They want it all, and they will call out the chariots and drive us into the Red Sea if necessary.

Fundamentalists have always known that they could not shove creationism in any form down the throats of state universities and colleges. They have never even tried to do this. They stage campus debates instead. So much for "equal time for Jesus." But for sixty years, they kept returning to the public day schools, banging on the doors to get in, trying to keep out Darwinism (the Scopes trial), and, when that approach failed, trying to get "equal time for a Jesus-ignoring doctrine of creation." When will they ever learn?

The Humanists' Long-Term Strategy

This Creatorless creation argument blew up in their faces when the Supreme Court responded that "there can be no valid secular reason for prohibiting the teaching of evolution, a theory historically opposed by some religious denominations. The court further concluded that 'the teaching of "creation-science" and "creationism," as contemplated by the statute, involves teaching "tailored to the principles" of a particular sect or group of sects.'"[6] The fact that the statute had not mentioned God or the Bible fooled no one.

Neither evolution nor creationism is religiously neutral, because *nothing* is religiously neutral. The public schools are founded legally on a lie. But evolutionists have always understood that if they could successfully appeal to neutral facts (a myth) and totally neutral scientific logic by which facts may be interpreted (a myth), they could take over the public schools. They relied on selling the idea of educational neutrality to the Christians, who controlled the schools and financed them. They were eminently successful in this sales job. Scientific Creationism is proof that the humanists' sales job was still believed by Christians as late as 1987.

The humanists pursued for over 150 years a successful program for secularizing American education. First, the schools were to be declared by law as officially neutral religiously. Second, after the passage of the Fourteenth Amendment, the courts step by step began to impose the First Amendment's provision of religious neutrality on the states. This was crucial to the humanists' plan for

---

6. *Edwards v. Aguillard*, p. 2.

The End of Illusions: "Creationism" in the Public Schools

capturing the United States. Those who would subsequently seek to control taxpayer-financed schools would be compelled by state and federal law to operate in terms of humanism's worldview, the myth of religious neutrality. By law, humanists would automatically gain control of American public education. They fully understood that if they could take over the public schools, they could then use their control over the schools to capture every human institution, for they would shape the thinking of succeeding generations of students.

The humanists' goal has always been conquest. They seek the establishment of the kingdom of man. The early progressive educators were self-conscious in their strategic planning. This is why R. J. Rushdoony called his 1963 study of the founders of modern progressive education, *The Messianic Character of American Education*.[7] Stephen Jay Gould, Harvard's paleontologist and *Scientific American* columnist, has summarized the history of Creation Science's attempt to get Creatorless creationism into the public schools:

> The legal battle over teaching evolution in public schools has passed through three broad phases. The laws of the Scopes era simply barred the teaching of evolution outright. The Supreme Court finally struck down this strategy in 1968, but only after these laws had enjoyed 40 years of effectiveness in muzzling the presentation of evolution in public schools.
>
> Since they could no longer ban evolution, fundamentalists then adopted a new strategy of legislating equal time for teaching the sectarian, literal interpretation of the Book of Genesis that they call "creationism." The initial "equal time" laws were, at least, honest in the sense that they properly identified creationism as a religious alternative to evolution. These statutes were soon struck down.
>
> The phase-two defeats restricted the legal options of fundamentalists to a third strategy. They invented a bogus subject called "scientific creationism" — simply the old wolf of Genesis literalism, lightly clothed in a woolly patina of supposed empirical verification.
>
> But a new name couldn't hide the unaltered content and context. Only Arkansas and Louisiana passed laws mandating equal time for "evolution science" and "creation science." The Arkansas law was struck down after a full trial that included my own testimony as a witness. Federal District Court Judge Adrian Duplantier then struck down the Louisiana law without trial. The state appealed to the United States Supreme Court.
>
> On June 19 [1987], the Supreme Court declared the Louisiana act unconstitutional. Justice Byron White, in his one-page concurrence with the

---

7. Philadelphia: Presbyterian and Reformed.

majority, expressed the heart of the matter with beautiful succinctness. "This is not a difficult case. . . ." he wrote. "The teaching of evolution was conditioned on the teaching of a religious belief. . . . The statute was therefore unconstitutional under the Establishment Clause."

We who have fought this battle for so many years were jubilant. The Court, by ruling so broadly and decisively, has ended the legal battle over creationism as a mandated subject in science classrooms. I do not think the fundamentalists can invent a fourth strategy.[8]

The Fourth Strategy: "Shut Them Down!"

He is wrong. There is a fourth strategy: to shut down all taxpayer-financed schools. That step has not been taken by fundamentalists, who still believe in taxpayer-financed education with all their hearts. They send their children to be educated by their enemies, in order to save a few dollars in tuition money. This is the fundamentalists' equivalent of passing their children through the fire. "Moreover thou has taken thy sons and thy daughters, whom thou hast borne unto me, and these hast thou sacrificed unto them to be devoured. Is this of thy whoredoms a small matter, that thou hast slain my children, and delivered them to cause them to pass through the fire for them" (Ezek. 16:20-21)?

Cornelius Van Til argued throughout his career that problems of knowledge are always problems of ethics. When we find an error in logic, we should begin our search for the ethical origin of the logical error. The logical error of the Scientific Creation movement is its continual appeal to neutral principles of interpretation, an appeal to a common-ground epistemological system. But a common-ground epistemology necessarily implies the existence of a common-ground ethical system. There is no epistemological neutrality because there is no ethical neutrality. Creationists who appeal to a common-ground neutral scientific worldview do so in part because of ignorance. They are seldom even vaguely familiar with the history of theology, philosophy, or even science. But the underlying basis of this self-conscious appeal to a common-ground scientific epistemology, despite a hundred years of ridicule and defeat by Darwinians, is ethical. The fundamentalists will not give up the idea that the state is economically, legally, and morally responsible for the education of children. The Creation Science movement has been seeking to get in

---

8. Stephen Jay Gould, "The Verdict on Creationism," *New York Times Magazine* (July 19, 1987), p. 32.

bed with the evolutionists. In this sense, Ezekiel's language of whoredom is appropriate. They simply refuse to launch a full-scale attack on all modern humanist science because they will not launch a full-scale attack on the legitimacy of public education. They will not tell their people that the public schools should be closed, and that nothing short of this is acceptable.

So they spent three generations trying to keep evolution out of the schools, and then fell back to "equal time for Jesus," and then fell back to "creationism without a Creator." Gould is correct: there is no fourth alternative, *if* Creation Scientists refuse to give up the goal of getting access to the immoral public schools.

Thus, we must build a truly creationist science, a consistently Christian worldview, by proclaiming the illegitimacy of all taxpayer-financed education. To proclaim even a tiny shred of legitimacy for taxpayer-financed education is necessarily to proclaim a tiny bit of legitimacy for evolutionary humanism, which now controls the schools by law.

The fundamentalists have at last hit their skulls into an unbreakable brick wall. The game is over. It is time to declare a consistent Christian worldview. Such a worldview involves an implacable hostility to the public schools.

A Christian can measure his commitment to Christ (among other measures) by this hostility to taxpayer-financed education. To the extent that he still has faith in taxpayer-financed education, he still is governed by humanist presuppositions. He is still betraying his faith by a continuing commitment to a long-dead compromise of Christianity with Greek natural law theology. He is still proclaiming a worldview based on the naive goal of equal time for Jesus. Jesus deserves and demands far more than equal time.

It is time for Christians to stop proclaiming a stalemate religion. It is time to proclaim the crown rights of King Jesus in every area of life.

Academic Freedom: Paying Your Own Way

Humanists have appealed since the early nineteenth century to a doctrine of academic freedom. It was first developed by God-hating humanist professors in Prussian universities who feared getting fired from their posts if their apostasy was revealed to the civil authorities. In a tax-supported world financed by Christians, the pagan professors needed something to cover their attempt to steal the minds of

Christian students. They needed legitimacy. They invented the doctrine of academic freedom.

The doctrine of academic freedom is today and has always been a bogus moral appeal devised by unscrupulous people who live on wealth confiscated from others. They use this bogus doctrine to defend their right not only to this confiscated wealth but also their right to steal the allegiance of the children of those taxpayers whose money has been stolen from them. What "academic freedom" meant (and still means) was simple: a license for taxpayer-supported teachers to steal the minds of the next generation at the expense of this generation of taxpayers. Specifically, it meant (and still means) the right of atheists and humanists *who promise to obey the State only when the State is based on humanism* to teach anti-Christian worldviews to the children of Christians who pay their salaries.

This is all that academic freedom has ever meant. It rests, unquestionably, on the myth of neutrality. Rather than resting on the earlier eighteenth-century version of the myth of neutrality, namely the philosophy of natural law, the modern version of academic freedom has always rested on the twin notions of cosmic evolution and moral relativism. Darwinism came late to the scene, and was appropriated by the evolutionists because Darwinism seemed to bring scientific sanctions to their earlier philosophical evolutionism.

Classroom professors in American private colleges picked up the doctrine of academic freedom during the last century. They, too, wanted protection, not from voters but from parents of tuition-paying students. Even more obviously than the Prussian professors, they were nothing more than parent-hired tutors. The Prussian professors were agents of the State; the American teachers were employees of parents. So they grabbed the doctrine of academic freedom as their life preserver in a sea of uncertainty about their jobs. They, too, wanted to shape the minds of students without interference from "narrow-minded" parents. They used the doctrine of academic freedom to shield themselves from parents, college presidents, and boards of trustees. Because of the doctrine of academic freedom they carved out what basically are trade union monopolies, with appropriate trade union jurisdictions, which in academia are called "departments." The faculty members have become the true economic owners of higher education throughout the world.[9]

---

9. Henry G. Manne, "The Political Economy of Modern Universities," in Anne Husted Burleigh (ed.), *Education in a Free Society* (Indianapolis, Indiana: Liberty Fund, 1973).

The End of Illusions: "Creationism" in the Public Schools 215

Russell Kirk begins his book, *Academic Freedom* (1955), with this citation:

> "Academic freedom," says a distinguished editor, Mr. W. T. Couch, "is the principle designed to protect the teacher from hazards that tend to prevent him from meeting his obligations in the pursuit of truth." This is the best definition of the idea that I have come upon.[10]

Notice the focus of Mr. Couch's concern: *to protect the teacher*. This was exactly the concern of the Prussian university professors who sought autonomy from the political authorities whose tax money supported them. But who needs to be protected most, the teachers or their students? Who is to protect the students from indoctrination by a group of self-serving, taxpayer-supported humanists whose worldview is totally opposed to the opinions of most of the voters and most of the parents who send their children to the state-run schools?

Scalia Dissents

Who should speak for the students? Who defends their interests? This was the issue raised by Supreme Court justice Scalia in his dissent from his colleagues' decision:

> Had the Court devoted to this central question of the meaning of the legislatively expressed purpose a small fraction of the research into legislative history that produced its quotations of religiously motivated statements by individual legislators, it would have discerned quite readily what "academic freedom" meant: *students'* freedom from *indoctrination*. The legislature wanted to ensure that students would be free to decide for themselves how life began, based upon a fair and balanced presentation of the scientific evidence—that is, to protect "the right of each [student] voluntarily to determine what to believe (and what not to believe) free of any coercive pressures from the State."[11]

There is an unstated problem here, one which has long confounded all attempts to discover a neutral doctrine of academic freedom. One man's "fair and balanced presentation of the scientific evidence" is another man's "blatant indoctrination." One voter's view of what should be taught is the denial of another man's religion. *The*

---

10. Russell Kirk, *Academic Freedom* (Chicago: Regnery, 1955), p. 1.
11. Justice Scalia's dissent, Supreme Court of the United States, *Edwards v. Aguillard*, p. 18.

question of fairness cannot be solved apart from an appeal to legitimate authority: first, the authority of God; second, the authority of those to whom God has delegated the responsibility of speaking in His name and enforcing His law in any specific area. This is the issue that the Supreme Court cannot avoid, yet one which it refuses to face squarely. In the name of neutrality, the Court has defined God as the will of the people, and it has identified the agency responsible for voicing the will of the people as the civil government. The tenured, tax-financed, humanistic teachers insist that they alone lawfully represent the civil government in the classroom, and the Supreme Court has now upheld their claim against the legislators of the State of Louisiana and the taxpayers who elected them to office. The bureaucrats have become the voice of humanism's god. This is *the* lesson of modern democracy.

In short, the day the Constitution became religiously neutral was the day that the foundation of this Supreme Court decision was established. It was only a matter of time and effective lobbying by humanists who believe in salvation by politics and lobbying. The mythological doctrine of "equal time for Satan" eventually becomes "no time for God." Neutrality is a myth. The Scientific Creationists must learn this lesson. The Supreme Court has now given them a lesson that has overturned a quarter century of their misguided efforts to "save the public schools" and "make them fair" by trying to legislate "equal time" for an officially Creatorless doctrine of creation.

Who was W. T. Couch, whose statement of academic freedom so impressed Russell Kirk? I had the unpleasant experience in the summer of 1963 of working for three months as an associate of the late Mr. Couch. Couch was a dedicated anti-Christian humanist, a man who sneered at the very idea of the Bible as the infallible word of God. I was never impressed with his reputation as a "distinguished editor," but I fully understood his search for suitable academic employment. He never produced much of anything in the months that I worked with him, and he died leaving no visible mark on the conservative intellectual movement. He spent the three months I worked with him trying to get the multi-million dollar conservative foundation that employed us to spend a literal fortune to produce a modern version of the French *philosophes'* encyclopedia. He vehemently opposed any suggestion that the project should be straightforwardly conservative. It was the same old story: use money supplied by conservatives to produce academic materials that are officially neutral and inherently anti-Christian. I can understand why he was a firm supporter of the doctrine of academic freedom.

But why should conservative Russell Kirk affirm his faith in such a doctrine? Because Kirk is a defender of the medieval Roman Catholic philosophical compromise called scholastic natural law theology. He therefore plays into the hands of the God-haters whose expressed goal is to remove all traces of God from the classroom. It was a Protestant fundamentalist version of this same common-ground philosophy that led the Creation Scientists to invent a compromised hybrid doctrine of creation that self-consciously made no reference to the Creator. The Supreme Court threw it out anyway — in fact, because it made no sense. But like Dracula, it may rise again from the dead.

Gould Gloats

Thus, we should not be surprised to find Prof. Gould appealing once again to academic freedom as the justification for the Supreme Court's decision:

> But creation science is also a sham because the professed reason for imposing it upon teachers — to preserve the academic freedom of students to learn alternative viewpoints — is demonstrably false. Creationists are right in identifying academic freedom as the key issue, but they have the argument perversely backward.
>
> It was their law that abridged the most precious meaning of academic freedom, the freedom of teachers to follow the dictates of their consciences, their training and their professional commitments. . . .
>
> "Creation science" has not entered the curriculum for a reason so simple and so basic that we often forget to mention it: because it is false, and because good teachers understand exactly why it is false. What could be more destructive of that most fragile yet most precious commodity in our entire academic heritage — good teaching — than a bill forcing honorable teachers to sully their sacred trust by granting equal treatment to a doctrine not only known to be false, but calculated to undermine any general understanding of science as an enterprise?[12]

The answer to this familiar trade union appeal is simple: he who pays the piper calls the tune. The classroom evolutionists should be forced by economic necessity to persuade people to pay voluntarily for their time spent in the laboratory, classroom, and library. If there

---

12. Gould, "Verdict," p. 34.

is anything that Darwinists believe in it is the survival of the fittest. Let these Darwinian propagandists, these epistemological child molesters, find parents or private educational foundations to finance them. They should never again have an opportunity to fleece the taxpayers. They should face the same free market that creationists face. They have the academic freedom they need to find a buyer of their services. They are entitled to no other protection of their views.

They know what will happen. Not very many of them are sufficiently fit intellectually to survive the competitive challenge of the free market.

Conclusion

Unfortunately, there were a few lines in the Supreme Court's decision that have offered false hope to a few Scientific Creationists that yet another round of political lobbying for Creatorless creationism will somehow be successful. It is almost as if the Court deliberately intended this, in order to lure professionally naive Scientific Creationists into another round of expensive legal battles. It remains to be seen whether these lines will lead to another time-absorbing legislative attempt to get the first state-permitted, state financed "creationist" curriculum into the public schools. What is so discouraging is that Scientific Creationists have spent a quarter of a century and millions of donated dollars in this fruitless quest to make acceptable to Christians the legally neutral, innately humanist, inherently immoral public school system. Instead of now possessing a comprehensive creationist science curriculum for Christian schools, Scientific Creationists have nothing to show for their efforts except a pile a fee receipts from lawyers. When will this nonsense end? Only when fundamentalists at last abandon natural law theology and its presupposition, the myth of neutrality.

Let creationists cease playing into the hands of the evolutionists by vainly continuing to proclaim the existence of a nonexistent common-ground philosophy, a neutral scientific method that will lead all "truly logical" scientists, covenant-breakers and covenant-keepers, to an acceptance of a Creatorless creation and the abandonment of evolutionism. It was a hybrid concept in the first place. It has failed to get half-baked creationism into the public schools. It is time to scrap this epistemological equivalent of the Piltdown Man fossil: the myth of scientific neutrality.

Appendix C

COMPREHENSIVE REDEMPTION: A THEOLOGY FOR SOCIAL ACTION*

For God so loved the world, that he gave his only begotten Son, that whosoever believeth in him should not perish, but have everlasting life (John 3:16).

There is no more familiar verse in the Bible in today's evangelical world. This is the "verse of verses" in presenting the gospel of salvation to those outside the faith. It is this verse that is supposed to convey to the unregenerated the idea of the love of God. It is also the verse which most clearly offers to man the chief incentive to believe: eternal life. But it means much more: *Christ placated God's wrath against the world, so that God would sustain the world in history until the final judgment.*

It is common for men to point to the introductory phrase, "For God so loved the world," and to conclude that this verse teaches that God sent Christ to die to save all men. The term, "the world," supposedly refers to all the souls of all men on earth. In other words, when we speak of "the world," we mean the aggregate of mankind. The focus of concern is the conversion of souls. Evangelicals see their area of personal responsibility as essentially fulfilled when they deliver the gospel of personal salvation to the lost—salvation *out of* this world. The comprehensive gospel is, in their eyes, *comprehensive* with respect to *souls* (Christ died to save all men), but *limited* with respect to the effects of redemption, namely, *human actions and institutions*.

But men are never saved out of this world. Christ's prayer in John 17 is clear: "I pray not that thou shouldest take them out of the world, but that thou shouldest keep them from the evil. They are not

---

*A preliminary version of this essay was published in *The Journal of Christian Reconstruction*, VIII (Summer 1981): "Symposium on Social Action." P.O. Box 158, Vallecito, CA 95251, $7.50.

of the world, even as I am not of the world. Sanctify them through thy truth: thy word is truth. As thou hast sent me into the world, even so have I also sent them into the world. And for their sakes I sanctify myself, that they also might be sanctified through the truth" (John 17:15-19).

But Christians forget the crucial words of Christ, "even so have I also sent them into the world." Sent them *to do what?* To preach the gospel without expecting any visible results of the gospel in history?

Kosmos: The World

The Greek word, *kosmos* (world), is used in several ways, just as the English word "world" is used in several ways. ("What in the world are you talking about?") It frequently refers to something far broader than humanity. It often refers to the *present world order,* meaning the scheme of creation that man was designed to complete. "My kingdom is not of this world," Jesus said (John 18:36a). He was not referring to the souls of mankind, but to the creation, the total world order. This comprehensive world order is being steadily reconciled to Christ, in the dual sense that men are being reconciled to Him (II Cor. 5:19), and that Satan's kingdom is being overcome by the preaching of the gospel and the establishment of Christian institutions. "For he must reign, till he hath put all enemies under his feet" (I Cor. 15:25).

Satan's "world": The Bible speaks of Satan as the prince of *this world* (John 14:30). Premillennialists and amillennialists have argued that this means that God has delivered control of the world in history (or at least during the "Church Age") to Satan. Christians will be progressively under the temporal rule of Satan's human followers, we are told. This argument is incorrect. As Greg Bahnsen has argued so forcefully, the phrase, "prince of this world," does not mean that Satan runs the world. God runs the world, as the Creator and Sustainer of the world. So in what sense is Satan a prince of this world? What does "this world" mean in this context? I cite only part of Bahnsen's carefully developed argument, but this extract will be sufficiently detailed to give food for thought to anyone who has held to a misinterpretation of "prince of this world." Bahnsen argues that the word has an *ethical* frame of reference.

It is quite common for the term "world" to be used, not in a geographic sense, but in an *ethical* sense; here it denotes the *immoral realm of disobedience* rather than an all-inclusive, extensive scope of creation. The "world" represents the life of man apart from God and bound to sinful impulses. Thus, when scriptural writers speak of "the world," they often mean the world *in so far as* it is ethically separated from God. Paul contrasts *godly* sorrow to the sorrow of the *world;* the former brings salvation, while the latter leads to death (II Cor. 7:10). If "world" here meant the geographic scope of creation (embracing all men and things), then the "sorrow of the world" would include the sorrow of any and all men who live in the world — thus precluding the possibility of any earth-dweller repenting with godly sorrow and finding salvation. Furthermore, the juxtaposition of "godly" with "worldly" would require — if "world" denotes a location rather than an ethical state — that "godly" correspondingly denotes a physical realm or location; otherwise Paul's contrast would not be categorical and mutually exclusive (i.e., some sorrow could be simultaneously godly *and* located in the world). Paul is clearly using "world" for the unethical state of sinful rebellion, and thus can contrast it to the ethical state of godliness. In Colossians 2:8, Paul appositionally explains "the elementary principles of the *world*" as philosophy which is *"not according to Christ."* Hence the elements of "the world" (cf. Gal. 4:3) stand in direct antithesis to Christ. Here the world is the unethical sphere of opposition to Christ. In Philippians 2:15, Christians are called "lights in the *world*" — that is, "children of God without blemish in the midst of a *crooked and perverse generation.*" The "world" is not each and every human being, but rather the *generation* which is perverse and crooked; the term is *qualitative* rather than quantitative. It has an ethical, not geographical, focus. The world in its wisdom knows not God, and God makes the world's wisdom foolish (I Cor. 1:20, 21; cf. 3:19). The world is that realm which is under God's condemnation (I Cor. 11:32), for to walk "according to the course of this world" is to follow Satan and be a "son of disobedience" and therefore a "child of wrath" (Eph. 2:2-3). From these verses it is evident that "world" denotes the ethical sphere of sinful rebellion. . . .[1]

The world knows not God (I John 3:1) and therefore hates the Christian brotherhood (3:13) — which indicates that "world" denotes a *subclass of humanity*, one which is ethically qualified. Those who are worldly listen to those who are likewise worldly and not of God (I John 4:5-6). John summarizes this contrast between the saved and the lost, the realm of light and life and the realm of darkness and death, the sphere of righteousness and the sphere of wickedness, by saying, "We know that we are of God, but the whole world lieth in the evil one" (I John 5:19). "The world" is not the geographical, created order; nor is it the whole of humanity. It is that *aspect* of reality, that *portion* of humanity, which is in the grip of Satan and not of

---

1. Greg L. Bahnsen, "The Person, Work, and Present Status of Satan," *Journal of Christian Reconstruction*, I (Winter 1974), pp. 22-23.

God. The world is positioned in the evil one and does not have its source in God; the world is that realm which is dominated by Satan and his standards. It is correspondingly appropriate that Satan is designated by John as "he that is in the world" (I John 4:4). The world is in Satan, and Satan is in the world. This confirms the ethical understanding of the term "world" which has been discussed above, for the created realm certainly *does* have its origin in God and *has* God immanent to it. Thus, "the world" (which is not of God, but is characteristically in and occupied by Satan) cannot be identified with created reality or the whole of humanity. "The world" must be interpreted (in the above passages) as an unethical spiritual realm, the kingdom of darkness, the city of reprobate man.[2]

Bahnsen goes on for several more pages in order to correlate "this age" with "the world" in the same sense of ethics, but there is not space here to reproduce Bahnsen's brilliant insights. The point should be clear: "the world" can be taken in many passages to mean Satan's ethical realm, not the whole *kosmos* as such.

The riches of this "world": The word can also mean the riches and advantages of earthly life. The Bible asks, "For what is a man advantaged, if he gain *the whole world*, and lose himself, or be cast away" (Luke 9:25)? It can also mean Israel. The Pharisees stated of Jesus that "the world"—meaning a large number of Israelites—"is gone after him" (John 12:19b). Thus, in some instances, *kosmos* was used to refer to persons in a group, but the word usually referred to a much broader concept: *the world order*.

The love of this "world": When the Bible speaks of *God's love for the world*, it obviously does not include the prince of this world, Satan, for an everlasting fire has been prepared for him and his angels (Matt. 25:41b). God loves the world, meaning that which He created, but He nevertheless intends to visit the world with a cleansing fire (II Peter 3:10). The world today will, in part, survive that fire, yet elements of it will not. In other words, the world loved by God is *now*, but it also *will be*. There is both a present and future aspect, just as there was a separate world order prior to the Noachic Flood, yet God preserved elements of that world by His grace in the ark (II Peter 2:5). There is both continuity and discontinuity in the biblical concept of *kosmos*. It was, is now, and shall be, despite major changes.

The redemption of the "world": The theological question that has to

---

2. *Ibid.*, p. 24.

be dealt with is this one: What is the relationship between that *kosmos* that God loves and the work of redemption that Christ inaugurated, "that whosoever believeth on Him should not perish, but have everlasting life"? In short, *is the world being redeemed?* People certainly are. But what about the world? Is it being redeemed ("bought back") by Christ? The answer is *yes*. It is being redeemed by God's grace: special and common.

Grace: Special and Common[3]

Grace means *unmerited gift*. Or more precisely, it means a gift from God to those who do not merit such a gift, on the basis of the death of His Son, Jesus Christ, who did merit God's favor. When we speak of "common grace," we are not speaking of God's love of all humanity, but instead we are speaking of God's common gifts to humanity. God sends the blessings of sunshine and rain to all men, both the just and unjust (Matt. 5:45). Nevertheless, this does not mean that He loves all men indiscriminately. The gifts to the righteous are special; any gifts to the unrighteous are for their ultimate condemnation. As Paul writes, concerning our obligation to help our enemies (quoting Proverbs 25:22):

Therefore if thine enemy hunger, feed him; if he thirst, give him drink: for in so doing thou shalt heap coals of fire on his head (Rom. 12:20).

The fact that our enemies receive unmerited gifts from us, and therefore from God, who is our Supreme Commander, makes their unwillingness to repent all the more devastating to them on the day of judgment, for God punishes those who have received much from His hand with greater severity than those who have received less (Luke 12:47-48).

God loves the world, the created order. He loves his own people, but he also loves the cosmic order that sustains them. Without sun and rain, without life itself, His people could not be sustained. When Adam died by rebelling, he did not cease breathing immediately. He was physically sustained by God. Adam provided the seed of future generations. Adam was given the gift of life, so that there might be people born who would be beloved by the Lord,

---

3. Gary North, *Dominion and Common Grace: The Biblical Basis of Progress* (Tyler, Texas: Institute for Christian Economics, 1987).

chosen "before the foundation of the world, that we should be holy and without blame before him in love: having predestinated us unto the adoption of children by Jesus Christ to himself, according to the good pleasure of his will" (Eph. 1:4-5). Because of God's special grace in electing some to eternal life, those who have not been so elected have nevertheless enjoyed the blessings of life. All men have participated in the plan of God; all men have played a role.

This is the proper frame of reference for the misused passage, I Timothy 4:10: "For therefore we both labour and suffer reproach, because we trust in the living God, who is the Saviour of all men, specially of those that believe." This is not a defense of universal salvation, meaning universal election. It is a defense of the idea that God's grace—His *unmerited gift* of Jesus Christ—is the foundation of life itself. God's grace heals all men. It gives them life and power to work out their destinies with fear and trembling (Phil. 2:12). This is a two-folded grace: universal and particular. Particular grace refers to personal redemption. Universal grace, or common grace, refers to the providence of God: the very sustaining power that undergirds the arena of existence. God loves this arena, the *kosmos*. He loves it so much that he sent Jesus Christ into the world to die for it.

Sustaining the World

The *kosmos* is comprehensive. It includes the life-sustaining features of the creation. Christ's death is therefore comprehensive, for it is the very foundation for time itself. What could exist apart from God's grace? What benefits would Adam and all his heirs, including Cain, otherwise have enjoyed? God's love for the world order does not mean that the special favor of God is offered indiscriminately to all men, let alone to Satan and his angels. It means that God extends *external blessings* to those who are His *eternal enemies*.

God so loved the *kosmos* that He gave His only begotten Son to sustain it. He did not offer the blessings or even the possibility of eternal life to everyone in the *kosmos*, so the particularity aspect of His salvation is maintained. Yet He loved more than the souls of men in general, thereby preserving the comprehensiveness of His love. He loves the world order, which is the arena of the drama of history. He does not love the tares of the field, but loves the field. "The field is the world [*kosmos*]; the good seed are the children of the kingdom; but the tares are the children of the wicked one" (Matt. 13:38).

Evangelicals have restricted the meaning of *kosmos* to human souls in general, yet they have simultaneously broadened the frame of reference of God's love, namely to souls in general. The Bible does not teach this. God loves *souls in particular* and the *world in general*. The concern of the evangelical world has been on the saving of souls, and they have long neglected the healing of the institutions of the world. But God's Son died to save (heal) all men, even though He did not die to regenerate all men. By neglecting the task of healing the *kosmos* — the institutional world order — Christians are denying the comprehensive nature of Christ's salvation. (Salve: a healing ointment.)

The Trinity and Society

The Trinity is a uniquely Christian concept: one God, yet three Persons, each with exhaustive knowledge of the others, and each equal in substance with the others, in perfect harmony of purpose and authority. In other words, there is unity and diversity in God's being. God is absolutely personal. There is true communion among the Persons of the Trinity. God is simultaneously *one* and *many*.[4]

We see in the creation a reflection of the nature of God. Society is both one and many. The human race is a unity which is distinguishable from other species, yet each individual has special characteristics that separate him from all other humans. A consistently Christian social philosophy acknowledges the reality of both the one and the many. For example, individuals are responsible before God for all that they say or do in life, and they will be judged individually on the day of judgment in terms of their performance (I Cor. 3). At the same time, social aggregates are also responsible for their adherence to the laws of God that are relevant for the particular aggregates: families, civil government, businesses, ecclesiastical organizations, etc. An entire society can be found guilty before God, in time and on earth (Deut. 28:15-68). We cannot ignore the laws relating to individual behavior or social behavior. Both individuals and social aggregates are responsible before God.

If we take this approach to social analysis, we have to deal with institutions. We have to recognize the covenantal relationship between men, and also under God. When a man and a woman cove-

---

4. R. J. Rushdoony, *The One and the Many: Studies in the Philosophy of Order and Ultimacy* (Fairfax, Virginia: Thoburn Press, [1971] 1978). This book develops insights in the writings of Cornelius Van Til.

nant before God in establishing a family, they are responsible as individuals for the performance of their vows.[5] Men and women have different assignments in the marriage, different responsibilities, and different degrees of authority (Eph. 5:22-33; I Pet. 3:1-7). Covenanted families under God are institutions for social peace and the extension of God's kingdom on earth—helping the earth to reflect heaven.

When men establish a civil government, they are also required to impose the rule of God's law for the civil government (Deut. 8). Men benefit as individuals from social peace, and social peace is a product of a society's adherence to biblical law. Every covenant is a covenant under God's law. Without law, there is no covenant.[6]

The Danger of Overemphasis

There is always a temptation for men to overemphasize or even ignore either the one or the many in a social order. Radical individualism or anarchy is one perspective, while socialism or totalitarianism is the other. In fact, as Hannah Arendt, J. L. Talmon, Robert Nisbet, and other social philosophers have noted, the absolute totalitarian regime requires the abolition or absorption into the State of all intervening social institutions—institutional buffers between the State and the citizen—in order to exercise maximum power.[7] The absolute *one* of the totalitarian State is composed of the radically autonomous (and unprotected) *many*. A man is defined solely as a member of the State, a "citizen" and nothing else. The French revolutionaries made "citizen" the universal greeting. France's Committee for Public *Safety* was also the Committee on Public *Salvation;* either translation is valid.[8] The messianic State requires undefended and isolated citizens as its foundation.

In modern evangelical circles, the tendency has been to emphasize personal and individualistic responsibility before God, to the exclusion of institutional responsibilities. Men are seen as souls to be

---

5. Ray R. Sutton, *That You May Prosper: Dominion By Covenant* (Tyler, Texas: Institute for Christian Economics, 1987), ch. 8.

6. *Ibid.*, ch. 3.

7. Hannah Arendt, *The Origins of Totalitarianism* (rev. ed.; New York: Harcourt Brace Jovanovich, [1968] 1973); J. L. Talmon, *Origins of Totalitarian Democracy* (New York: Norton, 1970); Robert Nisbet, *The Quest for Community* (New York: Oxford University Press, [1953] 1962); Nisbet, "Rousseau and the Political Community" (1943), reprinted in Nisbet, *Tradition and Revolt* (New York: Random House, 1968).

8. Robert Nisbet, *The Sociological Tradition* (New York: Basic Books, 1966), p. 34.

saved from sin. Institutions are not seen to be in the need of salvation (healing). Perhaps some attention may be given to the institutional church and its various agencies. These may be understood as being in need of reform, but not the civil government or other human institutions. Men as believing souls are to be brought under the rule of God, but not institutions.

Evangelicals, especially American fundamentalists, have preached and planned as if they were convinced that institutional reform is either impossible in history or else an automatic product of transformed lives, especially the lives of the leaders of the organizations.[9] But no guidelines are set forth as being morally binding institutionally. (It is with this problem in mind that I began publishing my Biblical Blueprints Series in 1986, in which biblical principles and specific practical recommendations are offered, with chapter and verse.)

In contrast to the individualism of twentieth-century fundamentalism, we find that theological liberals have tended to become advocates of social reform. The institutions of society are corrupt, they argue. Social justice is lacking. There must be some sort of institutional reforms, they argue, before men can live in harmony with their brothers. The presupposition of *environmental determinism* is often the foundation of such social analysis. Until the institutions are reformed, there can be no hope of individual reform.

A second aspect of this form of theological liberalism is its commitment to the civil government as the primary agency of social reform and therefore of social justice. The State is a messianic institution. Somehow, the State and its agents can be trusted to exercise monopolistic power for the benefit of God's kingdom, not just in those limited areas specified by the Bible, but in every area of life. The State is an agency of social salvation (healing), and therefore of personal salvation (healing). Not much emphasis is placed on the special grace of God—personal regeneration for eternity through faith. By default, Christians hand over power to the State, since they believe that institutions cannot be reformed in history. So they are

---

9. George Marsden, *Fundamentalism and American Culture: The Shaping of Twentieth Century Evangelicalism, 1870-1925* (New York: Oxford University Press, 1980). Marsden emphasizes that this pietist strain was accentuated after 1920, in response to the increased emphasis on social change by advocates of the social gospel (Part III). The revivalism of 1870-1900 was at times concerned with social change, but far less so from 1900 to the First World War, focusing on the temperance movement, missions, and private charity to those in poverty.

unconcerned with comprehensive social reform through voluntary action—the only available alternative program to social reform by State power. The liberals inherit a political vacuum, and they work to fill it. The State grows at the expense of private institutions. Taxes go up as tithes and offerings go down.

The Bible teaches us that *salvation is comprehensive,* just as God Himself is comprehensive. The one and the many are redeemed by Jesus Christ. They are healed because of Christ's sacrifice on the cross. But we know the fruits of salvation: adherence to the law of God. A good tree yields good fruit (Matt. 7:16-20). God so loved the world that He gave His Son as a sacrifice. If this comprehensive nature of Christ's redemption is ignored, then either one side or the other will be overemphasized: individual redemption or social transformation. Evangelicals want men's lives healed; liberals want institutional structures reformed. Both groups may use biblical law (or some hypothetical working out of the principles of biblical law) as the standard to judge whether or not a man or an institution has been redeemed. But both sides select only certain aspects of biblical law as their criteria, a practice that R. J. Rushdoony has called *smorgasbord religion:* a convenient picking and choosing of those aspects of biblical law that appeal to the audience or the religious leaders.

The Dualism of Modern American Christianity

Late-twentieth-century evangelicalism and fundamentalism have begun to modify this earlier perspective as one-sided, that is, their concern for soul-saving to the exclusion of concern for reforming institutions. Some evangelicals (and a tiny but growing handful of fundamentalist leaders) have now begun to concern themselves with social reform. This is partially a revival of an older evangelical tradition in the United States: the pre-Civil War revivalism of the Western states. This revivalism, especially under the influence of Charles G. Finney, was emotionalistic and pro-abolition, although Finney himself did not become an abolitionist.[10] The abolitionist

---

10. Sydney E. Ahlstrom, *A Religious History of the American People* (Garden City, New York: Image Books/Doubleday, [1972] 1975), II, pp. 96-97. On Finney and Oberlin's perfectionist theology, see Benjamin B. Warfield, *Perfectionism*, Vol. II (Grand Rapids, Michigan: Baker Book House, 1981), VII, Pt. I. This is a reprint of the original Oxford University Press edition of 1932. This section of the book is also reprinted in the abridged version published by Presbyterian & Reformed, 1958, 1974.

movement was not simply the product of a handful of Boston Unitarians and Transcendentalists.[11] The Unitarians needed a transmission belt into churches in order to rally Christians in the North, and revivals become one such transmission belt. Finney's perfectionism became, at Oberlin College, a crusade for abolitionism. The slavery question became a passionate cause for many Western revivalists.[12]

However, once the great war was over, it was easy for this emotional commitment to dissipate into a reforming spirit, or else to dissipate into pietism. Both approaches were common in the North and West. The reforming spirit became a part of the Social Gospel movement, and pietism became part of a later revivalism. Christianity turned outward on the one hand, and inward on the other.

The same dualism marked the post-Civil War developments of the South. The antebellum religious leadership, especially the progress-minded and culture-minded Presbyterians, never fully recovered from the defeat of the Confederacy, which they had equated with Christian civilization.[13] The rise of the pietist and independent churches to positions of local leadership transferred political power from the kingdom-minded to the revival-minded. The Populist movement, with its uneducated leaders, was one substitute for older southern conservative leadership, but it had died out by the turn of the century.[14]

By the late twentieth century, the pietist position was being challenged by the political leftists within evangelicalism and by the newly recruited political right within fundamentalism. The political left within evangelicalism found an ardent promoter in Dr. Ronald Sider, whose prescriptions for social renewal are sufficiently vague on the specifics to keep the conservatives anesthetized, but sufficiently radical in language to gain him extensive support on seminary facul-

---

11. Gilbert Barnes, *The Anti-Slavery Impulse, 1830-1844* (Gloucester, Massachusetts: Peter Smith, [1933]). This is not to say that the leadership of the abolitionist movement came from the evangelicals rather than the Transcendentalists in Boston and the Northeast. See especially the book by Otto Scott, *The Secret Six: John Brown and the Abolitionist Movement* (New York: Times Books, 1979).

12. Benjamin P. Thomas, *Theodore Weld: Crusader for Freedom* (New York: Octagon, [1964] 1973). Cf. Donald W. Dayton, *Discovering an Evangelical Heritage* (New York: Harper & Row, 1976). Dayton is Ronald Sider's brother-in-law.

13. John P. Maddox, "From Theocracy to Spirituality: The Southern Presbyterian Reversal on Church and State," *Journal of Presbyterian History*, LIV (1976).

14. C. Vann Woodward, *The Strange Career of Jim Crow* (3rd ed.; New York: Oxford University Press, 1974); Woodward, *Tom Watson: Agrarian Rebel* (New York: Oxford University Press, 1963).

ties and within student movements. He has gained support as a result of his denial of the social adequacy of an older generation's commitment to personal regeneration. He writes:

THE BIBLE AND STRUCTURAL EVIL Neglect of the biblical teaching on structural injustice or institutionalized evil is one of the most deadly omissions in evangelicalism today. What does the Bible say about structural evil and how does that deepen our understanding of the scriptural perspective on poverty and hunger?

Christians frequently restrict the scope of ethics to a narrow class of "personal" sins. A few years ago in a study of over fifteen hundred ministers, researchers discovered that the theologically conservative pastors speak out on sins such as drug abuse and sexual misconduct. But they fail to preach about the sins of institutionalized racism, unjust economic structures and militaristic institutions which destroy people just as much as do alcohol and drugs.

There is an important difference between consciously willed, individual acts (like lying to a friend or committing an act of adultery) and participation in evil social structures. Slavery is an example of the latter. So is the Victorian factory system where ten-year-old children worked twelve to sixteen hours a day. Both slavery and child labor were legal. But they destroyed people by the millions. They were institutionalized or structural evils. In the twentieth century, as opposed to the nineteenth, evangelicals have been more concerned with individual sinful acts than with their participation in evil social structures.

But the Bible condemns both. Speaking through his prophet, Amos, the LORD declared, "For three transgressions of Israel, and for four, I will not revoke the punishment; because they sell the righteous for silver, and the needy for a pair of shoes — they that trample the head of the poor into the dust of the earth, and turn aside the way of the afflicted; a man and his father go in to the same maiden, so that my holy name is profaned" (Amos 2:6-7).[15]

Sider's appeal is based on several factors, not the least of which is his moral critique of the parents and pastors of those seminary students who are guilt-ridden and rebellious — students who are subsidized by those who have drawn Sider's criticisms. Another extremely important factor in his popularity is his promotion of dead programs of Lyndon Johnson's Great Society,[16] which is one more

---

15. Ronald Sider, *Rich Christians in an Age of Hunger* (Downers Grove, Illinois: Inter-Varsity Press, 1977), pp. 133-34.
16. Charles Murray, *Losing Ground: American Social Policy, 1950-1980* (New York: Basic Books, 1984).

example of how Christians climb on board discarded humanist programs of political salvation.[17] Because conservative fundamentalists have failed to develop a comprehensive world-and-life view based on biblical law, they are (or have been) unable to refute the latest humanist fads; and these fads, when worn out, become the "latest thing" on seminary campuses. Christian intellectuals are usually about half a generation behind the humanists, since they dine under the tables of the humanists, waiting hopefully for any scraps that might fall from the tables. What Harvard regards as passé, the "radical" evangelicals regard as the cutting edge of social regeneration. And the fundamentalists are seemingly unable to refute either group.

The "New Christian Right"

The 1980's have brought a revival of interest in the older conservative tradition of the nineteenth century within fundamentalist circles. Ideas and political programs somewhat reminiscent of the older Presbyterianism — the Hodges and Alexanders in the North, and men like Dabney in the South — have begun to gain attention. The same kinds of arguments that nineteenth-century conservative Protestant leaders might have offered against perfectionist revivalism and the Social Gospel movement are being heard again.

For years, liberal theologians decried the lack of political concern shown by the fundamentalists. They assumed, of course, that "political concern" would always be transformed into some version of New Deal nostrums. Now, however, the "New Christian Right" has become a major factor in American politics, a swing vote composing millions of potential voters.

The liberals in the churches are horrified, and almost daily some official of the National Council of Churches or a mainline liberal denomination blasts away at the fundamentalists' supposed denial of "the separation of church and State." The liberals have counted noses — an honored practice in any democratic nation — and have been startled to learn that the Moral Majority has more votes than the Barthians, Tillichians, Niebuhrians, and all the other robed humanists combined. Now they seem to think the nation would be far better off if the fundamentalists would simply return to their old

---

17. David Chilton, *Productive Christians in an Age of Guilt-Manipulators: A Biblical Response to Ronald J. Sider* (4th ed.; Tyler, Texas: Institute for Christian Economics, 1986).

ways, lock themselves in their churches, and ignore political matters that simply "do not concern them." It turns out that "Christian political concern" does not automatically mean pamphleteering for Franklin Roosevelt's New Deal. This revelation has shocked the theological liberals.

Church, State, and Society

The theological and political liberals have generally adopted some version of humanism. Humanism has, in turn generally adopted some version of statism. The State, as the most powerful of the institutions of man, and by far the most centralized, has been regarded as the agency of salvation. The messianic State has gained its faithful worshippers in the pews of liberal churches, or at least in the pulpits. The liberals believe in salvation by law—humanist law.[18] They believe (or have believed until recently) fervently in the beneficial nature of social legislation. *Politics has been the religion of humanism since the days of the tower of Babel.*[19]

The liberals have tended to propound solutions in terms of State power. This means that they define the problems of life in terms of politics. They regard political solutions as *the* solutions. This perspective is what has traditionally distinguished liberals from conservatives. Edmund Burke, in his *Reflections on the Revolution in France* (1790), provided modern conservatism with its statement of faith. Not politics, but tradition; not social upheaval, but social stability; not the rule of politicians, but the rule of law-abiding leaders in many institutions: here was Burke's manifesto. Society is not to be subsumed under the State. The State is not society. The State is simply one aspect of society, namely, the political. It is not a monopoly of authority. Churches, families, voluntary associations of all kinds, local civil governments, educational institutions, and numerous other institutions also have lawful authority. Men are not simply members of the State; they are members of many organizations, and they have multiple loyalties and responsibilities. Burke's perspective was generally Christian. The horrors of the French Revolution after 1792 had been predicted by Burke, and the Christian West finally

---

18. R. J. Rushdoony, "The Modern Priestly State: The Sociology of Justification by Law," in *Politics of Guilt and Pity* (Fairfax, Virginia: Thoburn Press, [1970] 1978), Pt. IV, ch. 2.

19. R. J. Rushdoony, "The Society of Satan" (1964), *Biblical Economics Today*, II (Oct./Nov. 1979). Published by the Institute for Christian Economics.

recognized the Jacobin movement as its mortal enemy. Jacobinism is a rival religion, the religion of humanity.[20]

The liberals have always tended to equate *social* reform with *political* reform. Social reform must be accomplished by top-down legislation imposed by the civil government. Only in this way, they believe, can the institutions of society be healed. Marx and the revolutionaries went one step beyond: the political orders of the old civilization must be shattered by revolutionary violence.[21] Lenin perfected this doctrine: capture the machinery of the old government and reform it. Then impose the will of the revolutionary cadre on the people. It was no accident of history that the French revolutionaries captured the bloated bureaucratic machinery of a monarchy and oligarchy that had lost faith in its own ability to lead, or that the Russian revolutionaries captured an even more bloated bureaucratic system, top-heavy and burdened by military defeats, economic crises, and loss of faith.[22] It is extremely difficult to capture a decentralized social order that resists both anarchy and centralization, and that retains faith in the moral validity and practical performance of its own institutions.

Religion and Politics Are Always Mixed

One criticism of churches that get involved in social action projects is that "religion and politics don't mix," a variation of the old doctrine of the separation of church and state. There are several comments that are in order. First, social action projects need not be political in nature. In fact, *in a social order based on the Bible, social projects would overwhelmingly be voluntaristic and privately financed.* By equating social action and politics, some conservative Christians have fallen into the ideological trap set by the liberals. Social action can involve political aspects from time to time, but it is not innately political, or even predominately political.[23]

---

20. R. J. Rushdoony, "The Religion of Humanity," in *The Nature of the American System* (Fairfax, Virginia: Thoburn Press, [1965] 1978), ch. 6. On the French Revolution, see Nesta Webster, *The French Revolution* (Box 2726, Hollywood, California: Angriss Publishers, [1919] 1969); [Anonymous], *Seventeen Eighty-Nine* (Belmont, Massachusetts: Western Islands, 1968). The author is a senior staff member in the U.S. Senate.

21. Gary North, *Marx's Religion of Revolution: The Doctrine of Creative Destruction* (Nutley, New Jersey: Craig Press, 1968).

22. Alexis de Tocqueville, *The Old Regime and the French Revolution* (Garden City, New York: Anchor, [1856] 1955); Richard Pipes, *Russia Under the Old Regime* (New York: Scribner's, 1975).

23. George Grant, *In the Shadow of Plenty: The Biblical Blueprint for Welfare* (Ft. Worth, Texas: Dominion Press, 1986); Grant, *Bringing in the Sheaves* (Atlanta, Georgia: American Vision, 1984).

Second, what about religion and politics? How can any political order be free of religion? Religion is a fundamental category of human life. Men live in terms of faith, a set of presuppositions that they regard as self-justifying, self-evident, and ultimate. These are therefore religious assumptions about the nature of life, man, law and causation. How can men legislate apart from basic presuppositions? How can the civil government say "no" to anything, unless there is something immoral about the act being prohibited? All legislation is ultimately *legislated morality*.

In a Christian social order, such legislation is not intended to redeem men from sin. It is intended to restrain the outward effects of sin. It is designed to protect the innocent. It provides a *predictable restraining framework* that enables individuals to make their contributions — in church service, in business, in the professions, in the neighborhood — without fear of arbitrary interference from State bureaucrats. A framework of civil law tells men what must not be done, so that they can devote their skills, capital, and efforts to those projects that can and perhaps should be done. It even allows them to devote their efforts to projects that cannot be done, but which might seem possible and worthwhile to attempt. *Civil law is not supposed to make men good; it is supposed to restrain external evil.* And evil is defined by means of a moral and religious perspective.

There is good politics and bad politics; there is never neutral politics. There is a political order based on the Bible, and there are numerous political orders based on religions opposed to the Bible; there is never a religion-free political order.[24] Until Christians finally reject all forms of the myth of neutrality, they will remain culturally impotent. Christ rejected all versions of the neutrality doctrine when He said: "He that is not with me is against me; and he that gathereth not with me scattereth abroad" (Matt. 12:30). Christians have been "neutralized" — made into ineffective gatherers — by means of the myth of neutrality. Those humanists and other religionists who are at war against the Bible and the god of the Bible have successfully promoted their religious systems at the expense of Christian orthodoxy by successful use of this preposterous myth. Some of the humanists have even believed in it in the past, although since the mid-1960's, the majority of thoughtful humanists have become more

---

24. George Grant, *The Changing of the Guard: The Biblical Blueprint for Politics* (Ft. Worth, Texas: Dominion Press, 1987).

consistent with their philosophy of ultimate relativism, in which no final truth is possible. They have admitted that they, too, are promoting positions that must alienate others. They have steadily abandoned natural law theory and other forms of universalism. But without some universally agreed-upon principles, there can be no neutral universe of discourse.

The Dying Myth of Neutrality

One of the best examples of a now-dead faith in human reason is found in a very popular book, *How to Read a Book*, by Mortimer Adler. It first appeared in 1939, and it has gone through at least 40 printings. As a book on how to read critically, it is excellent. As a book on philosophy, it is naive. It is based on a nineteenth-century view of human reason. The relativism of men like Karl Mannheim,[25] or the influential book by Thomas Kuhn, *The Structure of Scientific Revolutions* (1970), cannot be reconciled with the naive rationalism of Adler.[26] Here is Adler's faith:

One is hopeless about the fruitfulness of discussion if one does not recognize that all rational men can agree. Note that I said "can agree." I did not say all rational men do agree. I am saying that even when they do not agree, they can. And the point I trying to make is that disagreement is futile agitation unless it is undertaken with the hope that it may lead to the resolution of an issue.

These two facts, that men do disagree and can agree, arise from the complexity of human nature. Men are rational animals. Their rationality is the source of their power to agree. Their animality, and the imperfections of their reason which it entails, is the cause of most of the disagreements that occur. They are creatures of passion and prejudice. The language they must use to communicate is an imperfect medium, clouded by emotion and colored by interest as well as inadequately transparent for thought. Yet to the extent that men are rational, these obstacles to their understanding one another can be overcome. The sort of disagreement which is only apparent, resulting from misunderstanding, is certainly curable.

There is, of course, another sort of disagreement, which is due to inequalities of knowledge. The ignorant often foolishly disagree with the learned about matters exceeding their knowledge. The more learned, however,

---

25. Karl Mannheim, *Ideology and Utopia: An Introduction to the Sociology of Knowledge* (New York: Harvest, [1936]).

26. Thomas Kuhn, *The Structure of Scientific Revolutions* (2nd ed.; Chicago: University of Chicago Press, 1970); I. Lakatos and A. Musgrave (eds.), *Criticism and the Growth of Knowledge* (New York: Cambridge University Press, 1970).

have a right to be critical of errors made by those who lack relevant knowledge. Disagreements of this sort can also be corrected. Inequality in knowledge is always curable by instruction.

In other words, I am saying that all human disagreements can be resolved by the removal of misunderstanding or of ignorance. Both cures are always possible, though sometimes difficult. Hence the man who, at any stage of a conversation, disagrees, should at least hope to reach agreement in the end. He should be as much prepared to have his own mind changed as seek to change the mind of another. He should always keep before him the possibility that he misunderstands or that he is ignorant on some point. No one who looks upon disagreement as an occasion for teaching another should forget that it is also an occasion for being taught.

But the trouble is that many people regard disagreement as unrelated to either teaching or being taught. They think that everything is just a matter of opinion. I have mine. You have yours. Our right to our opinions is as inviolable as our right to private property. On such a view, communication cannot be profitable if the profit to be gained is an increase in knowledge. Conversation is hardly better than a ping-pong game of opposed opinions, a game in which no one keeps score, no one wins, and everyone is satisfied because he ends up holding the same opinions he started with.

I cannot take this view. I think that knowledge can be communicated and that discussion can result in learning. If knowledge, not opinion, is at stake, then either disagreements are apparent only—to be removed by coming to terms and a meeting of minds; or, if they are real, then the genuine issues can always be resolved—in the long run, of course—by appeals to fact and reason. The maxim of rationality concerning disagreements is to be patient for the long run. I am saying, in short, that disagreements are arguable matters. And argument is both empty and vicious unless it is undertaken on the supposition that there is attainable truth which, when attained by reason in the light of all the relevant evidence, resolves the original issues.[27]

Very few serious scholars really believe this any longer. They may do their best to make their arguments coherent, but when pressed, they really do wind up arguing that everything is simply a matter of individual opinion, individual prejudice, or individual class position. Marx believed that all philosophy is a class weapon used by the ruling social class to subjugate another.[28] Everything for Marx was a

---

27. Mortimer Adler, *How to Read a Book: The Art of Getting a Liberal Education* (New York: Simon & Schuster, [1940] 1967), pp. 246-48.
28. "Just as philosophy finds its *material* weapons in the proletariat, so the proletariat finds its *intellectual* weapons in philosophy." Marx, "Contribution to the Critique

question of ideology. Similarly, Van Til argued throughout his works that logical inference is always dependent upon one's starting point. If an argument is consistent, it must be circular. It cannot come up with a conclusion that is logically inconsistent with its presuppositions, unless there is a fundamental flaw in reason as such.[29] In short, we cannot use a system of reasoning that presupposes the intellectual autonomy of man, and then conclude that such a reasoning process demonstrates irrefutably the existence of the God of the Bible—a God who is absolutely sovereign, absolutely autonomous, and absolutely powerful. The existence of such a God denies the starting point of autonomous human reasoning.[30] Therefore, we cannot expect to see any reconciliation between rival systems of logic; since their presuppositions are irreconcilable, their conclusions will also be irreconcilable. In Dooyeweerd's words, these presuppositions are pre-theoretical, and therefore religious in nature.[31] They cannot be resolved by means of theoretical arguments.

The Bible says that the *work* of the law—not the law of God itself—is written on the heart of every man (Rom. 2:14-15).[32] There *are* universally shared ideas, but these ideas are *actively restrained or suppressed* by covenant-breaking men, as the first chapter of Romans argues (vv. 18-23).[33] There is a common ground of discourse among men, based on God's revelation of Himself through the creation, and also based on the image of God in man, but this common ground is ethically suppressed. No common human logic can overcome this suppression.

---

of Hegel's Philosophy of Right" (1843), in T. B. Bottomore (ed.), *Karl Marx: Early Writings* (New York: McGraw-Hill, 1963), p. 59. "The ruling ideas of each age have ever been the ideas of the ruling class." Marx and Engels, "Manifesto of the Communist Party" (1848), in *Selected Works*, 3 Vols. (Moscow: Progress Publishers, [1969] 1977), I, p. 125.

29. R. J. Rushdoony, "The Quest for Common Ground," in Gary North (ed.), *Foundations of Christian Scholarship: Essays in the Van Til Perspective* (Vallecito, California: Ross House Books, 1976), pp. 33-35; Greg Bahnsen, "Pragmatism, Prejudice, and Presuppositionalism," in *ibid.*, pp. 288-90.

30. R. J. Rushdoony, *By What Standard? An Analysis of the Philosophy of Cornelius Van Til* (Fairfax, Virginia: Thoburn Press, [1959] 1974); Richard L. Pratt, Jr., *Every Thought Captive* (Phillipsburg, New Jersey: Presbyterian & Reformed, 1979).

31. Herman Dooyeweerd, *In the Twilight of Western Thought* (Nutley, New Jersey: Craig Press, [1960] 1968), pp. 18-21. This is the thesis of Dooyeweerd's huge work, *A New Critique of Theoretical Thought* (Phillipsburg, New Jersey: Presbyterian & Reformed, [1954] 1969).

32. John Murray, *The Epistle to the Romans* (Grand Rapids, Michigan: Eerdmans, [1959] 1971), pp. 74-76.

33. *Ibid.*, pp. 36-37.

Whose Reforms?

What is the relevance of all this for social reform? Simple: all reforms are either consistent with the Bible or inconsistent with it. The Bible is our point of reference, our final court of appeal. The Bible, not natural law or natural reason, is the basis of evaluating the applicability or validity of any proposed social reform. When we lobby to have a law passed, we need not be embarrassed that it is a specifically Christian law—a law inconsistent with Marxist ideology, Islamic culture, or the latest findings of a Presidential commission. We must not allow ourselves to be paralyzed by doubts regarding the supposed unfairness of a particular law—"unfair law" being defined as any law that might restrain the self-proclaimed autonomy of man. There are always valid debates about timing, or the cost of enforcement, or the strategy of getting a law passed, but questions of fairness must not be decided in terms of humanistic law or humanistic assertions that a particular law "mixes religion and State." The more relevant question to be asked of any proposed law is this one: *Whose* religion does it promote?

Should the institutional church get involved in politics? The more relevant question is this: Can any consistent church *avoid* politics? Can it avoid discussing the decisions that men, including its members, make in life? Can a church stay silent in the face of legalized abortion? On a key issue like this, you would think that the most hardened "separator" would capitulate, but the vast majority of churches in any city are publicly unconcerned about abortion. They are not identified as pro-abortion or anti-abortion churches. They do not preach on the topic. They do not encourage members to get politically involved in the war against abortion. They stay silent. They remain *impotent*. They do not speak up when unborn children are aborted, and they remain culturally impotent—a fitting punishment, given the nature of the crime that they do not actively oppose.

The problem is not that of remaining outside of politics. If evil is entrenched in the land, all institutions that do not actively oppose it are part of that evil process. They become agencies for smoothing over the evil. Such churches give hope to men, calm the fears of men, and promote the blindness of men. They are important agents for the humanists. They perform their task of neutralization and castration quite well, and the humanists continue to reward such institutions by allowing them to retain their tax exemption.

Today when we speak of persecution, most pastors think of the threat of the loss of their churches' tax exempt status. They are not worried about prison sentences. They do not stay awake nights thinking about Klan-types burning down their homes or their churches. They worry about the loss of their tax-free status. *Satan buys off Christian leaders rather cheaply.* It is my opinion that tax-exemption, coupled with confiscatory tax rates and mass inflation, is one of the most important tools in the arsenal of the humanists in the late twentieth century. We must reaffirm tax-*immunity*.

There is no neutrality. Therefore, there is no neutral, undefined, common "moral law." There is one God, one law, and one plan of salvation, both social and individual. Plural laws, plural moralities, and plural religions are manifestations of a religious philosophy: *polytheism*. The god of any society is reflected in the law-order of that society. If society is officially *pluralistic* with respect to law, then it is officially *polytheistic* with respect to theology.

Why did God tell the Israelites to worship only Him, and to destroy the gods of the Canaanites? Was God being immoral? Was God being anti-democratic? Has God changed His mind?

The Whole Counsel of God

By bringing the churches back into prominence in the decision-making process at every level, Christian Reconstructionists would see an improvement in the preaching and teaching of the churches. Today's churches can afford to be irrelevant, since the pay-off for relevant preaching—the loss of tax-exempt status—is not very attractive. It pays a pastor to preach irrelevant sermons. Irrelevance is the watchword in most Bible-believing churches today. They fear loss of their tax status. They have a pessimistic eschatology that says that the church (at least in this "Church Age") cannot hope to see the reign of Christian law and culture. Most of them have even abandoned the concept of a uniquely Christian civilization (for without a law-order, there can be no civilization). The churches are socially irrelevant today precisely because *they have adopted a theology of earthly irrelevance*, and they have sold their institutional freedom for tax-exemptions.

Tax-exempt status is a weapon that Christians must use to undermine the enemy. It can be very difficult for the civil authorities to destroy the tax-exempt status of any given congregation. So tax-exempt status can become a weapon for churches on the offensive.

Tie up the bureaucrats in legal red tape. No compromise must ever be made solely as a result of some bureaucrat's threat (or the possibility of a threat) of removing the church's tax exemption. But it is easy to compromise, and not difficult to rationalize a compromise. Tax exemption is a very dangerous "gift" from the State. Use it prayerfully. We must reassert tax-*immunity*.

Every human institution is a possible topic in the church. Every human institution is capable of falling into sin, so the churches must always be alert to the degeneracy of the social institutions of the nation. There is no "King's X" from God and the rule of God's law. The church that hires a pastor who preaches the whole counsel of God must be prepared for him to lead them into deep waters, especially in the midst of a perverse generation. There are too many "court prophets" today. There are too many pastors who refuse to see the working arrangement between their own bland sermons and the degeneracy of the culture around them. They can remain irrelevant in "good times," meaning evil times with high per capita income. They will not survive in hard times, when the protecting institutions of society are collapsing or becoming openly tyrannical. People will subsidize irrelevance only while it is cheap.

The Necessity of God's Judgment[34]

We have to take seriously the outline of Deuteronomy 8 and Deuteronomy 28. If God's covenanted nation departs from His justice by departing from His law, it must be judged. This is not an option. Either men within a nation repent, and return to God's law, or else they will be destroyed. This is the *scattering process* spoken of by Jesus (Matt. 12:30). "And it shall be, if thou do at all forget the LORD thy God, and walk after other gods, and serve them, and worship them, I testify against you this day that ye shall surely perish. As the nations which the LORD destroyeth before your face, so shall ye perish; because ye would not be obedient unto the voice of the LORD your God" (Deut. 8:19-20). The scattering of Israel was God's threat against them. It is Christ's threat against men today. Men without a psychological center are regarded as crazy. Societies without a center become anarchistic, then tyrannical, and then are overcome by foreign invaders or domestic insurgents.

Ours is a *theocentric universe*. We must build in terms of this princi-

---

34. Sutton, *That You May Prosper*, ch. 4.

ple or be scattered abroad. God is in the center of all existence, as its Creator and sustainer. Individuals must acknowledge this fact, and so must institutions. They acknowledge this by covenanting with God, and there can be no binding, valid covenant without law, God's law.

There comes a time in the life of a covenanted nation that the judgment must come if that nation is to be healed. Without the chastisement of God—external, temporal cursings—God must give up the nation to the lusts of men's hearts, which means a casting away of the society. The *judgment* is therefore a form of *long-term grace*. Without it, there is no hope.

When is this necessary? First, when leaders ignore God and God's law. Second, when the people agree with their leaders. Third, when the sins have become so blatant that foreign nations ridicule God because of the sins of His people. This is the explanation Nathan gave to King David: ". . . by this deed thou hast given great occasion to the enemies of the LORD to blaspheme . . ." (II Sam. 12:14). God is jealous for His own name. Even an evil king like Ahab won a victory over the "invincible" Syrians because God was jealous of His own sovereignty. "And there came a man of God, and spake unto the king of Israel, and said, Thus saith the LORD, Because the Syrians have said, The LORD is God of the hills, but he is not God of the valleys, therefore will I deliver all this great multitude into thine hand, and ye shall know that I am the LORD" (I Ki. 20:28).

What is the function of God's external cursings on a society? First, to remind them that He is God. Second, to bring men face to face with the relevance of His law. Third, to humble them before Him and to repent. Fourth, to remind their children of the God of their parents. This is why all those in the generation of the wilderness perished, except Joshua and Caleb. They all were unfit to rule, being slaves mentally. But their children learned who God is, and they were fit to conquer in His name. Judgment is to demonstrate the sovereignty of God and the total dependence of His people on Him. Also, fifth, it is to provide sufficient fear so that men become willing to discipline themselves in terms of a chain of command. It is to raise up an army. Men must fear their heavenly Commander more than they fear the enemies of God. Sixth, judgment on His people is to warn the enemies of God about their own impending judgment. Isaiah (chapters 15 through 31) listed a similar set of woes that would befall the inhabitants of Israel. No one escapes, but restoration was promised to Israel, whereas no restoration was promised to the surrounding pagan cultures. The key differentiating factor is *restoration*.

What God's prophets prayed for and announced was *judgment unto restoration*. When the culture had departed so far that men had forgotten God, God struck them down. "Woe unto them that are at ease in Zion," the prophet Amos announced (Amos 6:1), and it is this warning that is supposed to awaken the sleepwalking members of His congregations. Judgment is one effective way to awaken them, to relieve them of their ease.

What are the basic forms of judgment? There are many. Deuteronomy 28 lists several: geographical (v. 16), financial (v. 17), agricultural (v. 18), pestilential (v. 21), drought (vv. 23-24), military (v. 25), dermatological (v. 27), psychological (vv. 28, 66-67), medical (vv. 60-62), demographic (v. 62). The general curse: "And it shall come to pass, that as the LORD rejoiced over you to do you good, and to multiply you; so the LORD will rejoice over you to destroy you, and to bring you to naught; and ye shall be plucked from off the land whither thou goest to possess it. And the LORD shall scatter thee among all people, from the one end of the earth even unto the other; and there thou shalt serve other gods, which neither thou nor thy fathers have known, even wood and stone. And among these nations shalt thou find no ease . . ." (vv. 63-65a.). The scattering process was designed to provide them with a most practical education in comparative religion. They would learn what it means to be a servant of a foreign god.

Judgement Is Comprehensive

This is the lesson of Deuteronomy 28. Judgment is comprehensive because sin and rebellion are comprehensive. Sin and rebellion infect every area of life. Satan is at work everywhere. He offers a challenge to God wherever he can. Because God requires His servants to exercise dominion in every area of life, across the face of the earth (Gen. 1:26-28; 9:1-7), His law is comprehensive. *Rebellion against His law is also comprehensive.*

If judgment is comprehensive, then in order for men to avoid comprehensive judgment, they must repent. This repentance must be as comprehensive as the sins had been during the period of rebellion. This also means that the standards of reconstruction must be comprehensive. If men are repenting in general, then they must be repenting from particular sins. *We do not sin in general without sinning in particular.* If men are to stop sinning, then they need to know which actions constitute sin before God. They need standards of moral behavior. Without a *comprehensive law structure*, men cannot know what God expects them to do. They also cannot know what God expects them to refrain from doing.[35]

Overcoming Corruption

When the institutions of society have been corrupted — corrupted in specific ways by specific individuals — then they need to be reformed by godly men who are reconstructing social institutions in terms of God's revelation of His standards in His law. It is not enough to see men regenerated. When they are regenerated, they must ask themselves: What things did I do before that were wrong, and what must I do differently to have my work acceptable to God? Unless these questions are asked and subsequently answered, the *fruit* of men's regeneration will be minimal. In some cases, it may continue to be evil. For example, what if some persecutor in the Soviet Union were converted to Christ? Would he be fulfilling God's law by becoming an even more efficient persecutor of God's people? No; he would have to get out of that calling. There is a book written about just such a convert, Sergei Kourdakov's *The Persecutor* (1973). He defected to the West, wrote the book and was murdered by Soviet agents (or so the evidence indicates). It is not enough, then, to call for men to turn to Christ. They must also *turn away from Satan* and all of Satan's works.

When a society is so at ease in Zion, when men and women no longer concern themselves about the specific nature of their sins, when social institutions are ignored as being beyond the scope of God's law, when preaching is no longer geared to helping specific Christians reform every area of life for which they are morally responsible, when leaders no longer read the Bible as a source of guidance in concrete decisions based on concrete laws in the Bible, when Christians no longer have faith in the long-term success of the gospel, in every area of life, in time and on earth, *then* the judgment of God is at hand. Then they must be awakened from their slumbers. When the steady preaching of God's law, week by week, institution by institution, is no longer present in a society that was once

---

35. *Ibid.*, ch. 3.

openly under a covenant with God, then God uses other means to reform that covenanted society. If men will not respond to honest preaching, or when the preaching is truncated (cut short) to suit a false theology or rich donors, then God reforms society by *some other means* than preaching. Judgment is that grim other means.

When should preachers begin to pray for comprehensive judgment? When they have a vision of the comprehensive nature of sin and the comprehensive nature of redemption. If they have seen that few preachers in society share this understanding, and that the rebellion of men in the society is accelerating, and that there is no way that preaching is likely to catch up with the rebellion, then it is time to begin calling for the comprehensive judgment of God.

Such judgment must be sufficient to scare Christians into action and to paralyze the sinners who are in control of the prominent institutions. It is to cause a shift in authority: from the ungodly to the godly, either by *conversion* of the ungodly or by their *removal* from positions of authority. This may require years of crisis or even servitude to a foreign power. It may require paying tribute to a foreign power, just as Israel paid tribute to a long line of foreign powers, culminating in the scattering (*diaspora*, or dispersion) of Israel under the Romans in the second century A.D. It does not matter how severe the judgment becomes, as long as the rebels within the society lose power, and the Christians eventually gain power. Only one thing must be preached: that *God's will be done*, that restoration come on God's terms, not on man's terms. Men pray down the judgment of God on a rebellious society the way that a platoon commander orders the artillery to lay down a barrage in his own sector, when the enemy is overrunning his platoon's position. It is not an act of suicide, but a painful act of aggression.

What the West Now Faces

Is the West at this stage? Yes. The single issue of abortion is proof enough. Murder of the innocent is the law of the land in most Western societies. As long as the slaughter of the innocents continues, societies store up a warehouse of wrath. If godly preaching and godly political mobilization are not enough to reverse the trend, then fear born of judgment will have to be the prayer of the saints. We must scare men into allowing the innocents to be born. (By "innocents," I do not mean sin-free; I mean *judicially innocent in human courts*—those who have committed no crimes.) We have lost on this issue. We have little time remaining to reverse the political process. Every year that we are delayed by the murderers in high places, a million babies die in the United States, and perhaps 55 million per year worldwide.[36] God's judgment is preferable to this.

What godly men must do is this: *prepare for a coming cataclysm.* They must offer valid alternatives to today's social degeneration, in every sphere of life. Each man need not attempt to provide guidelines for total reconstruction, but each man must find at least one area, preferably the one in which he possesses valid authority. Men must write, teach, and work to rebuild. They must prepare their families and churches for a coming cataclysm. They must do whatever they can to be in positions of leadership during and following a cataclysm. In fact, a series of cataclysms is likely, as sketched in Deuteronomy 28. We must be *ready to survive,* so that we will be *ready to lead.* We must confront the world with prophetic preaching, challenging those in authority to repent, to turn back from their *specifically* evil ways.

No Pity

One thing should be borne in mind: God will not pity the objects of His wrath. The prophets repeated this warning: God would not pity them. "And I will dash them one against another, even the fathers and the sons together, saith the LORD: I will not pity, nor spare, nor have mercy, but destroy them" (Jer. 13:14). Ezekiel was even more specific concerning God's lack of pity:

> Moreover the word of the LORD came unto me, saying, Also, thou son of man, thus saith the LORD God unto the land of Israel; An end, the end is come upon the four corners of the land.
> Now is the end come upon thee, and I will send mine anger upon thee, and will judge thee according to thy ways, and will recompense upon thee all thine abominations.
> And mine eye shall not spare thee, neither will I have pity: but I will recompense thy ways upon thee, and thine abominations shall be in the midst of thee: and ye shall know that I am the LORD.
> Thus saith the LORD God; An evil, and only evil, behold, is come.
> An end is come, the end is come: it watcheth for thee; behold, it is come.

---

36. *World Population and Fertility Planning Technologies: The Next 20 Years* (Washington, D.C.: Office of Technology Assessment, 1982), p. 63.

The morning is come unto thee, O thou that dwellest in the land: the time is come, the day of trouble is near, and not the sounding again of the mountains.

Now will I shortly pour out my fury upon thee, and accomplish mine anger upon thee: and I will judge thee according to thy ways, and will recompense thee for all thine abominations.

And mine eye shall not spare, neither will I have pity: I will recompense thee according to thy ways and thine abominations that are in the midst of thee; and ye shall know that I am the Lord that smiteth.

Behold the day, behold, it is come: the morning is gone forth; the rod hath blossomed, pride hath budded.

Violence is risen up into a rod of wickedness: none of them shall remain, nor of their multitude, nor of any of theirs: neither shall there be wailing for them.

The time is come, the day draweth near: let not the buyer rejoice, nor the seller mourn: for wrath is upon all the multitude thereof.

For the seller shall not return to that which is sold, although they were yet alive: for the vision is touching the whole multitude thereof, which shall not return; neither shall any strengthen himself in the iniquity of his life.

They have blown the trumpet, even to make all ready; but none goeth to the battle: for my wrath is upon all the multitude thereof.

The sword is without, and the pestilence and the famine within: he that is in the field shall die with the sword; and he that is in the city, famine and pestilence shall devour him (Ezk. 7:1-15).

Most people on earth have been refugees, captives, and tribute-payers in this century. Certainly, they have been tribute-payers to the messianic State. They have tasted the fruits of the religion of humanity. A few nations have avoided outright military invasion: the United States, Canada, New Zealand, Australia, and Latin America. Now Latin America is being threatened, and Central America has actually experienced Communist take-overs. No one is immune. The Chinese Communists went on the Long March in the early 1930's to escape from the military forces of the anti-Communists. They thought it no great sacrifice to retreat, in order to fight another day. A decade and a half later, they were victorious.

Responsible Christianity

What conquering ideological humanist armies have been willing to suffer for the sake of "the cause," few comfortable Christians are courageous enough even to contemplate as an outside possibility. They would rather die, they say. Better yet, they would rather be raptured to heaven above, sticking out their tongues on the way up at those nasty next-door neighbors who drink beer on Saturday night and play loud rock music on their stereos. After all, if drinking beer and listening to rock music in stereo doesn't constitute wickedness, what does? And if something else really is worse, it would probably be too controversial to preach against. It might involve getting personally involved. It might involve getting organized politically. It might involve donating hours to some cause, or some local charity. Worst of all, it might involve losing the church's tax exemption. No, drinking beer and listening to rock music on Saturday night are evils sufficient to the day. Do this, and you miss the Rapture.

The Israelites suffered captivity, tribute, and years as refugees. They tasted the fruit of unrighteousness. They saw what the judgment of God entails. They did not learn. They finally were scattered abroad. Having abandoned the redemptive concept of culture, they lost the land. Why should we expect better treatment? Why should we pray for better treatment? Why should we live our lives as if Deuteronomy 28 were not true? Why should we want it not to be true? Why should we prefer to live in a world in which there is no relationship between comprehensive rebellion and comprehensive judgment? Why should we want to preach a gospel that offers less of a challenge than comprehensive dominion through comprehensive redemption? *Why is our faith less than comprehensive?*

Here is the tragedy of modern preaching. Most Christians have given up hope for Christian dominion, in time and on earth. The premillennialists pray fervently for the Rapture. They buy endless books about prophecy, each one more colorful than the last, with the leading characters in the program changing constantly. (A remarkable study of the shifting interpretations of the "experts" in prophecy is Dwight Wilson's *Armegeddon Now: The Premillenarian Response to Russia and Israel Since 1917*, published by Baker Book House in 1977.) Take away their escape hatch, and they face a grim reality: they are going to die. A generation raised on Hal Lindsey's books does not really believe in death, since they fully expect to be raptured out of this world, before the trouble really begins. Why should men who believe they will personally escape the sting of death before the century ends be concerned with the problems of social reconstruction? They usually aren't.

Most amillennialists are even more pessimistic. They see no escape before things hit the low ebb for Christianity. They see external defeat, but without the delightful escape hatch of the Rapture. As Rushdoony has commented, they are premillennialists without earthly hope. At least the pretribulational premillennial dispensationalists expect to get out before the worst arrives. (The posttribulational dispenstionalists are not much better off than the amillennialists are. They believe that the church will go through a future Great Tribulation. The increasing popularity of posttribulational dispensationalism is an odd feature of recent American fundamentalism. Posttribs are the classic "stiff upper lip — grin and bear it" Christians. They really believe that things will get a lot worse before they get even worse. But at least very few of them have had the Dutch amillennial psychological burden of believing that it is the responsibility of every Christian to work to reform every area of life — and to do it without any reference to Old Testament law.) Dutch amillennialists burden themselves with the thought that they are personally and collectively responsible for building up the kingdom of God in every institution (the Kuyper-oriented Dutch amillennialists), but they know that they cannot possibly succeed. At least the fundamentalists and Lutherans are not guilt-ridden about not being able to extend the dominion covenant, since they do not believe in the dominion covenant.[37]

Comprehensive preaching against specific institutional sins is not in favor today, precisely because most Christians do not believe they are in any way responsible for, or able to exercise power over, the so-called secular institutions of society. They have no positive eschatology of victory, and they have no program for dominion based on the systematic application of biblical law. They lack both the tools of dominion — the laws of the Bible — and a forward-looking dynamic of history. As Rushdoony has said, the liberals believe in history, but not in God, and the conservative Christians believe in God, but not in history. Both liberalism and conservative traditional Christianity are losing influence. The end of their road is visible to both sides. The liberals face earthly Armageddon — nuclear war, or worse, the possible rule of unsystematic moralists (generally dismissed as fundamentalists) — while the fundamentalists see the impending crises and the Rapture, which makes them unreliable assistants in building up the kingdom of God by means of a generations-long strategy.

---

37. Gary North, *The Dominion Covenant: Genesis* (2nd ed.; Tyler, Texas: Institute for Christian Economics, 1987).

Hardly anyone preaches judgment for restoration's sake. Hardly anyone speaks of judgment as the prophets did, namely, as a painful means of moral and institutional restoration. The judgment that the liberals expect is that of historical defeat and impotence for liberal, humanistic values. The judgment that fundamentalists expect is one which Christians will escape, and which is not related directly to the post-resurrection rule of death-proof saints during the millennium. The judgment that amillennialists look forward to is the end of time, the last earthly event before the final judgment. None of these perspectives offers the biblical view of judgment, namely, that God chastises His people — covenantally, not just individually — as a way to restore them to faith in Him and to enable His people to engage once again in the task of Christian reconstruction: building the kingdom of God on earth, by means of His law. In short, no one preaches prophetic judgment any more.

Infiltration and Replacement

The French Revolution, like the Russian Revolution, relied heavily upon the existing bureaucratic structure for the implementation of social change. The revolutionaries recognized that the incumbent bureaucrats were vital, at least initially, for the consolidation of power by the new rulers. The stability of bureaucracy is perhaps its greatest strength. Loyalty of bureaucrats is directed toward the prevailing offices, not to individuals. When the revolutionaries replaced the king or czar, it made little difference to those holding bureaucratic positions. Lenin was the son of a minor Russian bureaucrat. Many of the French revolutionaries were lawyers and others who had worked with the various levels of the bureaucracy, either as employees or as hired representatives of business or the nobility.

The revolutionaries understood how bureaucracies operate. If Christians are to be equally successful in reshaping the civil government, they also must learn how the bureaucratic system works. Christians need to understand what motivates members of bureaucracies. They need to gain experience in working with bureaucracies. They need to have their own people inside bureaucracies, either as employees or as representatives of the civil government or business. Such an education must not be undertaken in order to make the present order function more smoothly, but the opposite: *to gum up the existing humanistic social order through its own red tape.* We need to infiltrate the bureaucracies in order to secure a foothold in the existing social order's transmission belts of power. We must be prepared to misdirect bureaucratic efforts against Christian organizations, and also to smooth the transition to Christian political leadership, thereby cutting short any attempted resistance movement within existing bureaucracies against such a transition of power to the Christians. Christians must begin to organize politically within the present party structure, and they must begin to infiltrate the existing institutional order.

Long, Hard Work

Unquestionably, the churches have no such long-term plan. They are not used to thinking in terms of long-term plans for social change. They have almost no comprehension of how civil government works. Only recently, as the threat to Christian institutions from secular humanists within the government has become more visible, have we seen the partial mobilization of Christians. They are pathetic in their vision, strategy, and execution, but they are numerous enough so that they have exercised considerable political strength. As they become more familiar with political techniques developed by the so-called New Right — such organizations as the Committee for the Survival of a Free Congress, the Conservative Caucus, and Richard Viguerie's direct-mail machine in Falls Church, Virginia — they will exercise even more power. When a few prominent "electronic church" preachers can mobilize tens of thousands of citizens and millions of dollars, the "old Left" has to be worried. A new political force is on the horizon [written in 1981].

Nevertheless, it is a long-term project. Max Weber, the prominent German social scientist, wrote back in 1918 about the difficulties of politics. It takes diligence combined with charisma, a knowledge of details and an understanding of widespread political forces, a willingness to become involved in the slow boring of holes.[38] Politics is not easy, and Christians (like ideological conservatives) want quick fixes. They, unlike the humanist liberals, do not believe in political salvation. They are interested in other aspects of life: education, family activities, business, church life, and so forth. The humanist liberals devote far more of their hearts and capital to politics, for pol-

---

38. Max Weber, "Politics as a Vocation" (1918), in H. H. Gerth and C. Wright Mill (eds.), *From Max Weber: Essays in Sociology* (New York: Oxford University Press, [1949] 1965).

itics consumes them. Therefore, they have succeeded in establishing a strong foothold in the bureaucracies, as well as in the political institutions. Those who wish to replace them have been unable to do so, even when elections have gone their way. The bureaucrats can afford to wait. They get paid to wait. All they need to do, they believe, it to wait out the latest political fad. They will be in control when the next batch of political novices is put into office.

This strategy works, until a really significant political change occurs. When a new political group comes into office which truly understands the ways of bureaucracies (mainly, through the control of their budgets), and which has sufficient support or control over the political process to rule as long as the bureaucrats can, the bureaucrats can be brought under control. But it takes time, dedication, skill, and great understanding. This is what the Christians lack. This is why a new generation of conservative Christian political operatives is needed. This is why Christians must begin training such young men to take over the reins of power, especially at the local level, when the crises shake the faith of men in the present humanist political order.

Power and Responsibility

So far, I have been discussing political power. But as I stated earlier, change is far more extensive than mere politics. The State is only one agency in the transformation process. We need to become active in another replacement process: the replacement of existing voluntary institutions. We know this much: *power flows in the direction of those who exercise responsibility,* especially in a major crisis. We must become prepared to lead during a humanist-created crisis. We need to be ready to provide leadership, food, clothing, and the necessities of life. The Mormons have understood this far better than any Protestant denomination. They have created institutions within their church to handle major crises. They will become even more formidable competitors to mainline churches in a crisis—and they are already formidable competitors. God's law works for everyone who imposes it, as the book of Jonah should reveal. The Assyrians in Nineveh who repented, through the king's person, became Israel's conquerors. Power flowed toward them. When men honor the external laws of society that God has set forth, they will be blessed externally. When they tithe, they will experience church growth. When they store up food, they will escape the ravages of famine. When they save, they will experience economic growth.

The Self-Conscious Defection of Pietists

Today's pietistic Protestants, with their emphasis on internal self-transformation to the exclusion of social responsibility, resent such teaching. There is enormous hostility to the idea that adhering to God's social laws brings external prosperity. Both the pietists and the Christian socialists refuse to consider such a proposition. If the proposition is true, then it places great responsibility on Christians to begin to rebuild Western civilization by reconstructing every institution in terms of biblical law. But Christians are embarrassed by biblical law. They are embarrassed by the God of the Bible who has imposed biblical law on His people, and who holds everyone responsible for obeying it.[39] Outraged by such a view of God, they stick their fists figuratively in the face of God, deliberately misinterpret both God and His law, and shout their defiance: "Is God really nothing more than the abstract, impersonal dispenser of equally abstract and impersonal laws?"[40] For this reason, *Christianity today is culturally impotent and irrelevant*. Christians are not in positions of leadership in any major social or political institution. They are fed by the scraps of power that fall from the humanists' tables.

Where are the Christian orphanages? I am not referring to Christian orphanages operated by Christians in Korea for some other foreign land. Where are the orphanages run by Christians in their own nations? Where are the Christian homes for the retarded? Where are the Christian schools for the deaf or blind? There are almost none. Why not? Because there is no tithing. Because there is no vision of a Christian social order. Because there is a futile faith in neutrality, Christians assume that the State has the right to educate the deaf and blind. They assume that education is essentially technical, and that as long as a competent instructor is located and financed by taxes, the handicapped children will receive all the education they need, irrespective of the theology of the technically competent instructor. In some perverse way, Christians assume that all that the deaf and blind kids need is the ability to read and write — the same preposterous error that enables the humanists to gain continuing support from Christian taxpayers for the humanist-controlled government school system. Their physical handicaps become an excuse for their theological neglect.

---

39. Greg L. Bahnsen, *By This Standard: The Authority of God's Law Today* (Tyler, Texas: Institute for Christian Economics, 1985).

40. Rodney Clapp, "Democracy as Heresy," *Christianity Today* (Feb. 20, 1987), p. 23.

The Christians have transferred power to the humanists because the humanists long ago recognized that power flows in the direction of those who exercise responsibility. And when you can get the majority to subsidize the program, while turning its administration over to you and your accomplices, you have pulled off a major coup. That is precisely what the humanists did, and are still doing. Just convince the Christians that the State, rather than the church or other Christian voluntary institutions, is responsible for the care of the poor, the education of the young, the care of the aged, the womb-to-tomb protection of the least productive members of society, etc., and you can get them to finance the religion of secular humanism with their own tax money.

This has many important benefits for humanists. First, the humanists control the institutions that certify competence (universities, colleges, accreditation boards). This means that only those people screened and certified by them will get the jobs. Second, the humanists believe in salvation by politics, so more of their efforts will be devoted to the capture and control of the State and all State-subsidized institutions. Third, the humanists are long-term builders, since they have no faith in the after-life. In their theology, "what you see is what you get," and all they see is life on earth. Fourth, by taxing Christians, they reduce the amount of money left to Christians for the financing of Christian social institutions—the alternatives to the State's institutions. Incredibly, the vast majority of Christian voters believe that this system is not only justified, but that it is the very best system possible. They rarely protest. They limit their protests to feeble, misguided, and ineffective efforts to "win back the public schools," as if public schools had ever been consistently Christian to begin with.[41] Such efforts must fail, precisely because the initial premise—that the State has the primary responsibility to care for the weaker members of society—is itself fallacious. *It is not the civil government, but the individual Christian, who is responsible.* He joins with other Christians to improve the delivery of services, since a group can make use of the division of labor principle, but he must always see himself as the responsible agent. He can withdraw financial support when he is convinced that the agency has sufficient funding or even too much. This keeps the salaried people in line, which is far

---

41. Robert L. Thoburn, *The Children Trap: The Biblical Blueprint for Education* (Ft. Worth, Texas: Dominion Press, 1986).

more difficult in a Civil Service-protected State bureaucracy that operates with funds confiscated by the monopoly of State power.

Conclusion

We need a new theology of dominion. We need to rethink the prevailing assumptions about the true locus of responsibility in social institutions. We cannot go on operating under assumptions that by their very nature transfer both power and responsibility to institutions that are coercive, tax-supported, and controlled by those whose primary skill is the capture and maintenance of political and bureaucratic power. We need to infiltrate existing organizations in order to make them less effective in carrying out humanist goals. We need to create alternative schools, orphanages, poorhouses, "half-way" homes, drug rehabilitation centers, day-care centers, and all the other institutions that bring the gospel of salvation and the message of *healing through adherence to God's law*. It is imperative that the issue of responsibility be faced. When we find what God's law says about the locus of responsibility, we can then determine who shall finance the program. Alternatively, when we find where God's word assigns the financial responsibility, there we have the locus of authority in that institution.

Social action is imperative. Without godly social action, the fundamental institutions of State power will remain in the hands of the humanists. They believe in salvation through politics. They are the ones most skilled at political manipulation. They have mastered the techniques of bureaucratic delay, as well as the politics of guilt and pity. Unless Christians create *privately financed alternatives to existing State agencies*, they will never counter the most crucial of questions: "Well, what would you people do about the care of the poor?" They recognize that Christianity is supposed to offer a "word and deed" evangelism.[42]

There is an old rule of politics: *you can't beat something with nothing*. For a century, Christians have ignored this rule. They have not only tried to fight something with nothing, they have even abandoned the fight altogether. They have allowed the humanists to capture the institutions of political power by default. They have allowed the humanists to increase the tax burden of the public to levels at least double that which was imposed by Pharaoh over Egypt, which was

---

42. Grant, *In the Shadow of Plenty*, ch. 1: "Word and Deed Evangelism."

"only" 20% (Gen. 47:26). They have allowed the humanists to increase taxes to four times (or more) the level warned against by Samuel in describing an evil State tax system of 10% (I Sam. 8:15). They have not only allowed this, they have hired ministers who actually approve of it, and they have financed so-called conservative seminaries to train up the next generation of ministers by assigning them books like Ronald Sider's *Rich Christians in an Age of Hunger*. Conservative Christians have adopted a theology of social responsibility that is essentially humanistic. They have retreated from the arena of social responsibility, but have failed to understand that this arena is basic to the world of fallen man. By so retreating, they have transferred power to those who have proclaimed the doctrine of salvation by politics. Without a theology of private social responsibility, without the doctrine of the mandatory tithe—no tithe-no full church membership (voting)—and without an understanding of the theology of humanism, the Christians have promoted the build-up of the society of Satan.

Both pietism and the Social Gospel have undercut Christian civilization. This retreat from the world of earthly responsibility, and this transfer of power to the State in the name of Christian charity, have led to the modern messianic State. The pessimism and retreatism of the pietists have given the field to the humanists and the Social Gospel defenders. The optimism of the Social Gospel theologians has died in our day, and possibly as early as the 1950's. The faith in salvation by politics is waning, but it is not being replaced by an orthodox theology. Instead of adopting a theology of salvation by God, the political and theological liberals have begun to adopt a theology of *no salvation at all*, since the State, humanism's only possible candidate for the office of God, has failed. The old quip about Unitarianism's dogma—"There is, at the most, one God"—is coming true for the spiritual heirs of Unitarianism. Their faith in the phrase, "at the most," is waning. But without a "holy State," there is only an unholy State. If the State is not God, in the theology of contemporary humanism, then the State is Satan. Men must worship something, and though their faith in the benevolence of the State is waning, they are not ready to cease worshipping it. They are only more likely to fear it, grovel before it, and curse it behind closed doors. They do not abandon it, if the alternative is *faith in God*. Today, that is the only remaining viable benevolent alternative. The old statist theology is losing its adherents. It is time for Christians to present them with a systematic, disciplined, tithe-financed alternative. And if they still will not repent, it is time to replace them in the seats of power.

Appendix D

ARE POSTMILLENNIALISTS ACCOMPLICES OF THE NEW AGE MOVEMENT?

I was not aware that I had written "books against Dominion Theology." I have made some mention of Dominion Theology in the final chapter of each of my last two books, but I doubt that it would require an entire volume to respond to what I have said.

Dave Hunt[1]

Mr. Hunt is much too self-effacing. He also underestimates just how much copy Christian Reconstructionists are capable of producing on their word processors. But it is a bit perplexing to find how little credit Mr. Hunt wants to take regarding the origin of the widely circulated accusation that I and those who work with me are implicit allies of the New Age movement. Given the amount of time that at least one television evangelist devotes Sunday evening after Sunday evening to attacking Dominion Theology, and given the fact that he admitted to me personally that he got his information originally from Mr. Hunt's books, this statement by Mr. Hunt was unexpected, to say the least. Like an arsonist caught in the act who insists that he lit only one small match, Mr. Hunt's reluctance to take full credit seems somewhat self-interested. I decided to go ahead and publish the book by DeMar and Leithart, *The Reduction of Christianity*.

Dave Hunt vs. Dominion Theology

Let us begin with the words of Jesus: "All power is given unto me in heaven and in earth" (Matt. 28:18). We should then ask the obvious question: Where is the earthly manifestation of Christ's power?

---

1. Letter to Gary North, July 20, 1987, in response to an offer to allow Hunt to read and respond to the first draft of a manuscript by Gary DeMar and Peter Leithart replying to his criticisms of Dominion Theology.

Dave Hunt is adamant: only in the hearts of believers and (maybe) inside the increasingly defenseless walls of a local church or local rescue mission. As he says, in response to an advertisement for my Biblical Blueprints Series: "The Bible doesn't teach us to build society but instructs us to preach the gospel, for one's citizenship is in Heaven (Col. 3:2)."[2]

It seems to me that he could have strengthened his case that we are citizens of only one "country" by citing a modern translation of Philippians 3:20. But this would only have deferred the question: Why can't Christians be citizens of two countries? After all, they are in the world physically, yet not of the world spiritually: John 17:14-16. Christians are, as Hunt (and all Christians) would insist, required to obey national laws, but also to obey the Bible. To be required to obey two sets of laws is to raise the question of dual citizenship.

Hunt's dispensationalist gospel is a gospel of the heart *only*. Jesus saves hearts *only*; somehow, His gospel is not powerful enough to restore to biblical standards the institutions that He designed for mankind's benefit, but that have been corrupted by sin. Hunt's view of the gospel is that Jesus can somehow save sinners without having their salvation affect the world around them. This, in fact, is the heart, mind, and soul of the pessimillennialists' "gospel": "Heal souls, not institutions." Prison evangelist (and former Nixon aide) Charles Colson has said it best (or worst, depending on your theology): "The real trouble is that we Christians are not willing to accept the gospel for what it is. It doesn't tell us how to save anything but our souls."[3]

Hunt separates the preaching of the gospel from the concerns of society. He separates heavenly citizenship from earthly citizenship. In short, he has reinterpreted the Great Commission of Jesus Christ to His followers: "All power is given unto me in heaven but *none* in earth." (A similar other-worldly view of Christ's authority is held by amillennialists.)[4] Christ's earthly power can only be manifested when He returns physically to set of a top-down bureaucratic kingdom in which Christians will be responsible for following the direct

---

2. Dave Hunt, *CIB Bulletin* (Feb. 1987), fourth page.
3. Cited in *Omega-Letter* (March 1987), p. 11.
4. "There is no room for optimism: towards the end, in the camps of the satanic and the anti-Christ, culture will sicken, and the Church will yearn to be delivered from its distress." H. de Jongste and J. M. van Krimpen, *The Bible and the Life of the Christian* (Philadelphia: Presbyterian & Reformed, 1968), p. 27; cited by R. J. Rushdoony, *The Institutes of Biblical Law* (Nutley, New Jersey: Craig Press, 1973), p. 14n.

orders of Christ, issued to meet specific historical circumstances. The premillenialist has so little faith in the power of the Bible's perfect revelation, empowered by the Holy Spirit, to shape the thoughts and actions of Christians, that Jesus must return and personally issue millions of orders per day telling everyone what to do, case by case, crisis by crisis.

For years, Christian Reconstructionists have argued that such a view of social affairs is inherent in premillennialism. In recent years, premillennial activists have denied this accusation. The intellectual roots of the recent rise of premillennial activism, however, can be traced back to the tiny band of postmillennial Reconstructionists. The premillennial camp is becoming divided, as Dave Hunt has noted. Hunt is the best representative of the older dispensational premillennialism of the 1925-1975 period: a consistent, no-nonsense (or all-nonsense) defender of the earthly defeat of the church. His book, *The Seduction of Christianity*, has become the number-one Christian best-seller of the 1980's, the biggest selling book on eschatology since Hal Lindsey's books.

Hunt is consistent. His premillennial peers are not. He spells out in no uncertain terms just what dispensationalism necessarily implies — precisely what we Christian Reconstructionists have been saying since before there was a Christian Reconstruction movement. In a taped interview with the publisher of the Canadian newsletter, *Omega-Letter*, Hunt says in response to Christian Reconstructionists: "You're looking forward to meeting Jesus, who when you meet him your feet are planted on planet earth. And He simply has arrived to take over this beautiful kingdom you've established for Him, then you've been under heavy delusion, you've been working for the antichrist and not for the true Christ."[5]

Back in the 1950's, J. Vernon McGee, the pastor of a very large dispensational congregation in Los Angeles, made the following classic statement about the futility of social reform: "You don't polish brass on a sinking ship." This phrase has become a favorite jibe against dispensational social pessimism and defeatism among Christian Reconstructionists. Rushdoony has quoted it for three decades. It is remarkable that Peter Lalonde, publisher of the *Omega-Letter*, repeats it favorably in his taped interview with Dave Hunt: "Do you

---

5. *Dominion and the Cross*, Tape #2 of *Dominion: The Word and New World Order*, a 3-tape set distributed by the *Omega-Letter*, Ontario, Canada.

polish brass on a sinking ship? And if they're [Reconstructionists] working on setting up new institutions, instead of going out and winning the lost for Christ, then they're wasting the most valuable time on the planet earth."[6]

Thus, *premillennialists deny the progressive maturation of Christianity and Christian-operated social institutions in history* (meaning pre-Second Coming history). The millennium ruled by Christ, Hunt says, will be a world in which "Justice will be meted out swiftly."[7] Jesus will treat men as fathers treat five-year-old children: instant punishment, no time for reflection and repentance. Christians today are given time to think through their actions, to reflect upon their past sins, and to make restitution before God judges them. Today, they are treated by God as responsible adults. Not in the millennium! The church will go from maturity to immaturity when Christ returns in power. And even with the testimony of the perfect visible rule of Jesus on earth for a thousand years, Satan will still thwart Christ and Christ's church, for at Satan's release, he will deceive almost the whole world, leading them to rebel against "Christ and the saints in Jerusalem."[8]

In short, the plan of God points only to the defeat of His church in history. Satan got the upper hand in Eden, and even the raw power of God during the millennium and at the final judgment at the end of history will not wipe out the kingdom of Satan and restore the creation to wholeness. Thus, Hunt concludes, *the kingdom of God will never be manifested on earth, not even during dispensationalism's earthly millennium.* I know of no pessimism regarding history greater than his statement, which is representative of all premillennialism (and amillennialism, for that matter): even the millennial reign of Christ physically on earth will end when the vast majority of people will rebel against Him, converge upon Jerusalem, and try to destroy the faithful people inside the city: "Converging from all over the world to war against Christ and the saints at Jerusalem, these rebels will finally have to be banished from God's presence forever (Rev. 20:7-10). The millennial reign of Christ upon earth, rather than being the kingdom of God, will in fact be the final proof of the incorrigible nature of the

---

6. *Dominion: A Dangerous New Theology*, Tape #1 of *Dominion: The Word and New World Order.*
7. Dave Hunt, *Beyond Seduction: A Return to Biblical Christianity* (Eugene, Oregon: Harvest House, 1987), p. 250.
8. *Idem.*

human heart."⁹ (Why these rebellious human idiots will bother to attack Jerusalem, a city defended by Jesus and His angelic host, is beyond me. I will let premillennialists worry about this, however. As to why they rebel, I have already provided a postmillennial answer as to what Revelation 20:7-10 means, including who rebels and where they come from, in my book, *Dominion and Common Grace*, which was written specifically to deal with this exegetical problem.)

Actually, this is one of the most astounding statements ever written by any dispensationalist in history. "The millennial reign of Christ upon earth, *rather than being the kingdom of God*, will in fact be the final proof of the incorrigible nature of the human heart."¹⁰ He argues that this rebellion is the final act of history. But if this reign of Christ is *not* the kingdom of God, then just what is it that Jesus will deliver up to His Father at the last day? How do we make sense of the following prophecy? "Then cometh the end, when he shall have delivered up the kingdom to God, even the Father; when he shall have put down all rule and all authority and power. For he must reign, till he hath put all enemies under his feet. The last enemy that shall be destroyed is death" (I Cor. 15:24-26). Hunt knows that Christ's destruction of the final satanic rebellion puts down death. So the kingdom spoken of in this passage *has* to be Christ's millennial reign, whether physical (premillennialism), spiritual (amillennialism), or covenantal (postmillennialism). That he could make a mistake as large as this one indicates that he is a weak reed for dispensationalists to rest on, at this late date, in their attempt to refute Christian optimism regarding the church's earthly future. The exegetical crisis of premillennial dispensationalism is becoming evident. It will not survive as a major evangelical force for much longer. That Dave Hunt, a man with a bachelor's degree in mathematics, is now the most prominent theologian of the dispensational movement, as immune from public criticism by dispensational theologians as Hal Lindsey was in the 1970's, indicates the extent to which the movement cannot survive. The amateurs give away the store theologically, and the seminary professors say nothing, as if these paperback defenders had not delivered mortal blows to the dispensational system.

He refuses to let go. In Tape Two of the widely distributed three-

---

9. *Idem.*
10. *Idem.*

tape interview with Peter Lalonde, he announces that God Himself is incapable of setting up a kingdom: "In fact, dominion—taking dominion and setting up the kingdom for Christ—is an *impossibility*, even for God. The millennial reign of Christ, far from being the kingdom, is actually the final proof of the incorrigible nature of the human heart, because Christ Himself can't do what these people say they are going to do. . . ."

Compare this with Hal Lindsey's comment under "Paradise Restored": "God's kingdom will be characterized by peace and equity, and by universal spirituality and knowledge of the Lord. Even the animals and reptiles will lose their ferocity and no longer be carnivorous. All men will have plenty and be secure. There will be a chicken in every pot and no one will steal it! The Great Society which human rulers throughout the centuries have promised, but never produced, will at last be realized under Christ's rule. The meek and not the arrogant will inherit the earth (Isaiah 11)."[11] Or again, "That time is coming when believers in Jesus Christ are going to walk upon this earth and see it in perfect condition. Pollution will be passé! Jesus Christ is going to recycle the late great Planet Earth."[12] All this "kingdom perfection" during the millennium is abandoned by Dave Hunt, in his desperate yet consistent attack on dominion theology. He has scrapped traditional dispensationalism's last remaining traces of optimism about history in order to paint a picture of inconceivable despair. Even God cannot set up a kingdom on earth. (Tough luck, God. Satan will overcome You again.)

Yet we Christian Reconstructionists are criticized by a minority of activist dispensationalists for saying that dispensationalism is inherently a pessimistic worldview. If it isn't, then why did Dave Hunt's books become the best-selling Christian books of the 1980's? *Because his traditional dispensational readers agree with him.* They recognize that the dispensational activists are no longer voicing the original theology of dispensationalism, but have adopted dominion theology, a postmillennial worldview.

If Hal Lindsey rejects Hunt's cultural conclusions, then why doesn't he say so publicly? If the professors at Dallas Seminary believe in world-transforming Christian social action rather than cul-

---

11. Hal Lindsey, *The Late, Great Planet Earth* (Grand Rapids, Michigan: Zondervan, [1970] 1973), p. 177.
12. Hal Lindsey, *Satan Is Alive and Well on Planet Earth* (Grand Rapids, Michigan: Zondervan, 1972), p. 113.

tural retreat, why don't they say so publicly. Silence is not golden, although it is a color somewhat close to golden.

Power or Ethics?

Here is the number-two message of pessimillennialism: *the gospel in history is doomed to cultural failure.* (The number-one message is that God's Old Testament law is no longer binding in New Testament times, which is why they are pessimistic: they no longer rest on the idea that God blesses His covenant people externally in terms of their faithfulness to His law, nor does He bring His enemies visibly low in history because of their covenantal rebellion.) In premillennialism and amillennialism, we see the underlying theology of the power religion: the issues of history will be settled in Christ's favor only through a final *physical* confrontation between God and Satan. The history of the church is therefore irrelevant: the conflict of the ages will be settled apart from the gospel, ethics, and the dominion covenant issued to Adam (Gen. 1:26-28), Noah (Gen. 9:1-17), and the church (Matt. 28:18-20). The conflict of the ages will be settled in a kind of cosmic arm wrestling match between God and Satan. The church is nothing more than a vulnerable bystander to this cosmic event.

Yet we all know who will win in a war based strictly on power. We know that God has more power than Satan. Satan knows, too. What Christians need to believe, now and throughout eternity, is that the earthly authority which comes progressively to Christians as God's reward to His people in response to their righteousness under Christ and under biblical law is greater than the earthly authority progressively granted by Satan to his followers for their rebellion against God. Unfortunately for the history of the gospel during the last century, both premillennialism and amillennialism deny this fundamental truth. They preach that the power granted to Satan's human followers in history will always be greater than the power granted by God to His people in history (meaning before Jesus' second coming). They preach *historic defeat for the church of Jesus Christ.* Why? Because they have denied the only basis of long-term victory for Christians: the continuing validity of God's Old Testament law, empowered in their lives by the Holy Spirit, the church's tool of dominion.

Jeremy Rifkin has understood this, and he has taken advantage of it.

Dispensationalism's White Flag

Rifkin has recognized clearly the social and intellectual problem for the consistent premillennialist or amillennialist: ends (*victory*) and means (*biblical law*). He understands that they lack both *motivation* and *strategy*. He has raised the institutional white flag to the devil, and he hopes to gain the position as the representative of the evangelicals in this program of surrender. But he has had to rush to the front of the evangelicals' army in order to become their spokesman. He was long preceded in leading this march to surrender by dispensationalism's leadership, who a century ago mentally and officially surrendered the future of the "Church Age" to Satan. In an interview in *Christianity Today* (Feb. 6, 1987), John Walvoord, a consistent representative of traditional dispensationalism, assures us: "We know that our efforts to make society Christianized is futile because the Bible doesn't teach it." He deliberately ignores the Old Testament prophets. He does not want Christians to preach prophetically, for the prophets called Israel back to obedience to biblical law, and *dispensationalism rejects biblical law*. Walvoord calls only for a vague, undefined "moral law" to promote an equally vague "honest government." Without specifics, this is meaningless rhetoric. This is *the theology of the rescue mission*: sober them up, give them a bath and a place to sleep, and then send them to church until they die or Jesus comes again. This is the "Christian as a nice neighbor" version of what should be "salt and light" theology: "Save individuals, but not societies."

Kantzer: Are we saying here that the Christian community, whether premil, postmil, or amil, must work both with individuals as well as seek to improve the structures of society? In other words, is there nothing within any of the millennial views that would prevent a believer from trying to improve society?

Walvoord: Well, the Bible says explicitly to do good to all men, especially those of faith. In other words, the Bible does give us broad commands to do good to the general public (p. 6-I).

Broad commands are worthless without specifics. A call to "do good" is meaningless without Bible-based standards of good. A Communist or a New Age evolutionist could agree with Walvoord's statement, since it contains no specifics. In response, Prof. John J. Davis of Gordon-Conwell Theological Seminary, a postmillennialist, replied:

But generally speaking, the premillennialist is more oriented toward helping those who have been hurt by the system than by addressing the systematic evil, while the postmillennialist believes the system can be sanctified. That's the basic difference with regard to our relationship to society (pp. 6-I, 7-I).

When dispensationalists are called pessimists by postmillennialists — as we postmillennialists unquestionably do call them — they react negatively. This is evidence of my contention that *everyone recognizes the inhibiting effects of pessimism*. People do not like being called pessimists. Walvoord is no exception. But his defense is most revealing:

Walvoord: Well, I personally object to the idea that premillennialism is pessimistic. We are simply realistic in believing that man cannot change the world. Only God can (11-I).

So, he objects to being called pessimistic. Well, what does he expect? Is this man totally self-deceived? Doesn't he read his own Seminary's scholarly journal, *Bibliotheca Sacra*? Listen to Lehman Strauss' dispensational assessment of today's world, in an article appropriately titled, "Our Only Hope":

We are witnessing in this twentieth century the collapse of civilization. It is obvious that we are advancing toward the end of the age. Science can offer no hope for the future blessing and security of humanity, but instead it has produced devastating and deadly results which threaten to lead us toward a new dark age. The frightful uprisings among races, the almost unbelievable conquests of Communism, and the growing antireligious philosophy throughout the world, all spell out the fact that doom is certain. I can see no bright prospects, through the efforts of man, for the earth and its inhabitants.[13]

Pessimism, thy name is Dallas Theological Seminary! Maybe Dallas Seminary did not invent fundamentalist pessimism, but it surely is the U.S. wholesale distributor.

Walvoord then insists: "We are simply realistic in believing that man cannot change the world. Only God can." Man cannot change the world? What in the world does this mean? That man is a robot? That God does everything, for good and evil? Walvoord obviously

---

13. Lehman Strauss, "Our Only Hope," *Bibliotheca Sacra*, Vol. 120 (April/June 1963), p. 154.

does not mean this. So what does he mean? That men collectively can do evil but not good? Then what effect does the gospel have in history? If he does not want to make this preposterous conclusion, then he must mean that *men acting apart from God's will and God's law* cannot improve the world long-term. If God is willing to put up with the victory of evil, then there is nothing that Christians can do about it except try to get out of the way of victorious sinners if they possibly can, while handing out gospel tracts on street corners and running rescue missions. The question is: *Is* God really willing to put up with the triumph of sinners over His church in history? Yes, say premillennialists and amillennialists. No, say postmillennialists.

What Walvoord is *implying but not saying* is that the postmillennialists' doctrine of the *historical* power of regeneration, the *historical* power of the Holy Spirit, the *historical* power of biblical law, and the *continuing validity* of God's dominion covenant with man (Gen. 1:26-28) is theologically erroneous, and perhaps even borderline heretical. But this, of course, is precisely the reason we postmillennialists refer to premillennialists as pessimistic. They implicitly hold the reverse doctrinal viewpoints: the historical *lack* of power of regeneration, the historical *lack* of power of the Holy Spirit, the historical *lack* of power of biblical law, and the *present suspension* of God's dominion covenant with man. (Carl McIntyre's premillennial Bible Presbyterian Church in 1970 went on record officially as condemning the doctrine of the cultural mandate of Genesis 1:28.)[14]

He says that only God can change the world. My, what an insight! *Who does he think postmillennialists believe will change the world for the better?* Of course God must change the world. Given the depravity of man, He is the only One who can. But how does He do this? Through demons? No. Through fallen men who are on the side of demons in their rebellion against God? No. So, what is God's historic means of making the world better? *The preaching of the gospel!* This is what postmillennialists have always taught. *And the comprehensive success of the gospel in history is what premillennialists have always denied.* They categorically deny that the gospel of Christ will ever change most men's hearts at any future point in history. The gospel in this view is a means primarily of *condemning gospel-rejecting people to hell*, not a program leading to the victory of Christ's people in history. The gospel

---

14. Resolution No. 13, reprinted in Rushdoony, *Institutes of Biblical Law*, pp. 723-24.

cannot transform the world, they insist. Yet they resent being called pessimists. Such resentment is futile. They *are* pessimists, and no amount of complaining and waffling can conceal it.

Pessimism regarding the transforming power of the gospel of Jesus Christ in history is what best *defines* pessimism. There is no pessimism in the history of man that is more pessimistic than this eschatological pessimism regarding the power of the gospel in history. The universal destruction of mankind by nuclear war—a myth, by the way[15]—is downright optimistic compared to pessimism with regard to the transforming power of the gospel in history. This pessimism testifies that the incorrigible human heart is more powerful than God in history, that Satan's defeat of Adam in the garden is more powerful in history than Christ's defeat of Satan at Calvary. It denies Paul's doctrine of triumphant grace in history: "Moreover the law entered, that the offence might abound. But where sin abounded, grace did more abound" (Rom. 5:20). In pessimillennial theologies, grace struggles so that sin might more abound in history.

Deliberately Deceiving the Faithful

What do pessimillennialists say in response? They accuse anyone who proclaims eschatological optimism as a heretical preacher of utopia. Dave Hunt writes: "A perfect Edenic environment where all ecological, economic, sociological, and political problems are solved fails to perfect mankind. So much for the theories of psychology and sociology and utopian dreams."[16] Here is the key word used again and again by pessimillennialists to dismiss postmillennialism: *utopia*. ("Utopia": *ou* = no, *topos* = place.) In short, they regard as totally mythological the idea that God's Word, God's Spirit, God's law, and God's church can change the hearts of *most* people sometime in the future. They *assume* (without any clear biblical support) that Revelation 20:7-10 describes a final rebellion in which *most people on earth rebel*, despite the fact that only *one-third* of the angels ("stars") rebelled with Satan, and only *one-third* of the earth is symbolically brought under God's wrath in the Book of Revelation's judgment passages (Rev. 8:7-12; 9:15, 18).

Over and over, pessimillennialists accuse postmillennialists of

---

15. Arthur Robinson and Gary North, *Fighting Chance: Ten Feet to Survival* (Ft. Worth, Texas: American Bureau of Economic Research, 1986).

16. *Beyond Seduction*, p. 251.

having too much confidence in man. This is really astounding, when you think about it, because all the primary defenders of modern postmillennialism have been Calvinists, and usually followers of Van Til. Normally, nobody accuses Calvinists of having too elevated a view of man, what with the Calvinists' doctrine of man's total depravity and fallen man's inability to respond in faith to the gospel without God's predestinating irresistible grace to force conversions. Postmillennialists are not arguing for confidence in "mankind as such." They are only arguing for the increasing long-term influence in history of *regenerate, covenantally faithful* people compared to *unregenerate, covenantally rebellious* people. What the amillennialists and premillennialists argue is the opposite: the steadily increasing long-term authority in history of unregenerate, covenantally rebellious people compared to regenerate, covenantally faithful people. It is not "confidence in man" that is the basis of postmillennial optimism; it is *confidence in the covenantal faithfulness of God* in rewarding covenant-keepers in history (Deut. 28:1-14) and punishing covenant-breakers (Deut. 28:15-68).[17] Listen to the words of Professor Thomas Sproull over a century ago regarding the coming period of millennial blessings:

> In order to accomplish this, the presence of the humanity of Christ is not necessary. The destruction of the kingdom of Satan cannot be done by a nature, but by a person. It is the work not of humanity, but of divinity. That kingdom extends over the whole world, and requires for its overthrow an omnipotent power. It received its death-blow when our Lord by his resurrection was "declared to be the Son of God."—*Rom.* 1:14. In his ascension "he spoiled principalities and powers, and made a show of them openly."—*Col.* 2:15. His manifestation in the flesh was necessary, that he might make atonement for sin; but by his incarnation he received no increase in strength, for vanquishing his enemies. It is indeed the God-man that gains the victory; not by human, but by divine power.[18]

How much plainer could he be? The basis of millennial blessings in history is the power of God in history, not the power of man in history. Yet dispensationalist intellectual leaders for over a century have boldly and unconscionably *lied* about the postmillennialists' explanation of the millennium, in order to score debate points with

---

17. Ray R. Sutton, *That You May Prosper: Dominion By Covenant* (Tyler, Texas: Institute for Christian Economics, 1987), ch. 4.
18. Rev. Thomas Sproull, *Prelections on Theology* (Pittsburgh, Pennsylvania: Myers, Shinkle, & Co., 1882), p. 411.

their poorly read followers. They are not ignorant men; they can read. They simply prefer to mislead their followers deliberately. It is not an intellectual defect on their part; it is a moral defect. Now that their followers have at last begun to read Christian books and newsletters written by people outside the dispensational ghetto, dispensational leaders are in deep, deep trouble. Their troops are deserting. (See Appendix E.)

Rifkin's Allies

We have seen in this book that a self-conscious liberal and New Age politician has used the premillennialists' own pessimistic eschatology, as well as the Creation Science movement's appeal to the second law of thermodynamics, in order to create a working alliance between Christians and the New Age movement. Rifkin's explicit pessimism concerning the future has led him to promote an attitude of "batten down the hatches," raise taxes, and create a controlled, government-directed, zero-growth economy. In short, he has seen the eschatological weaknesses of traditional premillennialism (evangelicalism and fundamentalism), and he has used these weaknesses as a kind of intellectual jiu-jitsu. The evangelicals have been silent about Rifkin for over seven years.

This is why it is annoying, to say the least, to read Walvoord's attack on postmillennialism as an ally of evolutionary liberalism:

> During the last part of the nineteenth century, evolution emerged as an explanation for why things were getting better. In those days, prophecy conferences included postmils, amils, and premils, but it became a battle between the premil view and the evolutionary view that seemed to fit postmillennialism. So premillennialism became a battle against the evolutionist, which ended up as a battle between fundamentalism and liberalism. I'm afraid the postmillennial position is still closely associated with evolution and liberalism (8-I).

He may be "afraid" of this, but anyone who has even a smattering of knowledge about twentieth-century postmillennialism needn't be afraid in the slightest. Here is the man who was president for thirty years of a seminary that has never offered a course defending the six-literal-day creation. He says that postmillennialism favors evolutionism, yet it was R. J. Rushdoony, a postmillennialist, who got Morris and Whitcomb's *Genesis Flood* into print with Presbyterian & Reformed Publishers after dispensationalist Moody Press made it clear to the authors that Moody Press rejected their literal day view of the Genesis week.[19] The intellectual leaders of postmillennialism in the United States are all six-literal-day creationists.

The "Gap Theory"

Dispensational premillennialists are hardly consistent defenders of this literal view of Genesis 1, given the fact that C. I. Scofield taught the "gap theory" in the notes of his famous reference Bible. This theory proposes two separate creations by God, the one described in Genesis 1:1, and then another preceding Genesis 1:2. (The "gap" refers to the supposed time gap between the two creations, although the word is more properly applied to the *gap of revelation* that this hypothesis inserts in between Genesis 1:1 and 1:2.) In between the two creations, there was enough time to absorb all the geological ages that the humanists can throw at us. (How the formless and void re-created world of Genesis 1:2 left geological traces of countless ages, with all those detailed fossil forms embedded in the rocks, is a bit of a problem, of course.) Scofield speaks of the "dateless past" as holding enough time to allow all geological eras.[20]

This "gap theory" had been developed in the early nineteenth century as a way to enable Bible-believing Christians to accept the findings of uniformitarian geology without giving up their faith in a literal Bible. Henry Morris, Duane Gish, and most other Scientific Creationists have long recognized the deadly threat that this compromising theory poses to biblical creationism.[21] It had been the acceptance by Christians of the ages-long time scheme of the pre-Darwin geologists that led to Darwinism in the first place, and made it far easier for Darwinism to be accepted by Christians.[22]

Premillennialism and Humanism?

There is no question that Jeremy Rifkin has seen the similarities between his "entropic" view of the universe and premillennialism's view. He self-consciously has pointed to these similarities. "The pre-

---

19. Henry M. Morris, *History of Modern Creationism* (San Diego, California: Master Book Pubs., 1984), p. 154.

20. C. I. Scofield, *Scofield Reference Bible* (New York: Oxford University Press, [1909] 1917), p. 3n.

21. Morris, *History of Modern Creationism*, pp. 41, 58-61, 92.

22. Gary North, *The Dominion Covenant: Genesis* (2nd ed.; Tyler, Texas: Institute for Christian Economics, 1987), Appendix C: "Cosmologies in Conflict: Creation vs. Evolution."

millennialists view history in much the same way as the second law of thermodynamics."[23]

There is also no doubt that the humanists have relied on the widespread fundamentalist faith in premillennialism to strengthen their hold over American life. The executive director of the American Humanist Association, Frederick Edwords, has made this plain in an article he co-authored for *The Humanist*, the AHA's magazine. It is an attack on Pat Robertson's unofficial campaign for the presidency. The article is filled with cartoons that picture men dressed in Nazi-type uniforms, but with a cross on the shoulder instead of a swastika. The article is a self-conscious attempt to link Pat Robertson's theology of Christian activism with the Christian Reconstruction movement—a link that Rev. Robertson publicly denies.

The authors say that "Robertson's position on the divine origin of human rights bears a striking resemblance to that of the most theocratic elements within the religious right."[24] What the two authors do not realize is that the head of Robertson's CBN University School of Law, Herbert Titus, wrote the appendix to R. J. Rushdoony's book, *Law and Society*, volume 2 of Rushdoony's *Institutes of Biblical Law* (Ross House Books, 1982). That really would have set them off! They did not do sufficient homework before going into print.

The authors devote the second half of their article to the question, "The Origin of the Religious Right," and they attribute it to someone named R. J. Rashdoony and his followers, the Christian Reconstructionists. (When some humanist scholar looks up "Rashdoony" at the library, he will find no entries. This will help to buy us Reconstructionists a little more time. "No such person; he must not have published very much.") The authors cite Rushdoony's 1972 speech to the Chalcedon Foundation:

> As one very, very prominent pre-millennial preacher in Los Angeles has repeatedly said, "You don't polish brass on a sinking ship." The world is a sinking ship, so waste no time on reform, on doing anything to improve the world, to bring about God's law order therein. No matter how fine a man says that, when any man believes it, he drops his future (p. 9).

---

23. Jeremy Rifkin, *The Emerging Order*, p. 236.
24. Frederick Edwords and Stephen McCabe, "Getting Out God's Vote: Pat Robertson and the Evangelicals," *The Humanist* (May/June 1987), p. 6.

Rushdoony has repeatedly cited this statement since I first met him in the early 1960's. Dispensationalist newsletter publisher Peter Lalonde has favorably cited this statement in his taped interview with Dave Hunt: "It's a question, 'Do you polish brass on a sinking ship?' And if they're working on setting up new institutions, instead of going out and winning the lost for Christ, then they're wasting the most valuable time on the planet earth right now, and that is the serious problem in his thinking."[25]

The humanist authors then go on to cite Rushdoony's conclusions:

> Consider the difference it would make to the United States if, instead of forty million or so pre-millennials, we had forty million post-millennials. Instead of having forty million people who expect the world is going to end very soon and that they are going to be raptured out of tribulation, consider the difference it would make if those forty million instead felt that they had a duty under God to conquer in Christ's name.

Then the two authors state the obvious — something denied repeatedly by a growing handful of Christian activists who are still premillennialists, and who have taken a long time to figure out why it is that most of their fellow premillennialists refuse to take their activism seriously: "And it is precisely this change in thinking, from premillennialism to postmillennialism, under the influence of Christian Reconstructionism, that has made possible the religious right and the political mobilization of millions of otherwise fatalistic fundamentalists" (p. 10).

These humanists understand that eschatology has consequences for people's worldview. They understand fully that it was *premillennialism's inescapably pessimistic view of Christians' earthly future* that long undergirded the fundamentalists' willingness to stay out of politics and let the humanists run the country for almost a century. This shift in eschatology has upset the alliance between humanism's power religion and fundamentalism's escape religion. It is this "political mobilization of millions of otherwise fatalistic fundamentalists" that these humanist authors resent. They end their article with a ringing challenge to their peers to read the writings of the Christian Reconstructionists, for if they avoid taking us seriously, humanists will fall into the same trap as those who failed to read and take seriously Hitler's *Mein Kampf* (p. 36).

---

25. *Dominion: A Dangerous New Theology*, Tape #1 of *Dominion: The Word and New World Order*.

Eschatology has consequences. While there are hundreds of thousands of fundamentalists, Pat Robertson among them, who have not yet abandoned the official doctrines of premillennialism, they have abandoned premillennialism's inherently pessimistic and retreatist social conclusions. They have become activists. Thus, it will be only for a few more years—less than a decade, I would guess—that those fundamentalists who remain as public activists will still cling officially to their premillennial theology. The humanists understand this. Dave Hunt understands this. Millions of premillennialists in the middle have not thought about this. When they do start thinking about it, there will be an ecclesiastical rupture over the timing of the Rapture (premillennial or postmillennial), and the Christian Reconstruction movement will inherit the best and the brightest of the younger (presently) premillennial activists.

We Reconstructionists need only to publish and wait patiently. Our eschatological adversaries will do our work for us. The premillennial activists will eventually be tossed out of their churches by outraged premillennial retreatists, who deeply resent being called retreatists, pessimists, and allies of the humanists—which they most certainly have been and continue to be. And once the activists see what their fellow premillennialists have done to them, and why, many of them will adopt postmillennialism. We Reconstructionists will at last recruit the shock troops we need. At that point, the humanists can kiss goodbye their monopoly over American political life.

Dominion Theology and the New Age Movement?

Christianity is the source of the idea of progress in the history of mankind. Other groups have stolen this vision and have reworked it along anti-Christian lines, from the Enlightenment[26] to the Social Gospel movement to the New Age movement, but this does not mean that postmillennial optimism is the cause of the thefts. It only means that Satan recognizes the motivating power of *orthodox* Christian theology. It surely does not mean that eschatological pessimism is in any way an effective shield against humanism, New Age philosophy, or socialism. Jeremy Rifkin is proof enough. He is a pessimist who appeals for support to pessimists within the Christian community.

---

26. Robert A. Nisbet, "The Year 2000 and All That," *Commentary* (June 1968).

What is even more galling is that dispensationalist author Dave Hunt has tried to link the Christian Reconstruction movement with the New Age movement, simply because Christian Reconstructionists, as dominion theologians, proclaim the legitimacy of social action along biblical lines.[27] What angers traditional premillennialists is that Reconstructionists say that the world is *not* going to hell in a handbasket. Satan's world is, but not the kingdom of God, which has manifestations on earth.

I wrote the first Christian book exposing the theology of the New Age movement in 1976, *None Dare Call It Witchcraft*,[28] years before Dave Hunt wrote anything about it. Yet the tape-buying public is tantalized by a direct-mail advertising piece for a three-tape interview with Hunt, in which the copywriter asks some legally safe but preposterous leading questions:

> Is Dominion Theology placing the church in allegiance with the New Age and Globalist groups who are trying to build a New World Order of peace and prosperity?
>
> Does Dominion Theology represent a rejection of the finished work of the cross?

Dave Hunt, citing II Peter 3:11 (and erroneously attributing to Peter the words of Isaiah 34:4), states categorically that theological optimism toward the gospel's power to transform this earth is a stepping stone to humanism. Instead, we should turn totally from this earth. Hunt separates heaven from earth so completely that the earth must show no signs in history of God's healing power. This is an explicit, self-conscious defense of the theology that undergirds that old line, "He is so totally spiritual that he's no earthly good." Hunt implicitly denies Jesus' required prayer: "Thy kingdom come. Thy will be done on earth, as it is in heaven" (Matt. 6:10).

---

27. "Closely related in belief are several other groups: the Reconstructionists such as Gary North et al, as well as Christian socialists such as Jim Wallis (of *Sojourners*), Tom Sine et al whose major focus is upon cleaning up the earth ecologically, politically, economically, sociologically etc. They imagine that the main function of the Church is to restore the Edenic state—hardly helpful, since Eden is where sin began. Many groups are beginning to work together who disagree on some points but share with the New Agers a desire to clean up the earth and establish the Kingdom." Dave Hunt, *CIB Bulletin* (Feb. 1987), front page.

28. Gary North, *None Dare Call It Witchcraft* (New Rochelle, New York: Arlington House, 1976). This has been updated as *Unholy Spirits: Occultism and New Age Humanism* (Ft. Worth, Texas: Dominion Press, 1986). See especially Chapter Eleven for a critique of Dave Hunt's eschatology.

Now you would say, boy, that's a pretty hopeless thing, well, but Peter didn't say that. He said, "Seeing that these things will all be dissolved, what manner of persons ought you to be in all holy conversations and godliness?" He said, "The day of the Lord is coming in which the heavens will be rolled up like a scroll. The elements will melt with a fervent heat," and so forth. And *that* in fact, Peter says, ought to motivate us to holy living, to turn *totally* from this world, from the materialization and all of the ambitions, and so forth, to a hope in the heavenlies, in a new creation, and it ought to motivate us to *godliness*. But these people are saying "no, the motivation we need is the desire to build, to reconstruct planet earth, to realize that ecologically we got problems." I mean we should be concerned about all that. I'm not denying that, but that's not our hope; that's not the primary goal of the church: social transformation. But the primary goal is to save souls, and to bring men to the cross of Jesus Christ, and I feel—I don't feel, I'm *convinced*—that the kingdom-dominion teaching is playing into the hands of the very lie that turns us from the cross and from the gospel and the true solution to a humanistic idea, but all done in the name of Jesus Christ, and for good cause.[29]

Hunt tries to protect himself. He makes an off-hand remark regarding ecology: "I mean we should be concerned about all that. I'm not denying that. . . ." Baloney. He is not concerned in the slightest. He shares this lack of concern (and lack of specifics, Bible-revealed answers) with dispensationalists in general. We are still waiting for the first study of "ecology and the Bible" written by any dispensationalist, with Bible-based answers to ecological questions. I devote more space to this topic than to any other in my third volume on the Book of Exodus, *Tools of Dominion*. Dispensationalists have written nothing about ecology because: 1) they would have to use Old Testament law to deal with the question, which their theology categorically rejects; and 2) they see no possibility of cleaning up the earth before the Rapture. The very idea of cleaning up the earth is a socialistic New Age deception, in Dave Hunt's view, as we have seen. He is quite specific about the link between the New Age movement and ecology:

But forgetting that for the moment, people will say, "Well I mean, you know, whether we are going to be taken to heaven, or whether the kingdom is on this earth, or, you know, whether we are going to be raptured, or whether we are not going to be raptured, those are future events. Let's not

---

29. *Dominion and the Cross*, Tape #2, of *Dominion: The Word and New World Order*.

worry about that; let's unite in our common concern for our fellow man," and so forth. That opens the door to a very deceptive lie which literally turns us from heaven as our hope to this earth, which is at the heart of the kingdom-dominion teaching, that we—man—was given dominion over this earth, and the problem is that he lost the dominion to Satan, and the big thing is that we need to regain the dominion. . . . But it opens the door to a marriage with New Age beliefs, as you know, with humanistic beliefs, so that we will all be joining together in working for ecological wholeness, working for peace, working for prosperity, because we are not concerned about heaven, or the return of Christ, or the Rapture, but we have got to be concerned about earth, the threat of ecological collapse, the threat of a nuclear holocaust.[30]

Here we have the continuing historical theme in all traditional dispensationalism: the radical separation of heaven and earth, which necessarily implies the increasing connection between hell and earth. The dispensationalists are promoting the spread of Satan's imitation New World Order when they protest the validity of Christ's New World Order, which He established definitively with His death, resurrection, and the sending of the Holy Spirit at Pentecost. Dispensationalism delivers the world to Satan and his followers *by default*, and all in the name of biblical orthodoxy regarding the Rapture—orthodoxy which began no earlier, they are forced to argue, than 1830.

Whose New World Order?

Now, let me say right here, as I have said earlier in this book: I believe in the New World Order of Jesus Christ, inaugurated at Calvary and visibly sanctioned in history by the resurrection and ascension of Christ to the right hand of God, where He now reigns in power and glory. What I reject is the imitation New World Order of humanism. But there *is* a biblical New World Order. There is a *new creation in Christ*. It was established *definitively* at Calvary. It is being established *progressively* in history. And it will be established *finally* at the day of judgment.

We cannot expect to beat something with nothing. We cannot expect to defeat the humanists' New World Order with a traditional (1830) theology of guaranteed historical defeat—the theology of traditional dispensational pessimillennialism. We must fight theological

---

30. *Dominion: A Dangerous New Theology*, Tape #1 of *ibid*.

hellfire with theological heavenfire, just as God fought it at the destruction of Sodom. The Sodomites lost that confrontation, not Lot, and certainly not Abraham. Pessimillennialists forget this. Nevertheless, just because Christian Reconstructionists preach victory for the church in history, we are now being linked to the New Age movement—a movement that I led the fight against long before traditional dispensationalists had ever heard of it, long before they discovered that they could sell paperback books about it, not to mention sensational audio tapes.

We have seen this strategy before. The Pharisees said that Christ was in league with Satan because He successfully cast out demons.

> Then was brought unto him one possessed with a devil, blind, and dumb: and he healed him, insomuch that the blind and dumb both spake and saw. And all the people were amazed, and said, Is not this the son of David? But when the Pharisees heard it, they said, This fellow doth not cast out devils, but by Beelzebub the prince of the devils (Matt. 12:22-24).

The Pharisees could not deny that Christ had achieved a visible victory over a demon. The blind man saw. Mute before, he could now speak. This called into question the *narrow, Palestine-bound religion of the Pharisees*. It meant that the son of David, the promised Messiah, had come among them. This was a threat to their nationalistic religion. It was a threat to their working alliance with the humanist Roman Empire. They had bowed the knee politically to Rome's humanist empire, and now Christ's manifestation of power was calling their compromise into question. The alliance between the Pharisees' escapist religion and Rome's power religion was being challenged by Christ's dominion religion. The escape religionists resented this, as they always do. Christ was challenging their theology of an exclusively *internalized* kingdom of God in the midst of a hostile, all-powerful kingdom of political humanism.

Christ replied in kind, showing them a new theology about the kingdom of God on earth:

> And Jesus knew their thoughts, and said unto them, Every kingdom divided against itself is brought to desolation; and every city or house divided against itself shall not stand. And if Satan cast out Satan, he is divided against himself; how shall then his kingdom stand? And if I by Beelzebub cast out devils, by whom do your children cast them out? Therefore they shall be your judges. But if I cast out devils by the Spirit of God, then the kingdom of God is come unto you (Matt. 12:25-27).

How do we know that *the kingdom of God is now on earth*, a doctrine that deeply disturbs Hunt? Because of this verse, among others. Jesus *did* cast out devils by the Spirit of God. He *did* use the power of God to overcome Satan. He *did* heal the sick. And He *will* conquer His enemies, through His church, in history, before He comes again in final judgment. He *now* reigns in heaven, at the right hand of God (Eph. 1:19-22). He reigns now, both in heaven and on earth (Matt. 28:18-20). Because He cast out demons by the Spirit of God, we know that the kingdom of God has come unto us. We also have that same Holy Spirit. The victory in principle is behind us: "For he *hath* put all things under his feet" (I Cor. 15:27a).

Anyone who denies this *denies the cross of Christ*. This is why it is preposterous to see the defeat-preachers ask: "Does Dominion Theology represent a rejection of the finished work of the cross?" No, dominion theology affirms *Christ's definitive victory over Satan at Calvary*. What outrages the escape religionists is that postmillennialists also preach *Christ's progressive victory over Satan in history, through His church*. Hunt categorically and self-consciously denies victory in history for the church of Jesus Christ. He affirms that Christ's chosen people are *losers in history*.

This is exactly what the Pharisees taught the Jews: that until the Messiah came, the Jews would be losers in history. This was the basis of the Pharisees' political compromise with the Roman Empire. Victory could not come until the Messiah came. Victory was always in the future. Victory was always on Messiah's shoulders, and always far ahead in time. And indeed, victory *was* on Messiah's shoulders, which was what Christ's miracles announced. But this meant that the Pharisees had to bow to Christ rather than Rome, that they would have to start preaching gospel victory and training redeemed people to exercise dominion. This was unacceptable to the Pharisees. It meant political trouble with Rome. It also meant that they would be responsible for working out in history the Bible's principles of social transformation, and on a worldwide scale, for they would have to begin preaching a comprehensive gospel of total healing.[31]

The Pharisees refused to accept this responsibility. They hated the very idea of worldwide responsibility. They wanted peace with Rome. But the church believed Christ, *which is why Christ's church took the gospel to the world in power*, while the Jews were scattered by the

---

31. See Appendix C: "Comprehensive Redemption: A Theology for Social Action."

Romans in a series of historic defeats, beginning with the fall of Jerusalem and the destruction of the temple.[32]

The postmillennial Christian Reconstructionists unquestionably teach that there will be a future era in which the gospel heals the souls of large numbers of people, and these healed people will then work to subdue the earth to the glory of God. But this is the offense, in Hunt's eyes. This optimism about visible manifestations of God's kingdom on earth, he says, is what the New Age movement is all about.

Tell it to Jeremy Rifkin.

Conclusion

While Dave Hunt denies calling postmillennial Christian Reconstructionists New Agers, there can be no doubt that he hints at this supposed relationship. His followers have picked up the accusation, and I have letters in my files that prove this.

We should not make eschatology the test of being a "fellow traveller" of the New Age movement. The New Age movement's three key doctrines are all anti-Christian: 1) reincarnation, 2) the divinization of man, and 3) techniques of "higher consciousness" as a means to divinization. There are optimistic New Agers, and there are pessimistic New Agers. Jeremy Rifkin is the most influential New Age social philosopher, and he is self-consciously pessimistic, and he self-consciously targeted premillennialists as those Christians closest to his worldview. I could make a far better case for Dave Hunt as a secret New Ager than he has been able to make concerning me. But either argument, and either innuendo, would be equally wrong, both morally and factually. Orthodox Christianity is inherently opposed to New Age doctrines. The early Christian creeds were statements of faith drawn up when proto-New Age theologians began to mislead Christian believers.

What I do argue here is that theonomic postmillennialism is more consistent in its opposition to Rifkin's version of New Age social theory than either premillennialism or amillennialism is. I argue that the worldview of Dave Hunt leads to a shortened view of time, a minimal view of Christians' authority in history and their responsibility in history. Dave Hunt is a self-conscious retreatist and expounder of the escape religion. Where views such as his pre-

---

32. David Chilton, *The Days of Vengeance: An Exposition of the Book of Revelation* (Ft. Worth, Texas: Dominion Press, 1987).

dominate, the church becomes temporarily what he says it will be in the future: a loser.

When Christians start winning in history, as they surely will, they will look back in amazement that anyone calling himself a Christian could have such a low view of the church in history and such a low view of the civilization-transforming power of the gospel in history. They will be amazed that any Christian could have believed that God would voluntarily transfer more power to Satan in history than to the Holy Spirit.

Let us not make Dave Hunt's theological mistakes. Let us abandon pessimillennialism in all its paralyzing forms. We were not intended by God to be historical losers.

I have made a series of very serious accusations. I have said that dispensationalists believe that the Christian gospel that saves men's souls will have no long-term positive effects in society at large. They therefore are forced to deny that the progressive sanctification of the church in history will produce positive results in society that will then lead to long-term social transformation of society at large. They therefore deny the cause-and-effect relationship between the church's progressive faithfulness and the progressive healing of society.

Dispensationalists look forward to the millennium as a period of reduced personal responsibility for Christians, for Jesus will issue orders to people and rule with an iron hand. Dispensationalists tend to see the historical battle between Christ and Satan in terms of cosmic power, not human ethics. This is because they reject the continuing validity of Old Testament law today. They therefore have to adopt "neutral" concepts of "natural law" that are shared by covenant-breakers and covenant-keepers. (This faith in common ground moral principles is another reason why the Creation Science movement appeals to supposedly shared common ground scientific principles in order to defend the doctrine of the six-day creation.)

In contrast, postmillennialists believe that God can and will transform social institutions for the better in the future. They believe that God will use Christians to achieve this improvement. Postmillennialists affirm the historic power of the church, the Holy Spirit, and God's law. They therefore believe in the culture-transforming power of the gospel in history. Christian Reconstruction postmillennialists have little confidence in man as such, but they do have greater confidence in redeemed, faithful men than in rebellious, satanic men.

In short, when Creation Scientists abandon the dispensational theology of either John Walvoord or Dave Hunt, they will find it far easier to do battle with the New Age theology of Jeremy Rifkin.

Appendix E

THE DIVISION WITHIN DISPENSATIONALISM

> *. . . I find the term Christian reconstruction to be a valid one; and certainly this concept is not the exclusive property of the postmillennialists. The Bible **does** apply to all of life. Christ **is** Lord of all the earth, and it **is** a valid task of all Bible-believing Christians to seek to bring every area of personal and corporate life into obedience to the Word of God. Rather than desert a good concept simply because it is misused, we should seek to be reconstructionists within the biblical eschatological framework.*
>
> David Schnittger[1]

Earlier in this study, I cited Rushdoony's summary of the difference between secularists and fundamentalists:

> **The humanists believe in history, but not in God. The fundamentalists believe in God, but not in history.**

Since about 1979, this description no longer applies as well as it did earlier. The dispensationalists are in the midst of a major division. The old conflict between pretribulationism and posttribulationism has revived, especially with the publication of posttrib Dave MacPherson's books on the origins of pretrib doctrine.[2] But now a major division has appeared within the pretrib camp: dominion theology vs. traditional dispensational pietism. Mr. Schnittger's well-written pamphlet is a good example of the newer dominion viewpoint.

---

1. David Schnittger, *Christian Reconstruction from a Pretribulational Perspective* (Box 1144, Oklahoma City, Oklahoma: Southwest Radio Church, 1986), p. 9.

2. Dave MacPherson, *The Incredible Cover-Up* (Medford, Oregon: Omega Publications, 1975); *The Great Rapture Hoax* (Fletcher, New York: New Puritan Library, 1983). MacPherson is a posttribulational dispensationalist.

Many Christians are coming to Christian Reconstructionism by way of eschatology; some are announcing their postmillennialism, while others adopt the language of postmillennial victory yet maintain that they have not abandoned their premillennialism. There is no question that since 1979, a growing minority of fundamentalists have abandoned their anti-historical outlook. They have begun to call for Christian dominion. Some have recognized that Christianity is the religion of historical optimism. They understand that if you deny this optimism toward the church's earthly future, you seriously impair the spread of the gospel. Others have recognized that Christianity's tool of dominion is biblical law. Dispensationalism is losing its younger leaders to Reconstructionism as they choose either of two forks in the road: postmillennial eschatology or biblical law. We Reconstructionists are happy to get them for either reason, but our preference is for the second road: ethics.

Defection Over the Question of Time

History is linear. It moves in a straight line, from creation to final judgment. But it is not only linear; it is progressive. *There is positive feedback in history.* Covenantal righteousness brings forth God's external, historical blessings (Deut. 28:1-14), while covenantal rebellion brings forth God's external historic curses (Deut. 28:15-68). This is why Christians can have confidence concerning the earthly success of the church *in history.* What this means is that the righteous efforts of each Christian have positive effects in the future.

This has been a popular idea. Humanists in the West have stolen it in every generation. The problem is that Christians from time to time abandon the very idea that the humanists have stolen: earthly optimism. The Christians sometimes become pessimistic about the earthly effects of their own hard work, and this leads to a "fortress church" mentality: "Form a circle with the wagons, boys: the satanists are getting closer!" They wait for God to intervene in history and pull them out of trouble, and even more important, *out of their personal responsibility for the future of the gospel.* In Appendix D, I cited Lehman Strauss in Dallas Seminary's journal *Bibliotheca Sacra:*

> We are witnessing in this twentieth century the collapse of civilization. It is obvious that we are advancing toward the end of the age. Science can offer no hope for the future blessing and security of humanity, but instead it has produced devastating and deadly results which threaten to lead us

toward a new dark age. The frightful uprisings among races, the almost unbelievable conquests of Communism, and the growing antireligious philosophy throughout the world, all spell out the fact that doom is certain. I can see no bright prospects, through the efforts of man, for the earth and its inhabitants.[3]

No Solutions; Therefore, No Responsibilities

This utter pessimism concerning the earthly future of the institutional church and Christian civilization is what lies behind the traditional premillennialists' lack of any systematic social policies. They think it is a waste of their time to think about such matters, since they believe that the Christians will never be in a position to implement them. Peter Lalonde's comments are representative of the mindset of traditional dispensationalism:

> Now, I'm thinking about a conversation I had here with a young Christian brother the other day. And he's much involved with the Reconstruction and Christian conservative movement in the U.S. And he's talking to me in terms of political change, social change, economic reform — in fact, he was talking to me in terms of revamping the entire Federal Reserve System in the United States. And I think he had a valid point, that the Federal Reserve is one of the most corrupt institutions on the planet. But it came to me, and the point he was making was this, he said: "Look, we're both sincere Christians. You're looking for a rapture, and I'm not. If I'm wrong," he said, "we will both go in the rapture anyway, but if you're wrong, I'm the only one of the two of us who has worked to set up the necessary institutions to run the world as God would have us do." In other words, what he is saying is, "My belief has nothing to lose; yours does."
>
> But there's a couple problems with this. It's not a case of a coin toss, of who's right and wrong; it's what the Word of God says. You just can't do it as a 50-50 option, because I don't believe the Word leaves that option. And the Word certainly does not teach anything about setting up institutions, and that's something we're going to talk more about. But this leads us to the central question. He's saying, in his view, his view has nothing to lose, where ours does. But it does, because the question is what do we do in the meantime? It's a question, "Do you polish brass on a sinking ship?" And if they're working on setting up new institutions, instead of going out and winning the lost for Christ, then they're wasting the most valuable time on the planet earth right now, and that is the serious problem in his thinking.[4]

---

3. Lehman Strauss, "Our Only Hope," *Bibliotheca Sacra*, Vol. 120 (April/June 1963), p. 154.

4. *Dominion: A Dangerous New Theology*, Tape #1 of the three-tape series, *Dominion: The Word and New World Order*, distributed by the *Omega-Letter*, Ontario, Canada, 1986.

Rushdoony has said, "A philosophy calling for an escape from time is not likely to involve itself in the battles of time."[5] Pretribulational dispensationalist David Schnittger has clearly recognized the danger of this dismissal of progress in history, the danger of the "we don't polish brass" analogy:

> North and other postmillennial Christian Reconstructionists label those who hold the pretribulational rapture position pietists and cultural retreatists. One reason these criticisms are so painful is because I find them to be substantially true. Many in our camp have an all-pervasive negativism regarding the course of society and the impotence of God's people to do anything about it. They will heartily affirm that **Satan is Alive and Well on Planet Earth**, and that this must indeed be **The Terminal Generation**; therefore, any attempt to influence society is ultimately hopeless. They adopt the pietistic platitude: *"You don't polish brass on a sinking ship."* Many pessimistic pretribbers cling to the humanists' version of religious freedom; namely Christian social and political impotence, self-imposed, as drowning men cling to a life preserver.[6]

Hal Lindsey: Before and After

The fact is, Hal Lindsey now says publicly that he *does* believe in Christian social action. I think we need to take him at his word. What he therefore needs to write is a systematic, Bible-quoting popular book that shows exactly how his stated position of 1970 is conformable to his new interest in Christian political and social activism. If he has not modified his earlier views — which he so obviously has, *because* of the growing influence of the Reconstructionists' worldview — then he needs to show why it was that for over a century, pretribulational dispensationalists refused to get involved in any kind of social activism, except for their ill-fated support of the Prohibition Amendment three generations ago.[7] Why did this only recently recognized error — Christian retreat as the logical and psychological outcome of eschatological pessimism — dominate the thinking of dispensationalists for a century? Why does the theology of zero public involvement still dominate Dallas Seminary, an institution that has yet to take a public stand against abortion, well

---

5. R. J. Rushdoony, *The One and the Many: Studies in the Philosophy of Order and Ultimacy* (Fairfax, Virginia: Thoburn Press, [1971] 1978), p. 129.
6. Schnittger, *Christian Reconstruction from a Pretribulational Perspective*, p. 7.
7. Douglas W. Frank, *Less Than Conquerors: How Evangelicals Entered the Twentieth Century* (Grand Rapids, Michigan: Eerdmans, 1986).

over a decade after the infamous 1973 *Roe v. Wade* decision, a case that originated in the city of Dallas? Why do the faculty members at dispensational seminaries still refuse to become vocal promoters of the Christian school movement? Why do they still send their own children to the public schools, and defend their moral right to do so (as one Dallas Seminary professor did to me)? Why, in short, do they do precisely what Christian Reconstructionists have always said was the only social action consistent with their theology, i.e., run rescue missions? For at least three-quarters of a century, 1900-1979, dispensationalism's major social concern was "demon rum," not demon humanism. Mr. Schnittger has well asked:

> I think it is time that these charges are addressed. As I read journals and magazines from organizations which hold the pretrib position, there is an eerie silence on these issues. Why aren't the leading schools like Dallas Theological Seminary, Grace Theological Seminary, or Moody Bible Institute undertaking a scholarly refutation of these charges? Why are pretrib Christian activities [activists] neglecting to integrate their eschatology with their strategies for Christian reform and reconstruction? Are the postmillennialists indeed the only ones who are consistent with their eschatology. . . .?[8]

He might also have added, "How could Talbot Theological Seminary in La Mirada, California have abandoned its original dispensationalism without a public word from anyone at Talbot or from the other dispensational institutions?" But this is what has happened. A major shift is in progress regarding the idea of progress, and Hal Lindsey is part of this shift.

Lindsey also says that he does not think we should try to date the rapture. This reluctance to date the rapture is a major reversal of what he was saying in the 1970's — "the generation of the fig tree" — and is another sign of the monumental shift in worldview that is taking place within dispensationalism today. Lindsey is the man who wrote these words regarding the restoration of Israel and the Second Coming of Christ: "It cannot be emphasized enough. This restoration would take place after a world-wide dispersion and long-term desolation of the land of Israel. However, it would occur shortly before the events which will culminate with the personal, visible return of the Messiah, Jesus Christ, to set up an everlasting

---

8. Schnittger, *Christian Reconstruction*, p. 8.

Kingdom and bring about the spiritual conversion of Israel."⁹ Lindsey was incorrect; it *could* be emphasized too much! It *was* emphasized too much. This misguided tactic of motivating their followers to wait rapturously for the Cosmic Escape Hatch that they promised would occur shortly after the creation of the State of Israel, has now blown a gaping hole in the side of traditional pretribulational dispensationalism. Lindsey, like all pretribulational dispensational rapturists prior to 1981, "bet the farm" on the creation of the State of Israel. The bet has not paid off yet. The longer it does not pay off, the more likely the younger fundamentalist troops are going to adopt the rhetoric of the Christian Reconstructionists and forget about their parents' prophecy charts. In this sense, *Hal Lindsey has made a fundamental psychological and motivational break with Dave Hunt, who still thinks that we can and should date the rapture, and who says privately that it is probably coming before 1990.*[10]

Hal Lindsey is the man who assured 20 million Christian readers: "There's nothing that remains to be fulfilled before Christ could catch you up to be with Him. . . . We should be living like persons who don't expect to be around much longer."[11] This was the rallying cry of Christians during the "Me decade" of the 1970's. He qualifies these words 43 pages later, on the last page of his book, telling people that it *may* be all right to finish school, or get married, and so forth. Nevertheless, it is not possible to erase the obvious implications of a worldview. Christians may finish high school or college, but what about grad school? Why suffer the rigors and expense of law school? He ended his best-selling book with the same old vision of Christian service: *tract-passing*. "So let us seek to reach our family, our friends, and our acquaintances with the Gospel with all the strength that he gives us. The time is short."[12] Peter Lalonde (cited above) is far more faithful to Hal Lindsey's 1970 theology than Hal Lindsey is today: "It's a question, 'Do you polish brass on a sinking ship?' And if they're working on setting up new institutions, instead of going out and winning the lost for Christ, then they're wasting the most valuable time on the planet earth right now. . . ."

You wonder why there are not half a dozen Christian law schools

---

9. Hal Lindsey, *The Late, Great Planet Earth* (Grand Rapids, Michigan: Zondervan, [1970] 1973), p. 52. This was the 35th printing.
10. He told this to my associate John Mauldin in the summer of 1987.
11. Lindsey, *Late, Great*, p. 145.
12. *Ibid.*, p. 188.

today turning out highly skilled men and women ready to defend Christian day schools and churches that have been zoned out of existence? Here is one very good reason: *a shortening of Christians' time perspective*. You wonder why Christians have been uninvolved in long-run strategies for changing the world? Here is why: *a shortening of Christians' time perspective*. Yet today leading fundamentalists bewail the fact that they have no books defending a consistent Christian worldview, except books written by neo-evangelical liberals and Christian Reconstructionists, neither of which accept pretribulational dispensationalism. They have no worldview books because their worldview militated against writing such books. They had a worldview, to be sure, a worldview that implicitly denied the importance of having any worldview. They had an *other*worldview instead.

Fighting Something With Nothing

The old slogan of American politics is correct: "You can't beat something with nothing." Christian Reconstruction is sweeping through the dispensational movement like a prairie fire in August. Dave Hunt's warnings against dominion theology have now begun to polarize the dispensational movement. He has made millions of Christians aware of another worldview, which was not known to them before, especially to the brighter younger ones. We Reconstructionists could not have done it without him. In the early stages of any movement, public criticism from opponents always does more good than harm. The publicity is of far greater value than the occasional defector. Most important, the initial critics are seldom well enough informed to inflict permanent damage; the opportunity that the criticisms provide for public response is a precious commodity.

Dave Hunt probably means well. He says that he wants to warn Christians about the antichrist. So does Mrs. Cumbey. This concern is perhaps the most peculiar concern of all. Not being well versed in the dispensational theology they profess, Mr. Hunt and Mrs. Cumbey have forgotten the obvious: *dispensational theology has always taught that the Antichrist will not appear until after the Rapture!* As Hal Lindsey wrote in 1970: "There will be no earthly advantage in being alive when the Antichrist rules. We believe that Christians will not be around to watch the debacle brought about by the cruelest dictator of all time."[13] Either Mr. Hunt has not thought through the teachings

---

13. *Ibid.*, p. 113.

of his theology, or else his motive is something very different from simply warning Christians about the imminent appearance of the Antichrist. Why bother ourselves about the antichrist? He and Mrs. Cumbey (*especially* Mrs. Cumbey) refuse to heed Lindsey's warning: "However, we must not indulge in speculation about whether any of the world figures is the Antichrist."[14] This needless fear of the antichrist is paralyzing Christians' required fear of God; God tells us to serve as prophets who are required to confront a sinful civilization with the ethical demands of God's covenant, but the Jonahs of this age are too busy packing for their trip to the heavenly Tarshish. "Antichrist fever" is being added to "Rapture fever."

Mrs. Cumbey actually speculates that the Antichrist may be Pat Robertson, and said so in her book that followed *The Hidden Dangers of the Rainbow*, titled *A Planned Deception*,[15] which is why her original publisher, Huntington House, wisely refused to publish it, despite the fact that her first book had been a runaway best-seller. She is doing this forthrightly in the name of the old fashioned (pre-1980) version of pretribulational dispensationalism. I debated Mrs. Cumbey regarding her allegations on Richard Hogue's satellite radio show in the fall of 1986. She has painted herself into a corner with her accusations against Rev. Robertson; no Christian leader has been willing to join her in this campaign. The good work she did in *Hidden Dangers* is being squandered away. This should be a warning to us all: Satan can disrupt our lives just as easily by encouraging us to immerse ourselves in a campaign to expose him as by any other of his planned deceptions.[16]

---

14. *Idem.*
15. Pointe Publishers, 1986.
16. After I finished my book on the occult New Age philosophy in 1976, *None Dare Call It Witchcraft*, I set aside occultism as a topic of study until I had to revise the book in 1985 (*Unholy Spirits*). I believe that anyone without a special calling by God, and without prayerful support from a local church, should not indulge himself or herself in a long-term study of the occult. It begins to affect adversely a person's judgment. It is all too easy to begin to take seriously the preposterous claims of crackpot occultists, and to believe that Satan and his followers are in control of events. Dispensational theology only adds fuel to this error. Mrs. Cumbey has spent far too much time studying the subject of the New Age movement. It is time for her to go back to practicing law. Better for her to use her skills to defend home schoolers from state bureaucrats than to read any more books by Alice A. Bailey. This was also Larry Abraham's suggestion to her. Larry was the co-author of *None Dare Call It Conspiracy*, so he is no shrinking violet when it comes to the danger of conspiracies.

Dispensationalism's Fig Tree Problem

The dating of "the terminal generation" by pretribulational dispensationalists for three and a half decades, 1948-1981, had been tied to the creation of the State of Israel in 1948. Hal Lindsey wrote in 1970: "The general time of this seven-year period [the future tribulation period] couldn't begin until the Jewish people re-established their nation in their ancient homeland of Palestine."[17] In his list of proofs that prophecy is being fulfilled in our day, the first one he lists is the return of the dispersed Jews to Israel.[18] But there is a major theological problem with such so-called prophetic fulfillments: they cannot possibly be going on today, according to original dispensational theory. The "clock of prophecy" stopped with the coming of the church, pretribulational dispensationalism always insisted. Only with the "69th week of Daniel," after the rapture, will it begin ticking again. The Church Age was never predicted in the Old Testament; it is "the great mystery"; the Church Age is the "great parenthesis" in Old Testament prophecy. The dispensational author Harry Ironside wrote a whole book on the topic, *The Great Parenthesis*. The entire dispensational system, with its self-conscious rejection of the continuing validity of Old Testament law, from the beginning rested on the crucial presupposition that the New Covenant church was a radical prophetic break from Old Covenant Israel.[19] As Charles Ryrie wrote, "If the Church is not a subject of Old Testament prophecy, then the Church is not fulfilling Israel's promises, but instead Israel herself must fulfill them and that in the future."[20] "The Church is a

---

17. *Late, Great*, p. 42.
18. Hal Lindsey, *There's a New World Coming: A Prophetic Odyssey* (Santa Ana, California: Vision House, 1973), p. 81.
19. The "ultradispensationalists" point out that since Peter cited Joel 2 as being fulfilled at Pentecost (Acts 2), Pentecost was obviously a fulfillment of prophecy. They quite properly conclude that Peter could not have been starting today's "Church Age" New Testament church, but rather an interim Jewish church. Paul alone started the New Testament gentile church, they argue. They then deny water baptism along with everything in Acts 1-8 (or all of Acts, say some ultradispensationalists who also reject the Lord's Supper). There is no consistent dispensational answer to this problem, and Charles Ryrie's desperate attempts to overcome it reveal just how exegetically bankrupt the dispensationalist system has always been. Ryrie appeals to the covenant theologians' arguments for continuity in order to refute the ultradispensationalists, and to the ultradispensationalists' arguments for discontinuity in order to refute the covenant theologians. It is an embarrassing performance. Charles Caldwell Ryrie, *Dispensationalism Today* (Chicago: Moody Press, 1965).
20. Charles Caldwell Ryrie, *The Basis of the Premillennial Faith* (Neptune, New Jersey: Loizeaux Brothers, [1953] 1972), p. 126.

mystery in the sense that it was completely unrevealed in the Old Testament and now revealed in the New Testament."[21]

Thus, original dispensationalism appears to teach that no event which has taken place since the establishment of the church until today could possibly have been predicted in the Old Testament. Obviously, the church is still around, and it is being affected by present historical events, such as the creation of the State of Israel. At best, what is happening today is a kind of "shadow" of *future, post-Rapture, tribulation era* fulfillments of Bible prophecy.[22] No Bible prophecy is actually being fulfilled in our day, according to scholarly, technically precise dispensationalism. John Walvoord admitted this in his 1963 address at the Congress on Prophecy. Pretribulational dispensationalists can legitimately speak only of "preparation for the world events predicted to follow the rapture. . . ."[23] Preparation, yes; actual fulfillment of prophecy, no. But if Hal Lindsey had emphasized this highly important qualification to dispensational theology in his *Late, Great Planet Earth*, it would never have made it into a second printing.

Pretribulationalists for many years predicted that the Rapture would take place in 1981: 1948 + 40 (one generation) − 7 (great tribulation period) = 1981. This was the 40-year "generation of the fig tree" (Matt. 24:32-35). When the Rapture did not take place as dated, the "generation of the fig tree" seemed to get a stay of execution.[24] *When the Rapture also does not take place in 1988, as it will not, the present restructuring of pretribulational theology will accelerate.* How many years can the generation of the fig tree be extended? Time has just about run out on dispensationalism's reliance on the creation of the State of Israel as *the* motivational cornerstone of their system. If Israel is ever defeated militarily, or if it should be converted to Christianity, the dispensational system will collapse. Dispensationalists have "bet the farm" on the State of Israel's continuing existence and its continuing

---

21. *Ibid.*, p. 136.
22. David Schnittger is careful to use this shadow terminology in his booklet. "I do think the shadows of tribulational conditions are lengthening, and we could very well live to experience the rapture." He goes on to warn his readers: "Such a hope should not cause us to falsely conclude the forces of evil are winning, and the church age must end in defeat. The evidence of Matthew 13 and church history indicates just the opposite. The church is moving forward in an unprecedented fashion." *Christian Reconstruction*, p. 15.
23. John Walvoord, "Is the End of the Age at Hand?" in Charles Feinberg (ed.), *Focus on Prophecy* (Westwood, New Jersey: Revell, 1964), p. 167.
24. Frank Goines, *Generation of the Fig Tree* (Tulsa, Oklahoma: By the Author, 1979).

apostasy. In short, dispensationalists have once again taken a strong stand in favor of a theologically perverse *predestination to reprobation*, but without also affirming predestination to salvation: "No significant number of citizens of the State of Israel will be converted to Jesus Christ prior to the Rapture and the great tribulation, no matter what Christians do." This is one more example of the dispensationalists' *soteriology of inescapable impotence*, a doctrine of the self-imposed and perpetual weakness of the Holy Spirit in the so-called "Church Age." The Christian gospel is doomed to failure, they insist, just as surely as the State of Israel is doomed to continued apostasy.

The historical worldview of dispensationalism is about to be transformed as the "generation of the fig tree" gets older and older. Dispensationalists are about to learn to lengthen their time perspective. This, in and of itself, will change the character of American fundamentalism. (God willing, it will also cure Christians of their willingness to go into long-term debt, with the Rapture as a way escape from their creditors.)

This shift in perspective has already begun. For one thing, dispensational leaders are now talking about a coming revival, possibly before the twentieth century is over, a revival greater than any other in man's history. *This substitution of the prophecy of worldwide revival for the prophecy of the imminent Rapture constitutes the best evidence of "creeping postmillennialism" that I can point to.* Yet it is all being taught so subtly that people in the pews or in front of their TV sets are unaware of the major transformation that is taking place in their own thinking. And the wonderful thing is that any old-line dispensationalist leader who sees exactly where such talk about worldwide revival is headed, and who calls attention to it, warning people to come back to the "old time religion" of the imminent secret Rapture, is in danger of being dismissed as anti-evangelical, someone opposed to the spread of the gospel. Thus, a major shift in time perspective is coming, from the short run to a much longer run.

The postmillennial Christian Reconstruction movement will be the primary beneficiary of this shift.

Defection Over the Question of Ethics

Traditional dispensationalists are also concerned about the ethical side of the theology of Christian Reconstructionism, because Reconstructionists place so much emphasis on biblical law as a tool of dominion.[25] The social policies of a biblically reconstructed world will rest heavily on Old Testament law, and virtually all Christian groups today deny the continuing validity of Old Testament law. Thus, they must also deny the possibility of a future reconstructed world. Ethics shapes eschatology. Thus, working to transform this world's "secular" institutions is viewed as a waste of time. Secular humanists are therefore seen as having a legitimate claim to "secular" institutions, as if these institutions were not under the claims of Christ. Peter Lalonde's view represents traditional dispensational premillennialism. Don't polish brass on a sinking ship. There is a guaranteed lifeboat for us Christians: the Rapture.

There has been a division within the dispensational ranks since 1979, as a direct result of the adoption of the worldview of postmillennial Christian Reconstructionism in the name of dispensationalism. The premillennialists have begun to shift their concern from the imminent Rapture to the ethical requirements of biblical law. We Christian Reconstructionists are all in favor of this shift. Our concern with biblical law is greater than our concern with eschatology. Biblical ethics, not Bible prophecy, is fundamental. Thus, we applaud dispensational author David Schnittger's statement regarding Christian responsibility: "We believe God's laws are both good in themselves and universal in their application; because far from being arbitrary, they fit the human beings God has made. This was God's claim for His laws from the time of their inception." Even better, he goes on to prove his case by appealing to one of our most-cited Old Testament books, Deuteronomy:

> Notice what God said to Israel in Deuteronomy 10:12,13: *And now, Israel, what doth the Lord thy God require of thee, but to fear the Lord thy God, to walk in all his ways, and to love him, and to serve the Lord thy God with all thy heart and with all thy soul, to keep the commandments of the Lord, and his statutes, which I command thee this day **for thy good**?* Then in Deuteronomy 12:28: *Observe and hear all these words which I command thee for ever, when thou doest that which is good and right in the sight of the Lord thy God.* Notice the close connection between that which was "good and right in the sight of the Lord" and that which was "well" with them. This is true of individuals and nations today as well. Keeping biblical standards of morality, while not meriting salvation, does work toward the well-being of both individuals and society.[26]

---

25. R. J. Rushdoony, *The Institutes of Biblical Law* (Nutley, New Jersey: Craig Press, 1973); Gary North, *Tools of Dominion: The Case Laws of Exodus* (Tyler, Texas: Institute for Christian Reconstruction, 1988).

26. Schnittger, *Christian Reconstruction*, p. 19.

I could not have said it any better. This *is* the Christian Reconstruction position. His recommended five-point program outlined in Chapter Four instinctively mirrors Ray Sutton's five-point covenant model.²⁷ Yet somehow I wonder where in Scofield's Reference Bible this view of biblical law (code name today: "biblical standards") is taught. I do not recall its being in there. Neither does the ever-safely silent faculty at Dallas Theological Seminary. What I do remember was the 1963 attack on the Ten Commandments by (then) Dallas Seminary professor S. Lewis Johnson, in *Bibliotheca Sacra*, Dallas Seminary's scholarly journal:

> At the heart of the problem of legalism is pride, a pride that refuses to admit spiritual bankruptcy. That is why the doctrines of grace stir up so much animosity. Donald Grey Barnhouse, a giant of a man in free grace, wrote: "It was a tragic hour when the Reformation churches wrote the Ten Commandments into their creeds and catechisms and sought to bring Gentile believers into bondage to Jewish law, which was never intended either for the Gentile nations or for the church."²⁸ He was right, too.²⁹

The Ten Commandments are Jewish law, not ethically binding general principles, said Barnhouse and Johnson. And if the Ten Commandments are Jewish law and no longer binding on New Testament Christians, there can be little doubt that *any attempt to justify the view that any aspect of Old Testament law is binding today is necessarily anti-dispensational in intent*. This is the essence of the ethical view held by traditional dispensationalists, as articulated by two of the movement's most important leaders, Barnhouse and Johnson. (I doubt that former professor, former pastor Johnson would still affirm such an idea; anyway, I hope not.)

There is a very good reason why the younger socially active dispensationalists such as Mr. Schnittger receive no teaching offers or lecture invitations at Dallas Seminary and Grace Seminary, at least not in the field of New Testament ethics: they have "departed from the true faith," which was delivered in 1830 by John Nelson Darby (or possibly Margaret Macdonald in her trances),³⁰ spread in the

---

27. Ray R. Sutton, *That You May Prosper: Dominion By Covenant* (Tyler, Texas: Institute for Christian Economics, 1987).
28. He cites Barnhouse, *God's Freedom*, p. 134.
29. S. Lewis Johnson, "The Paralysis of Legalism," *Bibliotheca Sacra*, Vol. 120 (April/June, 1963), p. 109.
30. This is Dave MacPherson's thesis: see footnote #2, above.

"colonies" after 1870 by "W.E.B." (William E. Blackstone), popularized at the turn of the century by C. I. Scofield, and codified by the founder of Dallas Seminary, Lewis Sperry Chafer, in his often purchased but seldom read *Systematic Theology* (8 volumes). Schnittger has accurately described reasons for the evangelical retreat from society:

> Fourthly, there was the spread (specially through J. N. Darby's teaching and its popularization in the Scofield Bible) of pretribulationism. This portrays the present evil world as being beyond improvement or redemption; and predicts, instead, that it will deteriorate steadily until the coming of Christ Who will set up His millennial reign on earth. If the world is getting steadily worse, and if only Jesus at His coming will put it right, the argument runs, there seems no point in trying to reform it.[31]

That is precisely how the argument runs: *away from social responsibility*. It is nice to hear a pretribulationist at last face up to it, and try to overcome it. His spirit is willing, but his system is weak.

Abandoning the 1830 Faith

It is quite possible for pretribulational dispensationalists to become hard-core Christian Reconstructionists. All they have to do is ignore the obvious fact that their view concerning the continuing New Testament validity of Old Testament law has rejected everything ever written by the founders and promoters of pretribulational dispensationalism. *These activist dispensationalists have already become theonomists.*

They are also steadily abandoning the number-one official doctrine of Scofield theology: the steady defeat of the church. Writes Schnittger: "The Scriptures teach that the **entire** church age is characterized by the simultaneous development of both evil and righteousness, rather than a steadily eroding church brought about by the ever-expanding encroachments of opposition from the outside and apostasy within. . . . Apparently the church will not be raptured in defeat and impotence but at the apex of its development and influence."[32] Yet he turns around and says on the next page that "regardless of the efforts of the church, the world will not be Christianized. The direct intervention and judgment of God in Christ will be neces-

---

31. Schnittger, *Christian Reconstruction*, p. 3.
32. *Ibid.*, p. 16.

sary to wrench the kingdoms of this world out of the grasp of persistently rebellious mankind. Unlike postmillennialists, premillennialists recognize their calling is not to Christianize all nations, but to evangelize all people (Matthew 28:18-20)."

How can anyone sort out these views? The church will be raptured by Christ "at the apex of its development and influence." Yet this development and influence will not be enough to be victorious culturally. It will be a glorious stalemate. (I cannot resist mentioning the pre-game pep talk of a football coach: "Playing to tie is like kissing your sister.") He says that we are to evangelize people, not nations, despite the fact that the Greek word in the New Testament for *people*, "ethnos," is the same as the word for *nation*. We also know that a new nation, the church, has inherited the kingdom (Matt. 21:43).[33] So what is Mr. Schnittger talking about? Mr. Schnittger and his followers are talking *theological* premillennialism and *psychological* postmillennialism.

We know which motivation will be victorious in the end: the psychological vision of victory that stems from Christians' confidence in the historical power of biblical law. *Obedience to biblical law inevitably brings cultural victory (Deut. 28:1-14), whatever the eschatological views of those who obey it.* May the socially activist theonomic dispensationalists persuade all their followers of their new position! Let them march under the banner of C. I. Scofield, just so long as we Reconstructionists control access to their drums, their maps, and their ammunition, which we presently do. (Consider Dominion Press' Biblical Blueprints Series. Where is the dispensational version? Where is the amillennial version? We produced ten volumes in two years, start to finish. The pessimillennialists, being antinomians, have nothing comparable to offer. They forget: "You can't beat something with nothing.")

We Reconstructionists provide the ammunition in the battle against humanism. By default, we are in charge of ordinance, much to the distress of Dave Hunt and Mrs. Cumbey. They recognize the implications of what is happening: *dispensationalists presently control the banners, but postmillennial Reconstructionists control the agenda.* Mr. Hunt and Mrs. Cumbey know that I am correct when I say that those dominion dispensationalists who still march under the traditional

---

33. Gary North, *Healer of the Nations: Biblical Blueprints for International Relations* (Ft. Worth, Texas: Dominion Press, 1987), Introduction.

Scofield banner have in fact switched to theonomy, which is why none of them is willing to write a systematic defense of his new version of dispensationalism. The radical break with Scofieldism would be too obvious. Such a systematic theology could not possibly be systematic. *Scofieldism and biblical law don't mix.* So they write motivational pamphlets instead, motivating their followers right into the theonomic postmillennial camp. For whatever reasons (mostly psychological, possibly financial), whole segments of the dispensational leadership have abandoned dispensationalism while valiantly proclaiming a "new, improved dispensationalism." This greatly upsets Mrs. Cumbey especially, but there is nothing she can do about it. The tide has turned.

A Transitional Hybrid: No Reproduction

Mr. Hunt and Mrs. Cumbey are equally correct about another thing: the transitional nature of the present commitment of premillennialists to the "old time religion." They fully understand that this theologically schizophrenic, halfway house commitment cannot survive very long. So do we Reconstructionists. The mediating theological position of these new converts to Reconstructionism simply cannot be held over the long term. Consider the two following appeals. Which do you think will win the minds of Christians in the long run?

1. A logical response to the pretribulational Christian Reconstructionist: "You tell me that I am responsible to obey and preach God's eternal legal principles, which used to be called theocracy, which the Reconstructionists call theonomy, but which you say are just biblical principles. You say that the old slogan that 'we're under grace, not law,' has been misinterpreted, just as the postmillennial Reconstructionists have long maintained. You say that I am responsible for trying to persuade people of the validity of God's revealed laws. Thus, the more I try to persuade sinners of the need to transform society by God's law, the more I will be persecuted for something other than passing out a tract that says, 'Jesus loves you, this I know, for the Bible tells me so.' My life's work will not have anything but shrinking influence in history prior to the rapture, and it will not survive the seven-year reign of the antichrist. Nevertheless, I am to sacrifice everything I possess to defend this theology of assured external *stalemate* (whereas Dallas Seminary assures the church of assured external defeat rather than stalemate). I become morally responsible for leaving a cultural legacy to the next generation, even though every tradi-

tional dispensationalist says that Jesus is coming very soon to relieve me of all my burdens, and they also assure me that I don't have any of these heavy earthly social responsibilities, because I'm under grace, not law. You offer the church a long, hard road to cultural stalemate, whereas the Scofield notes and Dallas Seminary offer the church a short, easy road to cultural defeat."

2. A logical response to the postmillennial Christian Reconstructionist: "You say that I am responsible for personally keeping God's law, through the empowering of the Holy Spirit. My obedience will lead to greater internal and external blessings (Deut. 28:1-14), giving me greater influence. This will lead others to respect God's law and seek to claim these blessings for themselves. This desire on their part will then be used by the Holy Spirit to bring billions of people to faith in Christ. The gospel of salvation will grow in influence, while the gospel of Satan will diminish. My covenant-keeping work will have its assured effects in history, combining with the short-term and long-term efforts of a growing army of faithful Christians. Not only will God empower me to obey the law, but this law is powerful, leading to transformed lives and transformed institutions. I no longer have to worry about the antichrist, because the antichrist is simply the New Testament's word for the spirit of apostasy, not a person. My life's work, if it is true to the Bible, will survive. There is no age other than the Church Age, from Pentecost to the end of time. I join the winning side in history when I join the church."

Which position makes more sense to you? Which position do you believe will gain the commitment of the next generation of socially active dispensationalists? Will they retain some peculiar version of dispensational Reconstructionism, and thereby suffer persecution from those who will use Dave Hunt's books to drive them out of their local pietistic, retreatist, abortion-ignoring churches? Or will they simply drop any pretence of holding to this completely rewritten and explicitly unfaithful version of the Scofield notes? I think the answer is obvious. So do Mr. Hunt and Mrs. Cumbey. *They know that this halfway house, socially activist dispensationalism, cannot survive, and that those who hold it today will probably be postmillennialists by the year 2000 if they remain activists.* They know that any spread of the comprehensive gospel within dispensationalism will inevitably lead to the abandonment of dispensationalism. We Reconstructionists know it, too. So we can afford to cheer on the dispensational activists, while Dave Hunt and Mrs. Cumbey remain silent, afraid to tell their followers to flee from activism. They are rightly fearful of appearing to be cultural ostriches, political stick-in-the-muds, and socially unconcerned retreatists, but they are equally afraid of pouring gasoline on the postmillennialists' fire by calling their followers to become politically and socially active, too. Heads, Reconstructionism wins; tails, Reconstructionism wins. This is the inescapable dilemma of today's dispensationalist. This is why the faculty of Dallas Seminary never says anything. Safety first.

To both of them I say: "You can't beat something with nothing. You will not command an army by waffling under fire. Fish or cut bait, Dave and Constance. Either tell your followers what you *really* think about how much time remains before the Rapture, and what you *really* think about the wisdom of getting involved specifically as Christians in a comprehensive lifetime program of political and social reform based on Old Testament law, or get off the playing field. No more mumbling. No more veiled grousing. Halfway house religion doesn't work." They fully understand this, and they don't know what to do.

They should do the smart thing: *abandon pretribulational dispensationalism*. Forget about the "old time religion" that was invented in 1830. Join the historic Christian faith instead. This is what ex-Dallas Seminary professor Bruce Waltke has done (now a covenant theologian teaching at Westminster Seminary in Philadelphia). This is also what Dallas professor Ed Blum did. S. Lewis Johnson also left. (Quite frankly, one of the best ways we Calvinists have found to gain academic converts to our system is to get inquisitive men to teach at Dallas Seminary. Our motto is: "You train 'em, we gain 'em.")

The Holy Spirit

Charismatics and Pentecostals who grew up with dispensationalism have now begun to recognize the schizophrenia of their position. They preach the continuing manifestations of the Holy Spirit: tongues and healing. Dallas Seminary will expel any student and fire any faculty member who openly affirms such Pentecostal doctrines, for this dispensational stronghold has long taught that these signs of the Spirit were limited to the transitional period of the Book of Acts. This view of the Holy Spirit has *always* been basic to dispensationalism. This is why Pentecostals were avoided by and ignored by dispensational fundamentalists during the early years of the twentieth century.[34]

---

34. George Marsden, *Fundamentalism and American Culture: The Shaping of Twentieth-Century Evangelicalism, 1870-1925* (New York: Oxford University Press, 1980), p. 94.

Pentecostals believe in miraculous healing. They teach that the Holy Spirit still gives sight to the blind, strength to useless legs, and health to the dying. They believe that the power of the Holy Spirit can overcome any sin-produced barrier in the life of every Christian. Yet they also preach that the gospel cannot convert this sin-filled world, that the power of the gospel, even though it is spread through the power of the Holy Spirit, will be successfully resisted by Satan's followers until Jesus comes again. Yet they also teach that the manifestation of the Holy Spirit in power was possible only because Jesus departed physically from the earth. They know that Jesus said: "Nevertheless I tell you the truth; It is expedient for you that I go away: for if I go not away, the Comforter will not come unto you; but if I depart, I will send him unto you" (John 16:7). They have until recently not noticed the obvious contradiction in their theology: that dispensationalists have hope only in the physical return of Christ to set up His kingdom. But then what happens to the Holy Spirit? Is He withdrawn by God the Father and God the Son because His work was needed only during the Church Age? If not, why not? From the beginning, dispensationalist theologians have remained discreetly silent on this problem.

Over a century ago, postmillennialist professor Thomas Sproull, of the Reformed Presbyterian Seminary in Allegheny, Pennsylvania, asked this question regarding the coming of millennial blessings: "How shall this change be brought about?" He answered: first, by God's judgment of the nations; third, by the establishment of righteousness on the earth. But his second explanation is relevant for understanding why charismatics are now abandoning premillennialism:

2. By the outpouring of his Spirit. We have already seen that the coming of the Son of man, in *Matt.* 16:28, meant the outpouring of the Holy Spirit on the day of Pentecost. He, though a distinct person from the Son in essential relation, identifies with him in his economic [relational—G.N.] work. What the Spirit of Christ does, that Christ does; where his Spirit is, there is he himself. There is a difference between the essential presence of Christ and his gracious presence. In the former he is everywhere, it belongs to his divine nature; in the latter he is where he wills to manifest himself by his Spirit: "If Christ be in you—the Spirit is life because of righteousness." —*Rom.* 8:10.

The work of the Spirit on the day of Pentecost was but a partial fulfillment of prophecy: "I will pour out my Spirit upon all flesh."—*Joel* 2:28. It was confined then to a number of converted Jews in Jerusalem. But it shall extend to all the world at the millennium. So soon as the Gospel of the kingdom shall have been preached in all the world for a *testimony* to all nations, then shall this grand consummation take place. — *Matt.* 24:14. The Spirit shall then be fully given.[35]

The modern charismatic movement is at last beginning to abandon its schizophrenic theology: a doctrine of the Holy Spirit that preaches His unstoppable miraculous healing power in personal history, and a doctrine of eschatology which preaches the unstoppable cultural and political power of Satan's forces in the so-called "Church Age." As charismatics become fully consistent with the first doctrine, they will inevitably abandon the second. This, in my view, is the best explanation of why the discovery of "dominion theology" or Christian Reconstruction took place first in postmillennial Reformed circles and second in charismatic circles: *both groups have a very high view of the authority of the Holy Spirit in history.* Resistance to dominion theology has been strongest in traditional non-charismatic dispensational circles and in amillennial circles, for the opposite reason.

Ethics Shapes Eschatology

Why do I attack dispensationalism? Not primarily because of its view concerning the timing of the second coming of Christ, although this view is opposed to what the Bible teaches, and it leads (and has led) straight to social pessimism, pietism, and world retreat. This prophetic emphasis has been the big recruiting point in the movement, but it has always been of secondary importance theologically. The heart, mind, and soul of premillennialism of all kinds, and of amillennialism as well, is the erroneous doctrine that Old Testament law is no longer covenantally binding in the New Testament. The heart of pessimillennialism is its *antinomianism* and its self-conscious *anti-covenantalism*. These people hate Old Testament law with every fiber of their being. They are at war with God's revealed law. They may mouth platitudes about "honoring God's moral principles," but they have for over a century categorically resisted every attempt to spell out specifically what these laws require, especially for society's institutions. "Social gospel, social gospel!" they shouted whenever

---

35. Rev. Thomas Sproull, *Prelections on Theology* (Pittsburgh, Pennsylvania: Myers, Shinkle, & Co., 1882), pp. 419-20.

they heard such a suggestion. "We're under law, not grace!" "No creed but the Bible, no law but love!" "We're People That Love," Jim Bakker announced. But love is the fulfilling of the law (Rom. 13:8). Mr. Bakker was not interested in fulfilling the law.

The New Pharisaism

Within the fundamentalist camp, leaders for a century preached against any consumption of alcohol, in blatant denial of the Old Testament requirement that God-fearing adults be allowed to enjoy strong drink as part of a formal, national celebration to the Lord: "And thou shalt bestow that money for whatsoever thy soul lusteth after, for oxen, or for sheep, or for wine, or for strong drink, or for whatsoever thy soul desireth: and thou shalt eat there before the LORD thy God, and thou shalt rejoice, thou, and thine household" (Deut. 14:26). When was the last time you heard a preacher expound on this verse? There is no hope of turning strong drink into soda pop, the way fundamentalists have tried to turn wine into grape juice. These personal holiness preachers wanted to be holier than God in their antinomian confidence, so they even dared to substitute grape juice for wine at the God's communion table. Welch's grape juice was created early in this century to meet the communion table demands of fundamentalist churches; the commercial product did not exist before this. Can you imagine Jesus' speaking of the kingdom, "Old grape juice skins cannot hold new grape juice"? Or how about a best-selling devotional book called, *A Taste of New Grape Juice*? Grape juice does not expand because it is not fermented, that is, because it is not wine. "Not expanding" is the cultural mindset of fundamentalism. A communion table that serves only grape juice accurately reflects the worldview of those taking it: no threat of bursting humanism's cultural wineskins.

Fundamentalists preached for a century against dancing, smoking, and going to movies — in the days before R-rated and X-rated movies, when every movie was G-rated. Only in the last two decades have many of them at last purposefully forgotten this anti-movie aspect of the fundamentalist past, just in time for PG-rated movies. The disappearance of this sort of preaching (and these sorts of requirements at Christian colleges) paralleled the decline of perfectionist theology. For a century, fundamentalists did exactly what the Pharisees did: they invented lots of preposterous man-made legal requirements to substitute for the law of God. It seemed easier to obey man-made requirements. Only one sin was excepted: gluttony. Diets are very hard work and involve lots of self-discipline for a lifetime. I have never heard a sermon against the sin of gluttony. The sin of gluttony is difficult to cover up, so it is not preached about.[36]

Meanwhile, adultery raged (and still rages) undisciplined in church after church. In the Old Testament, magistrates would have executed the pair of adulterers (Lev. 20:10); these days, the man (especially if he is a pastor, as he so frequently is) publicly repents, makes zero restitution, and is allowed to keep his pulpit, except in one tiny Calvinist denomination I know of, where the pastor is told to transfer to another Presbytery to seek a new pulpit. (An ecclesiastical position that can best be understood in terms of this principle: "At least get him far away from *my* wife!") What Jim Bakker did (at least with Miss Hahn) was run-of-the-mill stuff, and every pastor in the country knows it. At least Bakker resigned (for a few weeks). The evangelical world hates the law of God, and they have invented eschatologies to accommodate this fundamental hatred. They have denied any positive feedback between covenantal faithfulness and external blessing in history. They prefer to adopt pagan natural law principles in an attempt to escape God and God's revealed law.[37] And then along came AIDS. God will not be mocked — not at zero cost, anyway.

The Transforming Power of God's Law

Pessimistic eschatology is first and foremost *a denial of the Holy Spirit and His empowering of Christians to exercise dominion in terms of biblical law.* It is not that we Christian Reconstructionists are postmillennialists first and foremost; it is that we are theonomists who believe in the *inevitable* transforming power of the Holy Spirit

---

36. In the Old Testament, it was a crime punishable by death to be a rebellious post-adolescent son. The marks of this rebelliousness were drunkenness and gluttony (Deut. 21:20). In the 1909 Scofield Reference Bible, the concordance lists this verse under drunkenness but not gluttony. This is typical, not random. There is a story, possibly apocryphal, of a meeting between Old Testament scholar Robert Dick Wilson (died, 1921) and fundamentalist scholar Reuben A. Torrey. Wilson smoked a pipe. Torrey supposedly approached Wilson, and said, pointing to the pipe, "What would Jesus say if He were to come back today and find you with that?" Wilson took the pipe out of his mouth, jabbed its stem into Torrey's legendary girth, and said, "What would He say if He found you with *that*?"

37. Norman Geisler, "A Premillennial View of Law and Government," *Bibliotheca Sacra*, Vol. 142 (July/September 1985). Geisler is a professor at Dallas Seminary.

and God's law as the tool of dominion, and so have adopted postmillennialism as a covenantally inescapable corollary.[38] The primary issue for Christian Reconstructionists is ethics, not eschatology.

When we preach dominion, we do not narrow our focus, as fundamentalists have done for well over a century, to personal sins alone. These can more readily be steadily overcome (progressive sanctification). In any case, personal sins are easier to hide from the public. They can also be hidden away in the subconscious by various false theologies of perfectionism: the "higher life" type of thinking.[39] But when we talk about the responsibility of Christians to exercise dominion culturally, our present visible failure cannot be denied. We cannot cover it up. Thus, we face a decision: to get to work in terms of biblical law, or to continue our retreat, either into nearly total defeat culturally (amillennialism) or into a mental world of expectant deliverance (pretribulational dispensationalism). In either case, the result is the Christian ghetto. It is an ecclesiology of "a safe port in the storm." The end result is the Gulag archipelago, where power-seeking humanists select our ghetto for us. (The first stage of entering the Gulag archipelago is sending your children to a public school. Any Christian who willingly does this to his children has in principle accepted the Gulag as a legitimate institution: compulsory State re-education in terms of anti-Christian principles.)

A growing minority of Christians have at last begun to see where Christian ghetto thinking leads, and where the ethics of "spiritual victories only" leads. They have begun to understand that Christian freedom must be defended, which means that *Christian civilization must be extended.* We must go on the offensive culturally if we are to avoid the Gulag. This means that we need future-oriented motivation and Old Testament institutional blueprints—biblical law. Both have been denied by pietists for over a century. Alcoholics who have sobered up eventually realize that it is not enough to get sober and stay sober; they must do something with their sobriety. Christians must recognize the same thing. It is not enough to seek personal holiness; they must do something with that holiness. This belated recognition of a world of God-assigned responsibility beyond personal behavior is at the heart of the transformation that is going on

---

38. Greg Bahnsen has tried to separate the two doctrines, but unsuccessfully. See my rejoinder in North, *Dominion and Common Grace: The Biblical Basis of Progress* (Tyler, Texas: Institute for Christian Economics, 1987), pp. 138-45.

39. Frank, *Less Than Conquerors*, ch. 4.

inside the American Christian community today. A shift of eschatology is accompanying a shift in the vision of Christian responsibility, both personal and institutional. Ethics shapes eschatology.

When the fear of AIDS eventually starts clearing out the public schools, this realization of broad-based Christian responsibility will spread.

Conclusion

Contrary to Alva J. McClain's premature obituary on postmillennialism in 1956,[40] postmillennialism is alive and well on planet earth. It is McClain's own traditional ghetto dispensationalism that is dying. It no longer has articulate defenders. Its supporters are hard-pressed to find serious works of scholarship written self-consciously from a dispensational standpoint. As far as I know, there is still not a single comprehensive book that develops a self-consciously dispensational social ethics, yet it is now over a century and a half since the 1830 invention of dispensationalism. The system's few remaining public defenders are one or two major TV evangelists[41] and a dedicated man with a bachelor's degree in mathematics who has specialized in the study of cults. Talbot Seminary is quietly moving away from dispensationalism, converted (in part) by a 20-year-old Calvinist student at nearby Biola College; Dallas Seminary (as always) is judiciously silent, having lost several of its faculty members to the dreaded Calvinists; and Grace Seminary (as always) is not taken seriously as an intellectual center, even by dispensationalists. To escape this dying worldview, dispensationalism's younger followers are becoming theonomists and psychological postmillennialists. They are thereby announcing, "Dispensationalism is dead. Long live dispensationalism!"

From this point on, it's just a matter of time. And ethics. And the Holy Spirit.

---

40. Alva J. McClain, "Premillennialism as a Philosophy of History," in W. Culbertson and H. B. Centz (eds.), *Understanding the Times* (Grand Rapids, Michigan: Zondervan, 1956), p. 22.

41. Jimmy Swaggart is the obvious example, and he publicly describes himself as one of dispensationalism's few remaining defenders. So is Jerry Falwell, although he has not discussed eschatology very often for about a decade. Hal Lindsey also keeps the flag flying.

Appendix F

TIME FOR A CHANGE:
RIFKIN'S "NEW, IMPROVED" WORLDVIEW

*The pagan calendar had a nature-cycle; the festivals and events which governed the calendar were natural events, the equinox, the solstice, the death of vegetation, the birth of vegetation, and so on. The government of time was thus within time, from nature and man. The Christian calendar was the antithesis of all this: every year is "the year of our Lord"; time and the universe are his creation. Time and the cosmos are thus governed from before and beyond time and history. Not only are they absolutely controlled from all eternity, but God Himself enters history from the beginning by His revelation and His prophets, and supremely in Jesus Christ, so that history moves, not in terms of **nature-dates** but **historical-dates**. The old calendar celebrated nature and rites of nature; the new calendar celebrates God's year and the works of men under God.*

R. J. Rushdoony[1]

Jeremy Rifkin is to worldviews what Prof. Harvey Cox is to theologies: he adopts a new one about every four years. While *Is the World Running Down?* was at the typesetters, Rifkin's latest book appeared, *Time Wars: The Primary Conflict in Human History*.[2] It is notable, if for nothing else, because no co-author is listed anywhere. This is a true Jeremy Rifkin book.

So, time is the primary conflict in human history. Then what about entropy? What about the titanic intellectual struggle (1980) between the West's faith in technological progress and the scientific principle of entropy? What about Rifkin's prophetic announcement that "a new world view is about to emerge, one that will eventually replace the Newtonian world machine as the organizing frame of

---

1. R. J. Rushdoony, *The Revolt Against Maturity: A Biblical Psychology of Man* (Fairfax, Virginia: Thoburn Press, 1977), p. 229.
2. New York: Henry Holt & Co., 1987.

history: the Entropy Law will preside as the ruling paradigm over the next period of history."[3] It has disappeared from the pages of the prophet Rifkin's latest revelation. For that matter, it had already disappeared in *Algeny* (1983). It has gone down some sort of Orwellian memory hole; it has been blipped off the West's cosmological computer screen.

What now? Time. Time's the thing. Technological time. Computerized time. Split seconds, nanoseconds, picoseconds: they are going to destroy our way of life. Once again, Rifkin announces a titanic struggle. Like Don Quixote, he calls his shrinking army of still-devoted followers to join him in a life-and-death campaign against another newly discovered windmill. "A battle is brewing over the politics of time. Its outcome could determine the future course of politics around the world in the coming century."[4] Apparently, the evil windmill of entropy has been slain, as has the evil windmill of genetic engineering (*Algeny*). How these awesome challenges were overcome, he does not say. But he does not look back over his shoulder. He marches forward. Each victory always leads to another campaign. But each campaign always leaves a significant percentage of his followers stuck in the trenches, battling the last windmill, unaware that Rifkin has once again grabbed the regimental flag and marched off in a new direction to overcome a new windmill.

Rifkin sings a siren song to those who enjoy being whooped into a frenzy once every few years. The lyrics may be different, but the tune never changes: the evils of growth-oriented capitalism. Jeremy Rifkin knows that capitalism produces economic growth and technological change, and as a committed socialist, he resents this. He returns to this theme — the hidden dangers and moral evil of capitalism's economic progress — in book after book. "The new temporal warfare is a direct outgrowth of another, earlier battle — an economic, social, and political controversy centering around a long-revered spatial metaphor that 'Bigger is better.' This cardinal concept, which so dominated our thinking after World War II, started to come under attack from many quarters during the 1960s and 1970s. The industrial nations of the West had organized the future with bigness in mind."[5] He totally misunderstands free market capital-

---

3. Jeremy Rifkin (with Ted Howard), *Entropy: A New World View* (New York: Bantam, [1980] 1981), p. 6.
4. Rifkin, *Time Wars*, p. 2.
5. *Ibid.*, pp. 2-3.

ism; it is the leaders of socialist governments, not free market societies, that are so arrogant as to imagine that anyone or anything other than God can successfully "organize the future."

Nevertheless, Rifkin claims that "big is better" is the reigning orthodoxy of our era—which, on the whole, it is—and that this orthodoxy has now begun to be challenged. "A spatial heresy began to take hold, winning over legions of converts to a new vision. 'Small is beautiful' began to challenge the once-powerful myth that bigger is better."[6] Rifkin is still living in the light of the dying embers of the social fires of 1965-71, the world of youthful dreams about bug-free organic farms, safe political revolution, and chemical euphoria. Small looked good in those days, just so long as a tuition check from Daddy arrived on time each semester. But graduation day finally arrived, or Sonny dropped out of college, and Daddy is not sending checks any more. In fact, Daddy and his friends are fast approaching retirement, and the kids are now expected to ante up the retirement money, through endless increases in the Social Security tax. The checks are now supposed to flow in the other direction, and the West is facing a monumental and inescapable debt crisis.[7] Unfortunately, this is not a crisis that committed socialists like to discuss in detail, for it was their ideology of compulsory wealth redistribution that created this debt crisis. So they invent other crises that can be substituted for the real one.

Today, Rifkin announces, there is a far deeper conflict than the conflict over "big is better" vs. "small is beautiful." It is the concept of efficiency. Yes, folks, *efficiency*, that familiar bugaboo of anti-capitalist critics (who recognize belatedly that socialist economies are woefully inefficient), that ascetic religion of the Industrial Revolution, that hottest of hot topics (*circa* 1825), is with us still. We now know what is wrong with the West: ". . . efficiency and speed characterize the time values of the modern age."[8] The god of modern time is the goal of *faster*. And faster than you can say, "New, Improved Worldview," Jeremy Rifkin has written volume six (or is it seven?) of *The Prophet Speaks*, which exposes the evils of Western, technological time. Not linear time, this time, but computer time, which is *simulated time*. (Don't hold your breath for Rifkin to define this precisely). He an-

---

6. *Ibid.*, p. 3.
7. Lawrence Malkin, *The National Debt* (New York: Henry Holt, 1987); Peter G. Peterson, "The Morning After," *The Atlantic Monthly* (October 1987).
8. *Time Wars*, p. 3.

nounces: "The age of progress is about to give way to the age of simulation."[9] (But I thought the age of progress had been overcome in 1980 by the age of entropy, except that the age of entropy was overcome in 1983 by the age of algeny — genetic engineering.[10] I must be confused. Perhaps this is the sign of a coming worldview, the age of confusion. Maybe Rifkin will ask me to co-author a book on this topic. Or perhaps he will ask you.)

Rifkin's latest book asks his favorite question: What is the problem with our world? Its answer is the same: modern man's impulse to dominion. "Modern man has come to view time as a tool to enhance and advance the collective well-being of the culture. 'Time is money' best expresses the temporal spirit of the age."[11] *Time is money*: what an insight! Rifkin has really gone right to the heart of the matter, though perhaps he is just a tad late. This was Ben Franklin's timely (and profitable) advice to a young man back in 1748: "Remember, that *time* is money. He that can earn ten shillings a day by his labour, and goes abroad, or sits idle, one half of that day, though he spends but sixpence during his diversion or idleness, ought not to reckon *that* the only expense; he has really spent, or rather thrown away, five shillings besides."[12]

What old Ben was doing was what he did so well throughout his literary career: he took a fundamental biblical principle and transformed it into a popular aphorism. What is the underlying biblical principle of "time is money"? It is Paul's injunction to *redeem* (buy back) the time, because the days are evil (Eph. 5:16). So, a little over two centuries later, Jeremy Rifkin rides into town, six-shooter strapped on his hip, and announces, "Franklin, this town ain't big enough for both of us, and when I finish up here, it's going to be even smaller. Everything is going to be smaller, except for my book royalties. So, you had better clear out. And don't waste any time in getting out!"

---

9. *Ibid.*, p. 148.

10. "Accompanying this great technological transformation is a philosophical transformation of monumental proportions. Humanity is about to fundamentally reshape its view of existence to coincide with its new organizational relationship with the earth." Jeremy Rifkin (with Nicanor Perlas), *Algeny* (New York: Viking, 1983), p. 15.

11. *Time Wars*, p. 4.

12. Benjamin Franklin, "Advice to a Young Tradesman" (1748), in *The Autobiography of Benjamin Franklin and Selections from His Other Writings* (New York: Modern Library, 1944), p. 233.

It is odd that Jeremy Rifkin, self-proclaimed conservationist, should rebel against such a view of time. His book on entropy was a book about the modern humanist's view of time, "time's arrow," and how to conserve our world from the ruinous effects of energy-sucking, entropy-increasing technology. *Entropy* is a book, literally, on saving time: reducing the West's level of consumption so that mankind might save a fraction of a second (at the most) in the universe's inevitable dissipation of usable energy. (For man to use this usable energy, as we have seen in earlier chapters, is regarded by Rifkin as an implicit crime against an impersonal, meaningless cosmos.) What is the best way to conserve a scarce economic resource? Rifkin dares not say the words: *put a price tag on it*. If something is being wasted, it is being priced too low. If time is the object of cost-cutting, it is because it is so precious. If we are trying to save time, isn't this a sign of our rationality? Yet Rifkin lashes out against the time-consciousness of Western man. Where time is concerned, he wants waste. He believes that it is unnatural to save time.

What Franklin in particular, and capitalism in general, was trying to do was to remind us that there is scarcity in this world. At zero price, there is greater demand for scarce resources than there are supplies of them. In short, *time is not a free good*. Time must be paid for, wasted or not. But the genius of private ownership and its corollary, the legal right to appropriate the fruits of one's own productivity, is that this economic system more clearly penalizes anyone who refuses to place an accurate price on his own time. Like any system of allocation through competitive pricing, the free market reduces waste. It is *efficient*, for reducing waste is the textbook definition of efficiency. In short, *capitalism conserves resources* — in this case, mankind's only truly irreplaceable resource, time.

And Jeremy Rifkin hates capitalism with all his heart.

The Devil's Time Machines

Computers are taking over. Chapter One of Rifkin's book is titled, "The New Nanosecond Culture." He says that the modern world is committed to saving time, but we all feel increasingly deprived of it. Our time-saving technologies were supposed to free us from the clock, but in fact they have enslaved us as never before. "What time we do have is chopped up into tiny segments, each filled in with prior commitments and plans. Our tomorrows are spoken for, booked up in advance."[13]

---

13. *Time Wars*, p. 11.

What Rifkin never mentions is that it is mainly our tomorrow *evenings* that are scheduled in advance: the latest television shows and sports spectaculars. The United States is a nation devoted to the pursuit of leisure—leisure in such quantities that no other society has ever experienced anything like it. Common people have color television sets, videocassette players, stereo equipment, and access to more varieties of entertainment than the richest king on earth ever had, back when there were still kings on earth. We can bring the finest performances of the finest orchestras into our living rooms every evening. We can also bring the worst dramas ever written, the least humorous comedy skits ever produced, and pour out our lives, hour by hour, in the fruitless quest for meaningful amusement. We spin the dials of our television sets, or flip from channel to channel with our remote control units, vainly searching for something really worth watching. We seek ways to carve minutes off of our work days in order gain the extra time we need to bore ourselves into the wee hours of the morning.

Tired of scheduling your evening's entertainment? Then sit down with a videocassette recorder any time you want, and watch the program it recorded automatically a day or week ago. No matter how mediocre the televised programs may be most of the time, you can watch all you want, any time you want, for the price of a blank videocassette tape.[14] Yet Rifkin never mentions television. The fact that one or more television sets are on inside most American homes for over seven hours a day testifies to the enormous build-up of spare time, meaning easily wasted time. The lure of "free" entertainment is almost irresistible to most people.[15]

Rifkin ignores all this. This desperate quest for electronic entertainment reflects a crisis of man's soul, a crisis made cost-effective for

---

14. I once saw a cartoon of a delightfully pathetic character, Mr. Tweedy. A friend was looking in his closet, which was stacked floor to ceiling with videotapes of "Bowling for Dollars."

15. In 1974, my wife and I agreed to buy a television only on this basis: each of us promised to pay 25 cents per half hour of viewing when either of us selected a program to watch. We gave this money away to charities at the end of the month. The person who selected a program had to pay. We exempted only news broadcasts and documentaries. We cut our viewing time to a few hours a week, excepting (of course) news shows and documentaries. Just the measurable acknowledgment that our time was worth a few cents per hour was enough to get us to allocate our time far more rationally. We refused to watch junk, which made up the bulk of the scheduled programs. In our spare time, we started our publishing business, which eventually made us rich. This is redeeming the time.

the masses by technology, but which is not at bottom caused by technology. And it is *technology that serves the masses*, in book after book, that is Jeremy Rifkin's prime target. What Rifkin argues is that the computer makes possible a major transformation of time management in our capacity as producers rather than as consumers (which he self-consciously avoids discussing). "We are entering a new time zone radically different from anything we have experienced in the past. So different is the new computer time technology that it is creating the context for the emergence of a new language of the mind and an altered state of consciousness, just as the automated clock did in the thirteenth century when it laid open the door to the Age of Mechanism and the spectre of a clockwork universe."[16]

Precisely What Time Is It?

This has been a question men have asked from the beginning. For thousands of years, only priests knew the answer with any degree of accuracy. On cloudy days and nights, hardly anyone knew. Men's sundials and star-gazing techniques became useless.

There is no doubt that the advent of the central town clock, and then, five centuries later, of the factory whistle, and finally, in the nineteenth century, of the inexpensive portable watch, did in fact transform the West. There was, as David Landes puts it, a revolution in time.[17] It became economically possible for more and more people in the West to get a *usefully* precise answer to the question, "What time is it?" When this became possible at a price people could afford, they adjusted their lives accordingly, *when such adjustments proved sufficiently profitable to those who were willing to adjust*.

This revolution in time did not take place overnight. It took centuries, for it was a *comprehensive revolution*, as all true revolutions are — technologically, economically, socially, and psychologically. This is why Rifkin's argument in *Time Wars* is so implausible, namely, that the advent of today's more precise time measurement devices will have comparable transforming effects on civilization, and will have them within one generation. This is utter nonsense. Ask yourself this question: What fundamental change in anyone's life will be produced by the availability of cheap, battery-powered wristwatches that can accurately measure the seconds of a minute? Answer: only

---

16. *Ibid.*, p. 13.
17. David S. Landes, *Revolution in Time: Clocks and the Making of the Modern World* (Cambridge, Massachusetts: Belknap Press of the Harvard University Press, 1983).

the performance of athletes will be affected, and only just slightly.

It is true that my Japanese-manufactured wristwatch beeps on schedule when I set it to remind myself of an upcoming appointment. That I bought this watch for the money I earn in about twenty minutes is also remarkable. That I figured this out by using the watch's built-in electronic calculator is a marvel (or would have been five years ago). But the fact is, this watch has not changed my life very much. It simply makes me less dependent on my secretary, who reminds me of where I belong on special occasions, and less dependent on my mathematical computational skills, which are nothing if not mediocre. I have no doubt gained in knowing more precisely what time it is, but a minute or two one way or the other does not matter to me personally. It may matter for a production process, but all such highly rigorous production processes are governed by electronic calculators, not by people. And this is the whole point: the extraordinary increases in our machines' ability to measure time and adjust to time has very little to do with the way we live our lives. Traffic on the highways is just as clogged at peak driving hours as it was yesterday, and it will be equally clogged tomorrow, whether or not our employers buy a new computer software program.

The Decreasing Marginal Utility of Increased Speed

When railroad travel became common in the late-nineteenth century, it did transform the spatial reality of the masses. Inland food and equipment transportation became cheaper, mail delivery became faster and far cheaper, and long-distance travel over land became reasonably pleasant for the first time in man's recorded history. Trains went as fast as 60 miles per hour for long periods. With the exception of the sportsmen's iceboat, no other mode of transportation in man's history had ever approached this average speed. Since then, the jet airplane has made long-distance travel even more pleasant, but not fundamentally different, for most people do not use them very often. The magnitude of difference between a fast commercial train in 1860 and a fast commercial plane a century later did not have the same sort of impact on the average person (rather than business traveller) that the train had in comparison to the stagecoach the day that the first train arrived in a town. The impact of the automobile was stupendous — fast travel at your command, independent of externally imposed schedules.

Consider the town clock in comparison to the sundial. It made a major change in how businesses could be operated. It advanced the precision of work schedules, making possible new production processes. This was comparable to the magnitude of social change wrought by the advent of the train in comparison to the stagecoach. Then came the wristwatch. This was the private automobile of time measurement—decentralized, inexpensive, mass produced, life-changing. The impact that the wristwatch had on our lives in comparison to the town clock's chimes or factory whistle was very important—so important that it seems safe to conclude that it was far more important than any future technique in measuring *human* time will ever be. Improvements in watches have been made steadily, but their effects have been marginal in terms of the changes in our lives that they have wrought. A wristwatch that does not require winding is an improvement over one that does; one that has a little beeper alarm is also an improvement (except when it goes off at 12 noon on Sunday when you are sitting in church), but that beeper is not very significant in changing the way we work or live our lives. We even have a phrase for describing merely marginally useful improvements in technology: "bells and whistles." It applies very well to today's improvements in measuring time.

To argue that time-measurement technology has significantly changed our lives in this century is simply ridiculous. Rifkin grabs for any fact that might prove his case, and his desperation shows. He says that in 1927, Emily Post said that a widow should wait for three years before remarrying. By 1950, this had shrunk to six months. Today, Amy Vanderbilt says that the widow should resume the usual social course within a week.[18] He implies, but never is so foolish as to say, that this speeding up is in some way the product of improved time measurement. If he ever said this outright, the howls of derisive laughter would overwhelm him. Did the self-winding wristwatch shorten the widow's mourning period to six months? Has the quartz watch or the light-emitting diode watch now reduced it to a week?

In Puritan days, when life was shorter, harder, and more costly than today, widows were approached by suitors within a few weeks of the funeral of dear departed husbands. The widow inherited at least a third of her husband's land, plus whatever was being held in trust for his children. She could not work it well by herself; there were always unmarried men who wanted land, for it was income-

---

18. *Time Wars*, p. 51.

producing capital.[19] Traditions change for many reasons, but half-second or quarter-second improvements in time measurement surely are not the primary locomotives of social change, except when they lead to some major improvement in industrial production. This happened in industrial management studies at the turn of the twentieth century, as Rifkin knows,[20] but he cannot find anything comparable to these changes that have been produced by quartz watches. Yet Rifkin subtitles his book, *The Primary Conflict in Human History.*

The Supposed Evils of Saving Time

As always, Rifkin is the social critic. He attacks the late-nineteenth century time-management studies conducted by Frederick W. Taylor. "Taylor believed that the key to making a worker more efficient was to strip him of any capacity to make decisions regarding the conception and execution of his task. In the new scientifically managed factory, the worker's mind was severed from his body and handed over to the management. The worker became an automaton, no different from the machines he interacted with, his humanity left outside the factory gate."[21]

This, as you might expect by now, is sheer balderdash. Men are not machines, and if you treat them as machines, you will reduce their productivity. There is always an economic incentive in the free market to treat people well, for this is what pays. This is the way that Wayne Alderson took a nearly bankrupt steel fabrication plant and made it profitable within two years: treating people as people. His "Value of the Person" program became an industry objective because it produced profitable results.[22] Where managers and owners are allowed to take a portion of the workers' increases in productivity, they will have an economic incentive to improve relations within the factory or office. Only where they are not allowed to appropriate a portion of any increased production, as under socialism, will this incentive be absent.

Rifkin is a propagandist. He either doesn't know what he is talk-

---

19. Edmund S. Morgan, *The Puritan Family: Religion and Domestic Relations in Seventeenth-Century New England* (new ed.; New York: Harper & Row, 1966), pp. 58-59.
20. *Time Wars*, pp. 106-9.
21. *Ibid.*, p. 109.
22. R. C. Sproul, *Stronger Than Steel: The Wayne Alderson Story* (New York: Harper & Row, 1980).

ing about, or else he deliberately misinforms his readers. Peter Drucker tells us what Frederick Taylor accomplished, and it was not the creation of biological automatons in the workplace:

> Taylor did not start out (as most people believe who have never read him) with ideas of efficiency or economy, let alone with the purpose of making a profit for the employer. He started out with a burning social concern, deeply troubled by what he saw as a suicidal conflict between "labor" and "capital." And his greatest impact has also been social. For scientific management (we today would probably call it "systematic work study," and eliminate thereby a good many misunderstandings the term has caused) has proved to be the most effective idea of this century. It is the only basic American idea that has had worldwide acceptance and impact. Wherever it has been applied, it has raised the productivity and with it the earnings of the manual worker, and especially of the laborer, while greatly reducing his physical efforts and his hours of work. It has probably multiplied the laborer's productivity by a factor of one hundred.[23]

It is not true that Taylor took the skill out of manual work, though it has often been asserted. For he applied scientific management only to work that had never been skilled, i.e., to the work of the laborer. His most famous study, made in 1899, dealt with shoveling sand. And Schmidt, his shoveling laborer, was not skilled, had no pride in his nonexistent craft, no control over his work, no fun doing it, and a bare subsistence to show for his ten hours of back-breaking, but largely unproductive, daily toil. Taylor's study thus enabled the unskilled man to be paid handsomely, almost at the level of the skilled man, and to be in high demand. The laborer suddenly became productive. Taylor, in other words, repealed the "iron law of wages" under which the unskilled manual laborer had always lived. He did this by creating a skill that had never existed before, the skill of the "industrial engineer." It was the first skill to be firmly based on knowledge rather than on experience. The industrial engineer of scientific management is the prototype of all modern "knowledge workers" and, to this day, one of the most productive ones.[24]

Yet Taylor and "Taylorism" are the targets of Rifkin's wrath. Taylor's time and motion studies liberated unskilled workers by drastically increasing their productivity, something that Rifkin regards as perverse. Taylor's studies put man in greater control over nature, a sin in Rifkin's view. By paying close attention to saving time and

---

23. Peter Drucker, *The Age of Discontinuity: Guidelines to Our Changing Society* (New York: Harper & Row, 1969), p. 271.
24. *Ibid.*, p. 272.

effort, workers could increase their income. When instructed by profit-seeking managers, the workers did just that.

Rifkin quite properly traces this alien, clock-oriented worldview right back to the Puritans. He cites Richard Baxter's late-seventeenth century work, *A Christian Directory*: "A wise and skilled Christian should bring his matters into such order, that every ordinary duty should know his place, and all should be . . . as the parts of a clock or other engine, which must all be conjunct, and each right placed."[25] Rifkin exaggerates for effect: "The clock culture called forth a new faith: the future could be secured if everyone would only learn to be on time."[26] He says that modern society makes punctuality the key to man's self-salvation.

Progress: Productivity, Choices, and Freedom

What Rifkin fails to understand is that there is a process of development going on. Techniques of mass production make possible the spread of wealth to lower classes by means of price competition. Production for a mass market became more profitable than production for the court and the nobility. This was the process Max Weber called the democratization of demand.[27] Initially, a few types of products of fairly low quality are made available to the masses. By lowering prices, producers can create a mass market that will absorb the increased output of factories.

This is only the first stage of the process. Then comes greater product differentiation and increased consumer choice.[28] At first, price competition expands the market. New groups gain access to goods not previously available to them, either because prices were too high before, or because the products did not even exist. As participants in the production process, workers add to other people's wealth. Producers are buyers; step by step, as output per unit of input increases, as a result of the specialization of production, the wealth of all the participants increases. The initial expansion of buying alternatives itself expands as productivity increases. Some producers may specialize in producing for this newly improved buying

---

25. *Time Wars*, p. 96.
26. *Ibid.*, p. 97.
27. Max Weber, *General Economic History* (New York: Collier, [1927] 1961), p. 230.
28. Gary North, "Price Competition and Expanding Alternatives," *The Freeman* (August 1974).

public; others may branch out and aim at the still excluded buyers — the next level down.

The process of economic development increases the range of human choice. This does not happen overnight. Like the Model T Ford automobile that was available in any color in 1915, so long as you wanted it in black, so is the first stage of mass production. Ford became a billionaire through mass production, driving out of business many of his high-priced competitors. He changed the face of America. But by the late 1920's, the Model T was dead, and the Ford Motor Company fell into a long decline, because General Motors adopted a policy of inter-company competition through the creation of decentralized divisions: Cadillac, Buick, Oldsmobile, Pontiac, and Chevrolet. Each division offered consumers many product choices. Price competition became price *and* quality competition, as workers' productivity and therefore also their personal income increased. With this strategy of corporate decentralization, Alfred P. Sloan, Jr. revolutionized modern management.[29] He also created the major automobile company of his generation; it took him about five years.

Thus, the free market does not lead to a reduced number of choices, as the critics insist; on the contrary, it leads to far greater consumer opportunities. Freedom and increased capital investment increase people's productivity as workers, and therefore their ability to buy more of what they want. Free market capitalism, with its free mobility of labor, its right of voluntary contract, its emphasis on personal responsibility, and its supporting ethic of thrift and planning, opens new opportunities for men once locked in a far narrower universe economically. But this process is deeply resented by the aristocrats of the old society and by the intellectuals of almost all societies. A society that places considerable emphasis on considerations of personal and family status — name, rank, family heritage — does not react favorably to the *nouveau riche* "commoners" who, through a special skill of being able to produce for a mass market through cost-cutting and future-predicting, have become fabulously wealthy.

Discipline: External to Internal

Paralleling this development of commodity differentiation, workers in the initial stages of industrial development are tightly con-

---

29. Peter F. Drucker, *Management: Tasks, Responsibilities, Practices* (New York: Harper & Row, 1974), pp. 383-84.

trolled, doing only a few simple tasks.[30] As time goes on, production increases and markets expand. Production becomes far more complex, equipment becomes more expensive, and workers must receive greater training. With greater skills comes greater responsibility, a fundamental biblical principle (Luke 12:47-48). So, workers are steadily given more freedom to make decisions as companies are forced by growth and competition to decentralize the decision-making process. The modern "knowledge society" is heading for even greater decentralization, with more flexible work schedules.

The personal and social goal is self-discipline. This usually requires external social and institutional discipline in a pagan, rebellious society. As time goes on, people mature under this external discipline and become more responsive to other people's economic requests, as registered on a free, competitive market. Just as children need direct external discipline in the early years, so do God-hating societies require the discipline of long hours of work and tight factory schedules. Once the clocks are internalized, and the Puritan work ethic takes over a person's life, the external restraints become inhibiting and counter-productive.

Self-discipline under God is inescapably self-discipline under the constraints of time. We are temporal creatures. But self-discipline under time does not mean we are slaves to clocks, any more than self-government under law means that we are slaves to law. We are masters of time because we respect time as a *created* thing. God is sovereign, not time. Yes, if we lose this view of God, time can become a slave master. Anything that man substitutes for God becomes his slave master. But why single out time as the great villain? Why target the computer for vengeance? Only because Rifkin is an intellectual Luddite. Like the saboteurs of old, who tossed wooden shoes into machinery,[31] Rifkin tosses his wooden prose into everything technological that has become a tool of visible progress in the West.

Compùtopia

Rifkin hates "computopia." No wonder: he describes it in theological terms — the triumph of power-seeking man. Computopia is

---

30. Adam Smith, *Wealth of Nations* (1776), ch. 1.
31. *Sabotage* comes from the French word for shoe. A *sabot* is a wooden shoe, according to the first definition given in the *Oxford English Dictionary* (1971). Odd fact: the *OED* gives considerable space to various definitions of *sabot*, but does not include the words *sabotage* and *saboteur*. Strange.

the triumph of man, the immortal information-gatherer. He waxes eloquent—silly, but eloquent. "In computopia, there are no final judgments or end of history. In the new world, time is information, and information is immortal."[32] "Everything in the new computer world is temporary and fleeting. Everything is subject to continual edits, revisions, and modifications. . . . There is no well-established past, no preconceived future, no starting point or end of the line in this new world, just the unceasing process of simulation."[33]

No past? No starting point? No end of the line? Are you sure, Jeremy? Then I have a question for you: *What ever happened to entropy, your prophetic new worldview that you said in 1980 would shape mankind from now until heat death of the universe come?* Entropy has been tossed aside, like a mistress grown fat and wrinkled. Rifkin doesn't marry his worldviews; he wines them, dines them, collects his book royalties from them, and then moves on. For Jeremy Rifkin, a worldview is simply an irresistible opportunity for a weekend fling or two, and then he is off to new conquests.

Ah, but this new worldview sounds so, so . . . *apocalyptic.* "Now, a new journey begins. In the coming century our children are likely to redefine their environment using the language of information theory and cybernetics as they attempt to conjure up a view of nature that conforms with the operational principles of the new computer technology. We are entering a new temporal world where time is segmented into nanoseconds, the future is programmed in advance, nature is reconceived as bits of coded information, and paradise is viewed as a fully simulated, artificial environment."[34]

This is ridiculous. The world of nanoseconds is the realm of electronics and digital codes. It is not the world of human beings, nor is such a world the goal of human beings. Through computers, computer programs, and systems engineering we can make use of this speed-of-light world of energy, but we will never enter into it. We harness this invisible realm to fulfill our own purposes; we control it *representationally* through our tools. The world of electronic time no more will dominate us in the future than the speed of light presently dominates our ability to flip through television channels. It is the abysmal quality of the available entertainment, not the speed of the remote control sensor devices, that is the source of our dissatisfac-

---

32. *Time Wars*, p. 158.
33. *Ibid.*, p. 155.
34. *Ibid.*, p. 188.

tion. The highly sophisticated, inexpensive remote control sensor technology simply allows us to search the channels more efficiently for something worth watching. It exposes our cultural hopes as futile and naive without our having to leave our sofas, walk across the room, and start turning the channel selector manually. But Rifkin prophesies a future world where our children will spin simulated utopias out of electronic cloth, and somehow lose their freedom in the bargain. Men will be the prisoners of power, the programmed biological automatons of high technology.

The fault, dear Jeremy, is not in the electrons; but in ourselves, that we are underlings.

This apocalyptic, compuphobic vision comes from the self-anointed prophet who assured us in 1979: "For the past thirty years, the American economy has been relying on technological advances in specific growth industries, most of which are now maturing and showing signs of leveling off in terms of growth. Wonder drugs, the computer industry, photocopying and television immediately come to mind."[35] A most remarkable prophecy! *First*, wonder drugs were "leveling off" in 1979. Then, lo and behold, he went on to co-author a book called *Algeny* (1983), which warned us about a frightening new worldview, a radical vision of a future society based on science's ability to create new wonder drugs through genetic engineering. *Second*, the computer industry was also "leveling off." Now, lo and behold, he has written *Time Wars* (1987), warning us about a frightening new worldview, a radical vision of a future society based on science's ability to create a new view of time through computers and digital wristwatches.

What next? It is easy to predict. His next book (1991) will warn us about a frightening new worldview, a radical vision of a future society based on science's ability to mass produce photocopying machines. Perhaps he will call it *File Wars*. People will be terrified by the brave new world sketched in Chapter One, "See Attached Copy." They will be willing to sell their homes and move to Wyoming when they read Chapter Eight, "Paper Jammed in Roller." They will be tempted to move to a farm in Tasmania when the read the Conclusion, "A World Out of Toner."

---

35. Jeremy Rifkin (with Ted Howard), *The Emerging Order: God in the Age of Scarcity* (New York: Ballentine, 1979), p. 76.

New Age Rhythms

What Jeremy Rifkin is against, now as always, is man's exercise of dominion over nature. He remains faithful to the passive outlook of Eastern mysticism. "We have sacrificed wisdom for violence and used awareness as a weapon to secure our temporal domination."[36] What he wants, now as always, is a New Age metaphysical union with our environment. We must "make a choice to go forward to a new partnership with the rest of the living kingdom—a partnership based on a deep and abiding respect for the rhythms of the planet."[37] We also need a higher consciousness experience of our joining with nature. The following passage leads me to ask myself this key epistemological question: *What has this man been smoking?* "We have all experienced rapture, those special moments of undefinable time when we surrender control over the future, both our own and others'. We become our environment. Our time expands to encompass all other things; we become the world. We participate fully in a shared temporality where there exists no time hierarchy, no privileged minority, no inside and outside, no 'I' and 'they.' These are the moments of bliss we yearn for and that can only be attained by empathetic, shared participation."[38]

It gets worse. "Those who align themselves with the empathetic time dynamic are calling for the 'resacralization' of life at every level of existence from microbe to man. . . . The rhythm of the first constituency is slow-paced, rhapsodic, spontaneous, vulnerable, and participatory. Emphasis is on reestablishing a temporal communion with the natural biological and physical rhythms and of coexisting in harmony with the cycles, seasons, and periodicities of the larger earth organism."[39] In short, what Jeremy Rifkin wants what Western society has apparently denied to him: natural rhythm.

Then Rifkin proposes a reconstruction of public policy based on this new worldview. First, we must understand that "Time politics has become power politics."[40] You may have missed this, somehow. I know I did. Money politics, maybe; ego-trip politics, no question; but *time* politics? Second, time politics must be scrapped. "By trans-

---

36. *Time Wars*, pp. 192-93.
37. *Ibid.*, p. 194.
38. *Ibid.*, p. 195.
39. *Ibid.*, p. 199.
40. *Idem.*

ferring our private experience of empathy into public policy, we begin a new time journey, one in which temporal awareness is used to empathize with the future. In this new temporal world, time politics becomes empathetic politics."[41]

He is unfortunately silent about how we might transfer his vision of a new time politics into a specific political program. I suppose his first step will be to mount a grass-roots campaign against daylight savings time, which is clearly an assault of commercial time against natural time, and furthermore it was an invention of that capitalist time master, Ben Franklin. Never forget, "In an empathetic time world, our reality conforms to nature's."[42] Then we will no doubt need a ban against imported digital wristwatches. After that, it gets vague. How about local laws against beepers in public places?

To conduct a political transformation, you need constituents. You also need organizational allies. So, who are the representatives of this new empathetic politics? They are all those crazies who began to grab for political power in the late 1960's, meaning Rifkin's old constituencies. "Many new movements have emerged in recent years, each embracing aspects of the empathetic time vision. The environmental movement, the animal-rights movement, the Judeo-Christian stewardship movement, the eco-feminist movement, the holistic health movement, the alternative agriculture movement, the appropriate technology movement, the bio-regionalism movement, the self-sufficiency movement, the economic democracy movement, the alternative education movement, and the disarmament movement come readily to mind."[43] They come readily to *whose* mind? Have you ever seen one piece of literature, one single booklet, from any of these screwball movements that argues that the primary (or even secondary) reason for its existence is the world's desperate need for a new political order based on a totally new view of time? No? Neither have I. And neither has Rifkin. He cites no evidence. He just lists his hoped-for organizational allies.

One thing is sure: with this witches brew of a list, he has unofficially abandoned his expressed hope in *The Emerging Order* (1979) of capturing the evangelical movement and the charismatics. His future does not lie with the "Pat Robertson for President" crowd. So, he has returned to his old haunts, seeking to enlist at least part-time

---

41. *Idem.*
42. *Ibid.*, p. 210.
43. *Ibid.*, p. 206.

support from the few remaining shocked troops of the Nirvana Liberation Front, the mind-blown visionaries of social transformation who never quite recovered psychologically from the startling news that a jury in a U.S. courtroom actually did free Angela Davis.[44] There are not many of them left.

Like charismatics, Rifkin wants revelation, but clearly not Christian revelation. He wants to wait for the kind of higher consciousness that is sought after by New Age avatars: "In an empathetic time world, the mind places less emphasis on manipulative knowledge and more emphasis on revelatory knowledge. Manipulative knowledge gives us control but at the expense of wisdom. We become skilled craftsmen learning how to reshape surfaces without gaining any deep understanding of interiors. Manipulative knowledge is always exercised at the outer margins of reality. Revelatory knowledge is always experienced in the depths. . . . Revelation is experienced by a giving over, a reaching out. The essential why of things becomes revealed to us when we choose to surrender to them. . . ."[45]

Watch out, Mr. Rifkin. The things to which you want to surrender may turn out to be more than impersonal aspects of the universe.

Conclusion

When I decided to publish this book, I asked my cover designer to paint a split picture. On the left was an alarm clock with its back open and a broken coiled spring hanging out. It was sitting on a table in a dingy room with worn-out wallpaper. The clock's face would read five minutes to twelve. On the right hand side of the cover was a high tech digital clock on a table in a freshly wallpapered room. Its face would read twelve fifteen. The artist tried twice, but the designs never conveyed my idea clearly, the idea of cosmic restoration. Had I known of Rifkin's decision to write *Time Wars*, I would have stuck with the old design and asked the artist to try once again. Rifkin literally followed my book cover's original design: from a world doomed by entropy, running out of time, to a high tech world that has been visibly restored.

---

44. My favorite recollection of the "free Angela Davis" movement is a political cartoon of a store filled floor to ceiling with posters: "Free Angela Davis!" and "Free Sister Angela!" The store's owner is on the telephone, eyes bugging out. "They just did *what?*"

45. *Ibid.*, p. 209.

This is the cosmic message of Christ's resurrection. Entropy will be overcome. There is plenty of time remaining. A new world has come, and a better world is coming. Jeremy Rifkin refuses to accept this. In this, he is both consistent and predictable, book after book.

There is not one word in *Time Wars* on entropy, or the second law of thermodynamics, or the heat death of the universe, or time's arrow. Nothing. The "unstoppable, inevitable" new worldview of *Entropy: A New World View* is gone. There is nothing on genetic engineering, either. The unstoppable worldview of *Algeny* is also gone. Not a trace remains. What does remain are the basic themes of his earlier books: hostility to the Protestant work ethic, free market economics, economic growth, science and technology, dominion over nature, and Western civilization in general. What we have in *Time Wars* is a yet another prophecy of yet another imminent shift in worldviews that will be based on, of all things, the digital wristwatch. It's all true, he assures us. You'll see. Watch.

There is one thing I think we can safely conclude about *Time Wars*: this time, Jeremy Rifkin really did write a book all by himself. That a publisher could be found for this manuscript is mind-boggling. The publisher is apparently operating under a variant of the marketing assumption set forth two generations ago by H. L. Mencken: "Nobody ever went broke by underestimating the taste of the American public." The variant? "No New York publisher is likely to go broke by underestimating the gullibility of the liberal intellectual community."

SCRIPTURE INDEX

OLD TESTAMENT

Genesis
1:1	xxxiii
1:2	270
1:24-24	18
1:26-28	xvii, xxi
1:26-28	13, 35, 263
1:28	81, 266
2:15	152
3	186
3:15	112
3:17-19	xxi, 75, 147
3:19	93
8:20-22	35
9:1-7	263
15	112
47:26	254-55

Exodus
1:7-10	146
3:2	3
12:37	145
20:12	10, 157
23:25	157
23:25-26	1, 3, 111, 146, 168
23:26	37, 169, 185
23:29	11
23:29-30	146
36:1-6	150

Deuteronomy
8:4	1
8:17	42
8:18	42, 164
8:19-20	240
10:17-13	292
12:28	292
14:26	301

Deuteronomy
21:20	302n
28	186
28:1-14	xvii, xxiii, 45, 78, 108, 111, 127, 149, 164, 169, 268, 282, 295, 297
28:2	128
28:15-68	112, 127, 225, 268
28:16-67	242
28:63-65	242
29:29	31

Joshua
24:13	42

I Samuel
8:51	255

II Samuel
12:14	241

I Kings
20:28	241

Psalms
14:1	31
91:12	124
106:15	148
127:5	157

Proverbs
8:36	101, 198
13:22	42
21:1	157
25:22	223

Isaiah
11	262
22:12-13	122
22:13	121
34:4	274
65:20	8, 110, 124, 168

Jeremiah
6:14	44
13:14	245

Ezekiel
7:1-15	245-46

Ezekiel
13:10	44
16:20-21	212

Joel
2	289n
2:28	299-300

Amos
2:6-7	230
6:1	242

Malachi
3:6	199

NEW TESTAMENT

Matthew
5:45	223
6:10	274
6:33	110, 111, 160
7:16	155
7:16-20	228
12:22-24	277
12:25-27	277
12:30	234, 240
13:12	159
13:38	224
16:28	299
21:43	295
24:14	300
24:32-35	290
25:41	222
28:18	166, 257
28:18-19	112
28:18-20	xxi, 145, 278, 295

Mark
9:40	8

Luke
9:25	222
12:47-48	111, 318
19:13	165

John
3:16	219
12:19	222
14:16-17	132
14:30	220
16:7	299
17:14-16	258
17:15-19	150, 219-20
18:36	220
20:30-31	151

Romans
1:18	128
1:18-22	93, 99
1:18-23	237
2:14-15	237
5:19	131
5:20	267
8:10	299
8:18-23	iii
8:29	151, 157
12:2	151
12:20	223
13:8	301

I Corinthians
1:20-21	221

Scripture Index

I Corinthians
2:16	176
3	225
3:8-15	111
3:9	221
11:1	151
11:32	221
15:13-17	ix, 69
15:14-17	xi
15:24-25	160
15:24-26	261
15:25	220
15:26	100
15:27	278

II Corinthians
5:17	132
5:19	220
7:10	221

Galatians
4:3	221

Ephesians
1:4-5	157, 224
1:4-7	64
1:14	111
1:19-22	278
2:2-3	221
2:4-6	145
2:8-10	154
5:16	308
5:22-33	226
5:25-27	149
5:26-27	154

Philippians
2:12	224
2:15	221
3:20	258

Colossians
1:16-17	26
1:17	31
2:8	221
3:2	258

I Timothy
4:10	224

Hebrews
9:15-23	163
11:6	111

I Peter
3:1-7	226

II Peter
2:5	222
3:10	222
3:11	274

I John
1:8-9	153
3:1	221
4:4	222
4:5-6	221
5:19	221

Revelation
12:9-11	114
20:7-10	260-61, 267
22:3	166
22:20	160

INDEX

Abbey, Edward, 160
abortion, 238, 244-45, 284-85
Abraham, 277
Abraham, Larry, 288n
academic freedom, 213-18
Adam, ix, xxii, 125-26, 152
Adler, Mortimer, 235-36
agenda (control of), 295
agnosticism, 30
agreement, 235-36
AIDS, 83, 182, 302, 304
alcohol, 301
Alderson, Wayne, 314
Alice, 120
alternatives to welfare, 254
amateur theologians, 261, 287
amillennialism, 247-48, 263
anarchy, 226, 240
animism, 140
Antichrist, 123, 259, 287-88
antinomianism, 43, 170, 264, 289, 292-93, 300
apes, 21
apocalypticism, 176, 181-82
apologetics
  defined, x (note)
  creationism, xii, xvi, 189, 193
  Darwinists', xii
  neutrality (false), xxxiii
  shift in, xx
  Van Til's, xxxiii, 195
Arendt, Hannah, 226
arguments, 236
"arsonist," 257
asceticism, 159

Aspect, Alain, 26
authority, 216, 263
autonomy
  academic, 215
  apologetics &, xxxiii
  cosmology, 171
  Darwinism & New Age, xiv
  "fairness," 238
  nature?, 18
  power religion, 42
  presupposition, xxxiii, 237
  religion of, 42
  scientific, 84
  starting point, xii
  universe, 35, 171
  see also closed box
Asimov, Isaac, 6-7, 27, 53-54, 62, 73
Assyria, 251
astronomy, 40
atheism, 30, 59
automobile, 312

Babel, 232
Bahnsen, Greg, 220-23
Bailey, Alice A., 184
Bakker, Jim, 301-302
balance of nature, 147, 169
Barnhouse, Donald, 293
Baxter, Richard, 316
Bazarov, I. P., 59-60
beer, 247
Bell, John Stewart, 24-26
Bent, Henry, 51
Berkeley, Bishop, 30
Berkeley, Univ. of Calif., 26

Berman, Harold, 148-49
Bible-Science Association, 70, 77
Biblical Blueprint Series, 295
biblical law, 228, 300 (see also antinomianism, covenant, ethics)
Big Bang, 53, 63, 73-74, 109
"bigger is better," 306-7
biology, 185
black skull, 21
Blum, Ed, 298
Blum, Harold, 120
Bohm, David, 24-25
Boltzmann, Ludwig, 55, 56-58, 61
box (see "open box")
Brennan, Justice, 206
Bullinger, E. W., 149
bureaucracy, 86-87, 92, 157, 216, 233, 249, 254, 259
Burke, Edmund, 232
bush, 3

calendars, 305
Calvinism, 180, 268, 298
capitalism, 168-69
captivity, 247
carburetor, 128
cards, 125-26
Carson, Rachel, 141
cartel, xxviii
cataclysm, 245
cat experiment, 27-28
causality, 29, 37
CBN University, 271
Chafer, Lewis Sperry, 294
change, 159-60, 195, 196, 203-4
chaos, 31, 72
charismatics, 298-300
Chilton, David, 231n
Christ (see Jesus)
Christian Reconstruction
    covenantal, 47
    Dave Hunt &, 287
    ethics &, 117, 291-94, 303
    progress, 47
Christianity, x, 196, 228-32, 246-7 (see also church, covenant, creeds)

church
    cleansing, 154-57
    defeated?, 263
    no maturation?, 260
    politics &, 238
    progress, 154-55
    sanctification, 149-50, 154-57
    membership standards, 42
    state &, 232-40
    Wrinkles, 154
Church Age, 114, 149, 264, 289, 297, 299
church history, 263
classical liberalism, 178-79
Clausius, Rudolph, 52-54, 56
cleansing, 153, 154-57, 275
clock of prophecy, 289
clocks, 75, 91, 104, 311-13
closed box
    Darwinism, 191, 198
    debate, 204-5
    how big?, 96-97
    no observer, 30
    universe, 52, 61-62, 65, 75, 92, 109
    see also "open box"
closed systems, 52
circular reasoning, 237
citizen, 226
citizenship, 156, 258
Clauser, John, 26
Colson, Charles, 258
Columbus, 182
common grace, 223-24
common ground, xxxiii, 70, Appendix A, 212
complexity, 73-79, 191-92 (see also simplicity)
communism, 59-61
computopia, 318-20
condors, 140
consciousness, 137 (see also higher consciousness)
conservation, 85, 87-88, 122, 180, 309
constants, 115, 117, 184, 185 (see also uniformitarianism)
Constitution, 216
continuity, 2, 111, 176, 202-3

Index

contracting universe, 53-54, 64
Copenhagen School, 15, 23
corruption, 243
cosmology, 58, 60, 64-65, 68, 82, 171, 205
Couch, W. T., 215, 216-17
Council of Ephesus, 133, 150
Cournot, Sadi, 55
Courville, Donovan, 145
covenant
  blessings, 45, 128, 157, 163
  cause and effect, 45, 172, 185, 295
  constant, 115, 185
  creeds, 45
  dominion, 263, 266
  external world &, 12
  family, 157
  institutions, 78, 157
  national, 240-41
  natural law &, 169
Cox, Harvey, 305
creation, 58, 82-83, 85, 159-60
creationism
  apologetics, x, xvi
  autonomy, xii
  colleges &, xiv
  Creator-less, 206, 210, 213, 217, 218
  Darwinism vs., 5
  debates, xii
  defeatist, xviii
  denominations &, xiv
  despair &, xiii, 70-71, 128
  discontinuity, 170, 176-77
  entropy theory &, 9-11, 69-71, 119, 123, 129, 166-68, 186, 191, Appendix A
  epistemology, 67-68
  eschatology &, 70-71, 74-76, 78-79, 127, 188-89
  ethics & nature, 170, 173
  Gould vs., 198n, 211-12, 217
  methodology, xii, xv
  millennium?, 167
  nature & ethics, 170, 173
  neutrality &, 209, 212
  no influence, xix
  pessimism, 68, 70-71, 76, 88, 127, 172, 188-89, 302

  postmillennial, 167
  public schools, 200, 212-13
  resurrection &, xi, xix, xxi
  retreat, xxiii, 303
  revival &, 209
  Rifkin &, 123, 170
  sanctification, 152, 170
  second law &, 189-90
  shared presuppositions, 170, 187-88, 190, Appendix A
  social pessimism, 70-71, 88, 189
  social theory, 77
  weak points, xvi
  without God, 206-7
  worldview, xiv-xv
Creator-creature, 176
creeds, 45
crisis in faith, 184
cross, 278
Cumbey, Constance, 183, 184, 287, 288, 295, 296, 297
curses, 9, 170, 241-42
Custance, Arthur, 8
cycles, 63-64, 147, 148, 159

Dallas Seminary, 263, 265, 284-85, 293, 296, 298
Darby, John Nelson, 293-94
Darwin, Charles, 209
Darwinism
  autonomy, xiv
  control by, xvii, 5-6, 209
  despair, xiii
  education, 209-10
  energy, 201-2
  political, xvi
  power, xv
  religion, xi
  religious, 93
  shared presuppositions, 170, 187-88, 190, Appendix A
  soft underbelly, xiii
  subsidizing, 218
  sunshine evolution, 96, 192-93, 205
  taxpayers &, 218
  use of entropy, 192-93
  war with, xiv-xvi, 5, 8, 113

weak case, xiii
worldview, xv
Davis, John J., 264-65
DDT, 141-42
deaf, 252
death, 8, 42, 100-1, 109, 111, 121, 198
  (see also heat-death)
debates, xii, xiii
debt, 291, 307
decay, 159-60, 166-68, 170, 188
decentralization, 233
deductive logic, xiii
default, 253
defeat, 156, 171
democracy, 86-87, 216
despair
  alternative to, xiv-xv, xxiii
  creationism, 70-71, 128
  entropy &, 70-71, 128
  Darwinism, xiii
  heat death, 54-55, 109
  preferred to God, 63-64
  premillennialism &, 113
  pessimillennialism, 76, 113-14
  Rifkin, 107, 177
  Russell, Bertrand, 54-55
  zero growth, 112
dispensationalism
  activists in, 294
  allies of humanism, 272
  antinomian, 264, 289, 292-93, 300
  crisis of, 261, 269, 294
  division within, 261, 281, 294-99
  ethics &, 292
  "gap" theory, 270
  halfway house, 297
  Holy Spirit debate, 298-300
  hybrid system, 296
  pessimism of, 265-67
  rescue mission theology, 264
  responsibility, 292, 294
  Rifkin &, 264, 269-71
  social ethics, 304
  white flag, 264
  see also Rapture
determinism, 227
diets, 302

directionality, 51-52, 282
disagreement, 235-36
disasters, 109
discontinuity, 2, 4, 176-77, 201-2
disintegration, 32
doctrines of the faith, x
dominion
  biological?, 147
  creation &, 13-14
  ethical, 110, 146, 148, 155, 160
  God's laws &, 161
  institutions &, 156
  long-term growth, 160
  narrow?, 303
  religion, 44-46
  Rifkin vs., 80-81, 134, 138
  steady, 146
  stewardship, 85
dominion theology
  agenda, 295
  Dave Hunt &, 257, 275-76
  need for, 254
  utopian?, 267
Don Quixote, 306
Drucker, Peter, 315
dualism, 228-29
Dubos, René, 81-82, 94

earnest, 111
Eckhart, Meister, 133, 153
ecology, 141, 275
Eddington, Arthur, 19, 62, 91
Eden, 124-27
education, 506, 200, 209, 212-13,
  Appendix B (see also public schools)
Edwords, Frank, 271
Edwards v. Aguillard, 206
Einstein, Albert, 16-17, 19, 25, 27, 28, 32
electrons, 23-24, 29, 320
energy
  atomic, 126
  consumption of, 99
  evolution &, 201-2
  final dissipation of, 109
  garden of Eden, 126
  God-substitute, 199, 204

guilt &, 99
  redirected, 1-2
Engels, Frederick, 59-61
Enlightenment (Scottish), 178
entertainment, 310
entropy
  agreement, 188
  allegiance to, 100
  binding?, 191-94
  Claussius, 53
  closed systems only?, 193n
  creationism &, 9-11, 69-71, 119, 123, 129, 166-68, 186, 191, Appendix A
  cursed effects, 78, 126
  defined, xxiv, 49-51
  despair &, xiii, 54-55, 107
  destroys man, 97-98
  final judgment, 112, 127
  garden of Eden, 124-27
  god, 101, 107
  guilt &, 99-101
  law of, xxv, 67-68, 75, 107, 129, 175, 305
  life vs., 39n, 57, 99, 120, 123
  meaning &, 97-98
  measure, 191
  miracle vs., 10, 190
  Morris defines, 9-10
  "noise," 188, 191
  nothingness, xxv
  one-way street, 52-53, 62
  pessimillennialism &, 76, 186
  pessimism &, 40, 48, 52, 62-64, 92, 172, 189
  Satan &, 175
  second coming &, 79
  social, 92, 96-97, 98, 101, 110
  social pessimism, 68, 70-71, 76, 189
  sovereignty of, 157
  sting?, 114
  tendency, 77
  time scale, 71, 95
  universal?, 192
  "usually," 75, 79, 198
  worldview, 106-7
  see also equilibrium, heat death, social entropy

epistemology, 67-68, 77
equations, 27
equilibrium, 1n, 50, 53, 57, 193n, 203n
escape religion, 42-44, 47, 277
eschatology
  back door, 76
  consequences, 273
  creationism, 88, 188-89
  deferral, 46
  eternal life, 54
  ethics &, 292, 300-4
  New Age, 183
  scholarship &, xix
  science &, ix-xi, 188-89
  self-contained, 183
  shift in, xx
  social outlook, 68
  tactics &, xviii-xix
  worldview &, 48-49, 272
  see also dispensationalism
eternal life, 54
ether, 32
ethics
  "boxes," 118-19, 122
  Christian Reconstruction, 47, 291-94
  closed box, 108
  conquest &, 45
  de-emphasis, 76
  dominion &, 42, 45, 146, 148, 155, 160
  eschatology &, 292, 300-4
  evolution &, 118
  fixed order, 83, 117, 134, 184, 199-200
  knowledge &, 185, 212
  growth &, 160
  nature &, 83-84, 170
  power vs. dominion, 42
  primary topic, 110
  progress &, 77-78, 84-85
  reconstruction by, 132
  union with Christ, 133
  "world," 220-21
evangelicalism, 229
evolution
  ethics &, 118
  mathematics vs., 197

punctuated, 77
sunshine, 96, 192-93, 205
evolutionism (see Darwinism)

facts, 187, 208-9
failure of nerve, 137, 181-82
fairness, 215-16
faithfulness, 45
fact, 2n, 36, 187, 195
Fall
  entropy, 124-28
  power of, ix
  thermodynamics &, xi
family, 157, 226
fear, 244
feedback, 158-59 (see negative feedback, positive feedback)
Ferris, Timothy, 13, 19
fig tree, 289-90, 290
final judgment
  all religious, 113
  entropy, 127
  escape from, xiii, 54-55, 62-64, 131, 159
  evolutionism, 112
  march toward, 127
  stalemate vs., 108
  versions, 199
Finney, Charles, 229
Flood, xi, 207-8
fluctuations, 57
flux, 60, 195
Ford, Henry, 317
France, 226
Franklin, Benjamin, 308, 322
French Revolution, 226, 232-33, 249
"full bucket" analogy, 151-53
fundamentalism, 180-81, 212-13, 231, 272 (see also dispensationalism, escape religion, pietism)
future-orientation, 98

gap theory, 270
garden, 82, 124-27
gas, 1n, 50, 56
gasoline, 128
General Motors, 137, 317

Genesis Flood, xi, 269-70
Genesis Institute, 70
genetic engineering, 84, 204
Georgescu-Roeqen, Nicholas, 68n
ghetto, 303
Gish, Duane, 73
gluttony, 302
gnosticism, 43-45
God
  blessings of, 45, 128, 163
  center, 240-41
  character of, 199
  closed box vs., 30, 92
  curse, xxii-xiii, xxi, 37, 159, 170, 241-42
  death of, 63, 107
  delegates authority, 216
  equal time for?, 195, 209-10
  evaluator, 71
  existence of, 60
  glorious, 152-153
  Holy Spirit, 132, 186, 298-300
  intervention by, 33
  Jesus as, 133
  judgment, xiii, xxiii, 37, 49, 108, 127, 149, 282
  karma vs., 169
  kingdom of, 10, 111, 155-75, 260, 262
  law of, 43, 97, 146, 184, 291-92, 295
  love of, 219
  Newton on, 32
  observer, 30
  one-many problem, 37
  power of, 257-58, 263
  redirects energy?, 1-2
  regeneration, 63
  sanctuary, 150
  sovereignty of, 159
  speaking in the name of, 216
  this world's, 107
  trinity, 225
  unchanging, 203-4
  uniformitarianism of, 199
  union with, 133
  voice of, 216
  whole counsel of, 239
  wrath of, 219
  see also covenant, ethics, law

Index

Goldman, Marshall, 92
gospel
  condemnation &, 266
  effects, 266
  failure?, 263
  heart only?, 258
  power of, 157
  society &, 156
  transforming power, 114, 123, 266, 280, 299
Gould, Stephen Jay, 5, 198, 211-12, 217
government, 226, 227, 234, 238
grace, 223-25
grape juice, 300
graveyard society, 145
gravity, 23, 31
Great Commission, 166, 257-58
Greece, 137, 140, 148
Gribbin, John, 26-29
growth
  capitalism &, 168-69
  contraction, 120-21
  economic, 178
  ethical imperative, 112
  ethics &, 111, 128, 178
  future-orientation &, 98
  grace &, 145
  hatred of, 98, 121
  limits to, 11, 106-7, 148
  long term, 111
  population, 147, 158
  reward, 160
  zero, 98, 109, 138
guilt, 73-74, 99-101
Gulag archipelago, 303
Guth, Alan, 22

Hall, G. Stanley, 4
handicapped, 252
healing, 225, 299
health, 146
heat death, 52, 105, 109, 121, 123, 203n
heat loss, 51, 52
hedonism, 121
Heisenberg, Werner, 30
Hemingway, Ernest, 142
Henry, Patrick, 44, 129

Herbert, Nick, 15-16, 19-21, 23-26, 47
higher consciousness, 106, 134
history
  "full bucket" problem, 152
  liberty &, 113
  linear, 14, 109, 113, 147-48, 282
  man's conquest, 91, 132, 163
  man's defeat, 109
  meaning of, 152-53
  perfect Christ, 151
  progress, 77-78, 84-85, 91, 95, 164-66, 175, 177, 273
  resurrection &, 163-68
  see also time
Hitler, Adolph, 104
Hogue, Richard, 288
holiness, 303
Holy Spirit, 132, 186, 298-300
hope (see optimism)
Hubble, Edwin, 40-41
Huizinga, J., 181-82
humanism
  alliance with fundamentalism, 272
  death of man, 63
  dualism, 94
  fundamentalism &, 272
  religious liberals, 231
  responsibility, 253
  shift of, 136-37, 143
  understand eschatology, 272-73
  "What is man?", 93
  zero growth, 159
humility, 74
Humphrey the whale, 139
Humphries, D. R. 192-93
Hunt, Dave
  amateur theologian, 261, 287
  anti-optimism, 183, 274
  anti-dominion, 156-57
  "arsonist," 257
  citizenship, 258
  consistent, 259
  despair, 262
  kingdom denied, 260, 262
  immune from criticism, 261
  limited God, 262
  limited salvation, 258

Lindsey vs., 262, 286
New Age doctrine, 103, 274
polarization, 287
retreat, 279

ideology, 236-37
improvement, 71, 74, 152
incarnation, 2, 45
individualism, 226-27
indoctrination, 215
Industrial Revolution, 178
inferiority complex, 10
infiltration, 249-51
innocents, 244
institutions, 154-57, 227
irrational physics, 31
irrelevance, 239-40, 252
Israel, 286, 289, 290

Jaki, Stanley, 14, 55-57
Jeans, James, 40, 62-63
Jesus
  bureaucrat?, 259
  divinity of, 133
  equal time?, 209-10, 213
  failure of?, 260-61
  miracles of, 75
  natures of, 133, 150
  perfect humanity, 131, 133, 150-54, 167
  person of, 133
  placated God, 219
  resurrection of, ix, 2, 10, 68, 123, 168
  triumph, 172
  see also resurrection
jet planes, xxviii
Johnson, Lyndon, 230
Johnson, Paul, 15-16
Johnson, S. Lewis, 293, 298
Jordan, James, 35
Jubilee Year, xxxii
judgment
  comprehensive, 242-43
  escape, 49
  escaping, 159
  final, 108, 112, 113, 199

forms of, 242
meaning &, 54
national, 240
reasons for, 240-41
restoration, 242, 248-49
two-fold, 149
Jupiter effect, 26-27
justice, 227

Kant, Immanuel, 18
Kantzer, Kenneth, 165
karma, 169
Kelly, Don, 57-58
Kelvin, Lord, 55, 95-96
kingdom
  denied, 10, 260
  earthly, 278
  God's, 155-57
  impossibility, 262
  internalized, 277
  "Kingdom now", 76, 80n
Kitcher, Philip, 189n, 191n
Kittel, Charles, 53
Kirk, Russell, 215, 217
Kline, Meredith G., 124
knowledge society, 318
kosmos, 220-23, 224-25
Kourdakov, Sergei, 244
Kuhn, Thomas, 235

Lalonde, Peter, 259-60, 272, 283, 286
Landes, David, 311
law
  comprehensive, 243-44
  restraining evil, 234
  "unfair", 238
  work of, 237
law of nature, 34, 60, 169-70 (see also natural law)
law schools, 286
lawyers, 218
leap of being, 107, 143
legislated morality, 234
legs, xii-xiii
Lenin, 233
liberalism, 178-79, 227-28, 232-33, 269

liberty, 113
life
  community of, 135
  death &, 99-100, 121
  energy addiction, 100
  energy &, 99-101
  entropy vs., 57, 99-101, 120, 123
  expectancy, 8, 110, 124, 168
  meaning of, 97-98
  sunshine &, 96
  whose?, 99-100
Lindsey, Hal
  activist?, 284
  antichrist, 288
  before & after, 284-85
  dating Rapture, 285
  Hunt vs., 286
  no criticism of, 261
  tribulation, 289
logic, 195, 212
Long March, 246
losers, 280
Luther, 182
luxuries, xxviii

Macdonald, Margaret, 293
macroevolution, 198
Maddox, John
  Dubos &, 94
  entropy, 95-96
  meaning of life, 97-98
  Nature, 92
  "Why environmentalism?", 93
magic, 33
man
  caretaker over nature, 93
  death of?, 100-1
  destroyer?, 94-95
  ecology &, 94-95
  entropy's victim, 97-98
  hatred of, 140
  image of God, 93
  nature &, 93-95
  responsibility of, 44, 92-95
  time vs.?, 104
Mannheim, Karl, 235
Marx, Karl, 59, 93, 179, 233, 136

Marxism, 71, 179-80
maturity, 44, 151-53, 155
McClain, Alva, 304
McDonald's, 80
McGee, J. Vernon, 259
McIntyre, Carl, 266
McPherson, Dave, 281
meaning, 54, 97-98
methodology
  autonomy, xii, xxxiii
  shared, 170, 187-88, 190
  uniformitarianism, 194-200
  Van Til, xxxiii
millennium, 167, 260-61 (see also dispensationalism)
mind, 176, 236
miracle
  Bibles, 3
  entropy vs., 10, 110, 190, 201
  healing, 199
  Jordan on, 35
  Engels denies, 60
  natural law, 11, 34-35, 169-70, 195
  "rewinding," 75
  science vs., 168
  scientists vs., 3-4
  thermodynamics vs., 2
  uniformitarianism, xxii
  Van Til on, 5
  vs. entropy,j?0B?110
miscarriages, 3, 37, 147, 169
mistakes, 88
monkeys, 51
Moore, John, 207
Moral Majority, 231
morality, 234
Morris, Henry
  Bible prophecy, 189
  disorganization theory, 152
  entropy described, 191
  entropy in garden, 127
  entropy law, 129
  entropy repealed, 166-67
  epistemology of, 77
  gap theory, 270
  natural law, 194
  public schools, 200

presuppositions, 67
prophecy, 189
revolution, 67
thermodynamics, 201
uniformitarianism, 197
Mother Nature, 142
motivation, xvii
Motz, Lloyd, 64
Murray, Gilbert, 137, 181
mysticism
  antinomianism, 43
  capitalism vs., 169
  Christianity vs., 133
  ecology movement &, 95
  gnosticism &, 43
  metaphysical union, 43
  pietism &, 43, 95
  Rifkin's, 80, 82, 132-34
  science vs., 106
  statism, 43
  vs. time, 104

natural law
  abandoning, 235
  autonomous?, 11
  changes in, 185
  Christians &, 32
  compromise with, 209, 213
  covenant &, 35, 185
  dead faith, 15-19
  death &, 9
  debate over, 188
  evolving, 194
  fixed, 60, 184-85, 188, 194-200
  flux &, 60, 195
  Geisler &, 302n
  God &, 169-70
  miracles &, 11, 19, 34, 169-70, 195
  scholasticism, 217
  science (19th century), 4
Nature, 92
nature
  autonomous?, 34
  balance of, 147, 169
  complex, 34, 36
  dominion over, 82, 85, 94-95, 135
  eschatology &, 48-49

ethics &, 170
impersonal?, 34
independent?, 18, 35
intelligible, 13-14
man &, 93-95
"mother", 142
not normative, 147
one with, 134-35
purposeful, 135
re-sacralized, 135
resilient, 94
simple?, 34
sovereign?, 46, 159
subordination to, 135
negative feedback, 11, 148, 158-59
Neumann, John von, 29-30
neutrality
  academic freedom, 214
  apologetics, xxxiii
  creationism &, 209
  myth of, 8, 60, 70, 235-37
  politics &, 234
  public schools, 200, 210-11
  statism &, 252
  Van Til on, 8
New Age
  anti-history, xiv
  Christianity vs., 133
  ecology, 275-76
  escapism, 47
  "fellow travellers," 183
  New Left &, 136-37
  "paint," 183
  pessimism, 48, 183
  politics, xxviii
  Reconstructionism &, 257
  Rifkin, xxv, 107
  theology, 279
New Christian Right, 231-32
New Deal, 231-32
New Left, 136-37
New Reformation, 175-76, 177-80
New World, 182
new world order, 10, 183, 276
Newton, 17, 32, 36
Newtonianism, 15-19, 67, 69, 305
Nisbet, Robert, 136-7, 196, 226, 165n

Noah, 185
Nobel Prize, 7
nuclear war, 267

Oberlin College, 229
Occam (Ockham), 37
occupy, 165
oil, xxvii-xviii, 141
open box, 69, 96-97, 118, 122, 198, 204-5
open region (system), 191-93, 202-3
opinion, 236
optimism, xvii, 104-5, 110-11, 113, 183, 282
order
 energy &, 204
 garden of Eden, 125-26
 moral, 83-84
 original, 74
 pockets, 199
 source of, 205
origins, 207-8
other-worldview, xxiii, 287
ownership, 85-86

Paley, William, 209
pantheism, 107, 135
peace, 44, 157
Pentecostals, 298-99
Peoples Bicentennial Commission, xxix
perfection, 131, 150-54
perfectionism, 301
pessimillennialism
 antinomian, 300
 defeat for church, 263
 denies Holy Spirit's power, 302
 entropy doctrine, 76
 New Age &, 183
 Rifkin's ally, 177
 social progress impossible, 165
pessimism
 cosmic and historic, 11
 creationism &, xvii-xviii, 70-71, 88
 defined, 267
 entropy &, xxv, 40, 48-49, 54, 62-65, 70-77, 92

eschatology, 72, 123
fundamentalism, 72, 123, 180-81
Greece, 181
historic, 11
Hunt's, 260
inhibiting, 265
paralysis, xxxiv
pietism, 95, 255
Rifkin's, 68, 123
Russell's, 54, 65-66, 105
science &, 40, 66, 77, 105
social, 68, 70-73
ultimate form of, 172, 260, 267
Pharisees, 277, 278
pietism, 95, 229, 255 (see also escape religion)
pietists, 252-54
pity, 245-46
plague, 182
pluralism, 239
politics
 church &, 238
 hard work, 250
 New Christian Right
 Rapture &, 272
 salvation by, 253-55
politicians, 86-87
politics and religion, 233-34
politics (time), 321-22
pollution, 81-82, 92
polytheism, 239
population growth, xxix, 145-46, 158
Populism, 229
positive feedback, 158, 164, 178
Post, Emily, 313
postmillennialism, 104, 114, 267-68, 272, 295, 297
poverty, 230
power, 251, 243, 253, 268
power religion, 41-42, 46, 263, 277
preaching, 243-44, 248, 301
predestination, 291
premillennialism
 bureaucratic kingdom, 259
 despair, 113
 entropy &, 166-67, 270-71
 power religion &, 263

no sanctification, 170, 260
Rifkin's strategy &, 71-72
see also dispensationalism
Presbyterianism, 229, 231
presuppositions, xxxiii, 77, 208
prices, 88, 97, 168, 309, 316
priests, 311
production, 87, 100, 168-69, 316
progress, 77-78, 84-85, 91, 95, 164-66, 175, 177, 273
prophecy, 289, 290
providence, 33, 168-70
Prussia, 213
public schools, 195, 200, 209-10, 213, 253, 285
pumps, 51, 62
punctuated evolution, 77
Puritanism, 164, 313-14, 316

quantum physics
causation, 29
Einstein vs., 19
equations, 27
irrational, 31
theories, 20
questions (three key), 12

railroads, 312
randomness, 1n, 50-51, 53, 57, 124-26 (see also equilibrium)
Rankine, W. S. M., 56
Rapture
amillennialists vs., 248
antichrist &, 287
biblical view of, 166
dating of, 290-91, 298
debt &, 291
ethics &, 292
fever, 288
footnotes &, xix
Hunt's concern, 276, 298
"lifeboat," 292
politics &, 272
reason, 236 (see also methodology)
rebellion, 99-100, 108, 132-33, 148, 152, 267
reconstruction, 132, 245

red tape, 249
redemption, 161, Appendix C (see also gospel, restoration)
reform, 227, 229, 233, 238, 283, 298
Reformation, 175-76, 180
regeneration, 63, 157
regularities in nature, 35, 37
Reid, Tommy, 74-75, 76-77
reincarnation, 64
relativism, 214, 235
religion, 233-34, 238
religious right, 272
Renaissance, 182
rescue missions, 166, 264
resources, 96
responsibility
Christians', 251, 292
comprehensive, Appendix C
escape religion, 44
ethical cleansing, 156
hopelessness vs. 294
locus of, 254
optimism &, 10-11
personal and institutional, 225-27
power &, 251-54
retreat from, 255, 303
theology of, 255
time & 283, 292
Pharisees, 278
pietism vs., 255
restoration, 122-23, 131, 242
resurrection (of Jesus)
creationism &, xi, xix
discontinuity, 2
effects of, ix, xx-xxiii
entropy &, 10, 123, 168, 324
history &, 168
humanism's alternative, 64
liberation of nature, 176-77
life expectancy &, 8, 110, 124, 168
methodology, xvi
new world order, 10
random?, 2n
Rifkin denies, 177
Satan's defeat, 114
social theory, 68-69
theology of, xx-xxii

thermodynamics &, 2
touchstone, xi
retreat, 273
revival, 209, 291
revivalism, 229
revolution, 233
Rifkin, Jeremy
  allies of, 269
  anti-capitalism, xxvi-xxviii, 86, 88, 168, 306, 309
  anti-Christian, 76, 79, 136
  anti-computers, 309-14, 318-20
  anti-dominion, 80-81, 138, 308, 321
  anti-efficiency, 307
  anti-growth, 73, 85-86, 120-21, 168, 180, 306
  anti-progress, 91, 175, 180, 305
  anti-speed, 307-8
  anti-technology, 73, 91, 100, 177-78
  background of, xxix-xxxii
  bigness, 306-7
  bureaucracy, 86-88
  campaigns, 306
  clocks, 311
  closed box theory, 96
  conservation, 85, 180
  conservationist?, 309
  constituents, 322
  creationists &, 123, 170
  deception by, xxvi, 81
  denies resurrection's power, 177
  despair, 177
  dominion, 80-81, 85, 138
  dualism, 133
  energy addiction, 99
  energy flow, 120
  entropy law (see entropy)
  environmentalism, 134
  errors of, xxv-xxvi
  escape, 109
  forgets entropy, 306, 308, 319
  fundamentalism &, 180-81
  guilt-manipulation, xxvi-xxvii, 73, 99-101
  Henry Morris &, 10, 129
  hope, 105-6
  hopeless, 104-5
  humanist, 101
  liberalism, 178-79
  Luddite, 318
  Marx &, 179-80
  mysticism, 80, 82, 99, 105-6, 132-34, 135, 321
  nanoseconds, 319
  New Age, 133-34, 321
  New Left, 137
  New Reformation, 177-80
  one with nature, 118, 135
  ownership, 85-86
  pessimism, 48, 68, 114-15
  pollution, 81
  popularity of, xxiv
  population decline, xxix
  "premillennial," 71-72
  premils & entropy, 270-71
  propagandist, 48-49, 314
  prophecies, 320, 324
  purposeful nature, 135
  rapture (psychological), 321
  revelation, 323
  rhythm, 321
  sackcloth (metaphysical), 122
  schizophrenic, 105-6
  self-conscious, 164
  self-interest, 86
  sexual license, 136
  spatial analogy, 307
  stewardship, 73, 85
  strategy, 72-73, 180-81
  targets of, xxvi, xxxi-xxxii, 72-73, 128
  time, Appendix F
  waste, 309
  worldview, 48
  zero growth, 138
Robertson, Pat, 80, 271, 288
rock music, 247
Roe v. Wade, 285
Roman Empire, 277, 278
Rome, 158
Rushdoony, Rousas J.
  becoming, 117
  calendars, 305
  change, 159-60

clocks, 131
closed world, 118-19
conquest, 91
covenants, 163
creeds, 45
dates, 305
deity, 150
evil days, 131
evolution, 104
gnosticism, 43, 45-46
Genesis Flood &, 78n, 269-70
graveyard society, 145
growth, 145
history, 163
humanistic law, 118-19
incarnation, 163
judgment, 113
liberty, 113
mysticism, 104
science, 91, 160
smorgasbord religion, 228
state of grace, 145
time, 91, 104, 117, 131, 145, 305
"year of the Lord," 305
Ruse, Michael, 5-6, 34n, 65n, 192
Russell, Bertrand, 54, 65-66, 105
Russia, 233
Russian Revolution, 249
Ryrie, Charles, 289n

sackcloth, 122
saint, 150
salvation, 157, 219-23, 226, 228, 253, 255 (see also redemption)
sanctification, 82, 111, 149-50, 153-57, 160, 181, 265
Satan
  defeat of, 278
  entropy theory &, 175
  equal time, 200, 208-10, 216
  eschatological pessimism, 149
  myth of neutrality, 108
  myth of status quo, 108
  New World Order, 276
  power of, 263, 267
  prince of world, 220-22
  State &, 255

  turning away from, 244
  upper hand?, 260
Saul's armor, xv-xvi
Scalia, Justice, 215-17
scarcity, 110, 168
scattering, 240, 247
Schaeffer, Francis, 82
Schlossberg, Herbert, 109
Schnittger, David, 281, 284, 285, 290n, 292, 294
scholarship, xix
schools (see public schools)
Schrödinger, Erwin, 26-29, 57n
Schumacher, E. F., 132
Schweitzer, Albert, 101
science
  atheism of, 30, 31-32, 35, 92
  creation out of nothing, 58
  creationism &, 160
  eschatology &, ix-xi
  "humility" of, 74
  methodology of, 187
  Middle Age, 14
  miracles, 3-4
  neutrality myth, 171
  pagan, 58
  philosophy of, 187
  religion, 41
  smallpox, 84, 184-85
  subjectivism, 19
  textbooks, 49-51
  time, 55-59, 62-64, 91, 105
  true and false, 208
  worldview &, xx, 208
scientists
  eternal life, 54
  influence, 41
  narrow, 40
  pessimism of, 40, 52-66
  specialists, 40
Scofield, C. I., 270, 293, 294, 295
Scopes trial, 209, 211
Scott, Otto, 139
second coming, 79, 88 (see also rapture, eschatology)
secularism, 292
self-discipline, 318

self-interest, 86
seminaries, 304
Shakespeare, William, 51
shark, 142
shuffling cards, 125
Sider, Ronald, 229-30
simplicity, 34, 36, 78-79
Simpson, George G., 197n
sin (see rebellion)
sinking ship, 259-60, 271-72, 286, 292
slavery, 230
Sloan, Alfred, 317
smallpox, 83-84, 100, 184-85
smells, 125
snail darter, 141
social action, 233, 254
social change, 250-51
social entropy, 70-76, 78-80, 101, 108-10, 112
Social Gospel, 229, 255, 273, 300-1
social theory, Chapter 3, 170-71
Sodom, 277
solipsism, 30
South, 229
space-time relations, 25
spaceship earth, 95
spark of divinity, 133
speed of light, 25, 185
Sproull, Thomas, 268, 299
stagecoach, 312
stalemate, 102, 108-9, 161, 295 (see also status quo)
Stam, C. R., 149
State, 227-28, 232-40, 255
static society, 120
statistical correlations, 31
status quo, 108, 120, 159-60 (see also stalemate)
stewardship, 85-86
Strauss, Lehman, 265, 282-83
students, 215
subjectivism, 19
sun, 96, 126
sunshine evolution, 96, 192-93, 205
Sutton, Ray, 78, 293
syphilis, 182

Talbot Seminary, 285, 304
Talmon, J. L., 226
tax exemption, 238-39, 240, 239, 240
taxes, 254-55
Taylor, Frederick, 314-15
teachers, 215, 217
technology, 78, 91-92
technophobia, 91-92, 95, 100
teleology, 209
television, 310, 319-20
thermodynamics
  antinomy of, 203n
  apologetics &, xvi
  Bible vs., 2
  classical, 193
  constant?, xxii, 185
  creationism &, 189-90
  cursed effects, xxi-xxii
  equilibrium, 193, 203n
  first law, 1
  mysticism vs., 107
  open systems, 69, 191-93, 202-3
  pessimism &, 40
  repeal of?, xxii
  resurrection vs., 2
  textbook view, 49-51
  third law, 203n
  universal?, 2
  see also entropy, social entropy
theonomy, 295-96
time
  arrow of, 91
  conquest of, 91, 132
  contempt for, 43
  cosmic, 55-61
  cyclical, 57, 59-61, 148
  end of, 52, 60, 105
  eternal life &, 54
  heat death &, 52
  insufficient for evolution, 194
  is money, 308
  man vs., 117
  plenty remaining, 95-96
  politics, 321-22
  positive feedback, 282
  rebellion against, 104
  revolution in, 311

Rifkin on, Appendix F
running out?, 96
Rushdoony on, 91, 104, 117, 131, 145, 305
scarce, 168
short view, 287
wasting, 131
tithe, 252
Titus, Herb, 271
Torrey, Reuben, 302n
trade, 169
trade unions, 214
traffic, 312
tribulation, 166, 289
Trinity, 225
Tucker, William, 84n
typewriters, 51

uniformitarianism
anti-Christian, 196
covenant &, 115
creationism &, xxii, 196-97
discontinuities vs., 201-2
ethical, 83, 117
God's, 199-200
God's law, 184
Henry Morris, 197
miracles &, xxii
natural law, 188
shared faith, 194-200
unions, 214
Unitarianism, 229, 255
United Nations, 104
universe
autonomy (see closed box)
closed box, 52, 60-62, 65, 75, 109, 167, 171, 191n, 197-98
contraction, 53-54, 64
"open box," 122, 198
theocentric, 240-41
utopia, xxviii-xxix, 267

vacuum, 58
Van Til, Cornelius
apologetics, xii
circular reasoning, 237
consistency, 237

creation, 5
deductive vs. inductive, xiii
ethics, 132, 212
facts, 187
full bucket, 151-52
knowledge & ethics, 212
law vs. change, 195
methodology, 187
miracle, 5
neutrality, xxxiii, 8
providence, 5
resurrection, 5
sin, 132-33
Van Wylen, Gordon, 64-65
victory, xi, 111, 114, 172, 278, 282, 295, 303
vows, 226

Waltke, Bruce, 298
Walvoord, John
changing the world, 265
doing good, 165, 264-66
no Christianization, 264
postmils and liberals, 269
prophecy, 290
Ward, Lester F., 93
waste, 87-88
Watson, Lyall, 4n
wealth, 42
Weber, Max, 87, 250
welfare state, 253
West, 31-33
whale, 139
white flag, 264
White, Lynn, 2n
Wilson, Dwight, 247
Wilson, Robert Dick, 302n
Wigner, Eugene, 13, 36n
winding down, 75, 191
Wine, 300
work of the law, 237
work ethic, 180
world, 219-20
worldview
dominion &, 44-46
escape, 42-44
eschatology &, 272

    power, 41-42
    science &, xx, 47
    theological, 85
    three outlooks, 41-46
wrinkles, 154

wristwatch, 312, 313

Young, Willard, 193n, 194

zero economic growth, 98, 108-9, 112, 129, 138, 159-60